MEMBER FUNCTIONS
WINDOWS 95 PROGRAMMING

```
<no class>
                    int AfxMessageBox(char* pszText, UINT nType = MB_OK)
                    UINT SetTimer(UINT nIDEvent, UINT nElapse, void(CALLBACK EXPORT* pfnTimer)
                        (HWND, UINT, UINT, DWORD))

CObject
    CDC
                    void DPtoLP(POINT* pPoint, int nPoints=1)
                    rvirtual int GetClipBox(RECT* pRect) const
                    CSize GetTextExtent(char* pszString, int nCount) const
                    BOOL GetTextMetrics(TEXTMETRIC* pTextMetric)
                    BOOL IsPrinting() const
                    BOOL LineTo(POINT point)
                    CPoint MoveTo(POINT point)
                    CBitmap* SelectObject(CBitmap* pBitmap);
                    CBrush* SelectObject(CBrush* pBrush);
                    virtual CFont* SelectObject(CFont* pFont);
                    CPen* SelectObject(CPen* pPen);
                    int SelectObject(CRgn* pRgn);
                    virtual int SetMapMode(UINT nMode)
                    BOOL SetPixelV(POINT point, COLORREF crColor)
                    UINT SetTextAlign(UINT nFlags)
                    virtual COLORREF SetTextColor(COLORREF crColor)
                    virtual CSize SetViewportExt(SIZE size)
                    virtual CSize SetWindowExt(SIZE size)
                    virtual BOOL TextOut(int x, int y, CString& string)

    CCmdTarget
        CWinApp
                    protected void LoadStdProfileSettings(UINT nMaxMRU = _AFX_MRU_COUNT)
                    virtual CDocument* OpenDocumentFile(char* pszFileName)
                    protected void RegisterShellFileTypes( )
            C<app>App
                    virtual BOOL InitInstance()
        CDocument
                    virtual void AssertValid() const;
                    virtual void Dump(CDumpContext& dc) const;
                    BOOL IsStoring()
                    void SetModifiedFlag(BOOL bModified = TRUE)
                    void UpdateAllViews(CView* pSender, LPARAM lHint = 0L, CObject* pHint = NULL )
            C<app>Doc
                    virtual void AssertValid() const;
                    virtual void Dump(CDumpContext& dc) const;
                    virtual void Serialize(CArchive& ar);
        CWnd
                    void CreateSolidCaret(int nWidth, int nHeight)
                    BOOL DestroyCaret()
                    void GetClientRect(RECT* pRect) const
                    CDC* GetDC()
                    CFrameWnd* GetParentFrame() const
                    void GetWindowRect(RECT* pRect) const
                    void GetScrollRange(int nBar, int* pMinPos, int* pMaxPos) const
                    void HideCaret()
                    void Invalidate(BOOL bErase = TRUE)
                    int  ReleaseDC(CDC*)
                    void SetCaretPos(POINT point)
                    int  SetScrollPos(int nBar, int nPos, BOOL bRedraw = TRUE)
```

```
                        void SetScrollRange(int nBar, int nMinPos, int nMaxPos, BOOL bRedraw = TRUE)
                        BOOL ShowWindow(int nCmdShow)
        ┌ CDialog
        │               virtual int DoModal()
        │               protected virtual void DoDataExchange(CDataExchange* pDE)
        │      C<app>Dialog
        │               protected virtual void DoDataExchange(CDataExchange* pDE)
        └ CView
                        virtual void AssertValid() const;
                        BOOL DoPreparePrinting(CPrintInfo* pInfo)
                        virtual void Dump(CDumpContext& dc) const;
            ┌ CScrollView
            │           CPoint GetDeviceScrollPosition() const
            │           void SetScrollSizes(int nMapMode, SIZE sizeTotal,
            │              SIZE& sizePage = sizeDefault, SIZE& sizeLine = sizeDefault)
            └ C<app>View
                        virtual void AssertValid() const;
                        virtual void Dump(CDumpContext& dc) const;
                        C<app>Doc* GetDocument();
                        virtual void OnDraw(CDC* pDC)
─── C<TYPE>Array
                        int Add(TYPE newElement)
                        int GetSize() const
                        int GetUpperBound() const
                        void RemoveAll()
                        void SetAtGrow(int nIndex, TYPE newElement)
                        void SetSize(int nNewSize, int nGrowBy = -1)
─── C<TYPE>List
                        POSITION AddTail(TYPE newElement);
                        TYPE& GetAt(POSITION position)
                        int GetCount() const
                        POSITION GetHeadPosition() const
                        TYPE& GetNext(POSITION& rPosition)
                        BOOL IsEmpty() const
                        void RemoveAll()
                        void RemoveAt(POSITION position)
                        void SetAt(POSITION pos, TYPE newElement)
─── CString
                        int GetLength() const
                        CString Left(int nCount) const
                        CString Right(int nCount) const
                        CString operator+(CString&)
─── CMemoryState
                        void Checkpoint()
                        void DumpAllObjectsSince() const
ifstream
                        int eof() const
                        int fail() const
                        iftream& getline(char* pszString, int nCount, char cDelim = '\n' )
                        ifstream& operator>>(...)
ofstream
                        ofstream& operator<<(...)
```

IDG BOOKS
WORLDWIDE

TM

References for the Rest of Us

COMPUTER BOOK SERIES FROM IDG

Are you baffled and bewildered by programming? Does it seem like an impenetrable puzzle? Do you find that traditional manuals are overloaded with technical terms you don't understand? Do you want to know how to get your PC to do what you want? Then the ...For Dummies programming book series from IDG is for you.

...For Dummies programming books are written for frustrated computer users who know they really aren't dumb but find that programming, with its unique vocabulary and logic, makes them feel helpless. ...For Dummies programming books use a humorous approach and a down-to-earth style to diffuse fears and build confidence. Lighthearted but not lightweight, these books are a perfect survival guide for first-time programmers or anyone learning a new environment.

> *"Simple, clear, and concise. Just what I needed."*
> —Steve P., Greenville, SC

> *"Finally, someone made learning to program easy and entertaining. Thanks!"*
> —Diane W., Chicago, IL

> *"When I saw this book I decided to give programming one last try. And I'm glad I did!"*
> —Paul G., St. Louis, MO

Millions of satisfied readers have made *...For Dummies* books the #1 introductory-level computer book series and have written asking for more. So if you're looking for a fun and easy way to learn about computers, look to *...For Dummies* books to give you a helping hand.

WINDOWS 95 PROGRAMMING FOR DUMMIES™

WINDOWS 95 PROGRAMMING FOR DUMMIES™

Stephen R. Davis

IDG Books Worldwide, Inc.
An International Data Group Company

Foster City, CA • Chicago, IL • Indianapolis, IN • Braintree, MA • Dallas, TX

Windows 95 Programming For Dummies

Published by
IDG Books Worldwide, Inc.
An International Data Group Company
919 East Hillsdale Boulevard, Suite 400
Foster City, CA 94404

Library of Congress Catalog Card No.: 95-75056

ISBN 1-56884-327-5

Printed in the United States of America

Published in the United States of America

First printing, June 1995

10 9 8 7 6 5 4 3 2 1

Distributed in the United States by IDG Books Worldwide, Inc.

 is a registered trademark of IDG Books Worldwide, Inc.

For More Information...

For general information on IDG Books in the U.S., including information on discounts and premiums, contact IDG Books at 800-434-3422.

For information on where to purchase IDG's books outside the U.S., contact Christina Turner at 415-655-3022.

For information on translations, contact Marc Jeffrey Mikulich, Foreign Rights Manager, at IDG Books Worldwide; fax number: 415-655-3295.

For sales inquires and special prices for bulk quantities, contact Tony Real at 800-434-3422 or 415-655-3048.

For information on using IDG's books in the classroom and ordering examination copies, contact Jim Kelly at 800-434-2086.

The ...*For Dummies* book series is distributed in Canada by Macmillan of Canada, a Division of Canada Publishing Corporation; by Computer and Technical Books in Miami, Florida, for South America and the Caribbean; by Longman Singapore in Singapore, Malaysia, Thailand, and Korea; by Toppan Co. Ltd. in Japan; by Asia Computerworld in Hong Kong; by Woodslane Pty. Ltd. in Australia and New Zealand; and by Transword Publishers Ltd. in the U.K. and Europe.

ABOUT IDG BOOKS WORLDWIDE

Welcome to the world of IDG Books Worldwide.

IDG Books Worldwide, Inc. is a subsidiary of International Data Group, the world's largest publisher of computer-related information and the leading global provider of information services on information technology. IDG was founded more than 25 years ago and now employs more than 7,500 people worldwide. IDG publishes more than 235 computer publications in 67 countries (see listing below). More than fifty million people read one or more IDG publications each month.

Launched in 1990, IDG Books Worldwide is today the #1 publisher of best-selling computer books in the United States. We are proud to have received 3 awards from the Computer Press Association in recognition of editorial excellence, and our best-selling *...For Dummies™* series has more than 17 million copies in print with translations in 24 languages. IDG Books, through a recent joint venture with IDG's Hi-Tech Beijing, became the first U.S. publisher to publish a computer book in the People's Republic of China. In record time, IDG Books has become the first choice for millions of readers around the world who want to learn how to better manage their businesses.

Our mission is simple: Every IDG book is designed to bring extra value and skill-building instructions to the reader. Our books are written by experts who understand and care about our readers. The knowledge base of our editorial staff comes from years of experience in publishing, education, and journalism — experience which we use to produce books for the '90s. In short, we care about books, so we attract the best people. We devote special attention to details such as audience, interior design, use of icons, and illustrations. And because we use an efficient process of authoring, editing, and desktop publishing our books electronically, we can spend more time ensuring superior content and spend less time on the technicalities of making books.

You can count on our commitment to deliver high-quality books at competitive prices on topics consumers want to read about. At IDG, we value quality, and we have been delivering quality for more than 25 years. You'll find no better book on a subject than an IDG book.

John J. Kilcullen

John Kilcullen
President and CEO
IDG Books Worldwide, Inc.

IDG Books Worldwide, Inc. is a subsidiary of International Data Group, the world's largest publisher of computer-related information and the leading global provider of information services on information technology. International Data Group publishes over 220 computer publications in 65 countries. More than fifty million people read one or more International Data Group publications each month. The officers are Patrick J. McGovern, Founder and Board Chairman; Kelly Conlin, President; Jim Casella, Chief Operating Officer. International Data Group's publications include: **ARGENTINA'S** Computerworld Argentina, Infoworld Argentina; **AUSTRALIA'S** Computerworld Australia, Computer Living, Australian PC World, Australian Macworld, Network World, Mobile Business Australia, Publish!, Reseller, IDG Sources; **AUSTRIA'S** Computerwelt Oesterreich, PC Test; **BELGIUM'S** Data News (CW); **BOLIVIA'S** Computerworld; **BRAZIL'S** Computerworld, Connections, Game Power, Mundo Unix, PC World, Publish, Super Game; **BULGARIA'S** Computerworld Bulgaria, PC & Mac World Bulgaria, Network World Bulgaria; **CANADA'S** CIO Canada, Computerworld Canada, InfoCanada, Network World Canada, Reseller; **CHILE'S** Computerworld Chile, Informatica; **COLOMBIA'S** Computerworld Colombia, PC World; **COSTA RICA'S** PC World; **CZECH REPUBLIC'S** Computerworld, Elektronika, PC World; **DENMARK'S** Communications World, Computerworld Danmark, Computerworld Focus, Macintosh Produktkatalog, Macworld Danmark, PC World Danmark, PC Produktguide, Tech World, Windows World; **ECUADOR'S** PC World Ecuador; **EGYPT'S** Computerworld (CW) Middle East, PC World Middle East; **FINLAND'S** MikroPC, Tietoviikko, Tietoverkko; **FRANCE'S** Distributique, GOLDEN MAC, InfoPC, Le Guide du Monde Informatique, Le Monde Informatique, Telecoms & Reseaux; **GERMANY'S** Computerwoche, Computerwoche Focus, Computerwoche Extra, Electronic Entertainment, Gamepro, Information Management, Macwelt, Netzwelt, PC Welt, Publish, Publish; **GREECE'S** Publish & Macworld; **HONG KONG'S** Computerworld Hong Kong, PC World Hong Kong; **HUNGARY'S** Computerworld SZT, PC World; **INDIA'S** Computers & Communications; **INDONESIA'S** Info Komputer; **IRELAND'S** ComputerScope; **ISRAEL'S** Beyond Windows, Computerworld Israel, Multimedia, PC World Israel; **ITALY'S** Computerworld Italia, Lotus Magazine, Macworld Italia, Networking Italia, PC Shopping Italy, PC World Italia; **JAPAN'S** Computerworld Today, Information Systems World, Macworld Japan, Nikkei Personal Computing, SunWorld Japan, Windows World; **KENYA'S** East African Computer News; **KOREA'S** Computerworld Korea, Macworld Korea, PC World Korea; **LATIN AMERICA'S** GamePro; **MALAYSIA'S** Computerworld Malaysia, PC World Malaysia; **MEXICO'S** Compu Edicion, Compu Manufactura, Computacion/Punto de Venta, Computerworld Mexico, MacWorld, Mundo Unix, PC World, Windows; **THE NETHERLANDS'** Computer! Totaal, Computable (CW), LAN Magazine, Lotus Magazine, MacWorld; **NEW ZEALAND'S** Computer Buyer, Computerworld New Zealand, Network World, New Zealand PC World; **NIGERIA'S** PC World Africa; **NORWAY'S** Computerworld Norge, Lotusworld Norge, Macworld Norge, Maxi Data, Networld, PC World Ekspress, PC World Nettverk, PC World Norge, PC World's Produktguide, Publish& Multimedia World, Student Data, Unix World, Windowsworld; **PAKISTAN'S** PC World Pakistan; **PANAMA'S** PC World Panama; **PERU'S** Computerworld Peru, PC World; **PEOPLE'S REPUBLIC OF CHINA'S** China Computerworld, China Infoworld, China PC Info Magazine, Computer Fan, PC World China, Electronics International, Electronics Today/Multimedia World, Electronic Product World, China Network World, Software World Magazine, Telecom Product World; **PHILIPPINES'** Computerworld Philippines, PC Digest (PCW); **POLAND'S** Computerworld Poland, Computerworld Special Report, Networld, PC World/Komputer, Sunworld; **PORTUGAL'S** Cerebro/PC World, Correio Informatico/Computerworld, MacIn; **ROMANIA'S** Computerworld, PC World, Telecom Romania; **RUSSIA'S** Computerworld-Moscow, Mir - PK (PCW), Sety (Networks); **SINGAPORE'S** Computerworld Southeast Asia, PC World Singapore; **SLOVENIA'S** Monitor Magazine; **SOUTH AFRICA'S** Computer Mail (CIO),Computing S.A.,Network World S.A., Software World; **SPAIN'S** Advanced Systems, Amiga World, Computerworld Espana, Communicaciones World, Macworld Espana, NeXTWORLD, Super Juegos Magazine (GamePro), PC World Espana, Publish; **SWEDEN'S** Attack, ComputerSweden, Corporate Computing, Macworld, Mikrodatorn, Natverk & Kommunikation, PC World, CAP & Design, Datalngenjoren, Maxi Data,Windows World; **SWITZERLAND'S** Computerworld Schweiz, Macworld Schweiz, PC Tip; **TAIWAN'S** Computerworld Taiwan, PC World Taiwan; **THAILAND'S** Thai Computerworld; **TURKEY'S** Computerworld Monitor, Macworld Turkiye, PC World Turkiye; **UKRAINE'S** Computerworld, Computers+Software Magazine; **UNITED KINGDOM'S** Computing /Computerworld, Connexion/Network World, Lotus Magazine, Macworld, Open Computing/Sunworld; **UNITED STATES'** Advanced Systems, AmigaWorld, Cable in the Classroom, CD Review, CIO, Computerworld, Computerworld Client/Server Journal, Digital Video, DOS World, Electronic Entertainment Magazine (E2), Federal Computer Week, Game Hits, GamePro, IDG Books, Infoworld, Laser Event, Macworld, Maximize, Multimedia World, Network World, PC Letter, PC World, Publish, SWATPro, Video Event; **URUGUAY'S** PC World Uruguay; **VENEZUELA'S** Computerworld Venezuela, PC World; **VIETNAM'S** PC World Vietnam.

About the Author

Stephen R. Davis lives with his wife, son, and 1.5 dogs (two dogs, but one of them is pretty stupid) in Greenville, Texas. Stephen works for E-Systems, where he's been programming in and training others in C++ and Windows programming for seven years. Stephen has authored numerous books, including *Hands On Turbo C++*, *C++ Programmer's Companion*, and *C++ For Dummies*. His articles have appeared in *PC magazine*, *Micro/Systems Journal,* and the *Journal of Object-Oriented Programming*. Stephen can be contacted at srdavis@ACM.org.

Credits

Vice President and Publisher
Christopher J. Williams

Publishing Director
Amorette Pedersen

Editorial Director
Anne Marie Walker

Director of Production
Beth A. Roberts

Manuscript Editor
Betsy Wiggins

Technical Reviewers
Bob Bourbonnais
Don Hergert

Proofreader
T.L. Frazier

Indexer
Liz Cunningham

Composition and Layout
Publishers' Design and Production Services, Inc.

Book Design
University Graphics

Cover Design
Kavish + Kavish

Acknowledgments

I find it strange that only a single name appears on the cover of any book, especially a book such as this one. In reality, many people contribute to the creation of a *...For Dummies* book. From the beginning, acquisitions editor Trudy Neuhaus and my editorial agent, Claudette Moore, were involved in guiding and molding this book's content. During development, I found myself hip-deep in edits, corrections, and suggestions from editorial director Anne Marie Walker, manuscript editor Betsy Wiggins, and technical editor Bob Bourbonnais. T.L. Frazier did an outstanding job of proofreading the book in its final stage. This is a better book because of their involvement. And nothing would make it into print without the aid of the production department. Nevertheless, one name does appear on the cover, and that person must take responsibility for any inaccuracies in the text.

I also have to thank my wife, Jenny, and my son, Kinsey, for their patience and devotion. I truly missed those outings they went on by themselves so that Dad could make a deadline. Hopefully, we managed to strike a reasonable balance.

Finally, for those readers who have been following my family's pet population throughout my other *...For Dummies* books, I should mention our two new additions to the family: Beavis and Butt-head, our rabbits. Their presence, grazing on the lawn outside my office window every morning, makes the day that much more enjoyable.

If you want to contact me concerning Windows, C++ programming, or free-roaming rabbits on the lawn, feel free to drop me a line at srdavis@ACM.org.

The publisher would like to give special thanks to Patrick J. McGovern, without whom this book would not have been possible.

Contents at a Glance

Cartoons at a Glance
by Rich Tennant

page 231

page 83

page 157

page 259

page 379

page 453

Table of Contents

• •

Introduction

● ●

*W*elcome to *Windows 95 Programming For Dummies,* your entry into the wonderful and sometimes scary world of Windows programming. You will learn new concepts, new words for new concepts, new words for old concepts, and new reasons that you shouldn't have bought a computer. But, believe it or not, you will come out of this experience a better person (or maybe just a better programmer).

Who Are You?

As I do in all my books, I have made some completely unfounded assumptions about who you are and how much programming experience you have. In the interest of complete disclosure, let me fill you in on those assumptions.

First, I assume that you already know the basics of programming. These assumptions put you into one of these three groups:

✔ You've programmed in C or C++ in a non-Windows environment such as UNIX or DOS, and now you want to learn how to program Windows. Boy, is this book for you. I assume that you have no knowledge of Windows programming.

✔ You've written Windows programs in Visual Basic, but you're not familiar with C or C++. Visual Basic is a powerful tool, especially for writing small programs in record time. Maybe your applications are getting too big and too complicated, however, for Visual Basic to keep up. The time will come when you want to steer it out on the freeway, lock down the throttle, and move. You, too, are in the right place. This book builds on your knowledge of Visual Basic to teach you first C and C++ and then Windows. Little icons such as the one on the left flag special hints to VBers. ■

✔ You've programmed in some language long ago in college, but you don't remember the name of the language you used (all you remember is that you had to type lots of cards to get anything done). All you really want to do now is write a Windows program as easily as possible, and you have heard that Visual something-or-other is the way to go.

> ✔ You're probably in the wrong place. Despite the similarity of their names, it's not as easy to program in Visual C++ as it is in Visual Basic. If all you want to do is learn how to write a Windows program *as easily as possible,* look for *Visual Basic For Dummies* (from IDG Books Worldwide). It's available at all bookstores that have a clue. (If you're holding this book in your hands and still haven't purchased it, go ahead and buy it, and give it to your clever niece or nephew.)

I assume that you've already had some rudimentary experience in using Microsoft Windows. When I talk about dragging, therefore, you know that the topic is holding down the button while moving the mouse, not dressing up in women's clothing. I don't assume that you know anything about programming for Windows (or any other windowing operating system, for that matter).

In this book, you'll be using Microsoft Foundation Classes (MFC), which are based on C++; however, I don't assume that you know how to program in C++. I present enough C++ information to get you through. If you want to get the full treatment — to understand C++ in depth before learning to program Windows — you might consider purchasing *C++ For Dummies* (IDG Books Worldwide), by yours truly; my bankruptcy judge will thank you.

About This Book

Many *...For Dummies* books are meant to be used primarily as references. That is, you might be flying along just fine using, for example, Waning Interest, that hot, new package for calculating depreciation schedules, when — wham! — you slam directly into a pitfall you weren't expecting. At this point, you fling open your copy of *Waning Interest For Dummies,* look up the solution, and in minutes your book is back on the shelf (on your shelf, I hope, not on the bookstore's shelf), and you're back at work.

...For Dummies programming books aren't like that. Although they have a certain amount of "referenceness" to them, programming books such as this one are constructed more in the manner of a tutorial because they try to teach you something that is essentially difficult.

This book is divided into parts. Each part contains a group of chapters that teaches a set of skills which build on the skills of the previous parts. After you have completed a part, you'll want to reflect on what you've just read until you're sure that you understand it. To help you, I've included a quiz at the end of each part. If you can't answer the questions in these quizzes, you may want to return to the chapters and skim through them again.

By the time you've finished *Windows 95 Programming For Dummies,* you should have a firm foundation in Windows programming.

Windows 95 and Visual C++

This book concentrates on teaching you to write applications for Windows 95 in Visual C++. It may be obvious, but my lawyer suggests that I remind you that this subject has nothing to do with *using* Windows 95. That is, if you're a prospective user of Windows 95, look for *Windows 95 For Dummies.* That book is for people who need help using Windows 95 programs. This book is for people who want to *write* those nifty Windows 95 programs.

I had a choice: Write about Windows 95 or write about Windows 3.1. As you might imagine, the choice of Windows 95, Microsoft's newest version of Windows, was a no-brainer. First, it contains significant improvements over Windows 3.1 and earlier — enough so that Windows 3.*x* versions will melt away in the glow of Windows 95 faster than a snowfall in El Paso. I predict that within a year of Windows 95's entrance into the market, Windows 3.1 will be completely forgotten.

Second, for programmers, Windows 95 is somewhat simpler to program than Windows 3.1. Particularly in the area of memory management, Windows 95's support for 32-bit memory addressing greatly simplifies things.

Finally, for beginning MFC programmers, there really isn't that much difference between Windows 95 and its predecessors anyway. Most of what's in this book, therefore, applies directly to MFC programming for Windows 3.1.

The choice of tools was much more difficult. On one hand, I debated about whether to write all examples so that they stay completely generic and compile under all major brands of C++ compilers. The problem with this approach is what I call "the charades effect," in which I stand in front of you, grunting and pointing at different Windows features without being able to get specific.

With non-Windows C++, that wasn't a problem. C++ is pretty much standardized, so as long as the compiler implements the full language, there isn't a problem.

With Windows programming, the slavish adherence to commonality is a much larger problem.

Both Borland and Microsoft offer powerful class libraries and application generators that greatly simplify the job of writing a Windows application. Unfortunately, the two tools are not compatible.

To avoid those tools in the name of compatibility is similar to wearing Bermuda shorts in the winter just so that you can get by with only one style of clothing all year long.

I decided to focus on Visual C++ for two primary reasons. First, its powerful Microsoft Foundation Classes and AppWizard are supported by compilers from other companies, such as Watcom and Symantec (even Borland has announced that it will support the Foundation Classes). Second, Microsoft has promised to support other computers in its Foundation Classes, including MIPs, DEC Alpha, Power PC, and even Macintosh.

By the way, don't worry — I don't expect you to know now what Microsoft Foundation Classes are or what the AppWizard is. One of the purposes of this book is to teach you what these things are and how to use them.

How This Book Is Organized

This book contains six parts and a somewhat large appendix. Parts I and II are directed toward teaching Windows programming concepts. Sure, you write a few applications, but what those applications do is definitely secondary to how they do it.

Beginning with Part III, you begin working on three simple Windows programs. Obviously, the point of each of these exercises is not the program itself. The point is to *learn* something. In each case, you begin with a do-nothing program and add feature after feature until you have something useful at the end. By adding these features, you learn something about adding similar features to your applications, whatever they might be.

Part I, "Getting Started"

Part I uses the example of a manually generated Windows program that does nothing more than display the phrase "Hello, world" in a window. By following the trails laid out by our Windows programming forefathers, you learn what it was like when Windows programming separated the men from the nerds. This exercise gives you a handle on the parts of every Windows program and also what goes on "under the hood" in a Windows program.

Part II, "AppWizard Programming"

After you understand the basic principles of Windows programming, you back up and rewrite the "Hello, world" program with the help of the

AppWizard application generator and the Microsoft Foundation Class library. By comparing what the AppWizard generates with what you already know about Windows programs, you'll be able to decipher how AppWizard and Microsoft Foundation Classes work their magic.

Part III, "App 1: A Drawing Program"

In this part, you begin working on your first simple application. This application captures mouse movement to allow you to draw simple pictures on the screen much like an Etch-A-Sketch program does. It also lets you save these images to disk and recover them.

Part IV, "App 2: The Personal Scheduler"

In this part, you write a nifty scheduler application. This Windows application contains most of the neat features users expect of Windows programs: scrolling windows, opening and saving different file types, dialog boxes, menus, and toolbars — neat stuff like that. This program also supports print and print preview capabilities.

Part V, "App 3: A Text Editor"

In this part, you write a simple text editor. This application demonstrates how to manipulate text in a window, how to control the insertion cursor (the caret), and how to handle the scroll operation yourself.

You'll notice that this book does not cover DDE, OLE, ODBC, VBX, or OCX. Entire books are being written about each one of these topics, even as we speak. However, I do discuss print, print preview, and drag-and-drop capabilities.

Part VI, "The Part of Tens"

Part VI includes the ubiquitous Part of Tens, without which no book can claim to be a Dummy. The Part of Tens covers these subjects:

- Ten most common coding mistakes
- Ten most important Visual C++ compiler options
- Ten best sources of help when you get stuck

The Appendix

The Appendix contains an introduction to the C programming language for Visual Basic programmers. By building on your knowledge of Visual Basic, it can teach you the basics of the C language as quickly as possible.

I'll be happy if you finish this book with a good handle on the fundamentals of Windows programming, on which you can build later. Then, if you want to learn more after you finish this book, you can build on your Windows programming knowledge with the help of more advanced books about Windows programming.

Icons Used in This Book

As is standard practice in *...For Dummies* books, this book uses special icons in the margins to highlight particular sections as being either particularly important or particularly irrelevant:

Flags useful, helpful tips or shortcuts. ■

Marks an area you have to remember if you don't want to make a dumb mistake. ■

Flags a section of particular merit. Take note of this section and then continue. ■

Notes to Visual Basic programmers that relate what they already know to what's being taught. If you know Visual Basic, these sections can be a big help. If not, just skip over them.

(C programmers: Try not to be disdainful of your new Visual Basic brethren. Welcome these new converts from the dark side of the Force.) ■

Indicates a section that is so technical as to be useless to beginners, and, therefore, I probably shouldn't have even mentioned it; however, you can read or skip these sections — whichever you prefer. ∎

 Flags some point that is different between Windows 95 and Windows 3.1 (there are older versions of Windows, of course, but they have thankfully faded more or less into obscurity). These older versions of Windows are collectively called Win16. The Windows 95 way generally is presented first, followed by the Win16 way. Unless you must support Windows 3.1 also, just skip these sections. ∎

Part I
Getting Started

The 5th Wave   By Rich Tennant

"Unfortunately, C++ is not very fault tolerant."

In This Part...

In this part, you begin your study of Windows. You'll begin by learning a little background information and from there write your first Windows application: a simple "Hello, world" application.

This application seems a little strange at first to the Windows uninitiated. Don't despair, though. I'll take you through each section of the program until it seems almost second nature.

Chapter 1

Windows

• •

• •

Windows is Microsoft's family of windows-based operating systems for the IBM PC.

An *operating system* is the program that controls the overall computer. For example, MS-DOS is an operating system. Windows 95, the most recent member of the Windows family, is the operating system that enables an operator to execute other programs, called *applications,* or *"apps,"* for short. Applications written to execute under Windows are called *WinApps* by those in the know (which includes you). Word for Windows is an application; in fact, it's a WinApp. By extension, other app-types carry the name of the operating system for which they are written. DOSApps and UNIXApps are a couple of examples. ■

The purpose of this book is to get you started in writing boffo applications for Windows.

Specifically, you will write applications for Windows 95; most of the programs you write, however, should port to other versions of Windows without modification. ■

A Short History Lesson

Windows 95 didn't just spring into existence one day. It has a long and checkered past.

Prehistoric Windows

Microsoft first got into the operating-system business when IBM asked Microsoft to develop a disk operating system for the soon-to-be-released IBM PC. At the time, most personal computers were based on the 8-bit 8080 processor, which executed an operating system called CP/M-80, developed by Digital Research. IBM was planning to use the next-generation 16-bit 8086/8088 processor, however, which was not compatible with the 8080.

A version of CP/M, called CP/M-86, did exist for the 8086/8088 processor, but Digital Research was proving difficult to deal with. The IBM blue-suiters needed the extra frequent-flier miles anyway, so they decided to make a quick trip up to Redmond, Washington, to see whether Microsoft had something to offer instead. It didn't, but it did manage to keep the IBM people cooling their heels in the Redmondian waiting rooms long enough to go out and buy a CP/M look-alike, which Microsoft quickly renamed MS-DOS (Microsoft Disk Operating System) 1.0.

MS-DOS 1.0 was released in August 1981. It consisted of 4,000 lines of assembly code and could run in 8K of memory. It had to — the original PC came with only 16 kilobytes.

Originally, everyone thought that a battle between CP/M-86 and MS-DOS would ensue, but it never materialized. Microsoft managed to make a deal with IBM, in which a copy of MS-DOS came bundled with every PC that was sold. At that price, its success was ensured.

Technically, MS-DOS had two problems. First, it was definitely not built by anyone looking toward the future. Quite the reverse: MS-DOS was built with its gaze fixed firmly on the past.

Compatibility with CP/M was the order of the day. True, a CP/M program would not execute under MS-DOS; however, the differences were relatively minor. A vendor could easily port a CP/M application to MS-DOS. Applications existed for MS-DOS, therefore, almost from the first day of its existence. Technologically speaking, though, MS-DOS was a dated operating system almost from the first day it was offered. Its internal architecture limited its future growth.

In addition, MS-DOS was not intended for the average person. At the time the PC was introduced, only computer nerds had personal computers. I don't mean the semi-nerds of today who wear pocket protectors and practice safe cybersex. I'm talking about serious computer nerds who built their own computers in their garage.

Office computers generally consisted of remote terminals connected to mainframes. Neither IBM nor Microsoft had any idea that the PC was about to kick off a revolution in computing. Thank goodness MS-DOS didn't have the mind-bending commands of UNIX, such as *grep* and *awk*; however, even commands such as *cd * and *dir /w >lpt1:* were too difficult for the average nontechno-user to master.

Windows

As Adrian King says in his book *Inside Windows 95* (Microsoft Press, 1994), Windows is a "seven-year overnight success." In fact, the Windows 1.0 environment first appeared in November 1985. Windows was designed as a *graphical user interface,* or *GUI* (pronounced "gooey"): By using this interface, users can point at what they want and "shoot" by clicking it with the mouse. Computers such as the Apple Macintosh had shown that this picture-based interface was more intuitive for average users than was the cryptic MS-DOS command-line interface. Microsoft saw the potential for losing market share if it didn't come out in a hurry with its own GUI.

At one time, if someone had told me that my display was gooey, I would have begun looking for the glass cleaner.

Windows 1.0 was less than a resounding success — in fact, it was your basic failure. More than anything, it was too much operating system shoehorned into too little hardware. Windows 1.0 was slow, difficult to program, and prone to crashing — a winning combination in any programmer's book.

Windows was such an initial failure that Microsoft was prepared to abandon it. It set out to write OS/2 with the then still-alive computer behemoth IBM.

Bill Gates probably wishes that he hadn't written the following quote in his introduction to Ed Iacobucci's *OS/2 Programmer's Guide* (Osborne McGraw-Hill, 1988): "I believe OS/2 is destined to be the most important operating system, and possibly program, of all time." When IBM became recalcitrant, Microsoft slapped the resuscitators on its Windows program and managed to revive it. ■

Never one to admit a mistake, Microsoft continued to work away at Windows, releasing a major new revision every other year or so. First came Windows 2.0 (another failure), and then Windows 286, followed by Windows 386, and finally Windows 3.0 in 1990. Windows 3.0 was the first truly useful Windows environment. Luckily for Microsoft, during this same period PCs were becoming sufficiently powerful to handle Windows with something approaching reasonable response times.

Windows 3.1, released in early 1992, contained several enhancements, such as support for multimedia. This support gave Windows programs access to the inexpensive sound cards that were taking over the landscape. Windows-based applications, such as Grolier's Encyclopedia and Encarta, could play video clips from a CD in a window while generating realistic sound. But the main thing was that Windows 3.1 was much more crash-resistant. At last the popularity of Windows was ensured.

Windows 95

Windows 95, commonly referred to as Win95, got its start at about the time Windows 3.1 was released. As the decade of the '90s began, Microsoft wanted to break in to the workstation market. The problem was that Windows was written specifically for the Intel 80×86 chips found in the IBM PC family of computers. This family of processors is not typically found in workstations.

Microsoft decided to write a new version of Windows specifically for the workstation market; it hired DEC's number-one operating systems designer to spearhead the effort. The result, released in 1993, was dubbed Windows NT. To the application programs, Windows NT doesn't look much different from other versions of Windows. Internally, though, it was completely rewritten and was a significant departure. Versions of NT exist for workstations based on processors from MIPS, DEC, and Motorola as well as on Intel-based PCs.

NT originally stood for *new technology*, by the way. I guess that the implication is that all those other versions of Windows use *old technology*, or *OT*. After someone at Microsoft came to the same realization, the company decided that NT doesn't stand for anything. ■

The only problem was that Windows NT required significantly more computer power to run than did Windows 3.1. Microsoft decided that it needed a version of Windows that takes advantage of the new technology of NT but that still didn't require a small mainframe to execute.

So Microsoft rewrote a new version of Windows specifically for the PC. The result was eventually christened Windows 95.

Tying Windows 95 to the IBM PC and its Intel family of processors enabled Microsoft to take certain shortcuts compared to NT so that Windows 95 can execute as fast as Windows 3.1. Windows 95 takes advantage of many of the new features of Windows NT, including the use of 32 bits throughout much of the operating system.

The later Intel processors can execute in two modes: 16-bit mode, in which they look like the founder of the clan, the 8086, and 32-bit mode. The 32-bit mode instructions are considerably easier to use, especially for accessing the large amounts of memory that modern applications require.

Under MS-DOS and Windows 3.1, the microprocessor generally runs in 16-bit mode. Windows 95 is, by comparison, primarily a 32-bit mode operating system.

To hear Microsoft tell it, Windows 95 is almost completely 32-bit, whatever that means; research by outside code spelunkers, however, has revealed that a significant amount of 16-bit code still remains in Windows 95. Nevertheless, the WinApps that execute under Windows 95 do so in 32-bit mode, which makes it (for our purposes) a 32-bit operating system. This situation implies some significant simplifications for the code developer (that's you), especially in the area of memory management. ■

 Microsoft claims that the base machine for Windows 95 is an 80386-based PC with 4MB of RAM and a VGA video adapter. A more usable base configuration might be 8MB of RAM. By comparison, Windows NT requires at least 16MB of RAM just to get started. ■

This book is designed to teach you to write applications for Windows 95. Windows 95's compatibility with Windows 3.1 means that for the most part you will also learn how to program under Windows 3.1; however, several features in Windows 3.1 were greatly simplified in Windows 95 — in particular, memory management. I don't intend to confuse you any more than necessary by dredging up that old stuff, because it's largely irrelevant now anyway.

Windows for the User

In the early days of computerdom, just as is true today, people needed a convenient way of telling a computer what they wanted it to do and getting back the results. The first commonly used I/O (input and output) devices were teletypes.

A *teletype* (commonly known as a *TTY*) is basically an electric typewriter with a cable out the back that enables the computer to determine which keys the operator is pressing. TTYs, which had been around for decades in the Western Union-style telex business, were commonly available and cheap.

With a TTY, an operator effectively "telexed" the computer a command. The computer analyzed the command and telexed the response back to the TTY. Communication was limited to the type of information a telex could handle — letters of the alphabet, numbers, and a limited set of special symbols.

Technology continued to advance until, around the early '70s, TTYs were replaced by terminals. Terminals were much faster — because TTYs were mechanical, they could print only about 30 characters per second, tops, whereas a terminal could produce about 960 characters per second. In addition, because terminals don't require paper, the lives of a few trees were spared. Still, terminals were (in their heart of hearts) just electronic TTYs. I/O was still limited to a small character set.

The IBM PC came with something called *bit-mapped graphics:* The card that drove the video display was an integral part of the computer. A program could access the display directly and set or clear each individual pixel on the screen the way it wanted. Display output was not restricted to some limited character set, and pictorial output was possible.

Even so, like its CP/M predecessor, MS-DOS treated the keyboard and display as a terminal, expecting input from a command line and producing characters a line at a time.

Limiting the user interface to a single command line puts a significant burden on users. Users must constantly keep in their own mind a picture of the state of the system. In addition, they must remember which commands are available and how those commands are formatted.

In a graphical user interface provided by Windows, the program can constantly display the state of the system visually, the way people work. In addition, the program can offer options for users to choose with a pointing device, such as the mouse.

Windows provides, in addition to a graphical user interface, several other major enhancements over MS-DOS, which are described in this section.

A consistent user interface

Windows provides a consistent user interface. The DOS command-line prompt might not have been quite as difficult to master if the commands were at least consistent. Adding /P to the DIR directory listing command, for example, causes it to pause every 25 lines. Adding the same /P switch to the PRINT command causes it to do something completely different.

A graphical user interface doesn't have to be consistent. In fact, early Windows programs weren't always as consistent as they could have been. Standards were established quickly, however (Windows pretty much adopted the standards established for the Apple Macintosh). For example, the main menu is always at the top of the window, the first menu item is always File, the second menu is always Edit, and so on. Experience has shown that users begin to feel at home when things are where they expect them to be and when they don't have to relearn a new set of commands with each new application.

As you will see, windows look the same in different WinApps because Windows (rather than the WinApps) does the work of creating and handling windows and similar objects.

Multitasking, just to keep things hopping

Windows gives users the ability to execute several programs simultaneously, switching effortlessly from one to another by pointing at windows and clicking them with the mouse. This feature may not seem to be that big of a deal. After all, if there's only one user, why does the operating system have to support more than one program?

The ability to switch quickly from one program to another has proved to be extremely popular. Consider the following scenario. In the middle of editing a large file, you suddenly realize that a value you need is buried in a spreadsheet somewhere. With MS-DOS, you must exit from the word processor to enter the spreadsheet program. Having found the value you need, you must then exit from the spreadsheet, reenter the word processor, and find where you left off. (Just hope with all that switching back and forth that you didn't forget the number!)

With Windows, you can enter the spreadsheet program without exiting from the word processor. After you've found the number you want, you click the word-processor window to reactivate it virtually instantaneously. The value you want remains displayed in the spreadsheet window in the background.

Again, MS-DOS could have been multitasked. The problem is that there's only one display and that each DOS application expects to have complete control of it. In a windowed environment, each application is granted its own windows, but multiple windows can share the display.

Fixing proportional fonts

To keep things as simple as possible, TTYs used a fixed-width (nonproportional) font. Because not all letters are of the same width, fixed-width fonts have a stilted appearance. (Compare the nonproportional output of a typewriter to a book that uses proportional fonts.)

Because Windows "paints" characters on the display graphically, it is free to space them however it deems best. Windows can therefore support multiple, proportional fonts that enable users to create almost book-quality output.

Finally — other, much needed improvements

Windows 95 has a host of other user features. For example, MS-DOS limited filenames to eight characters followed by a three-letter extension, and Windows retained this limitation until now. Windows 95 introduces what it calls long filenames. Now, if you want, you can name your file Invitations To My Third Wedding rather than WEDINV3.DOC.

In addition, a feature called *plug-and-play* greatly simplifies the job of installing plug-in cards and peripherals: Users can simply plug in a new plug-and-play card. Communication between the card and the rest of the system during bootup enables the card to identify itself. No switch settings, IRQs, DMAs, or port settings to fuss with (whatever those things are). Even cards that don't support plug-and-play are easier to install with the new Windows 95 configuration utility.

A new, more intuitive shell eases the job of navigating. Windows 95 provides support for pen computing and telecommunications and also has enhanced LAN support.

Windows for the Programmer

Windows offers advantages to not only the user but also the applications developer. True, Windows has a sizable learning curve. In the early days of Windows programming, little could be done about it. Nowadays, Visual C++ provides several development tools that greatly simplify the job of creating Windows applications. (Compilers from other vendors, such as Borland and Symantec, provide similar tools; this book, concentrates on the tools that accompany Visual C++.)

DIG those device-independent graphics

One advantage of the PC has always been that it is an open system. Anyone with a garage and a soldering iron could build a plug-in card to go into the PC. The number and assortment of cards for the PC were rich and varied.

Although this variety is attractive to users, it has been a nightmare for developers. With printers, for example, developers of word-processing programs for MS-DOS were forced into the unenviable position of supporting hundreds of different printers (if you don't believe it, just look at WordPerfect for DOS).

Windows moves the support for different types of hardware back into the operating system. Hardware vendors provide drivers that can be installed in Windows to support their equipment. Hardware vendors create the driver at the same time they create the device. The driver is provided to customers with either the hardware itself or Windows.

For graphics devices, this device independence takes the form of the *graphics device interface,* or *GDI.* Using the GDI, individual applications see a consistent interface, irrespective of the type of printer that is attached. A well-written Windows application handles displays, printers, plotters, and most other output devices in essentially the same way.

Enhanced memory management, if I remember correctly

Users require more and more from their applications. It's not sufficient, for example, for a word processor to put words in a document and then print them on paper. Modern word-processing programs must support grammar checkers, spell checkers, multiple fonts, and page layout. These capabilities require prodigious amounts of memory.

The 8088 processor at the heart of the first PCs was a 16-bit chip capable of addressing, at most, 1 megabyte of memory. Because MS-DOS was built specifically to support this processor, the 1MB boundary became a limitation for all DOS applications.

This situation is inexcusable today when you consider that Intel has had a 32-bit processor, the 80386, on the market since 1988. Every processor since that time supports an addressing range of 4 gigabytes (GB).

All Intel processors support an 8088-compatibility mode, known as *real mode.* When you execute MS-DOS on a Pentium processor, you're using your modern, state-of-the-art Pentium as a very fast 8088 — it should be a crime. ▪

When memory came in 16-kilobyte chips, 1MB may have seemed to be a reasonable limitation, but by the time chips were dished out in 4MB sizes, that 1MB limit seemed ridiculous.

Although different vendors, including Microsoft, came up with various ways around the 1MB limit, these work-arounds were all inadequate. These kludges were generally difficult for programmers and slowed down the program. Even Windows 3.1, which relies on real mode MS-DOS for many of its features, wasn't really in a position to slip these bonds completely, either.

Windows 95 is a full 32-bit operating system: Its applications can access the full 4GB addressing range of the 80386 and later processors. Of course, it also means that Windows 95 does not run on anything less than an 80386.

The design of Windows 95 limits applications to 2GB of available addressing space, but this amount hardly seems like much of a limit. At the current rate of $50 per megabyte, that's still 100 kilobucks of memory! (I may live to eat my words. After all, at one time I thought that 1 megabyte would last me my natural programming life.) ■

Support for Intel's 32-bit addressing mode brings with it several other advantages as well. For one, it means that programmers no longer have to deal with Intel's segmented memory model. No more near pointers and far pointers to worry about. (If you don't know what a near or far pointer is, don't worry. With Windows 95, you don't have to learn.)

In addition, Windows 95 uses *protected-mode addressing* to keep each application in its own, separate address space. This type of addressing means that one poorly written application can't crash other applications that may be executing simultaneously.

Windows 3.1 tried to do some of this and had limited success. If one application made an illegal system call, it was likely to get summarily booted off the machine without affecting its neighbors. It wasn't completely successful, however. (It seemed to me that when one application crashed, there was about a 50-50 chance that I would have to reboot the machine.) ■

This discussion does not mean that Windows 95 is 32-bit throughout. Windows 95 inherits a good deal of 16-bit code from its ancestors. I imagine that, as time goes on, the amount of 16-bit code within Windows will continue to shrink. The important thing for programmers, however, is that our programs are operating in a 32-bit world, regardless of whatever might happen on the Windows side of the API fence.

Conclusion

Windows has had a long and checkered background. In its first incarnation, it was clumsy and slow. It seemed to be too much operating system for too little hardware. Basing Windows on MS-DOS limited its effectiveness.

As time has passed, however, Windows has grown to the point that Windows 95 seems to be a full-fledged operating system. The hardware necessary to run it is cheap enough. Windows 95, which is full-featured, has shed that toy feeling. (This is the first version of Windows I can personally get excited about. I've heard that sentiment expressed among many other programmers too.)

So, enough of this background material. Let's program something!

Chapter 2
Your First Windows Program

● ●

In This Chapter

▶ Introducing the code for your first Windows application (WinApp)

▶ Building and executing your first program

▶ Using Hungarian notation

▶ Accessing the Windows API

▶ Introducing handles

▶ Registering Window classes

▶ Creating and displaying windows

▶ Introducing *include* files

▶ Interfacing with APIs

▶ Declaring prototypes

▶ Executing *WinMain( )*

● ●

*I*t has become customary to begin an introductory programming book with a program that displays the phrase *Hello, world* and then quits. The reason for this custom is well known. One of the first (and certainly the most popular) introductory texts about the C language, *The C Programming Language,* by Brian Kernighan and Dennis Ritchie, started out this way, and it has been part of the culture ever since. ■

This chapter and the next one rip apart this most basic program piece by piece. Understanding this program is a painful process at times because you are introduced to a number of new concepts. But I know of no other way than to simply slug your way through it. Persevere, and we'll work through it together. I try to give you enough stopping points so that you don't become bleary-eyed and your bladder doesn't burst.

Say Hi to the "Hello, world" Program

The following program opens a window on the screen, displays the phrase *Hello, world* in the upper-left corner of the window, and then waits for you to do something. To begin, you open in Visual C++ a file called Prog1_1.cpp and enter the following program exactly as shown here.

If you don't want to type all this stuff, this program and all other programs in this book are available on the accompanying disk from SJ&K Software (see the disk offer in the back of this book). ■

```
// Prog1_1 - A Hello World program written by hand
//            without the aid of modern conveniences
//            like AppWizard

#include <windows.h>

// prototype declarations
int WINAPI WinMain(
    HINSTANCE  hInstance,     // handle of current instance
    HINSTANCE  hPrevInstance, // handle of prev instance
    LPSTR      pszCmdLine,    // command line
    int        nCmdShow       // show state of window
    );
LRESULT CALLBACK WindowProc(
    HWND    hWnd,   // handle of window
    UINT    uMsgId, // message identifier
    WPARAM  wParam, // first message parameter
    LPARAM  lParam  // second message parameter
    );

// WinMain -- this is where execution begins
int WINAPI WinMain(
    HINSTANCE  hInstance,     // handle of current instance
    HINSTANCE  hPrevInstance, // handle of prev instance
    LPSTR      pszCmdLine,    // command line
    int        nCmdShow       // show state of window
    )
{
    static char szAppName[] = "Prog1";
    HWND hWnd;
    MSG  msg;
    WNDCLASS wndClass;
```

```
// first register the window class
wndClass.style        = 0;
wndClass.lpfnWndProc = WindowProc; // callback fn
wndClass.cbClsExtra   = 0;
wndClass.cbWndExtra   = 0;
wndClass.hInstance    = hInstance;
wndClass.hIcon        = LoadIcon(NULL,IDI_APPLICATION);
wndClass.hCursor      = LoadCursor(NULL, IDC_ARROW);
wndClass.hbrBackground = GetStockObject(WHITE_BRUSH);
wndClass.lpszMenuName  = NULL;
wndClass.lpszClassName = szAppName;
if (RegisterClass(&wndClass) == 0)// register class...
{
    return 0;               // ...quit if it doesn't work
}

// now create the app's one window
hWnd = CreateWindow(
        szAppName,           // the window class name
        szAppName,           // the window caption
        WS_OVERLAPPEDWINDOW,// window style
        CW_USEDEFAULT,       // initial x and...
        CW_USEDEFAULT,       // ...y position
        CW_USEDEFAULT,       // window size in x...
        CW_USEDEFAULT,       // ...and y dimension
        NULL,                // parent window handle
        NULL,                // menu handle
        hInstance,           // program instance handle
        NULL);               // creation params
  if (hWnd == 0)
  {
      return 0;
  }
  ShowWindow(hWnd, nCmdShow);
  UpdateWindow(hWnd);

  while (GetMessage(&msg, NULL, 0, 0))
  {
      TranslateMessage(&msg);
      DispatchMessage(&msg);
  }
  return msg.wParam;
}
```

```
// WindowProc -- this function gets called to
//               process Windows messages
LRESULT CALLBACK WindowProc(
    HWND    hWnd,      // handle of window
    UINT    uMsgId,    // message identifier
    WPARAM  wParam,    // first message parameter
    LPARAM  lParam     // second message parameter
    )
{
    static char *pszHello = "Hello, world";

    // decide what to do with each different message
    // type
    switch (uMsgId)
    {
      // handle the window paint message by displaying
      // the string "Hello, world" in the upper-left
      // corner (coord 0,0) of the window
      case WM_PAINT:
        HDC hDC;
        PAINTSTRUCT paintStruct;
        hDC  = BeginPaint(hWnd, &paintStruct);

        TextOut(hDC,                    // the device context to use
                0, 0,                   // x,y location
                pszHello,               // string to write
                lstrlen(pszHello)); // string length

        EndPaint(hWnd, &paintStruct);
        return 0;

      // handle the window destroy message by quitting
      // the application
      case WM_DESTROY:
        PostQuitMessage(0);
        return 0;

      default:
        // let Windows handle all other message types
        return DefWindowProc(hWnd,uMsgId,wParam,lParam);
    }
}
```

Whew! Your first job is finished. This is definitely a good point to stop and take a break. ▪

Building and executing (aack!) the program

Let's begin by building and executing Prog1_1 so that you can see what it does. Build a project file, and add to it the single file Prog1_1.cpp. Then choose Project | Build. This action compiles Prog1_1.cpp and, if it has no errors, links the resulting object into an .EXE (*executable*) file. (Use as much or as little of Appendix B, "Visual C++ 2.0," as you need until the example program is compiled and running.)

As soon as you execute the program by choosing Debug | Go, a window like the one in Figure 2-1 is displayed, with the "Hello, world" message.

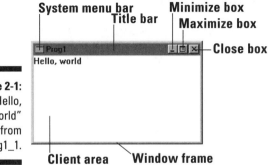

Figure 2-1:
The "Hello, world" output from Prog1_1.

Okay, so your window is not exactly like the window shown in Figure 2-1 — this figure shows the names of the parts of the window. You've already seen these parts when you've worked in Windows; however, you may not know the common names for these fixtures.

In particular, one term you may not be familiar with is *client area,* the part of the window in which the application normally writes. The client area is framed by the title bar on the top and the window frame on the other three sides. It's not that the application can't write outside the client area — it's just that it normally doesn't. (It's not something you can do accidentally.)

Before you shrug your shoulders and close the window, play with it a little. Notice that you can resize it by grabbing and dragging any of the edges of the window with your mouse. You can resize it in two dimensions by dragging one of the corners. If you make the window too narrow, the text is clipped to the available space instead of spilling out on the desktop.

You can move the window by grabbing the window by its title bar. You can "iconify" the window by clicking the Minimize box. When you do, the window "shrinks" down into its label on the task bar. You bring the program back by clicking the task bar button. You can maximize the window so that it takes up the entire screen by clicking the Maximize box.

Of course, this description is pretty mundane stuff. After all, all Windows programs do this stuff. But that's exactly the point. The "Hello, world" program is a real WinApp, entitled to all the rights and privileges thereof.

After you have finished playing with the program, terminate it by clicking the Close box. (Alternatively, the System menu box has a close option.)

Comparing the program with its evil non-Windows twin

Contrast the Windows "Hello, world" program with its MS-DOS or UNIX equivalent. First, the source code for that program is considerably simpler:

```
#include <stdio.h>
int main(void)
{
    printf("Hello, world\n");
    return 0;
}
```

Compared to the lengthy Windows listing shown earlier in this chapter, the preceding program is amazingly short. When I saw my first WinApp, I had the opposite reaction — I thought that this Windows program was amazingly *long* for a program that does nothing but display *Hello, world.* Perhaps that was your first reaction too.

Wait a minute. This WinApp does considerably more than just display some silly phrase. It supports windowing, which means that it supports moving, resizing, minimizing, maximizing, and closing that window — all the things we as users take for granted with any Windows program.

Think for a moment about how big the MS-DOS "Hello, world" program would be if it had to support all those same features. "But my "Hello, world" program doesn't need all that stuff," you argue. Yes, but "Hello, world" is not a reasonable program. Today, reasonable programs do have to support those features. Users want it. In particular, Windows users demand it.

Besides, it isn't nearly as difficult as it may seem. First, all Windows programs share this same "Hello, world" core. After you've mastered this core, you can reuse it on subsequent WinApps. Second, because this core code is common to all WinApps, Visual C++ includes tools to write this (and other common) code for you. But I'm getting ahead of myself.

You Visual Basic programmers are probably thinking, "My program supports windowing, and it's only a few lines long." That's not quite true, though. Your program is also rather large — it's just that Visual Basic writes most of it for you. Visual C++ can write much of this stuff too, as you will see later. ■

Including the Include Files

Now that you've seen "Hello, world" in action, this section describes what makes Prog1_1 tick. Let's follow a day in the life of this program by going through each section of code, one block at a time. This process lets you see what makes a Windows application work.

The first thing you see is the inclusion of windows.h. This *include* file is necessary in any Windows program. It contains the prototypes for all the Windows API functions.

What in the world is an API?

An *API*, or *application program interface*, is the interface between an application and Windows. That is, the API consists of the Windows functions an application can call.

Programming Windows by way of the API is also referred to as *SDK programming*. SDK is the Software Developers Kit, a package you had to purchase in the early days of Windows programming in order to do any Windows programming. ■

The interface to MS-DOS was assembly-language–oriented. Application programs accessed this interface by loading values into the CPU registers and executing Interrupt 21. Even if you are an experienced MS-DOS programmer, you may not have known anything about Interrupt 21 system calls. For the most part, the Standard C Library made these operating system (OS) calls for you. All you had to do was call the function you wanted from the library. When you wanted to produce output, you called *printf( )* without worrying what operating-system calls were going on underneath. If you called *getche( )* or *findfirst( )*, however, you accessed a C front-end to an MS-DOS call.

No Standard C Library calls support windowing functions. The concept of windowing didn't exist when the C library was conceived. The WinApp must therefore make the necessary Windows system calls itself. Thankfully, the interface to Windows is oriented toward languages such as C and not toward assembly language.

The API that Windows 95 supports is called the *Win32 interface,* which is essentially a 32-bit version of the Windows 3.1 interface. The API supported by Windows 95 is virtually identical to the Windows NT API. At one time, it was called the Win32c (*c* for Chicago) interface, but that name has fallen into disfavor with the Redmondian crowd.

The major differences between the Windows NT and Windows 95 API is that the Windows 95 API lacks support for some of the file-security features that Windows NT has and that it lacks support for multiple processors. ■

Okay, so what's a prototype?

Older C programs didn't usually contain function prototype declarations. Programmers simply invoked the function they wanted, and that was that. Experience with other languages showed that this was a bad idea, however. Consider the following snippet:

```
void MyFunc( )
{
    int nValue;
    nValue = AbsoluteValue(value);
}
```

The call to *AbsoluteValue( )* passing the integer *nValue* looks correct enough, but what if *AbsoluteValue( )* is expecting a floating-point value instead? The value is passed incorrectly, and the result is garbage.

To avoid this type of error, C++ requires function prototypes (C strongly encouraged the use of function prototypes, but you could still slack by).

A prototype declaration looks like a function definition without the body. The prototype defines the number and type of arguments the function expects to see. With a prototype added, the preceding code segment appears as follows:

```
double AbsoluteValue(double v);
void MyFunc( )
{
    int nValue;
    nValue = AbsoluteValue(nValue);
}
```

Now C++ can compare what the function expects to what is being passed.

In this example, you see that the *double* equivalent of *value* has to be passed to the function and the result converted back into an *int* before being stored in *value*. C++ makes the necessary conversions, and the program works as expected.

C++ requires prototype declarations to be written for every function. It is common practice to store these prototype declarations in .h *include* files, which are included in any source code that calls the functions.

The *include* file windows.h contains the prototypes for the Windows API functions.

Visual C++ uses many other Windows *include* files; just glance at the directory \MSVC20\INCLUDE. Most of the files necessary to access the Windows API are included by windows.h. ■

Prototypes are necessary in Visual Basic when you call Windows API functions, as the following example from the Visual Basic documentation demonstrates:

```
' The following declare must appear on a single line
Declare Sub FloodFill Lib "GDI"
(ByVal hDC As Integer, ByVal X As Integer,
 ByVal Y As Integer, ByVal Color As Long)

Sub Form_Click ( )
     ScaleMode = 3              ' Windows draws in pixels.
     ForeColor = 0              ' Set draw line to black.
     Line (100, 50)-(300, 50) ' Draw a triangle.
     Line -(200, 200)
     Line -(100, 50)
     FillStyle = 0              ' Set FillStyle to solid.
     FillColor = RGB(128, 128, 255) ' Set FillColor.
     FloodFill hDC, 200, 100, ForeColor
End Sub
```

The *Declare* statement describes to Visual Basic the number and arguments of the Windows function. Visual Basic uses this information in the same way C would, to make sure that the programmer is calling the function properly. The Windows API call appears as the last function in the subroutine. ■

Local prototypes

Following the windows.h *include* file in the Prog1_1 example are the prototypes for the two local functions. These prototypes appear as follows:

```
// prototype declarations
int WINAPI WinMain(
    HINSTANCE  hInstance,     // handle of current instance
    HINSTANCE  hPrevInstance,// handle of prev instance
    LPSTR      lpszCmdLine,   // command line
    int        nCmdShow       // show state of window
    );
LRESULT CALLBACK WindowProc(
    HWND    hWnd,   // handle of window
    UINT    uMsgId, // message identifier
    WPARAM  wParam, // first message parameter
    LPARAM  lParam  // second message parameter
);
```

Hungarian notation (no goulash)

Windows programs use a naming convention called *Hungarian notation* to make listings easier to read. Neither Windows nor Visual C++ enforces these rules, but if you don't follow them, you stand out like Rush Limbaugh at an ACLU convention.

The rules for Hungarian notation are as follows:

- ✔ *typedef*-created types appear in ALL CAPITAL letters (for example, an *unsigned int* is a *UINT* and not a *uint*).

- ✔ Constants and macros that have been defined in an *include* file are also in ALL CAPITAL letters (for example, 3.14159 is *PI*, not *pi* (and it's not *cornbread*, either).

- ✔ Function and structure names begin with a Capital Letter, as does each word in a multiword name. No underscores are used except for names that are covered in the first two rules (it's *MyFavoriteFood( )*, for example, not *My_Favorite_Food( )*; however, it is *GREEN_BURRITOS*).

- ✔ Object names begin with one or more lowercase letters. These letters indicate the type of the object. Therefore, *wMyIncome* is a (small) 16-bit integer.

Table 2-1 lists the indicators used for Hungarian notation. Notice that this table seems to contain some duplication. For example, both *u* and *w* designate an *unsigned int*. The difference is that, in the case of *u*, the size of the object (16 bits or 32 bits) is not important. The *w* specifies a 16-bit object.

Table 2-1 Prefixes Used in Hungarian Notation

Prefix	Data Type
p	Pointer
s	String
sz	String terminated with a zero byte
h	Handle
msg	Message
fn	Function (used with *p*)
c	*Char* (8 bits)
by	*Unsigned char* (*BYTE* or *UCHAR* — 8 bits)
n	*Int*
b	Boolean (used to hold *TRUE* or *FALSE*)
u	*Unsigned int*
w	*Unsigned int* or *short* (*WORD* — 16 bits)
l	*Long int* (32 bits)
dw	*Unsigned long int* (*DWORD* — 32 bits)

Now then, what's a handle?

You should be reasonably familiar with most of the types in Table 2-1 except for the handle entry. Like truckers on a CB radio, many objects in Windows are accessible only by their handle.

The concept of a handle is not new. Handles are used for file input and output (I/O) in the Standard C Library, as demonstrated in the following code fragment:

```
int fHandle;
fHandle = open("filename", "r");
if (fHandle)
{
    read(fHandle, block, bytesToRead);
}
close(fHandle);
```

The function *open( )* returns a handle when the file is opened successfully. This handle is presented to the *read( )* function call to read from that file. Notice that this handle is not a pointer. The program cannot use the handle directly to access information about the file. Other than passing it to a file I/O function call, the handle has no use.

Virtually the only thing about a handle a programmer can be assured of is that it cannot be zero. That is, if a function is supposed to return a handle and it returns zero, something went wrong.

Unlike the Standard C Library, which uses handles only for files, Windows uses handles for lots of different things. If the name of the object doesn't indicate the type of handle, often a few letters are tacked on to the prefix for this purpose. Thus, the variable *hwndMainDisplay* contains the handle of a window.

Handles are associated with properties such as images and pictures in Visual Basic as well. In addition, the *hDC* and *hWnd* properties are handles. ■

You're halfway through this chapter. This is probably a good time to check your fridge. ■

WinMain ( ): The First Act

The next thing in the example Prog1_1 program is *WinMain( )*. *WinMain( )* is always the first function to execute in a Windows application. It is the Windows equivalent of *main( )*. The prototype for *WinMain( )* appears as follows:

```
int WINAPI WinMain(
    HINSTANCE  hInstance,     // handle of current instance
    HINSTANCE  hPrevInstance,// handle of prev instance
    LPSTR      pszCmdLine,    // command line
    int        nCmdShow       // show state of window
    );
```

Using the Hungarian naming convention, you can see that this prototype declares *WinMain( )* to be a function that takes a handle, a second handle, a pointer to a zero-terminated string (often called an *ASCIIZ string*), and an *int*. Then it returns an *int*.

The *WINAPI* declaration means that Windows expects *WinMain( )* to use the same calling convention as other Windows API functions do.

After your program has been compiled and linked into an application, Windows doesn't know in which language the program was written. It can't know, therefore, to call *WinMain( )* using C++ calling conventions. Instead, Windows defines a calling convention for all languages, to which your C++ programs must adapt. If you were writing your programs in Pascal, for example, they would have to adapt to this same *WINAPI* convention.

At the time Windows 1.0 was conceived, Pascal reigned over the computer-language kingdom. Microsoft, demonstrating its amazing clairvoyance again, chose the Pascal calling convention for the Windows API just as C was beginning to dominate the language market. Declaring a C function *WINAPI* is telling it to use Pascal calling conventions. ■

The arguments to WinMain ( )

The *hInstance* argument to *WinMain( )* is the handle of the current program. This argument can be used by the WinApp to access information about the program's status. The second argument, *hPrevInstance*, is always zero and is ignored in Windows 95.

In Windows 3.1 and earlier, *hPrevInstance* contained the handle of any previous instance of the same program. If you started WordPad twice, for example, the second time you started it, *hPrevInstance* referred back to the first. (Why would you start it twice? I dunno — maybe you wanted to edit two files at the same time.) Because Windows 95 keeps each instance of a program completely separate from every other instance, it leaves this field at zero. ■

The *pszCmdLine* parameter points to any command-line parameters that are passed to the program. You can start a WinApp such as WordPad from the MS-DOS command line, for example, by entering the following command:

    WORDPAD MYFILE.TXT

If you do, *pszCmdLine* points to the string *MYFILE.TXT*.

It also points to *MYFILE.TXT* if the file has been dragged with the mouse and dropped on the WordPad icon or if you double-click the file MYFILE.TEXT and WORDPAD is registered to handle .TXT files. ■

You may have noticed that the type of *pszCmdLine* is *LPSTR*. *PSTR* stands for "a *p*ointer to a *str*ing," but what does the *L* stand for? Under 16-bit Windows, *pszCmdLine* is a long pointer to a string. Under Windows 95, no distinction is made between long and short pointers, so you can use the equivalent type *PSTR*; if you do, however, your programs do not compile properly under older versions of Windows. (I debated longer about whether to include the *L* than I did about whether my beer has good taste or is less filling, but it seems that adding an extra letter to the front of pointer types is not too much to ask in the name of compatibility.) ◼

The final *nCmdShow* argument to *WinMain( )* tells the application how to display the initial window will be displayed. Typical values for this variable are *SW_SHOW-NORMAL*, *SW_SHOWMINIMIZED*, and *SW_SHOWMAXIMIZED*, indicating that the application is being started in a normal window, a maximized window, or a minimized window (as an icon), respectively.

Minimizing is what the X-Windows world calls *iconifying*. That is, minimizing turns the window into an icon on the task bar, and maximizing makes the window fill the screen. ◼

Registering the Windows class (and no standing in line!)

WinMain( ) begins by registering the application's window class. This process is similar to introducing Windows to your application's main window: "Mr. Windows, I want to introduce you to my little window. Window, meet Mr. Windows."

The term *class* here is not used in the same sense as a C++ class. ◼

A window is always based on a registered window class. The window class tells Windows certain important properties about the window. More than one window can be created from a single window class. For example, all the menu windows can be created with the same window class.

WinMain( ) registers the window class by first filling in a *WNDCLASS* structure, which is defined as follows:

```
typedef struct _WNDCLASSW
{
    UINT         style;
    WNDPROC      lpfnWndProc;
    int          cbClsExtra;
    int          cbWndExtra;
    HINSTANCE    hInstance;
    HICON        hIcon;
    HCURSOR      hCursor;
    HBRUSH       hbrBackground;
    LPCWSTR      lpszMenuName;
    LPCWSTR      lpszClassName;
} WNDCLASS;
```

The *style* member controls certain redraw characteristics of the window. Constants carrying the prefix *CS_* are *#defined* in windows.h for this purpose. For example, setting *style* to *CS_NOCLOSE* before registering the class disables the Close box on the window frame and under the system menu icon.

Each of these *CS_* flags is defined as a constant with a single bit set to allow these properties to be combined. For example, the following expression combines three properties:

```
wndClass.style = CS_DBLCLK | CS_HREDRAW | CS_VREDRAW;
```

This assignment tells Windows to redraw the entire window whenever the window is resized in either the horizontal or vertical dimensions and to send double-click messages to the window. In this case, you don't need any of the preceding flags, so you set *style* to zero.

The second member, *lpfnWndProc*, is a pointer to a function that is associated with any window created with the newly registered window class.

In this example, you set it to point to *WindowProc* as follows:

```
wndClass.lpfnWndProc = WindowProc;
```

As you will see, this function handles messages for this WinApp. Because you don't have the foggiest idea what that means yet, skip it until the message loop is discussed later in this chapter.

The third and fourth members of the class define the class and the window extensions:

```
wndClass.cbClsExtra = 0;
wndClass.cbWndExtra = 0;
```

These members enable programmers to add data members to the end of the class structure and window structure definitions. Because C++ provides a much better way to store this type of information, set these values to zero and forget about them. (That was easy).

The fifth member, *hInstance*, is set to the instance handle of the current application passed to you as the first argument to *WinMain( )*:

```
wndClass.hInstance   = hInstance;
```

This member enables Windows to associate the window class with the proper program.

The *hIcon* member is set to the handle of the icon to be used for this application. The icon is the symbol (a small bitmap or picture) that is used when the application is minimized or when the program is examined in its folder. Visual C++ has a tool for creating bitmaps, but Windows has several default bitmaps. The following function call selects one of these default icons:

```
wndClass.hIcon = LoadIcon(NULL, IDI_APPLICATION);
```

Some other default icons are *IDI_ASTERISK*, *IDI_EXCLAMATION*, *IDI_HAND*, and *IDI_QUESTION*.

The *hCursor* member is set to the handle of the bitmap that will be used for the cursor:

```
wndClass.hCursor    = LoadCursor(NULL, IDC_ARROW);
```

Again, this application uses one of the defaults, the arrow cursor. Other default cursors are *IDC_CROSS* (a crosshair), *IDC_IBEAM*, *IDC_NO* (a slashed circle), and *IDC_WAIT* (an hourglass).

The next member, *hbrBackground*, identifies the background brush that will be used to paint the background in the client area of the window:

```
wndClass.hbrBackground = GetStockObject(WHITE_BRUSH);
```

This sounds a little strange to an old command-line programmer like me, but remember that windows are painted graphically. You paint with a brush. If you want the background to be white, therefore, you have to choose a white brush. (That makes sense.) Notice that, unlike real brushes, Windows brushes can paint patterns (such as checkerboard patterns). Part III, has much more to say about painting and brushes.

The *lpszMenuName* member points to the name of the menu class to be used with this window class:

```
wndClass.lpszMenuName   = NULL;
```

Because this WinApp has no menus, *NULL* works fine.

The final member, *lpszClassName*, is set to the name to be used for the window class:

```
wndClass.lpszClassName = szAppName;
```

Normally, for the main window in a program, you use the same name as the name of the program.

After the *WNDCLASS* is all dressed up, it's time to go to the party.

The window class is registered by passing the address of the *wndClass* object to the Windows API function *RegisterClass( )*:

```
if (RegisterClass(&wndClass) == 0)
{
    return 0;  // quit if it doesn't work
}
```

RegisterClass( ) returns a zero if it doesn't work (in that case, you should return from the program with a zero because there is no hope of progressing).

Creating the window

The next step after registering the window class is to create an instance of the window.

The relationship between a window class and a window is the same as the relationship between the class Author and me. There is only one class Author. I am an instance of the class Author (not a good instance, perhaps, but an instance nonetheless). There are lots of other authors, all instances of class Author (and all scurrying around looking for instances of class Contract with lots of instances of class Money attached, no doubt).

The *CreateWindow( )* API call is defined as follows:

```
HWND CreateWindow(
    LPCTSTR  lpszClassName, // registered class name
    LPCTSTR  lpszWindowName,// window name
    DWORD    dwStyle,       // window style
    int      nX,            // hor pos of window
    int      nY,            // ver pos of window
    int      nWidth,        // window width
    int      nHeight,       // window height
    HWND     hwndParent,    // handle of parent or owner window
    HMENU    hmenu,         // handle of menu
    HANDLE   hinst,         // handle of application instance
    LPVOID   lpvParam       // address of window-creation data
    );
```

Getting this type of information about the Window API functions is easy. From within Visual C++, place your cursor on the function you want information about and press F1. A help window should appear, showing the information you want.

If you want even more information, look under the Help window and choose Books Online. At first, the Books Online section is a little difficult to navigate. For API functions, look under Windows API, where you find the topic Alphabetical Function Reference. Within this section, just look up the function by name. The Quick Reference provides essentially the same information as Books Online does, but without the amplifying data, so it loads slightly faster.

See Appendix B, "Visual C++ 2.0," if you need additional assistance in using the Visual C++ help system.

After a while, as you begin to get the hang of it, you'll wonder how you ever survived without on-line help. ■

In the Prog1_1 example program, the call to *CreateWindow( )* appears as follows:

```
hWnd = CreateWindow(
          szAppName,           // the window class name
          szAppName,           // the window caption
          WS_OVERLAPPEDWINDOW,// window style
          CW_USEDEFAULT,       // initial x and...
          CW_USEDEFAULT,       // ...y position
          CW_USEDEFAULT,       // window size in x...
          CW_USEDEFAULT,       // ...and y dimension
          NULL,                // parent window handle
          NULL,                // menu handle
          hInstance,           // prgrm instance handle
          NULL);               // creation params
```

The first argument to *CreateWindow( )* is the name under which the window class was registered. *szAppName* is the same string that was used earlier, in the *RegisterClass( )* call.

The second argument points to the window title. This string appears in the title bar when the window is displayed. For simplicity, I use the same name as the window class.

The third argument specifies certain details about the type of window. Specifying *WS_VSCROLL*, for example, causes the window to be displayed with a vertical scroll bar. Specifying *WS_OVERLAPPEDWINDOW* (the most common selection) means that the window is conventional, with a title bar, system menu, and frame and with Minimize, Maximize, and Close boxes.

The next two arguments specify the initial *x* and *y* location of the window that is displayed. The two arguments after that specify the initial size of the window. The constant *CW_USEDEFAULT* enables Windows to choose the size and location of the window to best fit the existing window layout.

The next two arguments are the handles of the parent and menu windows, respectively. In this case, both are zero.

The next argument specifies the instance handle of the current application. Again, this argument was provided in the call to *WinMain( )*.

The final argument is always zero.

The return from *CreateWindow( )* is the handle of the window that is created. If the handle returned is zero, the program terminates because something went goofy.

Displaying the window

It may be surprising, but creating a window does not cause anything to be displayed on your monitor. Creating the window creates all the necessary structures within Windows; to make the window visible, however, the program must invoke *ShowWindow( )*, passing it the handle of the window and the *nCmdShow* parameter passed to *WinMain( )*. The first argument tells *ShowWindow( )* which window to display, and the second argument tells it how to display the window: minimized (as an icon), normal, or maximized (full screen).

The reason that creating a window does not display it is to enable the program to create all the windows it needs at the beginning of execution. When a program first starts up, people expect it to take a certain amount of time, so adding a small delay then is more acceptable. When the window is needed, the program can show the window quickly by popping it up without having to create it first. ■

Getting That Darned Message Out

The *ShowWindow( )* call puts the window on your monitor, but it *still* doesn't display the *Hello, world* message you've been trying so desperately to see. The *UpdateWindow( )* call that immediately follows the *ShowWindow( )* call uses a roundabout mechanism to display the message. Read the following sentence carefully: *The UpdateWindow( ) call causes a WM_PAINT message to be sent to the application to ask it to repaint the window.*

If the preceding sentence makes any sense to you, you already know something you haven't been telling me about. To understand what the phrase "causes a WM_PAINT message to be sent to the application" could possibly mean, you have to understand something about the Windows message loop and event programming, which are discussed in the next chapter.

Chapter 3

The Message Loop: "Hello, world" at Last!

● ●

In This Chapter

▶ Handling the message loop

▶ Introducing event-based programming

▶ Dealing with the *WM_PAINT* message

▶ Learning what a DC is (other than the nation's capital)

▶ Understanding the graphics device interface and device-independent output

▶ Responding to events and to different messages

▶ Introducing desktops

▶ Painting windows

▶ Learning about HDCs

▶ Introducing invalid rectangles

▶ Introducing the clipping region

● ●

*I*n Chapter 2, "Your First Windows Program," you registered your window class with Windows so that the two are on a first-name basis. You then created a window as an instance of the window class. But you still haven't succeeded in getting the *Hello, world* message out on your screen.

In this chapter, you learn how Windows and Windows applications (WinApps) work together through the message loop to get things done, such as displaying silly messages in windows. You also learn how Windows works with the application to handle appearing and disappearing windows.

Looping Around with the Message Loop

Consider the following seemingly trivial event. While working on this book, I was struck by a truly awe-inspiring process-improvement idea that I just had to send to all my colleagues. I popped up a mail window and began typing. (If you want to follow along, mail is one of the Network tools. Click the Start button, and then choose Programs, followed by Network and then Mail. Whew!)

After I had typed out my thoughts, I ended up with the screen shown in Figure 3-1.

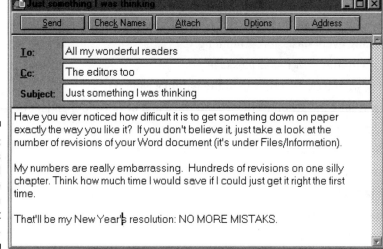

Figure 3-1: The author's initial message appears in its first incarnation.

Unfortunately, this window covered up my favorite Magic Eye calendar, which was sitting in the background (isn't Windows wonderful?), so I resized the window until it looked like Figure 3-2.

Then something extraordinary occurred to me. As I resized the mail window horizontally, the text of my message was not simply clipped off — it was wrapped to fit the confines of the window. Compare Figure 3-1 with Figure 3-2 more closely, and you'll see what I mean.

Understanding this extraordinary capability is central to comprehending the way Windows and Windows applications interact.

When a DOS application is executed, it essentially takes over control of the computer. It may ask MS-DOS to perform certain functions, such as reading a file from time to time by issuing system calls, but the DOS application retains control.

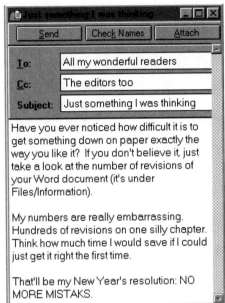

Figure 3-2:
This mail
message
has been
resized.

The situation with a Windows application is just the opposite: Windows stays in the driver's seat. With a word-processing program, for example, as you move the mouse, open windows, and so on, control stays primarily within Windows. It's only when you ask Windows to do something it doesn't already know how to do, such as reformat a document, that Windows must ask the word-processing program for help.

Coming from a command-line background, this process may seem backward, but look at its advantages. No matter how many WinApps may be executing at one time, none of them ever takes over complete control of your computer. You can jump back and forth between applications and between windows within an application. By retaining control, Windows can orchestrate between multiple WinApps, interpreting your mouse clicks and keyboard input by asking them for their help when necessary.

Basing events on event-based programming

What exactly does it mean that Windows asks the application for help? Does it walk up to the application and say something like, "Excuse me, but could you give me a hand with this?" In a way, it does exactly that.

First, you should understand that Windows is designed to react to external happenings, called *events*. For example, a mouse click is an event. Pressing a key is an event. Basically, nothing happens without an event happening first to kick it off.

A clock inside your PC creates timer events so that things can start even when you aren't doing anything. For example, screen savers are initiated from timer events. An *idle event* even occurs when absolutely nothing else is going on! ▪

When an event occurs, Windows generates a message and sends it to the proper application. How does Windows know which is the proper application?

For events related to the mouse, the proper application is the one that owns the window at which the pointer is pointing. For keyboard events, it's the foreground application. Usually this application is the one in the topmost window.

You can tell which application is the foreground application because the title bar at the top of its window is highlighted. The title bar in the window of any other application is a neutral color. ▪

Some messages are of general interest and are sent to all active applications.

How does an application receive a message? It must ask for it. It works much like a special-delivery mailbox does. After the application has worked off all previous messages, it reads its input mailbox. If nothing is in the mailbox, the application is suspended — there is no reason to waste perfectly good CPU cycles on an application that has nothing to do.

After an event occurs with which Windows needs help, Windows bundles up a message with the relevant information in it and puts the message in the application's mailbox. Windows then wakes up the application so that the reading can be completed and the application can process the message.

If another event occurs while the application is off processing the first event, the message goes into the mailbox and waits there until the application can return and read the mailbox again. An application can read only a single message at a time from the mailbox, no matter how many messages are stored there; by continually reading and processing messages from the mailbox, however, the application eventually exhausts the supply and is suspended again.

To speed things up, messages have priority (some messages are automatically added to the front of the queue, and others are shoved to the back). ▪

Okay, it's beginning to get good. If you need a break, take one now so that you can hold on throughout the next section. ■

Getting loopy with the "Hello, world" message loop

In the example WinApp Prog1_1, you see the message loop in action at the end of *WinMain( )*:

```
while (GetMessage(&msg, NULL, 0, 0))
{
    TranslateMessage(&msg);
    DispatchMessage(&msg);
}
return msg.wParam;
```

The function call *GetMessage( )* reads a message from the program's mailbox. Notice that you didn't have to create the mailbox — it was created for you when the application started up.

The first argument to *GetMessage( )* is the address of a MSG structure that will receive the message. *Defaulting* the next three arguments means that you are willing to accept all messages sent to any window that belongs to this application. *GetMessage( )* returns a *TRUE* when it receives any message other than the *WM_QUIT* message. (You can read more about this subject later in this chapter — sounds mysterious, doesn't it?)

A MSG is defined as follows:

```
typedef struct  _MSG
{
    HWND hwnd;
    UINT message;
    WPARAM wParam;
    LPARAM lParam;
    DWORD time;
    POINT pt;
} MSG;
```

The data members of the MSG structure are defined in this list:

✔ *hwnd* contains the handle of the window to which the message is being sent. In the sample program, this window is the one you created with the *CreateWindow( )* call. It's the only window you have. In an application with more than one window, however, you can use *hwnd* to determine which window will receive the message.

✔ *message* contains a number that uniquely identifies the type of message. Each type of message is identified by a constant defined in windows.h. These constants begin with *WM_*, followed by some name that describes the nature of the message. For example, Windows sends the application a *WM_QUIT* message when it's time for the program to collect its toys and go home. (This field really should be *uMessage*, but Microsoft doesn't always follow its own rules.)

✔ *wParam* is a 16-bit message parameter. The exact meaning of this value is message-dependent.

✔ *lParam* is a 32-bit message parameter. Ditto.

✔ *time* represents the time the message was written in the mailbox. This field is not like the date; rather, it's the length of time measured since Windows was booted. Windows uses this field to keep the messages in the proper order.

✔ *pt* contains the coordinates of the mouse pointer at the time the message was put in the mailbox. This location may or may not be useful, depending on the message.

GetMessage( ) returns a *FALSE* when it reads a *WM_QUIT* message and a *TRUE* when it reads any other message. The message loop that contains the *GetMessage( )* call continues, therefore, until a *WM_QUIT* message is received. The application returns the value stored in the *wParam* parameter of the *WM_QUIT* message.

After the message has been read (assuming that it's not a *WM_QUIT* message), it first goes through a translation process by passing it to the function *TranslateMessage( )*. This function converts some keyboard messages, but for most message types it has no effect, so you can ignore it for now.

The next function call, *DispatchMessage( )*, asks Windows to pass the message to the message handler for the window specified in the MSG structure. You told Windows to use the function *WindowProc( )* as the message handler for your window when you registered the window class (refer to Chapter 2, "Your First Windows Program," if you don't remember). That is, Windows calls the function *WindowProc( )* to process the message. After *WindowProc( )* finishes with the message, the code loops back up and gets another message, thus completing the message loop.

Responding Pleasantly to Events: WindowProc ( )

The function that handles messages is called the *window proc* (pronounced "prock"). It must be declared like *WindowProc( )* from the Prog1_1 example program, as shown here:

```
// WindowProc - this function gets called to process
//              Windows messages
LRESULT CALLBACK WindowProc(
    HWND    hWnd,    // handle of window
    UINT    uMsgId,  // message identifier
    WPARAM  wParam,  // first message parameter
    LPARAM  lParam   // second message parameter
);
```

The arguments to this function are the same as the first four members of the MSG structure returned from the *GetMessage( )* call discussed earlier. *WindowProc( )* returns a zero if it successfully handles the message.

Declaring the function *CALLBACK* makes it the proper storage class to be called from Windows.

Windows uses Pascal calling conventions. Declaring a function *CALLBACK* is virtually the same as declaring it *WINAPI*: It prepares it to be called like a Pascal function. ■

The window proc has the responsibility of handling any of the messages Windows might throw at it. Learning what these messages are and what they mean is your primary job when you learn to program in Windows.

Responding to Different Messages

The different messages your window proc receives have little in common. That is, different messages are processed in different ways. The window proc usually begins, therefore, with a *switch* statement followed by a *case* statement for each message ID the window proc intends to handle specifically. Most window procs have the following internal structure:

```
switch (uMsgId)
{
 case WM_<something or other>:
    //process the message here
    return 0;

   case WM_<something else>:
    //process that message too
    return 0;

   default:
    //let Windows handle all other message types
    return DefWindowProc(hWnd, uMsgId, wParam, lParam);
}
```

It's important to return a zero after you've processed the message — it tells Windows not to keep trying. For messages you don't intend to process, your window proc must pass them on to *DefWindowProc( )* for default processing. It's important to return whatever value that function returns as well.

A programmer never has to deal with the actual value of the *WM_* constants. (For example, I just looked up *WM_QUIT*. It has the value 0×12, but I didn't know that until just now, and I hope to forget it as soon as possible. To me, it's just *WM_QUIT*.) ■

Tagging your screen with the WM_PAINT message

Almost every WinApp must deal with two messages. The first one is the *WM_PAINT* message. This message is sent whenever Windows needs the current window repainted. The following statement may not be helpful to you, but I'll say it anyway: The window must be repainted whenever it is invalid.

The *WM_PAINT* handler repaints only the *client area:* the area inside the frame and underneath the title bar. Windows handles the rest of the window. ■

What is an "invalid window"? Is the data it contains incorrect? Maybe the window is crooked? The invalid window is another concept Windows programmers must master. (Will it never cease?)

Of desktops and white boards

Windows was built using what is called the "desktop metaphor." That is, the windows on your screen are supposed to look and act like sheets of paper on your desktop.

When you put a sheet of paper on your desk, it may cover up other sheets of paper so that the words and pictures they contain are obscured. As soon as you pick up the top sheet of paper, however, the obscured pages become visible again.

A video monitor is not like a three-dimensional desk, however. It more closely resembles a two-dimensional whiteboard (the modern-day equivalent of the chalkboard).

If your whiteboard is full of information, you must erase something before you can write a new page of text or graphics. Whatever information you erase is lost from the whiteboard. To restore the whiteboard to its former state after you've erased the new information, you must repaint whatever was there. But how do you do that? How can you know what was there?

Windowed environments have the same problem. When a window is obscured, the information that normally is on the screen is lost. When the window is unobscured, how can the lost information be restored? This problem is common to all windowing environments, and there are exactly two ways to solve it.

The first solution is for the operating system to save the window information (or at least the obscured parts) internally. If the operating system is really good, the application may continue to write to the window without caring whether the window is visible. After the window is unobscured, the operating system copies the necessary data to the screen for viewing. The X-Windows windowing environment for UNIX works in this way.

This solution is attractive for the person who writes the application because it places most of the burden on the operating system. The application doesn't have to keep track of anything — the operating system does. Programs written for these types of environments more closely resemble their command-line counterparts.

The main problem with this solution is that it consumes large gobs of memory. Storing a full-screen window meant for a multicolor, high-resolution monitor can consume a full 2MB of memory. Memory is a limited resource (and at my age, it's getting more limited all the time). You can't consume many 2MB chunks, even at today's low prices, before you run out. This solution is reasonable, therefore, only on UNIX workstations, on which 32MB of memory and more is typical, and in nongraphical environments (such as DesqView), in which the amount of data to be stored is less.

The second solution is to let the application regenerate the lost data as necessary. To return to the whiteboard analogy, when you need some portion of the whiteboard repainted, just get the person who put the information there in the first place to write it again.

This solution puts a slightly larger burden on the application programmer, but it considerably reduces the amount of memory that is necessary. (Remember that Windows 1.0 was designed to run in less than 512K of memory.) All WinApps work in this way.

In a few situations, to save time, Windows uses the X-Windows approach of copying information and restoring it without the application's help. The point is that Windows leaves the restoration work to the application the majority of the time. ∎

Getting back to the WM_PAINT message

A window is invalid when the data in the window is missing or out of date. This was also the reason for the call to *UpdateWindow( )* in the Prog1_1 example program. After you created the window, it was blank and therefore invalid. Calling *UpdateWindow( )* goads Windows into sending the application a *WM_PAINT* message, which is Windows' way of saying, "Hey, Prog1_1, please repaint that window for me."

Prog1_1 responds to the *WM_PAINT* message by displaying the *Hello, world* message (at last). The code to do so appears as follows:

```
// handle the window paint message by displaying
// the string "Hello, world" in the upper-left
// corner (coord 0,0) of the window
case WM_PAINT:
  static char *pszHello = "Hello, world";
  HDC hDC;
  PAINTSTRUCT paintStruct;
  hDC  = BeginPaint(hWnd, &paintStruct);

  TextOut(hDC,      // the device context to use
          0, 0,     // x,y location
          pszHello, // string to write
          lstrlen(pszHello)); // string length

  EndPaint(hWnd, &paintStruct);
  return 0;
```

The code begins by calling *BeginPaint( )*, which performs all the necessary steps to get ready to paint, including returning a handle you use for output. As mystical as that might sound, I'll leave it at that until you get to Chapter 4, "Painting Versus Writing."

The function then calls *TextOut( )* and passes it the handle to write with, the *x* and *y* location to write to, and the string and string length to write. The

Standard C Library function *strlen( )* returns the length of an ASCIIZ string in bytes; the *lstrlen( )* function is the Windows equivalent of the same thing. The only difference is that *lstrlen( )* accommodates 16-bit Oriental character sets when necessary.

TextOut( ) displays the specified string at the specified location and uses the current font. The x and y location is in units of pixels measured from the upper-left corner of the client area. The y value increases downward, and the x value increases to the right. (Other coordinate systems are possible, as discussed in Chapter 4, but this default is good enough for now.)

The call to *EndPaint( )* returns to the paint box all the paint supplies that *Begin-Paint( )* pulled out.

When is it necessary to repaint?
(When the paint begins to peel, of course)

All this paint stuff raises a question: Under what conditions is the program asked to repaint its window? You can easily answer this question by making a minor change to Prog1_1 to keep count of the number of times the window has been updated.

Because all manually generated WinApps look basically alike, I've reproduced only the window proc (to help you even more, lines that have been added or changed are shown in gray): ∎

```
// WindowProc - this function gets called to
//              process Windows messages.
//              Modified to display repaint count.
LRESULT CALLBACK WindowProc(
    HWND    hWnd,     // handle of window
    UINT    uMsgId,   // message identifier
    WPARAM  wParam,   // first message parameter
    LPARAM  lParam    // second message parameter
   )
{
    char buffer[128];
    static int nCount = 0;

    // decide what to do with each different message
    // type
    switch (uMsgId)
    {
       // handle the window paint message by displaying
```

```
// the string "Hello, world" in the upper-left
// corner (coord 0,0) of the window
case WM_PAINT:

    // make sure that the entire window is available
    // for writing
    InvalidateRgn(hWnd, 0, TRUE);

    HDC hDC;
    PAINTSTRUCT paintStruct;
    hDC = BeginPaint(hWnd, &paintStruct);

    // keep a count of every time you're asked to
    // update the window
    wsprintf(buffer,
            "Hello, world (number %03d)", ++nCount);
    TextOut(hDC,      // the device context to use
            0, 0,     // x,y location
            buffer, lstrlen(buffer));

    EndPaint(hWnd, &paintStruct);
    return 0;

// handle the window destroy message by quitting
// the application
case WM_DESTROY:
  PostQuitMessage(0);
  return 0;

default:
  // let Windows handle all other message types
  return DefWindowProc(hWnd,uMsgId,wParam,lParam);
  }
 }
```

These additions define a static variable *count*, which keeps track of the number of times the window has been redrawn by using the *WM_PAINT* message. The *wsprintf( )* call converts *nCount* into an ASCII string that is tacked on to your *Hello, world* message. (The Windows function *wsprintf( )* is similar to the Standard C Library function *sprintf( )* except that, by not supporting floating-point conversions, it does not cause the floating-point library to be loaded, thus rendering a smaller executable file.) The result of the conversion is stored in *buffer*, which is produced by way of the *TextOut( )* call, as you saw earlier in this chapter.

The call to *InvalidateRgn( )* makes sure that the entire window, including the area that contains the modified text, is repainted so that you can see the changes to the *nCount* variable. ▪

Watch what happens when you execute the program. When the window first appears, the count is one — that's logical. When you move the window slightly by grabbing its title bar, the count stays at one. The reason is that no information was added to the window when it was moved. Therefore, the application was not called on to repaint the window.

Try making the window slightly smaller. Again, the count stays at one because, again, no information was added. Minimize the window, and then reopen it. Aha! The count increases to two. Try making the window larger. Again, the repaint count increases.

Expanding the window creates the possibility that information will be added. Because Windows doesn't know what this extra information might be, it is forced to ask the application to redraw the window with the new window dimensions to supply the extra information.

Move the window so that at least part of it is off the screen. Then move it back into the middle of the screen. Again, the window is repainted. The portion of the window that hangs out beyond the end of the screen is apparently lost.

Experiment with other conditions. Partially obscuring your window with another window does not increase the count. After your window has been obscured, uncovering it (bringing it back to the top) does increase the count.

Try changing *wndClass.style* as follows:

```
wndClass.style = CS_HREDRAW | CS_VREDRAW;
```

This option asks Windows to redraw the window whenever it's resized.

Now a *WM_PAINT* message is generated whenever the window is resized, even if the window size is only decreased.

In a few cases, Windows retains the information necessary to restore the window. Moving the mouse pointer across a window, for example, does not cause it to be repainted. Windows temporarily saves the information obscured by the pointer and replaces it when the mouse pointer moves on. Windows saves the information obscured by a drop-down window as well.

The WM_DESTROY message

The Prog1_1 example program deals with only one other message: *WM_DESTROY*. This message is much easier to handle than the *WM_PAINT* message is.

The *WM_DESTROY* message is sent whenever a user closes the window (after the window has been removed from the screen). In the Prog1_1 example program, because this is the only window you have, there's nothing left to do but quit.

The program quits by sending itself a *WM_QUIT* message by way of the *PostQuitMessage( )* call. When *GetMessage( )* finds this message in the mailbox, it returns a *FALSE* that exits from the loop, thereby causing the program to terminate. The argument to *PostQuitMessage( )* is stored as the *wParam* parameter in the message. This value is eventually returned when the program terminates. Returning a value of zero means that all went well. ■

Are You with Me So Far?

To make sure that you're keeping up, this section presents a recap of what you've learned in the first part of this chapter:

- ✔ You should now be able to read Prog1_1 without assistance. If you don't understand some aspect of it, reread the relevant sections of this chapter until you do.

- ✔ Prog1_1 follows the pattern used in almost all Windows applications. The WinApp begins by registering a window class (maybe more than one), and then it creates an instance of the class with one or more windows. Finally, it sits back and waits for messages to come pouring in as a result of external events.

- ✔ The most important message all WinApps must handle is the *WM_PAINT* message, which is a request from Windows to the application to refresh some part of the window.

By the way, you might be wondering why Prog1_1 didn't display the *Hello, world* message when the window was first created. It certainly could have.

The problem is that the program must have the capability to restore the *Hello, world* message on request, so why repeat the code?

This situation is typical of the way all WinApps work. When an event occurs that would cause the displayed text to change, the program does not display the change immediately. Instead, it records the change and then invalidates the window to let the *WM_PAINT* code handle the output of the change.

Fortunately, it is possible to invalidate just a small section of the window to reduce the area that must be repainted. How do you do that? And why do they call it *WM_PAINT* and not *WM_WRITE*? And what's an HDC? And how do you know when to hold 'em and when to fold 'em?

This is another good stopping point, by the way, before you get into some more good stuff. ■

Interfacing with the Graphics Device Interface

As a graphical interface, Windows must support graphics on many different types of devices. Today, printers of all descriptions hammer, burn, lase, and jet both images and text in a variety of languages.

In addition, display screens come in different sizes and resolutions. Windows could have put the burden of supporting these different devices on the application, as MS-DOS did. Fortunately for us, however, Windows offers something called the graphics device interface, or GDI.

Have you ever noticed how SWDs (software developers) use an abundance of TLAs (three-letter acronyms)? I probably use at least 100 different TLAs in an NWD (normal workday). ■

A *GDI* is a set of functions that supports device-independent output. Using these GDI functions, a WinApp can perform output without knowing or caring exactly which type of device will receive it. This sentence means two things. First, you can write a WinApp so that it takes full advantage of the available screen resolution, whether it's 800×600 or 1024×768 and whether it has a palette of 16 colors or 16 million colors. Second, a WinApp doesn't even have to know that it's displaying things on a screen. In fact, in a properly written WinApp, the same code displays things on the screen, to a printer, to the print preview, or to any other graphics output device.

If the application doesn't know about the specifics of the different devices, what does? Windows itself? Not exactly.

Just as Windows defines an interface for the application software, it also defines an interface for hardware manufacturers. The manufacturer writes a device driver that is compatible with this interface and then supplies the driver either with the device or to Microsoft for inclusion in Windows. If you purchase a new LaserJet printer from Hewlett-Packard, for example, you will likely find a floppy disk in the box with a new Windows driver. You install the driver from the Control Panel.

The driver converts the generic requests from Windows into the specific language of the hardware device. ∎

More funny letters: the HDC

The *TextOut( )* function you used in the "Hello, world" program is one of the GDI functions. Like most GDI functions, the first argument to *TextOut( )* is an HDC. An *HDC* is a handle to something called a device context.

A handle is simply a way to get at something. Specifically, a handle is not a pointer. ∎

A *device context* is a data structure associated with a display device, such as a printer, a plotter, or a window on the screen. The device context describes the properties of the device to the GDI functions, such as the height and width of the monitor, the number of colors supported, and the resolution. (The device context is created and maintained by the device driver.) The device context, which is the computer equivalent of a picture ID, also describes temporary properties, such as the current background color.

Before a WinApp can write to a window, it first must get a device-context descriptor for that window — no display function can cash a check without a valid picture ID, handle to a valid device context.

In responding to the *WM_PAINT* message, the "Hello, world" program built a device context by calling the function *BeginPaint( )*.

BeginPaint( ) should not be called in response to any message other than a *WM_PAINT* message. ∎

When you use *BeginPaint( )*, your code looks like the following:

```
case WM_PAINT:
    HDC hDC;
    PAINTSTRUCT paintStruct;
    hDC  = BeginPaint(hWnd, &paintStruct);

    //...process the WM_PAINT message

    EndPaint(hWnd, &paintStruct);
    return 0;
```

The call to *BeginPaint( )* creates a device context for the window referenced by *hWnd* and returns its handle. The call to *EndPaint( )* returns the device context to Windows for destruction. Among other things, destroying the device context returns to the memory pool the memory occupied by the device context.

If you call *BeginPaint( )* to allocate a device context, you must call *EndPaint( )* to free that resource before returning from processing the message. ■

The device context must be returned to Windows after the *WM_PAINT* message has been processed. The device-context handle that is returned from *Begin-Paint( )* cannot be retained and used to process another message. By the time another message is received, the data in the device context may be invalid.

The call to *EndPaint( )* does one other thing. It tells Windows that the client area of the window has been updated (that it is no longer invalid). In Windows terminology, you say that the window has been *validated*.

Of course, we can lie. A WinApp can do something like the following:

```
case WM_PAINT:
    HDC hDC;
    PAINTSTRUCT paintStruct;
    hDC  = BeginPaint(hWnd, &paintStruct);
    EndPaint(hWnd, &paintStruct);
    return 0;
```

Here you see that the application has done nothing to restore the contents of the window; however, the act of calling *BeginPaint( )* followed by *EndPaint( )* is sufficient to fool Windows into believing that the window has been restored.

The following is *not* sufficient, however:

```
case WM_PAINT:
    return 0;
```

If the application returns without first validating the window, Windows peevishly sends another *WM_PAINT* message, asking it to go back and try again. Windows continues to send *WM_PAINT* messages until the application validates the window. In this case, Windows is just as stubborn in insisting that the window be validated as the application is in not validating it — an infinite loop results. (It resembles the situation at my dinner table when I tell my son that he can't get up from the table until he eats his Brussels sprouts.) ■

Use *BeginPaint( )* only when you're responding to a *WM_PAINT* message. Always call *EndPaint( )* before returning from the *WM_PAINT* message. ■

Validating the invalid rectangle

BeginPaint( ) returned one other thing in addition to a device-context handle: a *PAINTSTRUCT*. The *PAINTSTRUCT* structure has the following format:

```
typedef struct {
    HDC         hdc;
    BOOL        fErase;
    RECT        rcPaint;
    BOOL        fRestore;
    BOOL        fIncUpdate;
    BYTE        rgbReserved[32];
} PAINTSTRUCT;
```

Only the third member is of much interest. The first one is the same device-context handle that is returned from *BeginPaint( )*. The second one is a flag indicating whether Windows has already repainted the background. Because storing a brush in *wndClass.hbrBackground* ensures that Windows repaints the background for you, this one is always *TRUE* in this case. Windows uses the last three members internally; you shouldn't mess with them.

The phrase "used internally" is Microsoft code. It means one of two things: The field is used internally (unlikely), or (more likely) the field isn't there anymore or is used for some completely different purpose that only the authors of Word and other neat Microsoft products know about. ∎

The third member, the *invalid rectangle* (here we go with this invalid stuff again — did the authors of Windows have an inferiority complex or what?) is the smallest rectangle that completely encompasses all the invalid regions. (Wasn't that helpful?)

Okay, so what's an *invalid region?* It's a part of the window that Windows thinks should be updated.

Suppose that your window is obscured by two other windows, as shown in the configuration in Figure 3-3. If it is brought to the front (if the user clicked it with the mouse), your application receives a *WM_PAINT* message to repaint the two invalid regions previously obscured by window 1 and window 2. The invalid rectangle is then the single rectangle that contains both these regions, as shown on the right side of the figure.

The invalid region is of type *RECT*, which is defined as follows:

```
typedef struct {
    LONG left;
    LONG top;
    LONG right;
    LONG bottom;
} RECT;
```

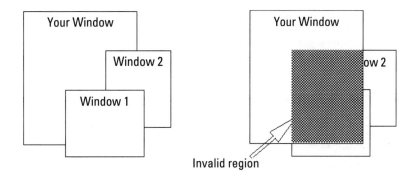

Figure 3-3:
The invalid
rectangle
contains
both
regions.

This definition is nothing more than the coordinates of the edges of the rectangle measured in units of pixels from the upper-left corner of the client area (y increases down the screen, and x increases toward the right).

The application can use this rectangle to avoid repainting the entire window. It is sufficient to repaint only the portions of the screen within the invalid region. The parts of the window that are outside this region are still valid.

Generating high-resolution graphical output can be a time-consuming process. Using the invalid region to reduce the amount of graphics information that is regenerated can significantly reduce the time it takes to repaint the window.

Clipping the clipping region

The device context has an area called the *clipping region*. Output is automatically clipped to fit within this region of the device context.

The clipping region for a normal window device context is never any larger than the client area. That's why output was automatically clipped to fit when the window was made smaller than the *"Hello, world"* string in the earlier Prog1_1 example program. This restriction keeps output from spilling out on the background.

It is possible (but not usually the case) to have a device context whose clipping area includes the entire window, for those times when you want to write to the title bar or scroll bars. ■

Calling *BeginPaint( )* sets the clipping region of the device context to be the same as the invalid region of the window. That is, even if the application attempts to repaint the entire window, somewhere within Windows this attempt is short-circuited so that only the parts of the window that need to be updated are then updated.

This short-circuiting doesn't save as much time as when the application uses the invalid rectangle to limit how much of the window it tries to update; because writing to screen memory is a slow process, however, this process can still save a considerable amount of time.

Can I see this invalid stuff in action?

To demonstrate the invalid rectangle and the invalid region at work, I made the following modifications to the "Hello, world" program.

```
// WindowProc - this function gets called to
//                process Windows messages
//                Modified to display invalid rectangle.
LRESULT CALLBACK WindowProc(
    HWND    hWnd,    // handle of window
    UINT    uMsgId,  // message identifier
    WPARAM  wParam,  // first message parameter
    LPARAM  lParam   // second message parameter
    )
{
    char buffer[128];
    static int nCount = 0;

    // decide what to do with each different message
    // type
    switch (uMsgId)
    {
      // handle the window paint message by displaying
      // the string "Hello, world" in the upper-left
      // corner (coord 0,0) of the window
      case WM_PAINT:
        HDC hDC;
        PAINTSTRUCT paintStruct;
        hDC = BeginPaint(hWnd, &paintStruct);

        //display the invalid rectangle
        HGDIOBJ hBackground;
        HGDIOBJ hOldBackground;
        int nNewBGColor;
        if (nCount & 0x01)
        {
            nNewBGColor = LTGRAY_BRUSH;
        }
        else
        {
            nNewBGColor = WHITE_BRUSH;
```

```
        }
        hBackground = GetStockObject(nNewBGColor);
        hOldBackground = SelectObject(hDC, hBackground);
        Rectangle(hDC, paintStruct.rcPaint.left,
                       paintStruct.rcPaint.top,
                       paintStruct.rcPaint.right,
                       paintStruct.rcPaint.bottom);
        wsprintf(buffer, "(%03d,%03d)x(%03d,%03d)",
                       paintStruct.rcPaint.left,
                       paintStruct.rcPaint.top,
                       paintStruct.rcPaint.right,
                       paintStruct.rcPaint.bottom);
        TextOut(hDC,
                200, 100, // output at random location
                buffer,
                lstrlen(buffer));
        SelectObject(hDC, hOldBackground);

    // keep a count of every time you're asked to
    // update the window
    wsprintf(buffer,
            "Hello, world (number %03d)", ++nCount);
    TextOut(hDC,    // the device context to use
            0, 0,   // x,y location
            buffer, lstrlen(buffer));

    EndPaint(hWnd, &paintStruct);
    return 0;

// handle the window destroy message by quitting
// the application
case WM_DESTROY:
    PostQuitMessage(0);
    return 0;

default:
    // let Windows handle all other message types
    return DefWindowProc(hWnd,uMsgId,wParam,lParam);
    }
}
```

The *WM_PAINT* handler function now displays the bounds of the invalid rectangle at a location chosen randomly in the middle of the window.

Just to make the program more visible, it paints the invalid rectangle alternately white and light gray so that you can see it.

It's critical in this version to remove the call to *InvalidateRgn( )* that you added in the second version; otherwise, the entire window is marked as invalid every time. If you play with this program, you notice that the dimensions of the invalid rectangle are not updated if the number is not within the invalid region. The reason is that output to the window is clipped by the device context so that only areas within the invalid region are updated. (Putting back the call to *InvalidateRgn( )* would solve this problem by invalidating the entire window, but then you couldn't see the invalid region.) ▪

The *if (nCount & 0x01)* conditional causes the program to paint the invalid region gray when *nCount* is odd, and white when it's even; otherwise, you would see gray on gray and never notice the difference.

The call to *GetStockObject( )* fetches a brush of the proper color, and *Select-Object( )* stores it in the device context. This process causes the background to be repainted with the specified color.

The first time I executed the program, the window was displayed with the dimensions of the entire client area displayed in the middle of a white background. This display is understandable because, when the window is first repainted, the entire window is invalid. I then resized the window to make it smaller so that the dimensions of the window were no longer visible; then I let go. The repaint count did not increment, and no invalid rectangle was drawn. Again, this situation makes sense because no information was added to the window. (So far, so good.)

I then resized the window outward to the right so that the dimensions of the invalid rectangle were visible within the window. The window then looked like the one shown in Figure 3-4.

Figure 3-4:
The window looks like this after it is expanded to the right.

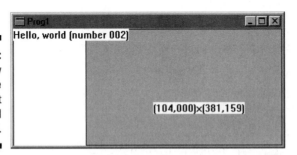

You can see that the window has been redrawn so that it is more than three times as wide as it was (from 104 to 381 pixels wide). You can also see that the invalid rectangle extends from 104,0 pixels in the upper-left corner to 381,159 pixels in the lower-right corner. (Great, so far.)

After a little experimenting, I decided to make the window smaller again and expand it, this time in both the *x* and *y* dimensions at the same time. The result is shown in Figure 3-5.

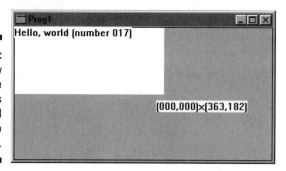

Figure 3-5:
The window looks like this after it's expanded down and to the right.

Figure 3-5 clearly shows the outline of the client area when the window was smaller (the white rectangle in the upper-left corner of the window). You can also see that the invalid region consists of two rectangular areas: one created by expanding the window downward and the other by expanding the window to the right. Finally, you can see that the invalid rectangle includes both those regions (in fact, it includes the entire window).

Other functions that return a device context

Other functions can be used to create a device context. One function of this type is the *GetDC( )* function. The handle returned from a call to *GetDC( )* is returned by calling *ReleaseDC( )*. This function pair is commonly used when your program responds to messages other than the *WM_PAINT* message.

Unlike *BeginPaint( )/EndPaint( )*, the *GetDC( )/ReleaseDC( )* function pair does not validate the window. In addition, *GetDC( )* sets the clipping region in the device context to be the entire client area, not just the invalid region.

Conclusion

This chapter is the single most important chapter in this book. If you understand the concepts of event programming and the message loop, the remainder of this book is mostly just a matter of conquering the details.

The *WM_PAINT* message was discussed in this chapter, along with a few of the ways in which you can cause Windows to generate the message. The chapter also discussed the invalid region that Windows uses to speed up program response.

In Chapter 4, "Painting Versus Writing," you finally get beyond "Hello, world" and learn how to print multiple lines to a window.

Chapter 4
Painting Versus Writing

•••

In this chapter

▶ Displaying proportional fonts

▶ Understanding source code

▶ Executing a program

•••

C hapter 2, "Your First Windows Program" mentioned that output is "painted" on the screen as opposed to being "written." The difference was neither obvious nor all that important in the "Hello, world" example program. This chapter looks at the distinction to help you see the effect it has on programs that print more than just a single, silly phrase.

Taking the Measure of Variable-Size Fonts

Unlike MS-DOS, Windows supports *proportional fonts,* which are fonts in which not every character is the same width. To old salts like me, proportional fonts were somewhat difficult to get used to, but only because of a historical aberration.

Typewriters use a ratchet mechanism to move the platen sideways after each keystroke. This simple device had to allocate the same amount of space for each character, regardless of whether it was the slim *i* or the UltraSlimFast-ready *W.* A special fixed-pitch font, Courier, was created to make the result as pleasing to the eye as possible. Because TTYs are mechanical devices and had the same limitation, they were stuck with Courier (or another fixed-pitch font). In retrospect, electronic terminals could have used a proportional font, but programmers were already used to seeing Courier, and it never occurred to them to change it. Courier was the font we all had grown up with.

Fixed-pitch fonts were never popular in the publishing industry, however. Even the earliest typesetters — I'm talking about Gutenberg's cronies here — knew about and understood proportional fonts (also known as *variable-pitch fonts*). To them, it was obvious that a *W* needed more space than an *i*. (It's obvious to me too, when it's stated that way.)

Displaying proportional fonts

To a programmer, proportional fonts raise more questions than a State of the Union address. First, you can no longer position text based on the column number. This concept doesn't exist because the characters no longer line up in neat columns. You can't "space over" by typing a set number of spaces — you don't really know how wide the space is.

For an initial foray into Windows programming, it was fine to place the line of text at location 0,0, the upper-left corner. No matter what the font size was, the upper-left corner stays at 0,0. But had there been a second line, where would it have gone? Before you answer that question, remember that the *x* and *y* location passed to *TextOut( )* is measured in units of screen pixels. (Other units are possible, as you will see later in this chapter.)

Before you can calculate the location of the second line, you have to know the height of the current font. To determine the height, you can call the function *GetTextMetrics( )* and pass it the handle of the device context you intend to use. If the function is successful, it returns a *TEXTMETRIC* structure that describes a number of properties about the current font.

TEXTMETRIC is defined as follows:

```
typedef struct _TEXTMETRIC {
    LONG tmHeight;
    LONG tmAscent;
    LONG tmDescent;
    LONG tmInternalLeading;
    LONG tmExternalLeading;
    LONG tmAveCharWidth;
    LONG tmMaxCharWidth;
    //...other stuff we're not interested in
    BYTE tmPitchAndFamily;
} TEXTMETRIC;
```

The first five of these fields are shown in Figure 4-1.

tmHeight refers to the overall height of the character measured in whatever units are in vogue — in this case, pixels. The height consists of two parts —

the portion above the baseline (*tmAscent*) and the portion below the baseline (*tmDescent*). (The baseline is the horizontal line under the letters.) An extra area at the top of some fonts, the *tmInternalLeading*, is used for accents, diacritical marks, and other pieces of punctuation and may be zero.

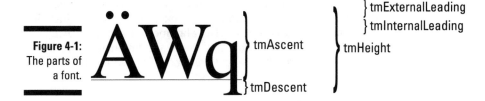

Figure 4-1:
The parts of a font.

In addition, *tmExternalLeading* specifies the amount of extra space to be inserted between lines. This field is similar to double-spacing, except that it has finer grain control.

The term *leading* stems from the fact that type was originally made of lead. (The first syllable is pronounced like the element, not like "lead me not into Windows programming.") To put a little extra space between characters or lines, the typesetter added a sliver of lead on one side of the type or the other. As you can tell, the term *leading* is literal. ■

The *y* offset of the top of each row is equal to the *y* offset of the top of the preceding row plus *tmHeight* plus *tmExternalLeading*.

Determining the width of each row is not as easy. The *TEXTMETRIC* structure gives both the maximum and average character width; your mileage may vary, however, depending on the mix of characters.

In a proportional font, a capital letter is about 1 1/2 times as large as the corresponding lowercase letter. In a fixed-pitch font, capital letters are the same width as lowercase letters (all letters have the same width). You can tell whether the font has a fixed pitch by ANDing *tmPitchAndFamily* with the flag *TMPF_FIXED_PITCH*. If the result is zero, the font is a fixed-pitch font — if not, it's a proportional font.

Notice that this result is exactly the opposite of what you might think at first. If the *TMPF_FIXED_PITCH* bit is set, the font is not fixed-pitch; if the bit is not set, the font is fixed-pitch. (It sounds like one of those programming screwups no one had the guts to change when it was first discovered, so now we're stuck with it.) ■

The average width of the lowercase characters is *tmAveCharWidth*; the average width of the capital letters can be calculated by using this formula:

```
avgCapWidth = textmetric.tmAveCharWidth;
if (tmPitchAndFamily & TMPF_FIXED_PITCH)
{
    avgCapWidth *= 1.5;
}
```

For most applications, the exact width information is not necessary. If you just want to make sure that there's enough room, use the maximum width. If you have an average mix of characters and the alignment is not that critical, use the average width. If you do need to know the exact dimensions of a specific string, you can use the function *GetTextExtentPoint32( )*, which is declared as follows:

```
BOOL GetTextExtentPoint32(
    HDC   hdc,                   // handle of device context
    LPCTSTR  lpString,           // address of text string
    int  cbString,               // number of characters in string
    LPSIZE  lpSize               // structure for string size
    );
```

The caller provides the relevant device context, the string in question, the length of the string, and an empty *SIZE* structure. If the function is successful, it fills in the *SIZE* structure with the dimensions of the string in the current font. ∎

Go on, give it a try

Okay, now you can try it out. Let's write a WinApp that prints multiple rows and multiple columns of information. In this case, have the application produce, for good measure, the size of the current font plus the location and width of the current window. You have that information at hand anyway.

Prog1_2: The source code

The following program, Prog1_2, is the window proc for your first attempt at producing this information:

```
// WndProc - Output the location and size of the current
//           window.  This involves calculating the line
//           spacing based on the font size
//           (First attempt -- the window doesn't update
//           properly when it's moved or resized.)

void OutputLine(
    HDC  hDC,                    // device context to output to
    int  nRowNumber,             // the row number to output to
```

```c
    char *pszDescription, // label string
    int  nValue           // data value
);

static int nRowSpacing;   // these two values are set...
static int nCharSpacing;  // ...by this function
LRESULT CALLBACK WindowProc(
    HWND   hWnd,          // handle of window
    UINT   uMsgId,        // message identifier
    WPARAM wParam,        // first message parameter
    LPARAM lParam         // second message parameter
  )
{
    HDC hDC;

    // decide what to do with each different message
    // type
    switch (uMsgId)
    {

      // when the window is created, find the character
      // size information for this font
      case WM_CREATE:
        hDC = GetDC(hWnd);

        TEXTMETRIC textMetrics;
        GetTextMetrics(hDC, &textMetrics);
        nRowSpacing = textMetrics.tmHeight
                    + textMetrics.tmExternalLeading;
        nCharSpacing = textMetrics.tmAveCharWidth;

        ReleaseDC(hWnd, hDC);
        return 0;

      case WM_PAINT:
        // set up for the paint like always
        PAINTSTRUCT paintStruct;
        hDC = BeginPaint(hWnd, &paintStruct);

        // output the current font size
        OutputLine(hDC, 1,
                   "Avg char spacing = ",
                   nCharSpacing);
        OutputLine(hDC, 2,
                   "Row spacing = ",
                   nRowSpacing);

        // get the size and location of the window
        RECT rectWindow;
```

```
                    GetWindowRect(hWnd, &rectWindow);
                    OutputLine(hDC, 4,
                            "Window x location = ",
                            rectWindow.left);
                    OutputLine(hDC, 5,
                            "Window y location = ",
                            rectWindow.top);

                    OutputLine(hDC, 7,
                            "Window x dimension = ",
                            rectWindow.right - rectWindow.left);
                    OutputLine(hDC, 8,
                            "Window y dimension = ",
                            rectWindow.bottom - rectWindow.top);

                    EndPaint(hWnd, &paintStruct);
                    return 0;

            case WM_DESTROY:
                    PostQuitMessage(0);
                    return 0;

            default:
                    // let Windows handle all other message types
                    return DefWindowProc(hWnd,uMsgId,wParam,lParam);
        }
    }


// OutputLine - this function outputs a string followed
//              by a value on the row specified. It uses
//              the global variables nRowSpacing and
//              nCharSpacing calculated earlier.
void OutputLine(
    HDC  hDC,                   // device to output to
    int  nRowNumber,            // the row number to output to
    char *pszDescription,       // label string
    int  nValue                 // data value
)
{
    int nCol1Offset = 20;
    int nCol2Offset = nCol1Offset + 25 * nCharSpacing;
    int nRowOffset = nRowNumber * nRowSpacing;

    // output column 1 - the label
    SetTextAlign(hDC, TA_LEFT | TA_TOP);
    TextOut(hDC,
            nCol1Offset,
```

```
                nRowOffset,
                pszDescription,
                lstrlen(pszDescription));

    // output column 2 - the data
    SetTextAlign(hDC, TA_RIGHT | TA_TOP);
    char szBuffer[16];
    wsprintf(szBuffer, "%d", nValue);
    TextOut(hDC,
            nCol2Offset,
            nRowOffset,
            szBuffer,
            lstrlen(szBuffer));
}
```

WinMain( ) is not shown because it's the same as the one that was already shown in Prog1_1; *WinMain( )* is required, however, in order for the program to be built and executed. Copy Prog1_1.cpp into Prog2_1.cpp, delete the *WindowProc( )*, and type the new *WindowProc( )* that was just shown. ∎

Now turn your attention to *WindowProc( )*. If you're going to print multiple rows and columns of information, you have to know the size of the current font. You have to call *GetTextMetrics( )* to get a *TEXTMETRIC* structure. You can do this within the *WM_PAINT* message handler, but your application may get numerous *WM_PAINT* messages, and the answer doesn't change. A better method involves calling *GetTextMetrics( )* one time and saving the result for use by the *WM_PAINT* handler.

The *WM_CREATE* message provides a convenient place to calculate the font-size information. The *WM_CREATE* message is sent immediately after the window is created (why is that not surprising?) and before the first *WM_PAINT* message is sent to display the window.

The *WM_CREATE* handler for this program appears as follows:

```
// when the window is created, find the character
// size information for this font
case WM_CREATE:
  hDC = GetDC(hWnd);

  TEXTMETRIC textMetrics;
  GetTextMetrics(hDC, &textMetrics);
  nRowSpacing  = textMetrics.tmHeight
             + textMetrics.tmExternalLeading;
  nCharSpacing = textMetrics.tmAveCharWidth;

  ReleaseDC(hWnd, hDC);
  return 0;
```

The *WM_CREATE* handler begins by getting a device-context handle using the *GetDC( )* function call. The handler uses *GetDC( )* rather than *BeginPaint( )* because it is not processing a *WM_PAINT* message.

The program then uses the device-context handle to get the *TEXTMETRIC* information, from which it calculates the row and character spacing. This information is stored in the global variables *nRowSpacing* and *nCharSpacing* for use later by the *WM_PAINT* handler. The final call to *ReleaseDC( )* releases the memory occupied by the device context.

The new *WM_PAINT* handler appears as follows:

```
case WM_PAINT:
  // set up for the paint like always
  PAINTSTRUCT paintStruct;
  hDC = BeginPaint(hWnd, &paintStruct);

  // output the current font size
  OutputLine(hDC, 1,
          "Avg char spacing = ",
          nCharSpacing);
  OutputLine(hDC, 2,
          "Row spacing = ",
          nRowSpacing);

  // get the size and location of the window
  RECT rectWindow;
  GetWindowRect(hWnd, &rectWindow);
  OutputLine(hDC, 4,
          "Window x location = ",
          rectWindow.left);
  OutputLine(hDC, 5,
          "Window y location = ",
          rectWindow.top);

  OutputLine(hDC, 7,
          "Window x dimension = ",
          rectWindow.right - rectWindow.left);
  OutputLine(hDC, 8,
          "Window y dimension = ",
          rectWindow.bottom - rectWindow.top);

  EndPaint(hWnd, &paintStruct);
  return 0;
```

As always, this *WM_PAINT* handler begins with a call to *BeginPaint( )* to get a device context and ends with a call to *EndPaint( )* to put it back.

The *OutputLine( )* function is an internal output function. Before you examine how it works, let's see how you get the data to print.

The function *GetWindowRect( )* returns a *RECT* structure that contains the coordinates of the upper-left corner and lower-right corner of the window. You use the coordinates of the upper-left corner as the location of the window. The distance from the upper-left to the lower-right corner of the window equals the size of the window. The units are measured in pixels.

 The units are something nebulous that the Windows documentation calls *device units,* or sometimes *physical units.* For a screen, device units are pixels. For the printer device, units may be something else. It doesn't really matter what a device unit is as long as it is applied uniformly. ■

The *OutputLine( )* function is the most interesting function in this program. It reappears as follows:

```
void OutputLine(
    HDC  hDC,                //device to output to
    int  nRowNumber,         //the row number to output to
    char *pszDescription,    //label string
    int  nValue              //data value
)
{
    int nCol1Offset = 20;
    int nCol2Offset = nCol1Offset + 25 * nCharSpacing;
    int nRowOffset = nRowNumber * nRowSpacing;

    // output column 1 - the label
    SetTextAlign(hDC, TA_LEFT | TA_TOP);
    TextOut(hDC,
            nCol1Offset,
            nRowOffset,
            pszDescription,
            lstrlen(pszDescription));

    // output column 2 - the data
    SetTextAlign(hDC, TA_RIGHT | TA_TOP);
    char szBuffer[16];
    wsprintf(szBuffer, "%d", nValue);
    TextOut(hDC,
            nCol2Offset,
            nRowOffset,
            szBuffer,
            lstrlen(szBuffer));
}
```

The function begins by calculating the coordinates of the specified row and two columns — column 1 is intended for the ASCIIZ string *pszDescription*, and column 2 is intended for the corresponding value *nValue*.

The string is displayed just as it was in Prog1_1, using the *TextOut( )* function, except that now, instead of being displayed at location 0,0, the *x* and *y* offset must be calculated. This program uses a fixed *x* offset of 20 pixels for column 1. It calculates the *y* coordinate by multiplying the specified row number by the height of a row, calculated in the *WM_CREATE* handler, discussed earlier in this chapter. Therefore, if the row spacing were 20 pixels, row 0 would be at *y* offset 0, row 1 at offset 20, row 2 at offset 40, and so on.

The integer *nValue* is first converted to a string by using the call to *wsprintf( )*. A small problem occurs in displaying this second column. Numbers are typically displayed right-justified with the columns of digits aligned. This alignment would be a serious problem in a variable-pitch font. To avoid this problem, the characters 0 through 9 are all the same width, even in a variable-pitch font, to enable the digits to line up.

If all the numbers had the same number of digits, there's no problem. You could start the second column at the same *x* offset, and the digits would automatically align. In this case, however, you can state with certainty that the different numbers will not have the same number of digits.

"I know," you say, "just pad on the left with spaces." That's fixed-pitch-think rearing its ugly head. That method doesn't work because the width of a space is not the same as that of a digit. Even if I got it to work for my font, it wouldn't work for your font, which is probably different. (I use a 15-point TrueType Magyar Bold sans serif with a half-gainer — what do you use?)

For each zero leading digit, you could move to the right by the width of a digit in the current font; however, this information is not available in the *TEXTMETRIC* structure. Besides, there's an easier way.

Rather than specify where you want the string to begin and then calculate it so that all the strings end at the same offset, you can specify the offset of the end of the string and let Windows perform all the calculations.

This technique is possible via the *SetTextAlign( )* function. The call *SetTextAlign(hDC, TA_LEFT | TA_TOP)* sets the alignment to be right-justified. In this mode, the *x* and *y* coordinates in the *TextOut( )* call specify the location of the right side of the number. This mode makes the numbers line up easily.

The call to *SetTextAlign( )* before printing the ASCIIZ string makes sure that it is returned to left-justification for the text output.

One other thing: Don't forget the prototype declaration of *OutputLine( )* at the beginning of the program. This declaration is required for all C++ programs.

Executing the program — a dreaded problem pops up

If you compile and execute the program, the window opens and displays the text shown in Figure 4-2, as expected. Notice that when I ran the program, the font was 7 pixels wide by 16 pixels high. That's approximately a 12-point font on my 800×600 display. Because the window was shoved all the way up into the left corner of the screen, the 0,0 location and the size seem reasonable. Notice also that all the ASCII strings are left-justified in the first column and that all the numbers appear right-justified in the second column.

Figure 4-2:
A display of font and window information; units here are pixels.

Prog1_2	
Avg char spacing =	7
Row spacing =	16
Window x location =	0
Window y location =	0
Window x dimension =	221
Window y dimension =	182

Everything looks good until you move the window. You would expect the window location to be updated, but it isn't. The displayed location stays firmly rooted at 0,650 even though you know that this is not the case.

Because you can learn more from a program that doesn't work than from one that does (or else I wouldn't have presented it), let's execute the program under the debugger to see what's wrong. Begin by setting a breakpoint in the *WM_PAINT* code.

Setting a breakpoint causes the application to stop when execution passes to that point in the program so that the programmer can examine variables and other items to see what's going on.

If you are already familiar with the concept of a debugger, you may find some of this explanation to be somewhat elementary. If you are still inserting *printf( )* statements in your code, it's about time for you to begin using a modern debugging tool. Fortunately, the debugger that is part of the Visual C++ IDE (Integrated Development Environment) is easy to learn. You're learning Windows programming anyway, so now is a good time to join the rest of us technonerds. ∎

To set the breakpoint, place the cursor on the first executable statement in the *WM_PAINT* code (the *BeginPaint( )* call works well) and then click Debug⏐Break-Points. This step should open a window that shows the current filename and line number. Click the Add button to add a breakpoint at the current line to the list of active breakpoints. Then click the Okay button to close the window.

If you've done everything properly, a small, reddish stop sign appears on the left side of the line that contains the cursor.

You can skip all this complicated stuff by placing the cursor where you want to set the breakpoint and then clicking the breakpoint button, which looks like this:

The debug toolbar is probably the most useful toolbar. ■

Resize the Visual C++ window so that it's small, and place it in a corner of the screen — far enough away that it does not intersect the application's window.

You must be careful when you set a breakpoint in the *WM_PAINT* handler. If the Visual C++ window intersects the application's window at all, the *WM_PAINT* handler is invoked every time you restart from the breakpoint. That's because the application is being asked to repaint the portion of the window that the Visual C++ window was covering. ■

Execute the program by choosing Debug | Go (or just press F5). You should hit the breakpoint. The application is being asked to paint the window the first time. Go again. If the application window does not intersect the Visual C++ window, the application should not hit the breakpoint again. Then move the window. Surprise! The program does not break. No *WM_PAINT* message is being generated.

Remember that moving a window does not generate a *WM_PAINT* message, because Windows has all the information it needs to redraw the window without the application's help.

You can reconfirm this as follows. With no breakpoints set, reposition the application's window so that the upper-left corner is near the middle of the screen. Notice that the reported location stays at 0,0. Minimize the window (click the Minimize button) so that the application shrinks to the task bar, and then redisplay it (click its icon on the task bar). When the window reappears, the location is displayed as something other than 0,0. It should be roughly half the screen resolution. If the screen is in 800×600 mode, therefore, the displayed value should be approximately 400,300.

Okay, so you have a moving problem. What about the other window functions? Try shrinking the window slightly. Again, no update. Setting a breakpoint in the *WM_PAINT* handler and resizing again confirms that a *WM_PAINT* message doesn't get generated. This confirmation makes sense because shrinking a window does not add any information. (Note the same restrictions about intersecting windows, as mentioned earlier.)

If you enlarge the window, however, the program stops at the breakpoint and confirms that a *WM_PAINT* message is sent. Even so, the size information is not uniformly updated. If you repeat the minimize-and-redisplay experiment, the size gets updated properly. What could possibly be going on? Why does Windows ignore your output request?

Here's a hint before you continue. Resize the window so that the *y* value is not visible but the *x* value is visible. Let go of the mouse. Resize the window outward so that both values change and both are visible. Notice that the *y* value gets updated but that the *x* value does not. Figured it out yet?

Here's another hint: Why was it necessary to add the call to *InvalidateRgn( )* to your second version of Prog1_1, back in Chapter 3. ■

Zeroing in on fixing your program

Remember that the invalid region in the device context includes only the parts of the window that need to be updated. When the window is expanded, these parts normally include only the new areas. Depending on how the window has been resized, the parts may not include the parts of the window that contain the *x* and *y* data you want to update. To save time, Windows clips any attempts to write to those parts of the window that are not included in the invalid region.

You have to make sure that the invalid region includes the area to which you are writing. In this case, you have to make sure that the entire window is updated whenever the window is either moved or resized, even if it's resized or moved only a little.

Making sure that the window is updated is easily done. A *WM_MOVE* message is generated whenever the window is moved, and a *WM_SIZE* message is generated whenever the window is resized. Capturing these messages enables you to invalidate the window. Invalidating the window causes a new *WM_PAINT* message to be created with the invalid region set to include the entire client area.

The following *WindowProc( )* has been updated to handle the *WM_MOVE* and *WM_SIZE* messages:

```
// WndProc - Output the location and size of the current
//           window.  This involves calculating the line
//           spacing based on the font size.
//           (Invalidate the window if it is moved or
//           resized to get the location to update.)
```

```
static int nRowSpacing;        //these two values are set...
static int nCharSpacing;       //...by this function
LRESULT CALLBACK WindowProc(
    HWND   hWnd,               // handle of window
    UINT   uMsgId,             // message identifier
    WPARAM wParam,             // first message parameter
    LPARAM lParam              // second message parameter
    )
{
    HDC hDC;

    // decide what to do with each different message
    // type
    switch (uMsgId)
    {

        // when the window is created, find the character
        // size information for this font
        case WM_CREATE:
          hDC = GetDC(hWnd);

          TEXTMETRIC textMetrics;
          GetTextMetrics(hDC, &textMetrics);
          nRowSpacing  = textMetrics.tmHeight
                     + textMetrics.tmExternalLeading;
          nCharSpacing = textMetrics.tmAveCharWidth;

          ReleaseDC(hWnd, hDC);
          return 0;

        // whenever the window is resized or moved, cause
        // a WM_PAINT message to be sent with the entire
        // client area invalidated
        // (By the way, you could have gotten the location
        // and size of the window from these messages.)
        case WM_MOVE:
        case WM_SIZE:
          InvalidateRgn(hWnd, 0, TRUE);
          return DefWindowProc(hWnd,uMsgId,wParam,lParam);

        case WM_PAINT:
          // set up for the paint like always
          PAINTSTRUCT paintStruct;
          hDC = BeginPaint(hWnd, &paintStruct);

          // output the current font size
          OutputLine(hDC, 1,
                     "Avg char spacing = ",
                     nCharSpacing);
```

```
        OutputLine(hDC, 2,
                   "Row spacing = ",
                   nRowSpacing);

        // get the size and location of the window
        RECT rectWindow;
        GetWindowRect(hWnd, &rectWindow);
        OutputLine(hDC, 4,
                   "Window x location = ",
                   rectWindow.left);
        OutputLine(hDC, 5,
                   "Window y location = ",
                   rectWindow.top);

        OutputLine(hDC, 7,
                   "Window x dimension = ",
                   rectWindow.right - rectWindow.left);
        OutputLine(hDC, 8,
                   "Window y dimension = ",
                   rectWindow.bottom - rectWindow.top);

        EndPaint(hWnd, &paintStruct);
        return 0;

    case WM_DESTROY:
        PostQuitMessage(0);
        return 0;

    default:
        // let Windows handle all other message types
        return DefWindowProc(hWnd,uMsgId,wParam,lParam);
    }
}
```

The call to *InvalidateRgn( )* invalidates some part of the window specified by *hWnd*. The second parameter specifies which part. If the second parameter is zero, the entire window is invalidated. The third parameter is set to *TRUE*, indicating that you want Windows to repaint the background.

The call to *DefWindowProc( )* passes the message on to Windows so that it can process the message as it does normally. Why bother? I didn't do that for the *WM_PAINT* message. The reason is that the *WM_PAINT* handler handles the *WM_PAINT* message. In this case, you aren't handling the *WM_MOVE* and *WM_SIZE* messages. You're just piggybacking your own functionality onto these messages. That's okay, but if you're not going to handle the message, you have to give Windows a chance to do so.

As it turns out, in the case of these two messages, Windows doesn't do anything with them either, but that isn't always the case. ∎

Using display units that are more convenient

For most applications, the display units are not important. As long as the font size was reported in the same units *TextOut( )* expected, it didn't make much difference. For some applications, however, everyone expects certain units. When someone asks me my age, for example, I can report it in fortnights. There's nothing wrong with that — it's just not what people expect. (People who go around asking my age deserve whatever they get.)

For a drawing application, for example, it makes more sense to specify the size of the window in units such as inches or centimeters. Reporting the font size in pixels is also a little strange. Font size is normally reported in a measurement called points. Other than something sharp, a *point* equals 1/72 of an inch (and they say programmers are strange).

Windows accommodates different display units through something called the *mapping mode.* By setting the mapping mode, the program can specify a logical unit for operations on the device context, which is different from the physical unit. The default mapping mode is *MM_TEXT.* In this mode, logical units and physical units are the same.

Some of the other mapping modes are shown in Table 4-1.

Table 4-1: Available Predefined Mapping Modes

Mapping Mode	Logical Unit	Y-Axis
MM_TEXT	Physical unit	Down
MM_LOMETRIC	0.1 mm	Up
MM_HIMETRIC	0.01 mm	Up
MM_LOENGLISH	0.1 inch	Up
MM_HIENGLISH	0.01 inch	Up
MM_TWIP	1/20 point	Up

A more natural mapping mode for font information is the *MM_TWIP* mode. (*Twip* is a made-up word that stands for "twentieth of a point.")

The following code shows *WindowProc( )* modified to use *MM_TWIP* mode.

```
// WndProc - Output the location and size of the current
//           window.  This involves calculating the line
//           spacing based on the font size.
```

```
//            (This version displays the font information
//            in points rather than in pixels.)

static int nRowSpacing;       // these two values are set...
static int nCharSpacing;      // ...by this function
LRESULT CALLBACK WindowProc(
    HWND   hWnd,              // handle of window
    UINT   uMsgId,            // message identifier
    WPARAM wParam,            // first message parameter
    LPARAM lParam             // second message parameter
  )
{
    HDC hDC;

    // decide what to do with each different message
    // type
    switch (uMsgId)
    {
      // when the window is created, find the character
      // size information for this font; this time, find
      // the size in TWIPs
      case WM_CREATE:
        hDC = GetDC(hWnd);

        // set the mapping mode for this device context
        // before requesting textmetric information
        SetMapMode(hDC, MM_TWIPS);

        TEXTMETRIC textMetrics;
        GetTextMetrics(hDC, &textMetrics);
        nRowSpacing  = textMetrics.tmHeight
                     + textMetrics.tmExternalLeading;
        nCharSpacing = textMetrics.tmAveCharWidth;

        ReleaseDC(hWnd, hDC);
        return 0;

      case WM_MOVE:
      case WM_SIZE:
        InvalidateRgn(hWnd, 0, TRUE);
        return DefWindowProc(hWnd,uMsgId,wParam,lParam);

      case WM_PAINT:
        // set up for the paint like always
        PAINTSTRUCT paintStruct;
        hDC  = BeginPaint(hWnd, &paintStruct);
        SetMapMode(hDC, MM_TWIPS);
```

```
                   // output the current font size
                   OutputLine(hDC, 1,
                           "Avg char spacing [points] = ",
                           nCharSpacing / 20);
                   OutputLine(hDC, 2,
                           "Row spacing [points] = ",
                           nRowSpacing / 20);

                   // get the size and location of the window
                   RECT rectWindow;
                   GetWindowRect(hWnd, &rectWindow);
                   OutputLine(hDC, 4,
                           "Window x location [pixels] = ",
                           rectWindow.left);
                   OutputLine(hDC, 5,
                           "Window y location [pixels] = ",
                           rectWindow.top);

                   OutputLine(hDC, 7,
                           "Window x dimension [pixels] = ",
                           rectWindow.right - rectWindow.left);
                   OutputLine(hDC, 8,
                           "Window y dimension [pixels] = ",
                           rectWindow.bottom - rectWindow.top);

                   EndPaint(hWnd, &paintStruct);
                   return 0;

               case WM_DESTROY:
                   PostQuitMessage(0);
                   return 0;

               default:
                   // let Windows handle all other message types
                   return DefWindowProc(hWnd,uMsgId,wParam,lParam);
           }
       }

// OutputLine - this function outputs a string followed
//              by a value on the row specified. It uses
//              the global variables nRowSpacing and
//              nCharSpacing calculated earlier.
void OutputLine(
    HDC  hDC,                 // device to output to
    int  nRowNumber,          // the row number to output to
    char *pszDescription,     // label string
    int  nValue               // data value
)
{
```

```
int nCol1Offset = 20;
int nCol2Offset = nCol1Offset + 35 * nCharSpacing;
int nRowOffset = -nRowNumber * nRowSpacing;

// output column 1 - the label
SetTextAlign(hDC, TA_LEFT | TA_TOP);
TextOut(hDC,
        nCol1Offset,
        nRowOffset,
        pszDescription,
        lstrlen(pszDescription));

// output column 2 - the data
SetTextAlign(hDC, TA_RIGHT | TA_TOP);
char szBuffer[16];
wsprintf(szBuffer, "%d", nValue);
TextOut(hDC,
        nCol2Offset,
        nRowOffset,
        szBuffer,
        lstrlen(szBuffer));
}
```

The call *SetMapMode(hDC, MM_TWIPS)* sets the mapping mode to *MM_TWIPS* before requesting the *TEXTMETRIC* information. If you write in *MM_TWIPS* mode, you have to make sure to get the font information in *MM_TWIPS* mode as well.

The remainder of the program is the same except that the font information is now in points rather than in the less useful pixels.

The *y* offset increases as you move up the screen in all the modes except *MM_TEXT*. As long as 0,0 is the upper-left corner of the window, the *y* offset passed to *TextOut( )* must be a negative number in order for the text to be visible — hence the minus sign in the calculation in *OutputLine( )*. ◼

Although the font-size information is now in points, the window dimensions remain in pixels. The reason is that the program is getting the window information from the function *GetWindowRect( )*, which thinks in physical units (pixels).

The mapping mode is a property of the device context and not of the window. Therefore, GDI calls, which accept the device-context handle, deal in logical units that are affected by the mapping mode. Window functions, which accept a window handle, generally deal in physical units. ◼

It is possible to convert manually from physical to logical units by using the *DPtoLP( )* function. This function accepts a pointer to a *POINT* structure that is assumed to be a coordinate pair in physical units. *DPtoLP( )* converts this physical unit coordinate pair into logical units and stores them back in the same *POINT* structure. (Actually, it accepts an array of coordinate pairs — the final parameter indicates how many pairs are in the array — but I'm trying to keep things as simple as possible.)

The *WM_PAINT* code that is converted to display the window dimensions in points appears as follows:

```
case WM_PAINT:
   // set up for the paint like always
   PAINTSTRUCT paintStruct;
   hDC = BeginPaint(hWnd, &paintStruct);
   SetMapMode(hDC, MM_TWIPS);

   // output the current font size
   OutputLine(hDC, 1, "Avg char spacing [points] = ",
                      nCharSpacing / 20);
   OutputLine(hDC, 2, "Row spacing [points] = ",
                      nRowSpacing / 20);

   // get the size and location of the window
   RECT rectWindow;
   GetWindowRect(hWnd, &rectWindow);

   // convert this from physical to logical units
   POINT ptConversion;
   ptConversion.x = rectWindow.left;
   ptConversion.y = rectWindow.top;
   DPtoLP(hDC, &ptConversion, 1);
   OutputLine(hDC, 4,
              "Window x location [points] = ",
              ptConversion.x / 20);
   OutputLine(hDC, 5,
              "Window y location [points] = ",
              -ptConversion.y / 20);

   ptConversion.x = rectWindow.right - rectWindow.left;
   ptConversion.y = rectWindow.top - rectWindow.bottom;
   DPtoLP(hDC, &ptConversion, 1);
   OutputLine(hDC, 7,
              "Window x dimension [points] = ",
              ptConversion.x / 20);
   OutputLine(hDC, 8,
              "Window y dimension [points] = ",
              ptConversion.y / 20);

   EndPaint(hWnd, &paintStruct);
   return 0;
```

The output from this function with the default system font is shown in Figure 4-3.

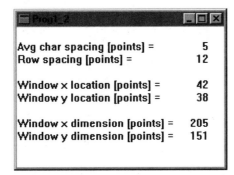

Figure 4-3: Some font and window dimensions with the units measured in points (1/72 inch — don't ask).

Knowing Where to Go from Here

By now you should be getting the flavor of Windows programming. If not, go back to the beginning of Chapter 2, "Your First Windows Program" and start over. If you think that Windows programming is difficult, you're right, but it's about to get much easier. If you think that this sort of thing just isn't your cup of tea, smooth out the pages, close the book, and see whether you can pawn it off on your brother-in-law for Christmas. (Why not? Think about what he got you for Christmas last year.)

So far, you have been doing what I call "old-style Windows programming." This is the way all Windows programming used to be done. I think it's important that you see it for yourself so that you can understand what's really going on.

Fortunately for everyone involved, Windows programming isn't done this way much anymore. All the major compiler vendors, including Microsoft and Borland, have in their compilers application generators that make the job of creating a WinApp much simpler. Beginning with Part II, you generate all your WinApps by using the Visual C++ AppWizard application generator.

20-Minute Workout

*T*his is the first in a series of quizzes designed to test your grasp of the material you just read. You can save yourself a great deal of time and trouble by just jumping directly to the answers — heck, you could just jump to the next chapter and forget this section entirely. Who would know? You would. Bad karma would haunt you for days. The loss of sleep alone would be enough to put you in a bad mood.

So grant yourself a good night's sleep and give the problems a go. Then you can flip to the answers and see how you did.

Questions

1 Explain the following statement. Exactly what is it, and what does it do? Explain each of the types. (What's a WINAPI, for example?) Where are these types defined?

```
int WINAPI WinMain(
    HINSTANCE  hInstance,      // handle of current instance
    HINSTANCE  hPrevInstance,  // handle of prev instance
    LPSTR      lpszCmdLine,    // command line
    int        nCmdShow        // show state of window
    );
```

2 Using Hungarian naming rules, give proper names for the following objects:

A. A pointer to a null-terminated string containing my name

B. The handle of a device context

C. A pointer to a 16-bit unsigned integer date

D. A binary flag containing pass/fail information

3 If you're in the middle of writing a program and you can't remember the arguments to *CreateWindow( )*, what's the best way to get information in a hurry?

A. Call Microsoft's customer-support hotline.

B. Call Microsoft Press, order the manual, and wait until it arrives.

C. Put your cursor on the function and press F1.

4 What's an invalid window?

5 What is the invalid region?

6 What is *DefWindowProc( )*, and when should it be called?

7 The *WM_PAINT* message count wasn't always updated when the window was enlarged; however, minimizing the window and then renormalizing it always caused the count to be updated. Knowing what you know now, explain what was going on.

8 Chapter 4 presented many problems in getting the size of the window to update when you resized it. You solved the problems by invalidating the window whenever a *WM_SIZE* message was generated. How else could you have solved the size problem?

Bonus: There are two solutions. Get bonus points if you can name both.

Answers

Hey, go back to the questions and at least try to answer them before you look here!

 This is a prototype declaration. It explains to the compiler the number and type of each argument the function expects and the type of value the function returns.

This particular function, *WinMain( )*, is the Windows equivalent of *main( )* (it's the first application to get control when the program starts up). Its argument types are shown in this list:

WINAPI: Declares the function to use Windows API calling rules

HINSTANCE: A handle to an instance of a program

LPSTR: A pointer to a string

These types are defined in windows.h.

2 My names are as follows:

  A. *pszDummy*

  B. *hDC*

  C. *pwDate*

  D. *bPass* (assuming that *TRUE* means pass)

3 The best way to get help with any function is to place your cursor on it and press F1. If your computer is turned off, you still get a faster response than if you call the customer-support hotline.

4 An invalid window is a window the application needs to update. It occurs when some part of the window that was previously covered up is exposed (when the window is made larger, for example).

5 The invalid region is a rectangle that encloses the areas of the window that need to be updated.

6 *DefWindowProc( )* is a new rock band that Bill Gates and a few of his friends are forming. It's also the name of the default message handler. This function should be called for any message your window proc doesn't intend to handle, including messages you intercept for your own purposes but don't handle (as you did with the *WM_MOVE* and *WM_SIZE* messages in Chapter 4).

7 If the invalid region of the window did not include the number area, the output was clipped so that the part of the string that contains the update count did not make it out to the window.

8 Setting *wndClass.style = VREDRAW | HREDRAW;* causes the entire window to be invalidated automatically when it is resized.

A second solution uses *GetDC( )* to fetch the device-context handle rather than *BeginPaint( )* because *GetDC( )* leaves the clipping region in the device context set to the entire client area. If you use this solution, the only problem is that you must remember to validate the window yourself before returning; otherwise, Windows insists on sending you another *WM_PAINT* message.

Part II
AppWizard Programming

The 5th Wave   By Rich Tennant

So, how do you like the performance of the new Windows 95?

In This Part...

*N*ow that you've seen how programs are built "by hand," you're probably thinking, "There must be a better way." Fortunately, there is.

Visual C++ provides a set of tools that help you generate better Windows applications faster and with much less hassle than doing it by hand. In this part, you learn how to use these tools. Even though the code generated by these tools may look different from what you wrote by hand in Part I, you learn how the code, at its core, isn't as different as you might think.

Chapter 5

Building Your First AppWizard Program

● ●

In This Chapter

▶ Building an application with AppWizard

▶ Making the application say "Hello, world" (again?!)

▶ Comparing the new application to the manual version

▶ Understanding what happened to *WM_PAINT* and the message loop

● ●

*A*s you've learned in this book, virtually all Windows programs start out in the same way. Even within the *WindowProc( )* routine, the programs have a great deal of similarity. All Windows applications (WinApps) register their window class in the same way, set up for *WM_PAINT* messages in the same way, and so on. Some clever people noticed these similarities and have come up with the idea of generating the framework for these applications automatically by using an application generator.

An application generator is a program, usually built in to the compiler environment, which asks the programmer a series of questions in the form of dialog-box menus. The application generator creates the framework for the eventual Windows application. This framework is adjusted depending on which options a programmer chooses during the creation process.

Both Microsoft and Borland offer an application generator with their Windows compilers. The two compilers have quite a few similarities; however, this book sticks with Microsoft's version, called AppWizard.

In this chapter, you generate the "Hello, world" program that was presented in Part I, except that this time you use the AppWizard tool to build the application framework for you. This process may seem like starting over (probably because it is); however, it enables you to compare the output from AppWizard with what you already understand. To continue the analogy, you've already done long division by hand — now learn how to use a calculator.

"Hello, world" AppWizard Style

To build an AppWizard application, you first must close any projects you may have open. Then choose File | New. When you see the question "New what?", choose Project. You then have the opportunity to choose MFC AppWizard (exe), which is what you want.

At this point AppWizard takes over and, through a sequence of six windows, asks a series of questions about the application you want to build. For this WinApp, Prog2_1, you want to keep things as simple as possible: Disable all fancy options. (Appendix B gives step-by-step instructions for building Prog2_1 with AppWizard.)

If you answer all the questions correctly, your New Project Information window (which appears as the last window before you actually build the project) should look like the one shown in Figure 5-1.

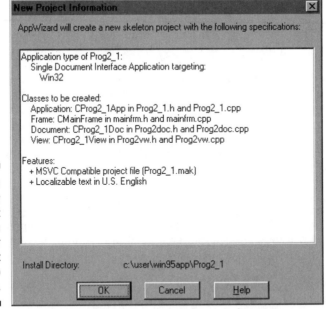

Figure 5-1: The New Project Information window for your first WinApp program.

Because the New Project Information window provides a complete description of the choices made during the preceding steps, I use it to describe the AppWizard setup for all subsequent applications in this book. ■

If your New Project Information window looks like mine, click OK to tell App-Wizard to generate the new application. At this point, AppWizard begins building a bewilderingly large number of files that contain a wealth of information, including a project file to tie together the other files.

Why do you need all those files for a program that doesn't do anything? The answer might surprise you: You need those files because this simple progtram can already do a number of things. To prove it, run it and see. The initial window from this "do nothing" WinApp is shown in Figure 5-2.

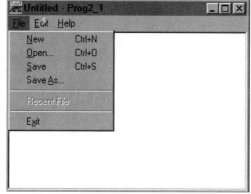

Figure 5-2:
Your first
AppWizard
program.

This program is already more sophisticated than the WinApps you created manually in Part I, and you haven't even done anything! For one thing, a menu is available with the standard File, Edit, and Help options. If you open the File menu, you see several options. If you then choose Open, a complete file-selection box is displayed. Opening the Help window displays an About dialog box, which describes your application and presents the application's icon.

Where's "Hello, world"?

Okay, as impressive as all this is (I was impressed, anyway), this program still doesn't display "Hello, world." Hey, AppWizard can't do everything. No problem. (The first sentence in the following paragraph is one of those leaps of faith you just have to tolerate for a minute until I can get around to explaining it.)

To display the phrase "Hello, world," all you have to do is edit the member function *CProg2_1View::OnDraw* in the file Prog2vw.cpp by adding the single call to the member function *CDC::TextOut( )*, as shown here:

```
void CProg2_1View::OnDraw(CDC* pDC)
{
        CProg2_1Doc* pDoc = GetDocument( );
        ASSERT_VALID(pDoc);
```

```
       // TODO: add draw code for native data here
    pDC->TextOut(0, 0, "Hello, world");
}
```

When you rebuild the program and reexecute it, out pops the "Hello, world" message as easy as 3.14159.

On one hand, this process certainly involves much less work: You had to answer only a few questions for AppWizard and then type a single line. That was even less than the Standard C version of "Hello, world," in which you had to type four lines.

On the other hand, what are all those files? Even the manual version, as difficult as it was, required only a single .cpp file. Admittedly, it was a rather large file, but it was just one file nonetheless.

And how did I know which line to add and where? AppWizard kindheartedly added the following hint:

```
    // TODO: add draw code for native data here
```

I then knew exactly where to put the call to *TextOut( )* (and I didn't have to be a rocket scientist). If you look in the .cpp files, you can see numerous *// TODO:* comments that goad you into adding code in all the right places.

But machines can lie. How did I really know? And who's handling the *WM_PAINT* message? It's the member function *CProg2_1View::OnDraw*.

What's a member function? And what did that gibberish about *pDC->TextOut(0, 0, "Hello, world");* mean?

Clearly, this program has raised many questions that need answers before you can continue. In Chapter 6, you get what you're looking for.

Conclusion

The application framework generated by AppWizard is a C++ rather than a C program, as was your first program. Its version of C++ code uses a class library called Microsoft Foundation Classes, commonly known as MFC — another one of those TLAs we're so DPO (darned proud of).

The purpose of this part of the book is to help you learn the basics of MFC programming. You will also study the relationship between the MFC Library and the Visual C++ tools, such as AppWizard.

Chapter 6

A Crash Course in C++

The Microsoft Foundation Class (MFC) Library is written in C++ and relies on many of (but not all) the features of C++ to get its work done. If you want to have a prayer of understanding MFC, you first must know something about C++ (at least the parts MFC uses).

One of the assumptions I did *not* make in writing this book is that you're an accomplished C++ programmer. (If you were, you would have been snatched up already by some telecommunications firm with too much money to spend, be getting paid lots of money to work all hours of the night and day filling in the potholes in Al Gore's information superhighway, and you wouldn't have enough time to even think about buying a *...For Dummies* book.)

This chapter teaches you the basics of C++. This crash course in C++ discusses only the features that are critical to understanding the MFC Library.

If you already know C++ (or think that you do), you can skip to Chapter 7, which tackles the MFC Library and the application framework.

C++ Is C Plus, Plus, Plus . . . .

The main thing to remember about C++ is that it's a superset of C. Being a superset means that a well-written ANSI Standard C program compiles properly when it is presented to a C++ compiler.

I'm not talking about when you're compiling in C mode. Most PC compilers (Visual C++ included) support a straight C mode in addition to C++ mode. To determine the type of code in the file, the compiler uses the same approach that is used to determine the gender of puppies: It lifts the source file by the tail and takes a look at its extension. If the file has only a .c extension, it's a C file; if PP is attached (as in .cpp), it's a C++ file. ∎

If you know C programming, you already know a great deal about C++ programming, because C++ is a superset of C.

The Features of Non-Object-Oriented Programming

Whether or not you're familiar with C++, you cannot possibly have gone through your programming life without having heard the terms "classes" and "object-oriented programming" (or "OOP") in connection with C++. However, some C++ features have nothing to do with classes or object-oriented programming. Because those features are conceptually simpler, let's begin with them.

Commenting on a new comment style

C++ defines a new comment style. Whenever two slashes (//) appear together, the remainder of that line is assumed to be a comment.

This new style may not seem to be a big deal, but you can tell that it's long overdue: After C programmers learn how to use the double slash, few of them ever return to using the slash-star (/*) method that is used in C. It's uncommon, in fact, to see C-style comments in a C++ program.

At will, declare!

Another new feature of C++ is that it offers the ability to declare a variable (almost) anywhere within a function. The following example code segment is legal, for example:

```
void AFunc()
{
    printf("Do 'bunch of stuff here\n");

    int i; // declare variable right before it's used
    for (i = 0; i < 10; i++)
    {
        // ...function continues on
}
```

There are a few places in your program where you can't declare a variable — for example, within the condition of an *if* statement. And of course, you must declare all variables before you use them. In addition, you can't declare a variable if there's a chance that control might branch around the declaration. Other than that, it's up to your imagination.

Referring to referential variables

One of the sometimes annoying features of C is that it passes arguments to functions strictly by value. The significance of that limitation is easy to demonstrate, as shown in the following example:

```
void Fn(int nAnotherVar)
{
    nAnotherVar = 10;
}

int main()
{
    int nAVar = 5;
    Fn(nAVar);
    // ...nAVar still has the value 5...
}
```

The variable *nAVar* is initialized to 5 when it is declared. When the function *Fn( )* is called, the value of *nAVar* is passed, not the variable itself (whatever that would mean). Therefore, *nAnotherVar* begins life with the value 5; when its value is changed to 10, however, it has no effect on the value of *nAVar* back in *main( )*.

C offered a manual way out of this dilemma, of course. *main( )* could have passed the address of *nAVar* rather than its value (this process, however, would require *Fn( )* to accept and manipulate a pointer to an integer rather than an integer itself):

```
void Fn(int *pnAnotherVar)
{
    *pnAnotherVar = 10;// store into the address provided
}

int main()
{
    int nAVar = 5;
    Fn(&nAVar);             // this time pass the address
    // ...the value of nAVar is now 10...
}
```

Now the program works as expected — the value of *nAVar* is changed to 10 after the program has returned from the call to *Fn( )*.

Because C++ is upwardly compatible with C, the C approach works just fine in C++; C++ provides a more convenient solution, however, by enabling one variable to refer to another:

```
void Fn(int &nAnotherVar)
{
    nAnotherVar = 10;
}
int main()
{
    int nAVar = 5;
    Fn(nAVar);
    // ...the value of nAVar is 10 here too...
}
```

In this example, *nAnotherVar* is called a *referential variable* (that's the significance of the seemingly out-of-place ampersand (&) — I wish that the designers of C++ wouldn't have reused symbols like that). A referential variable refers to another variable. After the referential has been declared and the reference established, all subsequent mention of the referential points back to the original.

When the function *Fn( )* is called, therefore, *nAnotherVar* is established as a reference back to *nAVar* (and not just to the value of *nAVar*); when *Fn( )* subsequently changes the value of *nAnotherVar*, it affects *nAVar*.

Passing by reference has an additional advantage. No matter how large a structure *nAVar* may have been, only its address is passed. This feature can save considerable time when *nAVar* is large.

Overloading on functions

Even the original old-style C enables programmers to declare the return type of a function in a function prototype declaration. ANSI Standard C expanded this ability by encouraging programmers to declare also the types of the function parameters. Look at the following line:

```
int AFunc(int nA, DWORD &dwB);
```

This prototype declaration defines *AFunc( )* to be a function that takes an integer followed by a reference to a double word and then returns an integer. Although *AFunc( )* may be the function's nickname, its full name is

```
int AFunc(int, DWORD).
```

Although C left function prototype declarations optional in order to stay compatible with older code, C++ makes full disclosure a requirement. That is, before the function can be called, a function's complete type must be declared, by using either a function prototype declaration or the function definition itself.

By requiring a prototype declaration of some sort, C++ can rely on its presence. This requirement enables C++ to differentiate between otherwise closely related functions.

For example, a C programmer may think that the following example contains an error because the three *Min( )* functions have been declared with the same name:

```
int   Min(int nX, int nY);
float Min(float fX, float fY);
char* Min(char *pX, char *pY);

void AFunc()
{
    int nA, nB, nC;

    nA = Min(nB, nC);    // is there any doubt which is
                         // intended?
    char *pD;
    pD = Min("string 1", "string 2"); // how about now?
}
```

The functions have only the same nickname, however: *Min( )*. Their full names are different:

```
int Min(int, int)
float Min(float, float)
char* Min(char*, char*)
```

This situation isn't all that unusual. For example, my son has several friends with the first name of Billy (and, naturally, with different last names). When he complains about them using their full name, I instantly know which Billy he's talking about. Even when he uses only the nickname, I can generally tell from the nature of the insult which Billy he means.

The same principle applies here. Is there any doubt about which *Min( )* is intended in the first call in the earlier example? Both arguments are integers — *Min(int, int)* clearly is the intended target. Just as clearly, the second call refers to *Min(char*, char*)*.

This capability, called *function overloading,* is strictly a compile-time decision that is made based on the declared types of the function arguments.

Mixed marriages: Mixing C and C++ in the same program

C++ can call C functions, but because C doesn't support function overloading, you cannot overload a C function name in this way.

To keep different functions with the same name separated during the link step, C++ adds the number and type of the function arguments to the function name in a process called *name mangling.* For example, *int Min(int, int)* might be rendered *Min$ii* (I say "might" because a standard way of performing name mangling doesn't exist.)

C doesn't perform any name mangling. Instead, the C compiler prepends an underscore to the name. The C function *SeaFunc(int, int)*, therefore, becomes *_SeaFunc.* (You might argue that any change to the function name

constitutes name mangling; C programmers are so accustomed to this simple change, however, that it just looks normal.)

These two transformations obviously are not compatible. If a C++ function attempted to reference *SeaFunc(int, int)*, the C++ compiler would look for *SeaFunc$ii*, not for *_SeaFunc.*

C++ defines the following construct to enable a C++ module to reference a C function:

```
extern "C" int SeaFunc(int, int);
```

The *extern "C"* declares *SeaFunc()* to be a C function whose name is not to be mangled. Because no name mangling is performed, however, C functions cannot be overloaded.

The return type isn't a factor in the decision about function overloading. You can't have a function named *int Min(int, int)* and another function named *char Min(int, int)*. ∎

Defaulting with default arguments

Another feature made possible by requiring prototyping is the ability to define default values for missing arguments to functions. In the following function, for example:

```
// default second argument to 10
double Log(double arg, double dBase = 10.0);

void MyFunc(double dArg)
{
    double dA;

    dA = Log(dArg, 2.0);    // log to the dBase 2
    dA = Log(dArg, 10.0);   // log to the dBase 10
    dA = Log(dArg);         // also log to dBase 10
}
```

the *= 10.0* means "use the value 10.0 for the value of *dBase* if no value is provided when the call is made." The third call, therefore, appears to the compiler exactly as though the programmer had entered *Log(dArg, 10.0)*.

Defaulted arguments must begin at the right and work their way toward the left. That is, the following construct is not allowed (and not just because it makes no sense):

```
double Log(double dArg = 1, double dBase);
```

The default-argument feature falls in the "Gee, that's nice" category more than in the "I gotta have it" category. Because the MFC Library makes use of it, however, I thought it best to mention it.

Inlining something other than skates

One of the more troublesome features in C is the *#define* macro. The principle is simple: The preprocessor expands macros into C statements before the compiler ever even sees them. Without going into all the details, suffice it to say that macros are prone to errors precisely because they are interpreted by a preprocessor that has different rules than does the compiler (and the preprocessor is not nearly as smart).

To avoid headaches, the designers of C++ wanted to stamp out macros. Using the carrot-and-stick approach, the designers couldn't use the stick and make macros illegal, because C++ had to remain compatible with C — so they were forced to use the carrot instead. The designers decided to ask programmers why they used macros. After all, a macro looks just like a function. Why not use a function instead? "It's simple," was the response. "Macros expand inline and don't involve the overhead of a function call." (C programmers are as sensitive to overhead as are corporate CEOs, ya know.)

No problem: The C++ developers simply added the *inline* keyword. The following code segment contrasts a macro, *MIN( )*, with an inline function, *Min( )*:

```
//MIN -- the macro version
#define MIN(x, y) (((x) > (y)) ? (y) : (x))

//Min -- the inline function version
inline int Min(int nX, int nY)
{
    // if nX is greater than nY...
    if (nX > nY)
    {
        // ...return nY; otherwise...
        return nY;
    }
    // ...return nX
    return nX;
}

void SomeOtherFunc(int nX, int nY)
{
    // ...some stuff...
    nX = Min(nX, nY); // this is expanded inline and
                      // does not generate a function call
    // ...continue...
}
```

Inline functions have the same syntax as normal functions do, except that they expand inline when they're invoked. They more closely resemble a *#define* rather than a normal function. So what's the advantage? Inline functions are part of the C++ language and are not handled by some dumb preprocessor with its own error-prone syntax.

Orienting Yourself to Object-Oriented Programming

Okay, so much for non-object-oriented features. What about the good stuff? Object-oriented programming is as much an approach to programming as anything else. That's why it's called the *object-oriented paradigm* (pronounced "pair a dime," as in 20 cents): Paradigm means "way of thinking."

Object-oriented programming, or as those in the know prefer to call it, OOP, relies on two principles we all learned way before we knew what a mouse was (other than a furry, little creature): encapsulation and classification. To explain these two topics, I like to begin with the learned example of object-oriented nachos.

Consuming object-oriented nachos

When my son and I watch Australian-rules football on the All-Southern Hemisphere Sports Channel, I sometimes whip up a plate of nachos. I dump some chips on a plate; throw on mashed-up beans, grated cheese, and lots of jalapeño peppers; and nuke the entire mess in the microwave for five minutes or so.

To use my microwave, I open the door, throw the stuff in, punch a few buttons on the front panel, and press the Start button. In a few minutes, for better or worse, the nachos are done.

Encapsulation

Think for a minute about what I don't do: I don't rewire anything inside my microwave to get it to work. I don't reprogram the software in the microwave oven, even if I cooked something different the last time I used it. The microwave has an approved interface — the front panel — that lets me do everything I want to do. It doesn't even occur to me to go around that interface.

This division of labor is not unimportant. For example, we live in a litigious society. If the microwave blows up because of something I enter from the front panel and my house burns down, I'm likely to do more than just stop buying products from the company that made the microwave. I shouldn't be able to do anything from the approved interface to cause it to do harm to me and my kin. If I take the lid off and start mucking with the insides, however, all bets are off.

Object-oriented programming takes the same approach to programming: It lets the programmer divide the job into separate sections, called *classes,* each of which is responsible for its own well-being.

Classification

Think about the object-oriented nachos for a minute, and consider what would happen if the microwave were on the fritz. I would follow all the same steps, except that, when it came time to cook the nachos, I would be forced to use the conventional oven instead. I may not like to cook my nachos in this way, but I can. (Of course, I might have to adjust the cooking time.)

Why can I use a conventional oven in place of a microwave oven? Because both are subtypes of some more generic type of oven.

In "object-oriented-ese," the strange and mysterious language of the object-oriented programmer, we say that the *class* ConventionalOven and the *class* MicrowaveOven are both *subclasses* of the *base class* Oven. We also say that a MicrowaveOven is derived from an Oven.

While I'm at it, let me introduce one more new word: My particular microwave is an *instance* of the class MicrowaveOven. ∎

As humans, we have an uncanny ability to classify. Sometimes it gets us in trouble. For example, prejudice is an example of overclassifying; most of the time, however, classification is a tremendous labor-saving device. When I had to teach my son what a microwave oven was, I could say, "A microwave oven is an oven that does whatever." Because he already knew what an oven is, this explanation greatly reduced the amount of information I had to convey and he had to store in order to understand microwave ovens. It has the additional advantage that things he learns later about ovens will be automatically attributed to microwave ovens.

Classification also affects the way we perceive the world around us. When we look at a forest, we see levels of abstraction. At first glance, we see plants and nonplants. The plants quickly divide themselves up into trees, grasses, bushes, and so on. A closer examination of the trees reveals oaks, maples, and elms, and then live oaks, red oaks, silver-leaf maples, and so on. In this way, we can make sense of a world too full of detail to be completely understood by our limited carbon-based computers (some, like mine, are more limited than others).

The functional programming microwave

Functional programmers don't see the world in this way. First, they would argue that building an entire microwave oven just to make nachos is a waste of time — we don't need the different power levels or a timer or a defrost cycle. Three cubic feet of space is certainly wasted on something as small as a plate of nachos.

To that, I would respond that, to a certain extent they're correct (even a blind pig finds an acorn once in a while). You certainly don't want a top-of-the-line microwave if all you ever do is make nachos with it. Because I use my microwave for much more than that, I bought a good model so that I can reuse it. (That word, *reuse,* is the Holy Grail of the software business.) If I intended to buy a microwave just to make nachos, however, I would undoubtedly get the smallest, simplest general-purpose microwave available. I would submit that this microwave would not be that much more expensive (if at all) than one built specifically for nachos.

Functional programmers would then argue that their nacho microwaves don't need an interface. Instead, they would just expose the insides to the user. Their recipe for making nachos would include instructions for how to make the internals of the functional microwave work. "Put nachos in the mouth of the Klystron tube. Connect the red wire to the black wire. Try not to stand too close if you intend to have children." Stuff like that.

The problem is that the recipe for making nachos quickly becomes hopelessly intertwined with the details of making the internals of a microwave work. This situation makes it more difficult for a programmer to get the overall picture with respect to nachos (by the same token, it makes the job of the microwave-oven programmer just as difficult). Consider what happens if you attempt to migrate this recipe to a conventional oven or use the microwave oven to make some other dish: "Make sure that the cheese is placed in the middle of the Klystron tube when the red wire is connected." Which parts of that instruction have to do with microwaves and which with nachos?

The OOP paradigm

Object-oriented programmers program in levels of abstraction, the way people think. They approach the problem to be solved by looking for the classes of things that are present. When they find them, they then set about coding each of these classes as stand-alone entities. When they code the final "recipe," they use these abstractions to get the job done.

This approach offers these advantages:

✔ *Divide and conquer.* It was good enough for Julius Caesar for a while, anyway. The manufacturer of my microwave did not have to get embroiled in all the possible recipes for which the microwave would be used. Even more important (for me, anyway) is that I, the user, don't have to get involved in the complexity of making a microwave work. All I have to understand is the interface, which is considerably simpler than what goes on inside.

✔ *Keep things divided.* Even if I'm the one building the microwave, when I have my microwave hat on, I can think about microwave things and forget about nachos, vegetarian hamburgers, kosher bacon, and my other favorite recipes.

✔ *Classify, classify, classify.* My understanding of what a microwave oven is and how it fits into the grand scheme of things is based on the simple principle that "A microwave oven is an oven that does blah blah blah." This type of relationship is so important that object-oriented programmers write it as one word — they call it the *IS_A* (pronounced "izzuh") relationship.

✔ *Reuse.* By building the microwave as generally as possible, a good chance exists that I can use it for other heating tasks. (A microwave oven meant specifically for nachos would be the ultimate novelty gift, wouldn't it?)

Programming with Class

So how does C++ support the object-oriented paradigm? First, you need some way to encapsulate into one structure all the properties of a type of thing (in the same way the term "oven" encapsulates the properties of that type of kitchen appliance with which I invariably turn nature's bounty into a blackened mass).

Even C allows disparate data properties about an item to be bound into a single structure, called a *struct*. For example, a *struct Window* might be defined as follows:

```
struct Window
{
    int    m_nWidth;
    int    m_nHeight;
    int    m_nX;
    int    m_nY;
    int    m_hDC;
    int    m_nColorPalette[256];
};
void TextOut(Window &w, int nX, int nY, char *pszString);
void Move(Window &w, int nDeltaX, int nDeltaY);
void Update(Window &w);
```

A struct is an effective way of describing the passive properties of a class of an item, such as a window.

But windows have active properties as well — they move, they appear, they disappear, they break, and they crash. You can define functions to perform these operations, as just shown. You can even form an informal association between these functions and the struct. The C language doesn't recognize this association, however. What you really want to do is bring these functions inside and make them a part of the structure. C++ enables you to do that by defining a *class:*

```
class Window
{
public:
    int    m_nWidth;
    int    m_nHeight;
    int    m_nX;
    int    m_nY;
    int    m_hDC;
    int    m_nColorPalette[256];
    void TextOut(int nX, int nY, char *pszString);
    void Move(int nDeltaX, int nDeltaY);
    void Update();
};
```

A class is defined with the new keyword *class.* (What would you expect, the keyword *knucklehead*?) Notice the presence of member functions included with the data members.

Card-carrying member functions

Member functions are accessed in much the same way as data members:

```
Window  w;
Window *pW = &w;

// access members through an object
w.m_nWidth = 100;
w.TextOut(0, 0, "Buy this book");

// access members through a pointer
pW->m_nWidth = 200;
pW->TextOut(0, 0, "Bargain at twice the price");
```

Just as it makes no sense to refer to *m_nWidth* without specifying a *Window* object, it makes no sense to call the member function *TextOut( )* without specifying an object with the call. (On which window should the output appear?) A member may be referenced from an object, as in the case of *w*, or from a pointer to an object, as in the case of *pW*.

A member function may be defined within the class definition; it is more common, however, to define the member function somewhere else. Therefore, the function *Move( )* might be defined as follows:

```
void Window::Move(int nDeltaX, int nDelayY)
{
    // update the location...
    m_nX += nDeltaX;
    m_nY += nDeltaY;

    // ...and then redraw the window
    Update();
}
```

The class name has now become part of the name of the function. Although its nickname may be *Move( )*, the full name of the function is *Window::Move(int, int)*. The new operator *::* is called the *scope-resolution operator*.

Notice that within a member function it isn't necessary to specify an object when you're referring to other members of the class. The "current" object is assumed. When *Move( )* is invoked, for example, it's invoked with the object *w*; the statement *m_nX* within *Move( )* refers to *w.m_nX;*, and *Update( )* refers to *w.Update( )*.

The current object has a name for those rare instances in which you have to refer to it explicitly. The current object is pointed to by the pointer *this*. Thus, you could have written the preceding function as follows:

```
void Window::Move(int nDeltaX, int nDelayY)
{
    // update the location...
    this->m_nX += nDeltaX;
    this->m_nY += nDeltaY;

    // ...and then redraw the window
    this->Update();
}
```

Thus, *this->m_nX* means "the *m_nX* member of the current object." The "current object" is the object with which the member function was invoked. If the function were called as *w.Move(1, 1)*, then *this->m_nX* refers to *w.m_nX*. If *Move( )* were called as *pSomeWin->Move(-1, 0)* then *this->m_nX* refers to *pSomeWin->m_nX*. And if — well, you get the idea.

In the function *Move( )* in this example, *this* doesn't have to be referenced explicitly because *this* is understood within a member function. When I say *m_nX*, it's understood that I mean *this->m_nX*. *this* is also a keyword, by the way. ■

Lock the doors, and hide the data!

In addition to providing active features such as Start and Stop, my microwave also has a metal box around it to keep prying fingers from intruding on its innards. C++ provides a similar feature, with the keywords *private* and *protected*. A private or protected member of a class is not accessible to nonmembers of the class.

For example, you could have declared the class *Window* as follows:

```
class Window
{
protected:
    int    m_nWidth;
    int    m_nHeight;
    int    m_nX;
    int    m_nY;
    int    m_hDC;
    int    m_nColorPalette[256];

public:
    void TextOut(int nX, int nY, char *pszString);
    void Move(int nDeltaX, int nDeltaY);
    void Update();
};
```

All the members defined after the private keyword are said to be private and are not available outside the class. The members defined after the protected keyword are similar to private members in that they aren't accessible from outside the class or outside any derived classes. The difference is that protected members are accessible from derived classes and private members are not.

You'll see later, in the section "Handling Your Inheritance," what a derived class is, but this difference is roughly akin to the following:

✔ *Public data* is data you're willing to share with everyone.

✔ *Protected data* is data you're willing to share with the kids and grandkids.

✔ *Private data* is data you're not willing to share with anyone (except maybe your spouse).

The member functions *TextOut( )*, *Move( )*, and *Update( )* may be accessed from other functions. The keywords *public*, *protected*, and *private* may be repeated as often as you want. (The initial state for a class is private, but you shouldn't rely on that.)

The class's public members make up the class's *public interface,* which is analogous to the microwave's front panel. It is necessary to document only the public members of the class to the general public because the other members are not accessible anyway. (After all, the manual for a microwave doesn't describe the microwave's innards.)

The advantages of restricting the interface to just a few of the member functions are numerous, but the most important one is the simplest: If a private or protected data member of a class gets screwed up, you can limit your search for the problem to the other member functions. They are the only functions that had access to the data member in the first place.

How do I get to the good stuff?

With all this data-hiding going on, you may be wondering how to get to the good stuff, such as the size and position of the window. The USDA-approved method is via *access functions,* as shown in the following example:

```
class Window
{
protected:
    int    m_nWidth;

public:
    int Width();
    int Width(int nNewWidth);

    // ...everything else the same...
};

inline int Window::Width()
{
    return m_nWidth;
}
inline int Window::Width(int nNewWidth)
{
    int nOldWidth = m_nWidth;
    if (nNewWidth > 0 && nNewWidth < MAX_WIN_WIDTH)
    {
        m_nWidth = nNewWidth;
    }
    return nOldWidth;
}
```

The access function *Width( )* merely returns the current width to the calling function. The access function *Width(int)* enables nonmember functions to set the width.

 This type of overloading is common for access functions. The function with no argument returns the current value of the data member. The function of the same name but with an argument sets the data member to the new value and returns the preceding value. The alternative is to append Get... and Set... to the front of the function name. ■

But why bother, you ask? Why not make the width public? When you program your classes, you have to be distrustful. If you give everyone access, they can change *m_nWidth* without the class's control. That's the purpose of the error checks in *Width(int)*: If a nonmember function tries to slip in some bogus value for width, the function catches the error and rejects it.

Doesn't data hiding cost a lot?

What about the overhead? Doesn't calling a function every time you want to read a data member from the class cost a great deal in terms of computer time? If you're worried about overhead, just declare the functions inline, as in the preceding example.

Here's an example of an inline function:

```
void MyExample(Window* pW)
{
    int nLocalW;
    nLocalW = pW->Width();  // this becomes:
                            //    nLocalW = pW->m_nWidth;
    // ...and the beat goes on...
}
```

Won't I mess up a good thing?

What if you don't want to play by the rules? What if you want your class to lift its hood just a little to its favorite function? Can it be done?

A class can declare another function or class to be a *friend*, as shown in this example:

```
class Window
{
    friend int SomeOtherFunction(int);
    friend class AnotherClass;

protected:
```

```
int    m_nWidth;
// ...class continues on like before...
```

This example declares the function *SomeOtherFunction(int)* and the class *AnotherClass* to be friends of the class *Window*. Declaring a function to be a friend gives it access to the private and protected members of the class. Declaring another class to be a friend makes every member function of the class a friend.

Getting off to a good start: The constructor

Because nonmember functions don't have access to the private and protected members of a class, it isn't possible to initialize an object in the conventional C manner:

```
Window w = {200, 150, 0, 0}; // not allowed
```

It is possible to define a member function (*Window::Init( )*, for example) to initialize these members:

```
Window w;
w.Init(200, 150, 0, 0);
```

The only problem with this solution is that the class must rely on the application software to call the *init* function properly. This solution goes against object-oriented philosophy, which states that each class should be responsible for its own well-being.

C++ therefore defines a special member function called the *constructor,* which is called automatically when an object is created. Rather than use the name *Init( )* for the name of the constructor (which got my personal vote), the constructor carries the name of the class.

The class might be defined, therefore, as follows:

```
class Window
{
    // ...as before...
public:
    Window(int nW, int nH, int nX, int nY);
};

// declare an object of class Window
Window w(200, 150, 0, 0);// invokes the constructor above
```

The constructor has no return type — not even void. (Why they added this little bit of inconsistency, I'll never know.) The constructor can be overloaded. C++ invokes the constructor that matches the types of the arguments provided in the declaration of the object.

One special constructor bears mention. If an object will be created without any arguments, an "argumentless" constructor, called the *default constructor,* must be provided:

```
Window w; // calls the constructor Window::Window()
```

Just as with any other function, it is possible to default the arguments to the constructor.

What C++ giveth, C++ taketh away. A programmer can also provide a function, called the *destructor,* which is called automatically whenever an object is destroyed. (You might say that the destructor stays after class to clean up. Or maybe not.) The destructor carries the name of the class, but prepended with a tilde (~). Because the destructor is not invoked with any arguments, it cannot be overloaded:

```
class Window
{
public:
    // destructor - invoked when object destroyed
    ~Window();

    // ...everything else the same...
};
```

When are objects created and destroyed?

When exactly is an object created, and when is it destroyed? The answer depends on the type of object. *Global objects,* which are objects declared outside any function, are created when the program starts up and before *WinMain( )* gets control. They are destroyed when the program terminates, after *WinMain( )* exits.

Objects declared within a function are created when control reaches their declaration. They are destroyed when control passes outside the block that contains their declaration, as shown in this example:

```
void AFunc()
{
    // ...whatever code...
    Window w;      //object w created here
```

```
        // ...processing continues...
}   // object w destroyed here
```

Introducing a new keyword

The parameters passed to a class create a problem for memory that is allocated dynamically.

To allocate memory dynamically, a C programmer uses the following function:

```
void* malloc(int nBytes)
```

where *nBytes* is the number of bytes to allocate. This memory is returned by using this function:

```
void free(void* pBlock)
```

where *pBlock* points to the block to de-allocate.

The problem with this approach is that *malloc( )* cannot possibly know which constructor to call or how. To solve the problem, C++ introduces a keyword, *new*, which allocates memory dynamically, like *malloc( )*, and then initializes it by calling the appropriate constructor. The keyword *delete* is used to invoke the destructor and de-allocate memory allocated with *new*.

In use, it looks like the following:

```
void SomeFunction()
{
    // ...lots of silly expressions...

    // Allocate a new Window dynamically
    Window* pW = new Window();

    // ...use the Window object allocated above...

    // when you're finished with it, put it back
    delete pW;
}
```

Handling Your Inheritance

Suppose that you've defined a neat-o class *Window* with all the fancy features you want, including double-pane glass — the works.

Now suppose that you want to adapt this class into a special type of window class, called a *ScrollingWindow*. Thinking like a functional programmer for a minute, you probably would copy all the *Window* code into a new file, make a global change of *Window* to *ScrollingWindow*, and then begin editing.

C++ provides a better way, and one that's much more similar to the way we humans approach such real-world things as microwave ovens and nachos: You can let the new class *ScrollingWindow* inherit from the class *Window*. This statement can be restated as "A *ScrollingWindow* is a *Window* that does blah blah blah." In C++ code, it looks like the following:

```
class ScrollingWindow : public Window
{
protected:
    ScrollBar sb;

public:
    ScrollingWindow(int nW, int nH, int nX, int nY,
        BOOL bScrollBar = TRUE) : Window(nW, nH, nX, nY);
    void Scroll(int nLines);
    void Update();
};
```

The following declaration means "*ScrollingWindow IS_A Window:*"

```
ScrollingWindow : public Window
```

It means that all the members of *Window* are also members of *Scrolling-Window*.

That is, *ScrollingWindow* has a height, a width, an *x* offset, and a *y* offset — just like a window. But *ScrollingWindow* also has a data member, *sb*, and a member function, *Scroll( )*, which Window does not have. *ScrollingWindow* is the subclass, and *Window* is the base class.

Notice also the constructor for *ScrollingWindow*. Most arguments to the constructor are passed on to the constructor for *Window* by way of the *:Window(nW, nH, nX, nY)* construct.

Although *ScrollingWindow* has direct access to the *Window*-ish data members, it's better to let each class take care of itself. Let the *Window* constructor initialize the *Window* part of the *ScrollingWindow* and let the constructor for *ScrollingWindow* concentrate on those members that are unique to the *ScrollingWindow*.

A subclass, such as *ScrollingWindow*, has access to the protected members of a base class, such as *Window*; it does not have access, however, to the private members. That's the difference between protected and private. ∎

Virtual Member Functions: Are They for Real?

The presence of the member function *ScrollingWindow::Update( )* introduces an interesting problem, as shown in this function:

```
void SomeFunction(Window &aw)
{
    // ...function does whatever...
    aw.Update();
    // ...function continues...
}

void AnotherFunction()
{
    // this is clearly legal
    Window w(100, 100, 50, 50);
    SomeFunction(w);

    // but so is this because a ScrollingWindow IS_A Window
    ScrollingWindow sw(200, 100, 75, 30, TRUE);
    SomeFunction(sw);
}
```

The call *SomeFunction(w)* is clearly legal and allowed. But the call *Some-Function(sw)* brings up a couple of interesting questions.

First, is the call even allowed? After all, *SomeFunction( )* is expecting a *Window*. Can you pass it a *ScrollingWindow*? The answer is, "Yes. A *ScrollingWindow IS_A Window*."

If the call is allowed, the second question becomes "To what function does the call to *Update( )* refer: *Window::Update( )* or *ScrollingWindow::Update( )*?" A C programmer's initial reaction would be that it must refer to *Window::Update( )* because the parameter aw is declared to be of type *Window*. But an object-oriented programmer would counter that, because aw refers to the object sw, the type is *ScrollingWindow*, and so the function call must refer to *Scrolling-Window::Update( )*.

Who's right? The answer is that it depends. The way the classes are written, the C programmer is correct. Object-oriented programmers can have their way however, with the simple addition of the new keyword *virtual*:

```
class Window
{
    // ...all else the same as before...
public:
    virtual void Update();
};
class ScrollingWindow : public Window
{
    // ...all else the same as before...
public:
    virtual void Update();
};
```

Now the decision about which *Update( )* function to call is made based not on the *declared* type of the object but rather on its actual type, also known as its *runtime type.*

This capability is known as *polymorphism.* Poly means "many or various," and morph means "action" (*ism* means "confusing Greek technical term.") Another name for this feature is *late binding* because the binding to the function is made late in life, during execution, or C, as opposed to normal C-style binding, called *early binding,* which takes place at compile-time. ■

Whoa! This feature is one that you're not likely ever to have seen in a language. The compiler cannot know which function to call in advance. It has to put the code in the program to decide during execution to which function to jump.

Late binding is a powerful feature. A function such as *SomeFunction( )* may have been written without any knowledge of class *ScrollingWindow. ScrollingWindow* may not even have existed, in fact, at the time the function was written. Even so, by inheriting *ScrollingWindow* from *Window,* all the recipes that previously worked with *Window* now automatically work with *ScrollingWindow.*

No Second-Class Citizens Here

Just as C defines operators for the intrinsic types, such as *int* and *double,* C++ enables programmers to add to the existing operators the capability to operate on user-defined types. You could create a class called *point,* for example, and then add a + operator to enable you to add two points together by using a command such as the following:

```
ptNew = ptFirst + ptSecond;
```

Consider the class *CSize*, which is used to measure the size of a window or the displacement from one point to another. It might make sense to add a *CSize* to another *CSize* object.

In C++, the declaration of the addition operator for *CSize* looks like the following:

```
CSize operator+(CSize, CSize);
```

You can see that the name of the operator is the keyword operator, followed immediately by the operator's symbol. Following this are the types of the two arguments and the return type of the operator.

You don't overload the operators for any of the classes in this book, but the MFC Library does overload a few of the operators, as you'll see later, in the discussion of the MFC classes. In addition, C++ overloads the left and right shift operators (*operator<<( )* and *operator>>( )*) to perform I/O.

Hey! The I/O Just Comes Streaming out

The C language is somewhat unusual in that it has no keywords for performing input and output. Instead, it relies on functions from the standard library for this purpose, most notably *printf( )* for output and *scanf( )* for input.

This situation has certain advantages. It's possible, for example, to rewrite the I/O handlers for different types of hardware by modifying only the library and not mucking with the compiler proper. This technique has a big disadvantage, however, in that it is error-prone. Consider the following code segment (if you're not a big C expert, don't worry — you don't use these functions much anyway):

```
// at top of file
#include <stdio.h>

// ...farther down...

// read the input character from the keyboard
char cInput;
scanf("%d", cInput);
```

As one of my college professors used to say, "As is painfully obvious to even the most casual observer," this statement has problems. First, the format field, *%d*, indicates that the variable is an *int* when it is in fact a *char*. An even more subtle bug is that *scanf( )* expects a pointer to the *char* and not the *char* itself. (How about that? Two bugs in a single statement.)

The correct statement is shown here:

```
// read the input character from the keyboard
char cInput;
scanf("%c", &cInput);
```

The designers of C++ decided to use function overloading to make errors such as this one impossible. The function they chose to overload was *operator<<( )* for input and *operator>>( )* for output. To enter a character from the keyboard in C++, therefore, you use the following:

```
// at top of file
#include <iostream.h>

// ...farther down...

// read the input character from the keyboard
char cInput;
cin >> cInput;

cout << "Thanks for the input\n";
```

Notice that the *include* file stdio.h, which contained the prototypes for the standard C I/O functions, has been replaced with *iostream.h*, which describes the overloaded *operator<<( )* and *operator>>( )* functions.

Stream I/O not only stamps out certain types of bugs before they can become a household problem, but it also is *extensible,* which means that you can overload either operator to perform input or output of a class of your own design. You see this feature in action later, during the discussion of file I/O of the MFC Library objects.

Conclusion

This chapter has attempted to quickly present C++ in enough detail that you can understand the examples throughout the remainder of this book. By mimicking these examples, you should also become familiar enough with the C++ features just discussed to be able to use them effectively.

If you're going to get serious about using C++ capabilities in your programs, however:

Buy *C++ For Dummies* or *Borland C++ For Dummies* (both from IDG Books).

Chapter 7

A Firm Foundation: MFC

· ·

In This Chapter

▶ What is MFC?

▶ What's an application framework?

▶ Where have all the functions gone (long time passing)?

▶ What are all those files in the AppWizard version of "Hello, world"?

· ·

So now you should have a handle on the C++ language. This understanding should help explain some of the symbols and a few of the terms used in the description of Prog2_1. For example, you should now understand what a member function is and that *CProg2_1View::OnDraw( )* is one of them.

This new understanding still doesn't explain what all those files are about. And why does the AppWizard creation Prog2_1 look so different from the manually generated Prog1_1? This chapter relates the pieces that make up Prog2_1 to its Prog1_1 cousin and helps explain a great deal about the interaction between AppWizard and MFC.

The MFC Explained

Different types of application generators exist. Some application generators work essentially by themselves, generating all the code they need without reference to predefined, canned external libraries. An application generator might be designed, for example, to work with just the Standard C Library.

Because the Standard C Library is standard across almost all platforms (hence, the name Standard C Library), an application generator based on this library has the advantage that it can be transported to many different platforms.

The disadvantage is that the Standard C Library functions don't do much individually. Application generators based solely on Standard C Library calls must therefore generate a great deal of source code to build an application that does anything.

By comparison, AppWizard-generated applications rely on a large body of C++ code called *Microsoft Foundation Classes,* or *MFC,* for the majority of their functionality. The inclusion of a large amount of functionality in MFC enables the applications generated by AppWizard to be much smaller than they would be otherwise.

MFC comes bundled with the Visual C++ compiler (and some other compilers, such as Symantec's). To keep you on your intellectual toes, MFC carries a version number that is independent of the compiler's version number. For example, Version 1.5 of Visual C++ comes with Version 2.5 of MFC, and Visual C++ 2.0 comes with MFC 3.0. Compilers from other vendors include various versions of the MFC.

There are some notable differences between MFC 1.0 and MFC 2.0; the differences between MFC 2.0 and MFC 3.0, however, are primarily in the area of enhancements. ■

The code that AppWizard generates is called the *application framework.* The term *framework* refers to the fact that the user classes AppWizard defines are relatively standard from one application to another.

This commonality offers several advantages:

- ✔ The application framework rapidly orients programmers to the program at hand. In programming, as in life, you can get the job done in many different ways. This flexibility can make understanding a Windows application (WinApp) more difficult than usual. Maintenance programmers first must figure out the general approach taken by the program's author. This isn't the case with a program generated by AppWizard, however. A programmer schooled in the use of the AppWizard can easily pick up and follow a new program created by AppWizard because of the standard application framework.

- ✔ A common application framework enables other tools, such as Class-Wizard, to work within that framework to take even more of the programming burden from the programmer's shoulders.

- ✔ The application framework generated by the AppWizard offers a common user interface that is compliant with the Windows 95 suggested interface standards.

Understanding the MFC Interface

Back in 1983, object-oriented programming was not the big thing it is today. Although Windows has some object-oriented features, its interface was built for functional programming languages, such as C and Pascal. Sure, you can access the Windows API from C++ — you did it throughout Part I — but when you do, you're using only the C subset of the C++ language.

MFC is a set of classes that overlay the Windows API to give it an object-oriented interface. You might say that MFC *is* the C++ Windows interface. MFC enables Windows programmers to make effective use of the object-oriented features of the C++ language. MFC makes the paradigm shift for you (sounds like a '50s dance, doesn't it? — sort of like the functional foxtrot or the protected interface promenade).

The MFC classes are application classes, just like any classes you or I might write. They have no special privilege. Windows is completely unaware that anything called MFC even exists. In addition, remember that although MFC encapsulates the Windows API, it doesn't preclude programmers from accessing Windows directly whenever they want. This capability is shown in Figure 7-1.

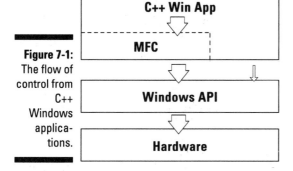

Figure 7-1: The flow of control from C++ Windows applications.

Suspicious readers might complain that introducing the MFC classes adds even more functions for beginners to master. This complaint would be valid, except that the MFC classes do such a good job of encapsulating the Windows API that it rarely becomes necessary for programmers to resort to accessing the Windows API directly.

This situation is good because there were, at last count, 2,132 API system calls in the Windows 95 repertoire. A C-based Windows 95 programmer doesn't have to know them all, of course, to be able to write sophisticated WinApps, but that's still a large number of functions. By comparison, MFC consists of 132 classes; you routinely deal with only 15 to 20 Windows classes in addition to another 20 to 25 general-purpose non-Windows classes. This reduction is a sizable one.

Learning what else MFC can do

In addition to encapsulating the Windows API interface, MFC provides the following features:

- ✔ A set of general-purpose (non-Windows) classes for manipulating strings, lists, collections, time, and so on
- ✔ Support for editable drop-down menus
- ✔ Support for the File Open, File Save, and File Save As menu options, including a file-selection box and a list of the most recently used files
- ✔ Print and print-preview support
- ✔ Scrolling windows and splitter windows
- ✔ Dialog boxes
- ✔ Toolbars
- ✔ Context-sensitive help
- ✔ Support for advanced features, such as ODBC (Open Database Connectivity) and OLE (Object Linking and Embedding) 2.0

These features aren't trivial. For example, Charles Petzold, in his API-oriented book *Programming Windows 3.1* (Microsoft Press, 1992) uses more than 50 pages to discuss printer support but — but MFC practically gives it to you for free.

How Does MFC Work?

Okay, so how does the encapsulation of the Windows API help explain the apparent differences between the MFC-dependent Prog2_1 and its Prog1_1 stand-alone predecessor? I started out by claiming that all WinApps must perform the following essential tasks performed by Prog1_1:

- ✔ Register a window class
- ✔ Create a window with that window class
- ✔ Dispatch messages to that window
- ✔ Field messages sent to the window and perform the requested operations, such as repainting the window's contents

I'm ignoring in this discussion the small minority of Windows applications that have no window. ■

So far, it isn't clear that Prog2_1 did any of those steps except the last one: It did display the "Hello, world" message from within the *OnDraw( )* member function (whatever that is).

The other operations, the ones not visible in Prog2_1, must be contained within MFC itself. Let's go looking for them. The search for these functions demonstrates a good deal about MFC and how it works with your classes to build a complete WinApp.

Registering the window class

The entry point into any Windows application is called *WinMain( )*. This is as good a place as any to begin your search.

The easiest way to find *WinMain( )* is to use the debugger. Load and compile Prog2_1. Be careful to choose Win32 Debug as the target (by choosing Project | Targets | Win32 Debug). Set a breakpoint at the entry into *WinMain( )*: Choose Debug | Breakpoints, enter *WinMain( )* in the Location window, and click the Add button.

Normally you set a breakpoint by selecting a line with the mouse and then clicking the "set breakpoint" icon on the toolbar. This icon looks like a policeman's hand held up to stop you. This point-and-shoot method requires that you know which source file contains *WinMain( )*. Using the Debug | Breakpoints window, you can enter a breakpoint without knowing which source file the function is in. ■

Execute the program that's under control of the debugger by choosing Debug | Go or clicking the "go" icon. The program stops as soon as it gets started. (I mean that literally, by the way.) The debugger should open a window to display the file winmain.cpp; the file contains a function that, after being simplified and cleaned up by me, looks like the following:

```
_tWinMain(HINSTANCE hInstance,
         HINSTANCE hPrevInstance,
         LPTSTR lpCmdLine,
         int nCmdShow)
{
    // AFX internal initialization
    if (!AfxWinInit(hInstance, hPrevInstance,
                   lpCmdLine, nCmdShow))
```

```
    {
        // On failure, just give it up
        goto InitFailure;
    }

    // Perform user-specific initializations
    CWinApp* pApp = AfxGetApp();
    pApp->InitInstance();

    // Read and dispatch messages
    int nReturnCode = pApp->Run();

    // Now terminate MFC stuff
InitFailure:
    AfxWinTerm();
    return nReturnCode;
}
```

Winmain.cpp is one of the many source files that make up the MFC library.

If the debugger can't find the source file winmain.cpp, it opens a window that asks where the file can be found. The file should be in the directory \msvc20\mfc\src on either your hard disk or the Visual C++ CD-ROM. ∎

Don't be concerned about the slight name change — the symbol _tWinMain is defined to be int WINAPI WinMain( ) in one of the include files. If you compare this function to your beloved WinMain( ) from Prog1_1, you see that the arguments are just what you would expect.

MFC functions that aren't members of an MFC class begin with the letters Afx. Thus, the first function WinMain( ) calls is AfxWinInit( ). Single-step through WinMain( ) until control reaches this function by either clicking the debugger toolbar button that looks like an arrow pointing inside a set of braces, by pressing F8, or by choosing Debug|Step Into. Stepping into this function reveals the following function contained in the file appinit.cpp (this file is just another of the many that make up MFC). Again, remember that I've cleaned up this function a little, to remove details that, for the purposes of this discussion, are unimportant:

```
BOOL AFXAPI AfxWinInit(HINSTANCE hInstance,
                       HINSTANCE hPrevInstance,
                         LPTSTR lpCmdLine,
                       int nCmdShow)
{
    // Perform some MFC initialization
    AFX_WIN_STATE* pWinState = AfxGetWinState();
    AFX_CORE_STATE* pCoreState = AfxGetCoreState();
```

```
pCoreState->m_hCurrentInstanceHandle = hInstance;
pCoreState->m_hCurrentResourceHandle = hInstance;

// Windows-specific initialization
CWinApp* pApp = AfxGetApp();
pApp->m_hInstance = hInstance;
pApp->m_hPrevInstance = hPrevInstance;
pApp->m_lpCmdLine = lpCmdLine;
pApp->m_nCmdShow = nCmdShow;
pApp->SetCurrentHandles();

// Register basic WndClasses
WNDCLASS wndcls;
memset(&wndcls, 0, sizeof(WNDCLASS));

// Common initialization
wndcls.lpfnWndProc = DefWindowProc;
wndcls.hInstance = hInstance;
wndcls.hCursor = afxData.hcurArrow;

// Child windows  — no brush, no icon,
//                  safest default class styles
wndcls.style = CS_DBLCLKS | CS_HREDRAW | CS_VREDRAW;
wndcls.lpszClassName = _afxWnd;
if (!AfxRegisterClass(&wndcls))
{
    return FALSE;
}

// Control bar windows
wndcls.style = 0;   // don't handle double-click
wndcls.lpszClassName = _afxWndControlBar;
wndcls.hbrBackground = (HBRUSH)(COLOR_BTNFACE + 1);
if (!AfxRegisterClass(&wndcls))
{
    return FALSE;
}

// MDI Frame window (also used for splitter window)
wndcls.style = CS_DBLCLKS;
wndcls.hbrBackground = NULL;
if (!RegisterWithIcon(&wndcls,
            _afxWndMDIFrame, AFX_IDI_STD_MDIFRAME))
{
    return FALSE;
}
```

```
// SDI Frame or MDI Child windows  — normal colors
wndcls.style = CS_DBLCLKS | CS_HREDRAW | CS_VREDRAW;
wndcls.hbrBackground = (HBRUSH) (COLOR_WINDOW + 1);
if (!RegisterWithIcon(&wndcls,
            _afxWndFrameOrView, AFX_IDI_STD_FRAME))
{
    return FALSE;
}

return TRUE;
}
```

AfxWinInit( ) begins by initializing a few MFC internal structures, such as something called *pApp*, which is returned by *AfxGetApp( )*.

The function then turns its attention to registering window classes. The function *AfxRegisterWindow( )* is just your old Windows API friend *RegisterWindow( )*, with proper MFC *Afx...* attire. The function *RegisterWithIcon( )* first attempts to load a suitable icon before calling *AfxRegisterWindow( )*.

Rather than register just one window class, as Prog1_1 did, *AfxWinInit( )* registers several different window classes for different purposes. Any single application may not need all these classes, but having them ready simplifies the MFC code.

It's clear that the first part of the puzzle is solved. The window class registration occurs in *AfxWinInit( )*. Let's continue to see whether you can figure out the rest.

Creating windows

After the window classes have been registered, *AfxWinInit( )* returns to *WinMain( )*. This function then makes the call *pApp->InitInstance( )*. At the time of the call, *pApp* points to the current application object. This object is used to describe the current program. It contains such information as the *hInstance* handle passed to *WinMain( )*.

The call to *pApp->InitInstance( )* is polymorphic, and ends up, in this case, at *CProg2_1App::InitInstance( )*. How can this be?

Getting from MFC to the program and back

The class *CProg2_1App*, which (as its name implies) is part of the application framework for the Prog2_1 application, inherits from class *CWinApp*, one of the classes that makes up the MFC Class Library. This inheritance is clear from the definition of *CProg2_1App*, contained in Prog2_1.h (notice the new line in the code):

```
class CProg2_1App : public CWinApp
{
public:
    CProg2_1App();

    // Overrides
    // ClassWizard-generated virtual function overrides
    //{{AFX_VIRTUAL(CProg2_1App)
    public:
    virtual BOOL InitInstance();
    //}}AFX_VIRTUAL

    // ...class definition continues . . . .
```

You can also see that the function *InitInstance( )* is declared virtual (it's declared virtual in *CWinApp* as well, by the way). *InitInstance( )* has been high-lighted to make it easier to find.

Because the function *InitInstance( )* is declared virtual, the call *pApp->Init-Instance( )* invokes the member function based on the runtime type of **pApp*, which is *CProg2_1App*. This gives the application a chance to influence the way initialization is performed.

This use of virtual functions is how the generic MFC classes mate with the application framework classes that make up your particular WinApp. Figure 7-2 shows this relationship for *CProg2_1App* and the other classes that make up the application framework.

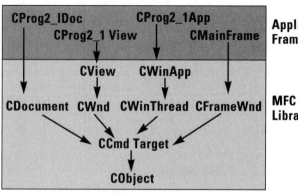

Figure 7-2:
The relationship between the application framework classes and the MFC classes.

What does CProg2_1::InitInstance( ) do?

The following is a slightly simplified version of *CProg2_1::InitInstance( )*:

```
BOOL CProg2_1App::InitInstance()
{
    // Load standard INI file options (including MRU)
    LoadStdProfileSettings();

    // Register the application's document templates.
    // Document templates serve as the connection between
    // documents, frame windows, and views.

    CSingleDocTemplate* pDocTemplate;
    pDocTemplate = new CSingleDocTemplate(
        IDR_MAINFRAME,
        RUNTIME_CLASS(CProg2_1Doc),
        RUNTIME_CLASS(CMainFrame),  // main frame window
        RUNTIME_CLASS(CProg2_1View));
    AddDocTemplate(pDocTemplate);

    // create a new (empty) document
    OnFileNew();

    return TRUE;
}
```

After loading the initial settings by calling *LoadStdProfileSettings( )* (don't worry — Chapter 12 explains this subject in detail), *InitInstance( )* uses the *RUNTIME_CLASS( )* macros to create instances of the classes *CProg2_1Doc*, *CMainFrame*, and *CProg2_1View*.

During the call to *OnFileNew( )*, the window is created through a call to *CreateWindowEx( )*. *CreateWindowEx( )* is just a slightly enhanced version of the *CreateWindow( )* function you used in Prog1_1 to create a window.

You generally have little reason to modify the code within *InitInstance( )*; however, AppWizard does customize the function calls made from within this function, depending on how you answer the questions posed in creating the application.

Dispatching messages

When control returns from *InitInstance( )*, *WinMain( )* passes control to *CWinApp::Run( )*. If you single-step into this call, you find that *CWinApp::Run( )*

eventually calls the function *CWinThread::PumpMessage( )*, shown in simplified form in the following code. *PumpMessage( )* contains the message-dispatch loop. (Remember that this loop is the one that reads messages from the input queue and sends them to the *WinProc* function.)

```
BOOL CWinThread::PumpMessage()
{
    if (!::GetMessage(&m_msgCur, NULL, NULL, NULL))
    {
    // Control comes here if WM_QUIT received
    return FALSE;
    }

    // process this message
    if (m_msgCur.message != WM_KICKIDLE &&
        !PreTranslateMessage(&m_msgCur))
    {
        ::TranslateMessage(&m_msgCur);
        ::DispatchMessage(&m_msgCur);
    }
    return TRUE;
}
```

Remember that a *::* by itself is part of the formal name of a function that is not a member of a class. Thus, *::GetMessage( )* refers to the nonmember function otherwise known as *GetMessage( )*. ■

Because *::GetMessage( )* returns a *FALSE* when it reads a *WM_QUIT* message and a *TRUE* otherwise, *PumpMessage( )* returns a *FALSE* immediately when it receives a *WM_QUIT* message. Other messages are passed to the *Translate-Message( )* function and then sent to the *WinProc* function via *DispatchMessage( )* in the same manner as in the manual Prog1_1 example.

Ignore for now the special consideration given to the *WM_KICKIDLE* message and the *PreTranslateMessage( )* function. These are just some features MFC has added for its own, internal purposes. You revisit the *Run( )* and *PumpMessage( )* functions again later in this book.

Run( ) continues to call *PumpMessage( )* in a loop until *PumpMessage( )* indicates, by returning a *FALSE*, that it has received a *WM_QUIT* message. At that point, *Run( )* returns to *WinMain( )*. After receiving control again, *WinMain( )* invokes *AfxWinTerm( )*, which cleans up a little and then exits, thereby terminating the program.

Finding where the message went

The call to *::DispatchMessage( )* sends the message to the window's *WindowProc*. In the case of the client window, the *WindowProc* is *CWnd:: WindowProc( )*. This function pulls out the *wparam* and *lparam* parameters and passes them to the function designated to handle that message, in a process called *message dispatching*.

Message dispatching is described in detail in Chapter 8.

The User Classes

By stepping through *WinMain( )*, you can see the relationship between the MFC class *CWinApp* and the application framework class *CProg2_1App* contained in the file Prog2_1.cpp.

The other main classes you deal with in creating MFC WinApps are *CProg2_1Doc* and *CProg2_1View*. You only occasionally deal with the *CMainFrame* class as well. (Obviously, the Prog2_1 portions in the preceding class names change from one application to another.)

Table 7-1 describes the relationship between these classes and their MFC base classes.

Table 7-1 Primary Application Framework Classes

Application Framework Class	Base Class in MFC	Source File	Purpose
CProg2_1Doc	CDocument	Prog2doc	Contains the application's data
CProg2_2View	CView	Prog2vw	Describes the client area of the application's window
CProg2_1App	CWinApp	Prog2_1	Describes the current instance of the program
CMainFraime	CFrameWnd	mainfrm	Describes the window frame of the application's main window

Let's look more closely at how this relationship works, by examining a class you've already dealt with (if only in passing): *CProg2_1View*.

Checking out the view

You've seen something of the relationship between *CProg2_1App* and *CWinApp*. You can see this same relationship in the class *CProg2_1View*. Begin by taking a peek at the *include* file, Prog2vw.h.

 When you look at the output of the AppWizard, it doesn't look exactly like this — okay, it hardly looks like this at all (remember that I've cleaned things up and removed a great deal of complexity for now): ■

```
//////////////////////////////////////////////////////////
// Prog2vw.h : interface of the CProg2_1View class
//

class CProg2_1View : public CView
{
public:
    CProg2_1View();

    virtual void OnDraw(CDC* pDC);

    virtual ~CProg2_1View();
};
```

The inheritance relationship shown here matches Figure 7-2. *CProg2_1View* inherits from the MFC class *CView*, and *CView* is derived from the base class *CWnd*. *CWnd* is the class that MFC uses to describe all windows.

The most interesting member function of *CProg2_1View* for now is *OnDraw( )*, which is called as a result of receiving the *WM_PAINT* message.

The code for CProg2_1View.cpp is straightforward:

```
// Prog2vw.cpp : implementation of the CProg2_1View class
//

#include "stdafx.h"
#include "Prog2_1.h"

#include "Prog2doc.h"
#include "Prog2vw.h"

//////////////////////////////////////////////////////////
// CProg2_1View

//////////////////////////////////////////////////////////
// CProg2_1View construction/destruction
```

```
CProg2_1View::CProg2_1View()
{
    // TODO: add construction code here

}

CProg2_1View::~CProg2_1View()
{
}

//////////////////////////////////////////////////////////
// CProg2_1View drawing

void CProg2_1View::OnDraw(CDC* pDC)
{
    // TODO: add draw code for native data here
    pDC->TextOut(0, 0, "Hello, world");
}
```

The constructor and destructor are empty — you didn't add any new members to the *CProg2_1View* class. You defined the *OnDraw( )* function to display the "Hello, world" message as a result of the *WM_PAINT* message. How did the *WM_PAINT* message get there?

The *WM_PAINT* message is first routed to the function *CView::OnPaint( )*, which appears as follows:

```
void CView::OnPaint()
{
   // standard paint routine
   CPaintDC dc(this); // create a device-context object
   OnPrepareDC(&dc);  // initialize it; like BeginPaint(),
   this->OnDraw(&dc); // the "this->" is unnecessary but
}                      // is added to demonstrate the point
```

OnPaint( ) begins by creating a device-context object (of class *CPaintDC*). The call to *CWnd::OnPrepareDC( )* initializes the object in the same way *BeginPaint( )* did, back in Prog1_1.

The call to *OnDraw( )* is "bound late," which means that it ends up, in this case, calling *CProg2_1View::OnDraw( )*. As you already know, *CProg2_1View:: OnDraw( )* uses the device-context object provided in *dc* to display the "Hello, world" message.

Remember that *this* is the address of the current object. It is a keyword and is defined only within a nonstatic member function. ∎

Again, this is an example of how the C++ late-binding feature is used as a bridge between the function *CView::OnPaint( )*, which is part of MFC and common to all WinApps built with MFC, and the application-specific function that is part of the application framework code unique to this application.

A word about the other application-framework classes

Let me mention another class you deal with frequently: *CProg2_1Doc*. This class is based on the MFC class *CDocument* and is used to contain any data the application may store. Because Prog2_1 has no data, it has little reason for a document class; skip over this class, therefore, until you get to Chapter 12.

MFD (Microsoft Foundation Details)

Although the preceding discussion left unexplained a few minor differences between Prog1_1 and Prog2_1, this section describes them for you now.

Getting a handle on your objects

Prog1_1 tends to deal in handles. It has *HINSTANCE* variables, *HWND* variables, and other types of handles. Prog2_1 thinks in terms of MFC objects. But why?

MFC generally doesn't use handles the way Windows does. Instead, MFC uses pointers to class objects. The argument to *OnDraw( )*, for example, was a pointer to an object of class *CDC* and not the handle of a *CDC* object. The change was necessary to make use of C++ syntax. You want the *CDC* class to have member functions in order to enable you to do things with device contexts; however, C++ knows nothing of handles. You also want to invoke member functions so that you can use the late-binding feature mentioned earlier.

In practice, the difference is unimportant. Because you don't have access to the data members in the device context (they're protected), even if you knew what they were — which you don't — you can't use the pointer as anything more than a handle anyway.

Finding things

As mentioned, MFC has more than 130 classes. The tear-out card in the front of this book shows the most common MFC classes used in this book.

With so many classes and with each class having its own set of member functions, how can you know where to find the member function you need for a particular application?

The best way to find a function is in the on-line documentation. To see how this process works, try looking up a member function now. Choose Help|Books Online from within the Visual C++ environment. Double-click MFC, then Class Library Reference, and then Alphabetical Reference. You'll see a list of groups of classes.

Suppose that you're looking up the *CView* class. To do so, double-click U Through W. (Because all the MFC classes begin with a *C,* it is left off the alphabetical listing, so you're looking in the *V*s.) Then double-click *CView.* The available options are CView, which means an overview of the class itself; Class Members, which means the public data members; and Member Functions, which when you double-click it, opens a list of all the member functions for this class. Be careful: This list doesn't include any member functions inherited by *CView* from its parent class *CWnd.*

Double-clicking the function opens a separate window with a description of the function, arguments to the function, return value, marital status, number of dependents, and any related functions.

If this process seems pretty involved, it *is* until you learn your way around. Give it a chance, though. It quickly becomes second nature.

If the help system is too slow or doesn't seem to work, you haven't installed Visual C++ properly. Check out Appendix B for more assistance in using Help.

The MFC functions tend to model similar functions in the API. The *TextOut( )* invoked in the *OnDraw( )* function, for example, wasn't the same as the API function. The full name of the member function invoked here is *CDC::TextOut(int, int, char*).* The full name of the API function is *::TextOut(HDC, int, int, char *, int).*

The pattern demonstrated by *TextOut( )* is common. If the first argument to the API function was a handle of some sort, the corresponding member function has similar arguments, except that it is a member of the class to that handle and the handle will be gone.

If you're familiar with the API calls, this rule can be helpful in reading MFC code and in helping you find a particular MFC function. ∎

Introducing the Prog2_1.rc file

The application framework included another file, Prog2_1.rc. This file, called the *resource file,* has a description of the number and arrangement of menu items and such items as the toolbar, dialog boxes, and help information. Because Prog1_1 doesn't have a menu or an About dialog box, it doesn't have a resource file (described briefly in Chapter 9). You'll be using the resource file to build a large part of the application in Part IV.

Learning about stdafx.cpp

One other .cpp file associated with your project, stdafx.cpp, doesn't appear in Prog1_1. This name is strange for a file, but it's contents are even stranger. All it contains is the following:

```
// stdafx.cpp : source file that includes just the
//      standard includes: Prog2_1.pch will be the
//      precompiled header, stdafx.obj will contain
//      the precompiled type information

#include "stdafx.h"
```

The comments tell the story. The Windows and MFC *include* files are extremely large; even with a fast processor, it can take some time for the compiler to work its way through. Because each .cpp file contains the same *include* files, it seems silly to duplicate the effort of processing these files for each .cpp file.

To avoid this waste, the AppWizard and the Visual C++ compiler work together as follows:

✔ The AppWizard builds the file stdafx.h, which contains all the MFC *include* files the current project needs. This file may vary depending on the options that are chosen.

✔ The AppWizard then builds the file stdafx.cpp, which was just listed. This file is always the same.

✔ The AppWizard then sets up the project file so that stdafx.cpp is compiled first.

✔ When Visual C++ compiles the stdafx.cpp file, it saves the results in a file named stdafx.pch. (The extension .pch stands for *p*recompiled *h*eader.)

✔ When Visual C++ compiles each subsequent .cpp file, it reads and uses the .pch file it generated earlier. Unless you've edited stdafx.cpp or stdafx.h, Visual C++ doesn't reparse the Windows *include* files.

Neat trick, don't you think? (By the way, Microsoft wasn't the first company to offer this feature — Borland was.)

The moral to this story is shown in this list:

- ✔ Any .cpp files you write should include stdafx.h first.

- ✔ If you have .h files, which most of the .cpp files in your project need, feel free to add them to stdafx.h (at the end) and then recompile stdafx.cpp.

- ✔ Because the .pch file contains a great deal of symbol information, it is by far the biggest file in your project. If you're having disk space problems, you'll want to delete the .pch files of projects you haven't played with for a while. They aren't necessary to execute the program, and they get rebuilt automatically when the project is rebuilt.

Conclusion

You've seen how the AppWizard conspires with Microsoft Foundation Classes to build an application framework and thus make the programmer's job easier. At first blush, the application framework doesn't seem to have all the parts a Windows application must have; by stepping through MFC, however, you begin to see that the same features common to all Windows applications (such as registering the Window class, creating the window, and reading messages from the message queue) are built in to MFC.

In Chapter 8, you continue your examination of the application framework by converting your second Windows program into an MFC application. In that chapter, you see how the final step, message dispatching, falls into place.

Chapter 8

Passing Messages in Class: The ClassWizard

● ●

In This Chapter

▶ Using the ClassWizard to add message handlers

▶ Why do you need message handlers?

▶ How does the message-dispatch mechanism work?

● ●

*W*riting a single "Hello, world" program by using the AppWizard, as you did in Chapter 7, doesn't exactly make you an expert in the use of MFC. Let's continue digging into the program by converting your second Windows program, Prog1_2, into its MFC equivalent.

Creating a Good View

Create the application framework for Prog2_2 by using the AppWizard. Tell AppWizard to turn off all cutesy options (just as you did in Prog2_1). Figure 8-1 shows the new project information you should end up with. (If you have any trouble getting your information window to look like this one, follow the instructions for Prog2_1 in Appendix B.)

As before, you know that you have to write the *OnDraw( )* member function. Using Prog1_2 as a pattern, I came up with the following (again, the lines in gray are the ones I added):

```
// Prog2vw.cpp : implementation of the CProg2_2View class
//

#include "stdafx.h"
#include "Prog2_2.h"
```

```
#include "Prog2doc.h"
#include "Prog2vw.h"

#ifdef _DEBUG
#undef THIS_FILE
static char BASED_CODE THIS_FILE[] = __FILE__;
#endif

/////////////////////////////////////////////////////////
// CProg2_2View

// ... other stuff went here ...

/////////////////////////////////////////////////////////
// CProg2_2View drawing

void CProg2_2View::OnDraw(CDC* pDC)
{
    // TODO: Add draw code for native data here

    // first set the mapping mode to MM_TWIPS
    pDC->SetMapMode(MM_TWIPS);

    // output the same type of stuff as before
    OutputLine(pDC, 1,
            "Avg char spacing [points] = ",
            m_nCharSpacing / 20);
    OutputLine(pDC, 2,
            "Row spacing [points] = ",
            m_nRowSpacing / 20);

    CRect rectWindow;
    GetWindowRect(&rectWindow);

    CPoint ptConversion = rectWindow.TopLeft();
    pDC->DPtoLP(&ptConversion);
    OutputLine(pDC, 4,
            "Window x location [points] = ",
            ptConversion.x / 20);
    OutputLine(pDC, 5,
            "Window y location [points] = ",
            -ptConversion.y / 20);

    CSize szConversion = rectWindow.Size();
    pDC->DPtoLP(&szConversion);
    OutputLine(pDC, 7,
            "Window x dimension [points] = ",
```

```
                    szConversion.cx / 20);
    OutputLine(pDC, 8,
               "Window y dimension [points] = ",
               szConversion.cy / 20);
}
```

This function would be somewhat complicated to understand if not for the
fact that you've already seen virtually the same code, in the form of Prog1_2.

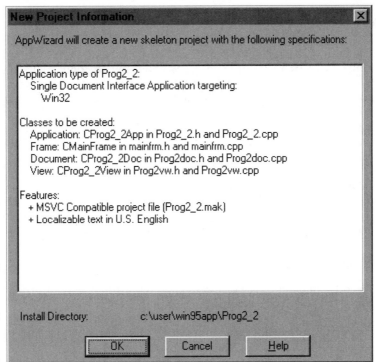

Figure 8-1:
The new
project
synopsis for
Prog2_2.

The following points have been mentioned, but they bear repeating:

☞ Because the device context is provided to you as an argument to *OnDraw( )*,
there is no need to call *BeginPaint( )* and *EndPaint( )*.

☞ *pDC* is not a handle to a device context, but rather a pointer to an object of
class *CDC*. *CDC* is the all-device-context class. It enables you to use C++
syntax in invoking member functions.

☞ The function *CDC::DPtoLP( )* is the member function equivalent of the API
device context handle function *::DPtoLP( )*. ■

Initiation rites: Adding members to the club

Like its API cousin, *Prog2_2* defines a function, *OutputLine( )*, to perform the output. I decided to write *OutputLine( )* as a member function of the class *CProg2_2View*.

I wrote the function for two reasons. The first reason is more or less a judgment call. You have to ask yourself whether this function is a property of the view. In my opinion, it is, so I made it a member of the class. If I had decided that it was not a property of the class, I might have left it a nonmember.

The second reason is that you don't want other functions writing willy-nilly to the client area of your window. As you know, the only civilized way to write to a window is to put the data somewhere for *OnDraw( )* to find it and then invalidate the window, causing *OnDraw( )* to be invoked. A nonmember function cannot be protected from the prying opcodes of other functions. Making *OutputLine( )* a protected member of the class keeps the electricity to the security fences turned on so that unwanted non-*CProg2_2View* functions can't call it.

I also made the decision to create the width- and character-spacing variables members of the view class. Clearly, the dimensions of the characters in the view are a property of that view. Other views with different fonts may have entirely different character dimensions. (This program has only one view window, but that isn't always true. You want to program for future expansion, don't you?)

To add a member to the class, you first must add it to the CProg2vw.h file, in which the view class is defined:

```
// Prog2vw.h : interface of the CProg2_2View class
//
/////////////////////////////////////////////////////////////

class CProg2_2View : public CView
{
protected:
    int m_nRowSpacing;   // these are now members
    int m_nCharSpacing;

    void OutputLine(CDC* pDC, int nRowNo,
                    char *pszDescr, int nVal);

        // ...the rest just like before...
```

Notice a few points about this code:

✔ Because the function *OutputLine( )* is declared protected, it is not part of the public interface of the class. Other functions have no business writing directly to the view.

✔ The names for the variables *m_nRowSpacing* and *m_nCharSpacing* now have an *m_* prepended to them. The *m_* stands for "member" and is something of an MFC standard, like the Hungarian notation.

✔ The new members should be initialized in the constructor in this way:

```
/////////////////////////////////////////////////////////////
// CProg2_2View construction/destruction

CProg2_2View::CProg2_2View()
{
    // TODO: Add construction code here

    // don't do any real initialization until the
    // OnCreate message is sent
    m_nRowSpacing = 0;
    m_nCharSpacing = 0;
}
```

Here's the code for the *OutputLine( )* function:

```
// OutputLine -- your old friend rewritten as a member
//                of the view class
void CProg2_2View::OutputLine(
    CDC   *pDC,
    int   nRowNumber,
    char *pszDescription,
    int   nValue
)
{
    int nCol1Offset = 20;
    int nCol2Offset = nCol1Offset + 35 * m_nCharSpacing;
    int nRowOffset = -nRowNumber * m_nRowSpacing;

    // output column 1 — the label
    pDC->SetTextAlign(TA_LEFT | TA_TOP);
    pDC->TextOut(nCol1Offset,
                 nRowOffset,
                 pszDescription);

    // output column 2 — the data
    pDC->SetTextAlign(TA_RIGHT | TA_TOP);
```

```
    char szBuffer[16];
    wsprintf(szBuffer, "%d", nValue);
    pDC->TextOut(nCol20ffset,
                 nRowOffset,
                 szBuffer);
}
```

This function appears almost identical to its API cousin.

What's a CPoint? A small CCircle? A good CArgument?

I glossed over it earlier, but *OnDraw( )* makes use of some heretofore unknown classes, such as *CPoint*, *CRect*, and *CSize* (it's enough to make you *CSick*). What are these classes, and why did I use them?

These classes clearly were designed to take the place of the API structures *POINT*, *RECT*, and *SIZE*; they are, in fact, C++ versions of the same thing. But what was wrong with those structures? Nothing, really. It's just that the C++ equivalents introduce member functions for manipulating the classes. The C versions do not (and could not) have these type of features.

If you prefer using the older versions, however, they're still available. Most of the functions that take *CPoint* are overloaded to accept a *POINT* as well. The function *CDC::DPtoLP( )* offers more flavors than Baskin-Robbins:

```
void DPtoLP( LPPOINT lpPoints, int nCount = 1 );
void DPtoLP( LPRECT lpRect );
void DPtoLP( LPSIZE lpSize );

void DPtoLP( CPoint *pPoints, int nCount = 1 );
void DPtoLP( CRect  *pRect );

void DPtoLP( CSize  *pSize );
```

The class *CPoint* is derived from *POINT*; *CSize,* from *SIZE*; and *CRect,* from *RECT*. It's not necessary to offer a separate *DPtoLP(CPoint*)* — the *DPtoLP(LPPOINT)* works fine because a *CPoint* IS_A *POINT*. Anywhere a *POINT* is required, a *CPoint* may be used. The same is true, of course, for *CSize* and *CRect*. ■

Which operations are defined for CPoint, et al.?

A *CSize* is the difference between two *CPoint*s. The following operations, therefore, are defined:

```
CSize delta;
CPoint point1, point2;
delta = point1 - point2; // distance from pt1 to pt2
point1 = point2 + delta; // pt1 is pt2 plus a delta
point1 += delta;         // scoot point1 over by delta
if (point1 == point2)    // true if point1 and point2 are co-located
```

The *CRect* class offers an assortment of different operations. For example, *CRect::UnionRect( )* calculates the minimum rectangle that contains two rectangles, and *CRect::IntersectRect( )* calculates the maximum rectangle that is fully contained within two rectangles (the area in which the rectangles overlap), as shown in Figure 8-2.

Union

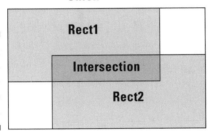

Figure 8-2:
The inter-
section and
union of two
rectangles.

The use of these classes gives programmers even more to learn (and you need to learn more right as much as I need to gain weight!), but the resulting code is easier to write, read, and maintain.

Adding a Message Handler: More Wizardry

If you look back at the constructor for *CProg2_2View*, you'll notice that although it does initialize the data members *m_nRowSpacing* and *m_nChar-Spacing*, it doesn't initialize them to anything useful (you can't fit much in a 0-by-0 window).

Why not calculate the character spacing in the constructor? To C++ programmers, this would seem to be the logical place. Unfortunately, MFC isn't ready to entertain such questions as "How big is my window?" during construction of the view object. Instead, the program must wait for the *WM_CREATE* message, just as you did with the API version in Prog1_2.

The reason the program can't calculate the character spacing in the constructor is simple: The window doesn't exist when the *CWnd* object is created. To understand how this can be true, you must understand that the *CWnd* object is *not* the same as the window itself.

Remember that MFC is *not* the Windows API — it is a shell around the Windows API. Because MFC is linked with your program's code, it is definitely on your side of the Windows API, as shown in Figure 8-3.

Figure 8-3:
The relationship between MFC objects and Windows objects.

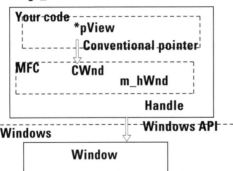

Therefore, although the *CWnd* object is created by MFC, a parallel window object is within Windows itself. Your code accesses the *CWnd* object directly, for example, through a C++ pointer; the *CWnd* object controls the window object by using a handle (of type *HWND*) exactly like an API-only program would. ∎

Although you can create a *CWnd* object at program start-up, the window to which the *CWnd* object refers doesn't exist until the *WM_CREATE* message is generated.

Snagging WM_CREATE

Okay, so you have to add a message handler to snag the *WM_CREATE* message. Ah, but this situation introduces a problem. The default framework the

AppWizard generates doesn't process the *WM_CREATE* message. To add the handler for this or any other message, you use the ClassWizard.

Unlike the AppWizard, the ClassWizard can be executed as often as you want. The ClassWizard saves information about your project in a special file, Prog2_2.clw, that enables it to reenter an existing project and know where it left off. (This file was created by the AppWizard.)

To add the *WM_CREATE* message handler, enter the ClassWizard and select *CProg2_2View* as the class to change and *WM_CREATE* as the message you want to grab. (Appendix B has detailed instructions on how to use the Class-Wizard.) To handle the message, the ClassWizard adds a new member function, *CProg2_2View::OnCreate( )*.

The name of the handler of a *WM_X* message is always *OnX( )*, where *X* is some arbitrary string. To fit Hungarian naming rules, *X* is in all caps in the message name and only the first letter is capitalized in the function name. ■

The list of events is similar to, but more extensive than, the list of event procedures you can define in Visual Basic. In addition, in Visual C++ you may add your own messages, as you'll see later in this chapter. ■

Now you can add the code to fetch *TEXTMETRIC* and read the size of the current font, just as you did in Prog1_2:

```
/////////////////////////////////////////////////////////////
// CProg2_2View message handlers


int CProg2_2View::OnCreate(LPCREATESTRUCT lpCreateStruct)
{
    if (CView::OnCreate(lpCreateStruct) == -1)
        return -1;

    // TODO: Add your specialized creation code here

    // Set the mapping mode to MM_TWIPS
    CDC *pDC = GetDC();
    pDC->SetMapMode(MM_TWIPS);

    // now get the font information
    TEXTMETRIC textMetrics;
    pDC->GetTextMetrics(&textMetrics);
    m_nRowSpacing  = textMetrics.tmHeight
                   + textMetrics.tmExternalLeading;
    m_nCharSpacing = textMetrics.tmAveCharWidth;
```

```
        ReleaseDC(pDC);
        return 0;
}
```

CProg2_2View::OnCreate( ) first passes the *WM_CREATE* message to the parent
class's member function *CView::OnCreate( )*. Just because *CProg2_2View*
intends to use the member function doesn't mean that its parent class
doesn't want it as well. How did I know to pass the message to the parent?
I didn't — the ClassWizard knew and generated the appropriate call for me.
(What a wizard.)

If all goes well with the *CView::OnCreate( )* call, control passes to the call to
GetTextMetrics( ). Because *OnCreate( )* isn't automatically provided with a
device context, it must get one on its own. Notice that the call to *GetDC( )*
doesn't refer to your old friend *::GetDC(HWND)* but rather to the MFC version
CWnd::GetDC( ) that *CProg2_2View* inherited from its grandparent, *CWnd*.

After fetching the *TEXTMETRIC* information and initializing the two data members, the function releases the device context by calling *ReleaseDC( )* before
returning a success indication.

You Can't Route Your Messages Without a Map

If you look more closely at the code generated by the ClassWizard, you'll
notice some strange things. In particular, at the top of the CProg2vw.cpp
source file is something that looks like the following:

```
BEGIN_MESSAGE_MAP(CProg2_2View, CView)
    //{{AFX_MSG_MAP(CProg2_2View)
    ON_WM_CREATE()
    //}}AFX_MSG_MAP
END_MESSAGE_MAP()
```

This code is indeed strange-looking. What could it possibly mean?

MFC uses this set of macros to set up something it calls a *message map* to
process the different messages the class may receive.

How does the message map work?

Each class is assigned a message map that describes those messages the class is prepared to handle. The message map is defined in this way:

- ✔ The *BEGIN_MESSAGE_MAP( )* macro begins the message map. It also specifies the name of the class and the class's parent.

- ✔ The ClassWizard needs the cryptic comment that follows the *BEGIN_MESSAGE_MAP( )* in order to find the beginning and end of the message-map definition. This comment enables the ClassWizard to find its way around the message map in order to edit it properly.

- ✔ The *ON_WM_CREATE( )* macro adds the *WM_CREATE* message to the message map for this class and associates it with the *OnCreate( )* member function.

- ✔ The comment at the end and the *END_MESSAGE_MAP( )* macro both signal the end of the message map.

When a Windows message is received, *CWnd::WindowProc( )* first searches the message map for *CProg2_2View* to see whether the class has registered an interest in that message. If so, it invokes the associated member function of the class. If not, it proceeds to the parent class indicated in the *BEGIN_MES-SAGE_MAP( )* (*CView*, in this case) and repeats the process.

If you look within MFC, you see that the message map for *CView* looks more or less like what you would expect:

```
/////////////////////////////////////////////////////////
// CView

BEGIN_MESSAGE_MAP(CView, CWnd)
    //{{AFX_MSG_MAP(CView)
    ON_WM_PAINT()
    ON_WM_MOUSEACTIVATE()
    ON_WM_CREATE()
    ON_WM_DESTROY()

    // ...other stuff...

    //}}AFX_MSG_MAP
END_MESSAGE_MAP()
```

This is a list of the messages the *CView* class is prepared to handle. For each of these messages, there is a corresponding *CView::On...( )* member function. If *WindowProc( )* can't find the message in this list, it continues with that *CView*'s parent, *CWnd*, and so on.

If *WindowProc( )* completes its search of the chain of message maps and still hasn't found a function to handle the message, it passes the message back to the Windows default message handler, *::DefWindowProc( )*.

All message-dispatch roads lead to *CCmdTarget*, which is the root base class for all classes that can receive a message through the message-dispatch scheme used by MFC. (If you flip back to Figure 7-2, you'll notice that the classes *CDocument*, *CView*, *CWinApp*, and *CFrameWnd* all inherit from *CCmdTarget*.) Classes such as *CString* do not and, therefore, cannot be sent messages. ∎

Let's see that in action

Let's follow a couple of messages through the winding streets and alleys they must traverse to end up at their proper destinations. Again, the idea is to look at the big picture.

In the example of a *WM_PAINT* message sent to the client area, MFC picks up the message and realizes that it was intended for the window associated with your view class object. It therefore looks in the message map for *CProg2_2View* for a *WM_PAINT* handler. It doesn't find one, so it looks in the message map for the parent class, *CView*. There it finds an entry for *WM_PAINT*. The message is passed to the handler *CView::OnPaint( )*. (So that's how control got to *CView::OnPaint( )*!)

Now consider the example of the *WM_CREATE* message. Again, MFC picks up the message from the input queue and examines the message map for the *CProg2_2View* class. Finding an entry there, it calls the function *CProg2_2View::OnCreate( )*. Because it straightaway finds a match, it never looks in the message map for *CView*. If it had looked, it would have found a match there as well.

In another example, Windows sends the *WM_LBUTTONDOWN* message when you press the left mouse button. If the mouse is within the client window when the mouse button is pressed, Windows sends the *WM_LBUTTONDOWN* message to your window's mailbox, where MFC reads it. It looks first in the message map for *CProg2_2View*. After finding nothing there, it looks in the message map for the base class, *CView*. Again, it finds nothing, so it looks in *CView*'s base class, *CWnd*. After coming up dry, it finally gives up and passes the message to the API function *::DefWindowProc( )* to take whatever default processing Windows sees fit.

Why a different mechanism?

What compelled the kind souls at Microsoft to introduce a different message-dispatching scheme? What was wrong with good ole C++ virtual functions? Why not just define a virtual function for each different message and let C++ sort it out?

The use of virtual functions to handle Windows messages presents two problems. The first problem is size. For each class that contains virtual functions, C++ must create a table that contains the address of every virtual function in the class. For conventional classes containing perhaps 10 or 20 virtual functions, this isn't an issue; however, there are hundreds of Windows messages. If each one got its own virtual function, it would add up to some relatively large tables.

The message-mapping scheme adopted by Microsoft remedies this situation by including in the map only those messages which that class intends to process.

The second problem involves memory. Memory is cheap, so there must be some more compelling reason. And there is. To dispatch the messages properly by using virtual functions, MFC's *WindowProc( )* would have to know about every possible message ID. That is, somewhere there would have to be a *switch* statement like the following:

```
LRESULT CWnd::WindowProc(UINT uMsgId, ...)
{
    // ...whatever preliminary processing
    switch(uMsgId)
    {
      case WM_PAINT:
        return OnPaint();  // this call bound late

      case WM_CREATE:
        return OnCreate(); // so is this

      // ...etc....
    }
}
```

If the *On...( )* functions were declared virtual, the calls to *OnPaint( )*, *OnCreate( )*, and the other *On...( )* functions would be bound late. This process would allow the message to be intercepted in a subclass, if necessary, which is just what you would want.

The hitch, though, is that Windows allows programmers to define their own message IDs. In addition, Microsoft adds new message types all the time. The virtual-function mechanism makes no provision for calling *On...( )* functions for message IDs that the MFC *WindowProc( )* function doesn't already know about at compile-time.

In object-oriented-ese, you say that the virtual member function-based message-dispatch scheme is not *extensible*. ■

The message-mapping system solves this problem by enabling a user's class to declare its intention to process a message ID that the class has made up itself.

With all these benefits, what disadvantages are there? There's really only one: Searching a chain of message maps to look for the correct message handler is considerably slower than executing a late-bound call to a virtual function. Slow enough to make a perceptible difference? Probably not. To be on the safe side, though, Microsoft minimizes the delay by including several optimizations in the dispatch code, such as hand-coded assembly language routines in key places.

Visual Basic uses the same type of memory-mapping scheme to route *WM_* messages to the different procedures; by the time you see them, however, the *wparam* and *lparam* portions of the message have already been interpreted and appear as arguments to the event procedure. ■

The Home Stretch

All you have to do now to complete the *Prog2_2* example is to add the *WM_MOVE* message handler. This process is straightforward. Return to the ClassWizard, and select the *CMainFrame* class. In the window on the right, click *WM_MOVE*. The ClassWizard obediently adds the proper function, which should be edited as follows:

```
void CMainFrame::OnMove(int nX, int nY)
{
    CFrameWnd::OnMove(nX, nY);

    // TODO: Add your message handler code here

    // invalidate the window whenever it is moved
    // to force the OnDraw to display the new window
    // location
    Invalidate();
}
```

You don't need to add a *WM_SIZE* handler because MFC creates the view window with the *CS_HREDRAW* and *CS_VREDRAW* style.

 You may have wondered why you add the handler to the *CMainFrame* class and not to the *CView* class. The answer is that it's the window frame that moves around the screen. Any movement of the view window would be with respect to the window frame that contains it. ■

Conclusion

Let's step back and compare this second MFC effort with its strictly API counterpart. The amount of programming required was slightly less, but similar. You had to get the *TEXTMETRIC* information as you did earlier, and you still had to put it in the display by using the *OutputLine( )* function.

The AppWizard simplifies the task a little by building the application framework. All you had to do was stick your code in the right places. The ClassWizard helps even more by inserting empty message handlers in the proper places and by adding these handlers to the class message map.

If you program Windows day in and day out for six months, that may not seem like a big deal. Heck, you could set up the necessary framework in your sleep. But if you program in Windows only occasionally, remembering when to cross the *t*'s and dot the *i*'s can be a problem. Help like this is well worth the money, especially when it's free.

Chapter 9

Managing Your Resources

• •

In This Chapter
▶ Enjoying natural resources (such as icons)
▶ Using AppStudio to edit a resource file

• •

*B*efore pushing on with other programming examples, this chapter presents one other thing Prog2_2 can teach you: how to use and edit resources.

 This chapter presents just a quick overview of the resource file. You'll get a complete baptism of fire in Part IV, in which you edit the resource file to change the About box, add menu items, add menu accelerators, build a dialog box, and change the toolbar. ■

Introducing the Ever-So-Helpful Resource File

Not all the files the AppWizard generated were conventional C++ source files. The file Prog2_2.rc is known as a *resource file,* or *resource script.*

When you open Prog2_2.rc, you can tell that it's not your grandmother's ordinary file anymore. Rather than display text, which is what happens when you open a C++ source file, the window instead shows a hierarchical representation of the resources in your program. This windodow, which resembles the window you see when you open a project file, is shown in Figure 9-1.

Why bother with a resource file?

You're probably asking, "What are resources? Do you mean water and oil and stuff like that?" Windows *resources* are properties that determine the look

Figure 9-1:
The
contents
of the
resource
file as
displayed
from the
Visual C++
environ-
ment.

and feel of the program. Some examples of resources are the position of the menu items, the menu text, the speed keys used to access the menu items, and the program icon.

Elements such as menu text can be hard-coded, but it's much better to encode these elements into the resource file. It's the old divide-and-conquer gambit again. If you think about it, the text that is displayed in a menu has nothing to do with the act of displaying the menu or retrieving the message that results from choosing one of the menu options. Putting such secondary information as the placement, size, and text of menus in a resource file gets it out of the mainstream of the logic of displaying and interpreting the menu.

In addition, if the resource-type information is buried within the part of the code that handles menus, it can be difficult to edit that information. You might think that you just won't change the menu, but experienced program-mers know that the only constant in programming is change. Everything that can be changed *will* be changed; the details of the look and feel of the pro-gram are the most likely to change. Placing this type of information in a resource file that can be separately and conveniently edited makes a great deal of sense.

Some programmers have to support multilingual versions of their software. Although this situation doesn't happen often, when it does, resource files are a lifesaver. Although a programmer must build different text resources for each language, the program code can remain identical.

Really, what is a resource file?

The resource file is just a text file written in a C-like resource language. The resource language is so C-like, in fact, that it includes many of the .h files your C and C++ programs include. The AppStudio editor might define a constant it inserts in the .h file that both the resource .rc and the source .cpp file can include.

In the old days, programmers used a conventional text editor to build and edit the resource file. Editing the resource file with a text editor was not only just one more thing to learn about, but, because it wasn't something programmers used every day, the process was also error-prone. The AppStudio resource compiler makes editing the resource file much easier by interpreting the contents for you.

After a programmer edits the resource file, he uses the resource compiler (RC) to compile it. Again, in the old days, using the RC compiler was a manual exercise. When you use a project file, however, you invoke the RC compiler automatically — so automatically, in fact, that unless you pay careful attention to the messages, you might not even notice it running.

After the resource file has been compiled, the linker binds the output with the rest of the program during the link step.

So show me

To see the AppStudio resource editor at work, try editing the icon associated with the Prog2_2 sample program. This resource is the most visible and certainly the most fun to edit. Double-click the icon folder. When the icon appears, double-click it; a Paint-like utility pops up, enabling you to set the bits in the standard 32-bit-by-32-bit icon (Appendix B provides detailed instructions).

After you finish editing the program icon, close the icon editor and rebuild the application. You should notice that only the Prog2_2.rc file is recompiled before the entire application is relinked. When you execute the program, the program icon reflects your changes. (This is easy to see in the About box in the Help menu.)

Conclusion

You've certainly been busy in this part of the book. This list shows some of the things you learned about in Part II:

- ✔ Using the AppWizard to build an application framework
- ✔ Getting up to speed with C++ programming
- ✔ Understanding the relationship between the AppWizard and Microsoft Foundation Classes
- ✔ Filling in the application framework
- ✔ Adding a message handler with the ClassWizard
- ✔ Using the AppStudio resource editor

Now that you know the basics of using the Visual C++ tools, it's time to learn how experienced Windows programmers make their Windows programs perform all those neat tricks by using MFC. In Part III, you build a simple drawing application. Each chapter concentrates on some new feature you may want to use in your Windows applications.

20-Minute Workout

Questions

1 Of the following prototypes:

```
int MyFunction(char *pString);
int MyFunction(int nX, int nY = 100);
```

which of the following three calls is different from the other two?:

```
int n;
n = MyFunction(10, 100);
n = MyFunction("10");
n = MyFunction(10);
```

2 Why are inline functions normally defined in a .h *include* file?

3 What are the disadvantages of a functional microwave (as opposed to an object-oriented microwave)?

4 Define the following terms:

A. OOP

B. Base class

C. Subclass

D. Instance of a class

E. Runtime type

F. Late binding

5 What's the difference between a *protected* and a *private* member of a class?

The MFC member function *CView::OnPaint* contains the following lines:

```
LRESULT CView::OnPaint()
{
    CPaintDC dc(this);  // what does this mean?
    // ...function continues...
```

Explain the line *CPaintDC dc(this)*.

Suppose that there is an event named *crash* (which all my programs should have).

    A. What is the name of the MFC event?

    B. What is the name of the associated message?

    C. What is the name of the function to handle the event?

In Chapter 8, you captured the *WM_MOVE* message to allow the *x* and *y* coordinates displayed in the window to be updated properly. You didn't have to grab the *WM_SIZE* message; because it does no harm, however, use the ClassWizard to add a handler for the *WM_SIZE* window.

An API function has the following prototype. What might the corresponding MFC Library function prototype be?

```
int IntersectClipRect(
    HDC  hdc, // handle of device context
    int  nLeftRect, // x-coord of upper-left of rectangle
    int  nTopRect,  // y-coord of upper-left of rectangle
    int  nRightRect, // x-coord of lower-right
    int  nBottomRect // y-coord of lower-right
);
```

Answers

The first and third function calls are identical. The second call is different.

Inline functions are expanded inline during compilation. This means that the definition of the inline function must be available during the compilation step. If an inline function is called in one source file, a.cpp, but defined in another, b.cpp, the definition of the function is not available to the compiler when a.cpp is compiled.

(It is possible to define an inline function at the top of a module if it's called only from within that module.)

In a nutshell, the problems with functional microwaves are as follows:

✔ It's difficult to reuse the microwave for other recipes.

✔ The recipe gets confused with instructions for operating the microwave.

✔ Problems are difficult to isolate.

A. Object-oriented programming.

B. To define by analogy, if *Cat* publicly inherits from *Feline*, then *Feline* is the base class of *Cat*.

C. In the *Cat* example, *Cat* is the subclass. Another term for subclass is "publicly derived class."

D. In the *Cat* class example, a particular cat (for example, *catGarfield*) is an instance of class *Cat*.

E. The actual type of an object rather than its declared type. The runtime type may be (and usually is) the same as the declared type, but it may also be a subclass of the declared type.

F. The process of deciding which of several virtual member functions to call based on the runtime type of the class and not on the declared type. (It also means getting married late in life.)

A private member of a class is accessible only from the class itself. A protected member of a class is also accessible from a subclass.

CPaintDC is a subclass of *CDC* that constructs a screen-based device context, which can be used for painting.

The class *CPaintDC* has a constructor *CPaintDC::CPaintDC(CWnd*)*, which constructs a *CPaintDC* object by using the current settings of the window object that is provided.

CPaintDC dc(this) declares an object *dc* of class *CPaintDC*, using the *CWnd* object pointed at by *this* to construct it.

Remember that *this* always points to the current object. Because the example is within a member function of class *CView*, *this* is of type *CView**. Remember also that *CView* is a subclass of *CWnd*.

The (a) *ON_WM_CRASH* event generates the (b) *WM_CRASH* message, which is fielded by the (c) *OnCrash( )* member function.

The code should look identical to the code added to handle the *WM_MOVE* message:

```
void CMainFrame::OnSize(UINT nType, int cx, int cy)
{
    CFrameWnd::OnSize(nType, cx, cy);

    // TODO: Add your message handler code here

    // same for the resize message as for move
    Invalidate();
}
```

In this case, unlike in the *WM_MOVE* case, you have the option of adding this message to the window frame (as shown here) or to the view. The reason is that the client area is resized whenever the window frame is resized.

Problem 9 has two solutions. The more straightforward solution is shown here:

```
int CDC::IntersectClipRect(
    int  nLeftRect,  // x-coord of upper-left of rectangle
    int  nTopRect,   // y-coord of upper-left of rectangle
    int  nRightRect, // x-coord of lower-right
    int  nBottomRect // y-coord of lower-right
);
```

The only things that have happened are that the initial device-context handle has been removed and the function has been made a member of the class that corresponds to the device context, *CDC*.

A more convenient solution is provided by replacing the four different arguments with the single object of type *CRect*.

```
int CDC::IntersectClipRect(
    CRect *pRect    // the rectangle
);
```

Part III
App1: A Drawing Program

The 5th Wave   **By Rich Tennant**

"...AND TALK ABOUT MEMORY! THIS BABY'S GOT SO MUCH MEMORY, IT COMES WITH EXTRA DOCUMENTATION, A HARD DISK—AND A SENSE OF GUILT! I MEAN I'M TALKIN MEMORY!"

In This Part...

*N*ow it's time to write the first of three Windows applications. This application, a simple Etch-A-Sketch program, teaches you how to read the mouse, draw on the current window, save your data to disk and restore it later, and scroll.

Chapter 10

The Ultimate Mousetrap

● ●

In This Chapter

▶ Keeping track of the mouse pointer

▶ Trapping button events

▶ Drawing with the mouse

● ●

*N*othing is more fundamental to Windows programming than tracking the mouse. The MFC Library handles normal mouse interactions, such as menu choices and button-presses; it's useful, however, to be able to drop back and manage the mouse yourself whenever you need to. The drawing program you're preparing to build gives you a chance to track the mouse and see the results. This chapter explains how to locate the mouse and transform that information into the Super VGA equivalent of cave drawings.

The Big Event: Moving the Mouse

Whenever the mouse changes location, a *WM_MOUSEMOVE* message is sent to the window to which the mouse pointer points to notify the window of the move. The following program, Prog3_1a, demonstrates how to snag the *WM_MOUSEMOVE* message and report the mouse coordinates (in this case, in text form at location (0,0) in the client window).

I use the letter at the end of the program name (the *a* in Prog3_1a, for example) as a minor version number. You can be sure that if there's a Prog3_1a, a Prog3_1b follows and — I hope — improves on it. I use the minor version designations to make clear which version of the program I'm describing in the text.

I suggest that you use the AppWizard to create the first program without the minor version indication (Prog3_1, for example). After you have version *a* working, you can make the indicated changes to convert that program into version *b*, from there into version *c*, and so on, all the while retaining the name

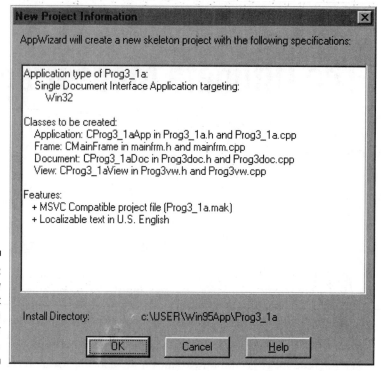

Figure 10-1:
The new project information summary for Prog3_1a.

New Project Information

AppWizard will create a new skeleton project with the following specifications:

Application type of Prog3_1a:
    Single Document Interface Application targeting:
    Win32

Classes to be created:
    Application: CProg3_1aApp in Prog3_1a.h and Prog3_1a.cpp
    Frame: CMainFrame in mainfrm.h and mainfrm.cpp
    Document: CProg3_1aDoc in Prog3doc.h and Prog3doc.cpp
    View: CProg3_1aView in Prog3vw.h and Prog3vw.cpp

Features:
    + MSVC Compatible project file (Prog3_1a.mak)
    + Localizable text in U.S. English

Install Directory: c:\USER\Win95App\Prog3_1a

[OK]   [Cancel]   [Help]

Prog3_1. That way, you don't have to rerun AppWizard for each minor version. This technique saves you a great deal of disk space and typing time. ■

Build a new AppWizard project for Prog3_1a by using the information shown in Figure 10-1. (This is the same way you've built all the AppWizard projects in this book — with all "fancy features" disabled).

Use the ClassWizard to add a handler for the *WM_MOUSEMOVE* message to the *CProg3_1aView* class. Figure 10-2 shows the ClassWizard display in action.

Figure 10-2 should look familiar to you by now, but maybe you got bored and jumped ahead. If you have any trouble adding the message handler, see Appendix B for a blow-by-blow description of how it's done. Chapter 8 explains how message handlers work. ■

The definition of the *CProg3_1aView* class is contained in the *include* file Prog3vw.h, which appears as follows (again, my additions are marked in gray):

```
// Prog3vw.h : interface of the CProg3_1aView class
//
/////////////////////////////////////////////////////////////

class CProg3_1aView : public CView
{
protected:
    // the current location of the mouse
    CPoint m_pntMouseLoc;

protected:      // create from serialization only
    CProg3_1aView();
    DECLARE_DYNCREATE(CProg3_1aView)

// Attributes
public:
    CProg3_1aDoc* GetDocument();

// Operations
public:

// Overrides
    // ClassWizard generated virtual function overrides
    //{{AFX_VIRTUAL(CProg3_1aView)
    public:
    virtual void OnDraw(CDC* pDC);
    protected:
      //}}AFX_VIRTUAL

// Implementation
public:
    virtual ~CProg3_1aView();

// Generated message map functions
protected:
    //{{AFX_MSG(CProg3_1aView)
    afx_msg void OnMouseMove(UINT nFlags, CPoint point);
    //}}AFX_MSG
    DECLARE_MESSAGE_MAP()
};
```

If you've followed my advice, your class will be called simply *CProg3_1View*, without the minor version number. ∎

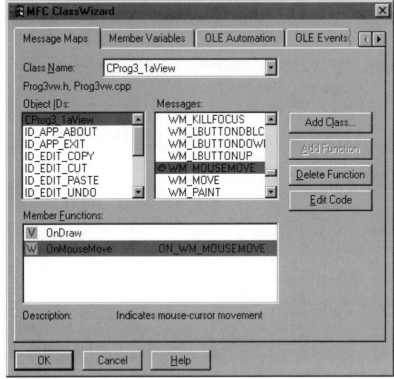

Figure 10-2:
Adding the
mouse-
move
message in
Class-
Wizard.

The class *CProg3_1aView* has all the parts you've come to know and love. It declares a constructor *CProg3_1aView( )* to enable you to initialize any members you might add to the class.

Remember that the view window doesn't exist when the constructor is invoked. The constructor must limit itself to initializing the data members to benign values on its own. Any functions that rely on the actual window attached to the view object must wait until the window exists. The best place for window-dependent initialization code is generally in the *InitialUpdate* member function.

CProg3_1aView defines a *GetDocument( )* member function that you need later, but not now. Next is the virtual *OnDraw( )* member function, which (as always) you must overload. Finally, you see the message map for this class that contains the entry for the *OnMouseMove( )* function, which receives the *WM_MOUSEMOVE* message.

I manually added the new member *m_pntMouseLoc* of class *CPoint* to contain the location of the mouse pointer within the window. *CPoint* objects are used to record locations within a window.

The code for class *CProg3_1aView* appears in Prog3vw.cpp as follows. (The diagnostic code that appears within the *#if _DEBUG* checks has been removed here to shorten the listings and highlight the important points. Otherwise, the key elements tend to get lost in a sea of detail.) Don't remove this diagnostic code from the application framework generated for you by AppWizard — just leave it there. The diagnostic code is discussed in Chapter 14.

```
// Prog3vw.cpp : implementation of the CProg3_1aView
//                class

#include "stdafx.h"
#include "Prog3_1a.h"

#include "Prog3doc.h"
#include "Prog3vw.h"

/////////////////////////////////////////////////////////
// CProg3_1aView .

IMPLEMENT_DYNCREATE(CProg3_1aView, CView)

BEGIN_MESSAGE_MAP(CProg3_1aView, CView)
    //{{AFX_MSG_MAP(CProg3_1aView)
    ON_WM_MOUSEMOVE()
    //}}AFX_MSG_MAP
END_MESSAGE_MAP()

/////////////////////////////////////////////////////////
// CProg3_1aView construction/destruction

CProg3_1aView::CProg3_1aView()
{
    // initialize the current mouse location to null
    m_pntMouseLoc = CPoint(0, 0);
}

CProg3_1aView::~CProg3_1aView()
{
}

/////////////////////////////////////////////////////////
// CProg3_1aView drawing

void CProg3_1aView::OnDraw(CDC* pDC)
{
    char szBuffer[80];
```

```
      wsprintf(szBuffer, "Mouse loc = (%3d, %3d)",
                      m_pntMouseLoc.x,
                      m_pntMouseLoc.y);
   pDC->TextOut(0, 0, szBuffer);
}

//////////////////////////////////////////////////////////
// CProg3_1aView message handlers

void CProg3_1aView::OnMouseMove(UINT nFlags,
                                CPoint point)
{
   // Save off the location of the mouse
   m_pntMouseLoc = point;

   // Now repaint the window
   Invalidate();
}
```

As always, the *ON_WM_MOUSEMOVE( )* macro adds the *OnMouseMove( )* function to the message map as the recipient of the *WM_MOUSEMOVE* message.

The constructor for *CProg3_1aView* initializes the data members I've added to the class to something reasonable. (Otherwise, they contain garbage.) In this case, you have only one new data member, *m_pntMouseLoc*, which is initialized as follows:

```
   m_pntMouseLoc = CPoint(0, 0);
```

This statement creates a temporary object of class *CPoint* by using the *CPoint::CPoint(int, int)* constructor. It then uses the assignment operator to copy that object into the *m_pntMouseLoc* member. The point (0,0), which is in the upper-left corner of the client area, is a reasonable value for *m_pntMouseLoc*.

How did I as a programmer know that a *CPoint(int, int)* constructor is in the MFC Library? I didn't know until I looked up *CPoint::CPoint* in the help system. There I found a list of the available constructors.

In Prog2_1 and Prog2_2, I used the constructor to initialize the data members to 0. I knew that this step wasn't necessary, but I was just being a good citizen. A *WM_CREATE* message was sent, which caused the program to calculate the real values before the *OnDraw( )* function tried to use them anyway. That isn't the case here. A *WM_MOUSEMOVE* message isn't sent until the mouse is moved around somewhere in the program's client area, which is likely to be long after the first output from *OnDraw( )*. ■

It isn't necessary to initialize Visual Basic variables. Visual Basic initializes them for you when the object is created — C++ does not. Analogous to the fundamental law of navigation ("Everybody's gotta be somewhere") is the law that all variables have a value. If you don't assign the object a value, you should consider the object's value to be either random or the worst possible value, whichever is worse. ◼

The actual location of the mouse is stored in *m_pntMouseLoc* in the *OnMouseMove( )* function at the bottom of the module. After the location has been stored, the call to *CWnd::Invalidate( )* causes the window to be repainted with the new value.

Because *CProg3_1aView* inherits from *CView*, which inherits from *CWnd*, any member of *CWnd* is also a member of *CProg3_1aView* — remember that a subclass inherits all the members of its base class. *CWnd::Invalidate( )* is therefore also a member of *CView* and *CProg3_1aView*. For this reason, *CProg3_1aView:: OnMouseMove( )* can call *CWnd::Invalidate( )* and not refer to the class explicitly. The window object to be invalidated is the current view. ◼

The output is performed in the *OnDraw( )* member function. The call to *wsprintf( )* generates the ASCII string in the local variable *szBuffer*, which is then displayed by using the *CDC::TextOut( )* function, as was done earlier.

The output from this program is shown in Figure 10-3.

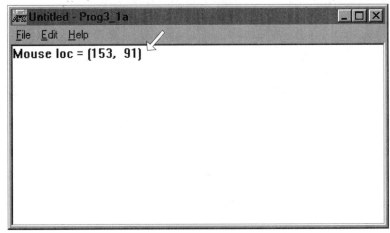

Figure 10-3: The output of Prog3_1a shows the location of the mouse (in pixels measured from the upper-left corner).

Drawing with the Mouse (No Other Pets Allowed)

If you can track the mouse, it should be relatively easy to build a simple drawing tool. As the mouse moves along, rather than print the location of the mouse in text form, you can simply set the pixel at that address to black.

There's a slight problem, of course. (Isn't there always?) You probably don't want the program to draw if the user isn't holding down one of the mouse buttons. How can you tell whether one of the buttons is pressed? You can certainly grab the button-down and button-up messages, but it turns out that this isn't necessary. MFC passes the button status in the *nFlags* argument passed to the *OnMouseMove( )* function. If the *MK_LBUTTON* bit is set, the left button is pressed; if the *MK_RBUTTON* bit is set, the right button is pressed (these constants are defined in windows.h).

Bits exist for other conditions too. Because each condition is represented by a different single bit, multiple conditions can be set simultaneously.

The following Prog3_1b is a first attempt at this type of drawing program:

```
// Prog3vw.h : interface of the CProg3_1bView class
//
/////////////////////////////////////////////////////////////

class CProg3_1bView : public CView
{
protected:
    // the current location of the mouse
    CPoint m_pntMouseLoc;
    UINT   m_nMouseFlags;

    // ...the remainder of the file unchanged
    // Prog3_1a...
```

Notice the addition of *m_nMouseFlags*, which is used to hold the *nFlags* passed to the *OnMouseMove( )* function.

The Prog3vw.cpp source file is also similar:

```
// Prog3vw.cpp : implementation of CProg3_1bView class
//

#include "stdafx.h"
#include "Prog3_1b.h"
```

```
#include "Prog3doc.h"
#include "Prog3vw.h"

#ifdef _DEBUG
#undef THIS_FILE
static char BASED_CODE THIS_FILE[] = __FILE__;
#endif

/////////////////////////////////////////////////////////
// CProg3_1bView

IMPLEMENT_DYNCREATE(CProg3_1bView, CView)

BEGIN_MESSAGE_MAP(CProg3_1bView, CView)
    //{{AFX_MSG_MAP(CProg3_1bView)
    ON_WM_MOUSEMOVE()
    //}}AFX_MSG_MAP
END_MESSAGE_MAP()

/////////////////////////////////////////////////////////
// CProg3_1bView construction/destruction

CProg3_1bView::CProg3_1bView()
{
    // initialize the current mouse location
    // and flags to null
    m_pntMouseLoc = CPoint(0, 0);
    m_nMouseFlags = 0;
}

CProg3_1bView::~CProg3_1bView()
{
}

/////////////////////////////////////////////////////////
// CProg3_1bView drawing

void CProg3_1bView::OnDraw(CDC* pDC)
{
    // If the left button is down, select black...
    COLORREF nColor = RGB(0, 0, 0);
    if (m_nMouseFlags & MK_RBUTTON)
    {
        // ...if the right button is down, red
        nColor = RGB(0xFF, 0, 0);
    }
```

```
        // Now put a dot there if either left or
        // right button is down
        if (m_nMouseFlags & (MK_LBUTTON | MK_RBUTTON))
        {
            pDC->SetPixelV(m_pntMouseLoc, nColor);
        }
    }


    /////////////////////////////////////////////////////////////
    // CProg3_1bView message handlers

    void CProg3_1bView::OnMouseMove(UINT nFlags,
                                    CPoint point)
    {
        // Save the location of the mouse
        m_pntMouseLoc = point;
        m_nMouseFlags = nFlags;

        // If either the left or right button is down,
        // repaint the window
        if (m_nMouseFlags & (MK_LBUTTON | MK_RBUTTON))
        {
            Invalidate(FALSE);
        }
    }
```

The *OnMouseMove( )* function records the current mouse position, as it did earlier, but now it also records the condition of the mouse flags. If either of the mouse buttons is pressed, it then calls *Invalidate( )* to force the *OnDraw( )* function to be invoked.

The phrase "if either of the mouse buttons is pressed" is written in C++ as

```
    if (m_nMouseFlags & (MK_LBUTTON | MK_RBUTTON))
```

MK_LBUTTON | MK_RBUTTON builds a word with just the two specified bits set. This word is then bitwise ANDed with *m_nMouseFlags*. If either of these two bits is set in *m_nMouseFlags*, the result of this ANDing is nonzero (*TRUE*). If neither is set, the result is zero (*FALSE*). ■

In the past you called *Invalidate( )* with the default argument of *TRUE*, which erases the screen before redrawing it. This argument is not acceptable now because you want to retain whatever was drawn earlier and just add to it. This is the significance of the *Invalidate(FALSE)*.

OnDraw( ) uses the *CDC::SetPixelV( )* function to set the pixel at the current mouse location to the specified color. The program uses black if the left mouse button is pressed and red if the right button is pressed.

Colors are constructed by using the macro *RGB(r, g, b)* to mix the primary colors red, green, and blue in varying degrees. Each of the arguments to *RGB( )* is a 1-byte value that represents the relative strength of that color. Therefore, *RGB(0xff, 0xff, 0xff)* is all three colors full on or bright white; *RGB(0, 0, 0)* is black (all colors off); and *RGB(0xff, 0, 0)* is bright red (all-ahead red; all other colors off). *RGB(0, 0xff, 0)* is bright green, and *RGB(0, 0, 0xff)* is bright blue. Other colors are created by using intermediate values for *r, g,* and *b* between 0 and 0xff. (Remember that the hex value 0xff is the largest unsigned byte value. In decimal, this value would be 255.)

The Visual Basic equivalent of *SetPixelV( )* is the *PSet* method. ▪

The result of executing this program on my 66MHz 80486 is unsatisfactory, as shown in Figure 10-4.

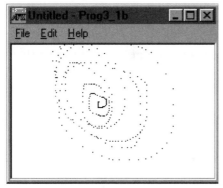

Figure 10-4: The funky result of executing Prog3_1b. Ouch!

In this case, I began drawing in the middle of the screen and spiraled outward, slowly at first, but I gathered speed as the radius increased. As long as I move the mouse pointer extremely slowly, the pixels combine to draw something that looks vaguely like the spiral I expect. As soon as the mouse picks up speed, however, large gaps begin to appear between pixels — the faster the mouse scurries across the screen, the larger the gaps. (What I ended up with looks more like mouse droppings than mouse drawings.) The program apparently cannot keep up with the mouse.

There are two reasons the mouse cannot keep up. First, if you move the mouse from point A to point B on the screen, Windows doesn't guarantee that your program will receive an *OnMouseMove( )* message for every pixel location in between. Even if it did, another effect would conspire to keep the preceding program from working as expected.

Repainting a window is assumed to be a painful process in terms of computer time. You've already seen how Windows maintains an invalid region to limit the size of the area in the window that has to be repainted. Windows also takes precautions to make sure that a window doesn't get repainted more often than necessary. For example, the *WM_PAINT* message has one of the lowest priorities in the system. If a *WM_PAINT* message is queued up to be processed and some other event occurs (such as a *MOUSEMOVE* event), the other message is placed in front of the *WM_PAINT* message in the queue.

If that event causes a new *WM_PAINT* message to be generated, the event replaces the old *WM_PAINT* message — the queue never has more than one *WM_PAINT* message in it at a time.

Why does this process make the screen get displayed faster? Consider what happens when a user changes the display font from within that popular Windows word-processing program MissingWord.

Changing the font causes MissingWord to generate a *WM_PAINT* message to repaint the display window in the new font. It also causes a *WM_FONTCHANGE* message to be sent to recalculate the word spacing within the paragraph. Because the new font is slightly larger than the old one, MissingWord must reposition the text as well. This repositioning of text also generates a second *WM_PAINT* message to display the text in its new location in the window.

The point is that it makes little sense to repaint the screen in the new font before the text has been repositioned only to be forced to repaint the window again to update the text locations.

To avoid repainting, Windows processes the font-change message before the *WM_PAINT* request, even if the *WM_PAINT* request was generated first. In addition, the second *WM_PAINT* request to move the text is combined with the first *WM_PAINT* message to repaint the window (with the new font) one time. ■

Drawing with the Mouse: A Second Attempt

So what can you do to Prog3_1b to make it a reasonable drawing program? The problem was that the mouse locations sent to the program weren't dense — there were holes between them.

Rather than set just a single pixel at the current mouse location, how about drawing a line from the preceding mouse location to the current mouse location, in a software version of connect-the-dots? This process sets all the intermediate pixels, making the drawn line appear solid no matter how far apart the mouse locations are that you get in the mouse-move messages. The next version, Prog3_1c, does exactly that.

Before you look at Prog3_1c, you have to understand how the Windows line-drawing tools work. The Windows application (WinApp) begins by building an imaginary pen of the proper color and type. The WinApp then places this pen in the window with the *MoveTo( )* function. The function *LineTo( )* draws a line from the pen's current position to the position specified in the call.

VBers will probably recognize that *MoveTo(x)* followed by *LineTo(y)* is equivalent to *Line x-y* in Visual Basic. ■

The Prog3vw.h *include* file looks the same as it did earlier except for the addition of the *m_nDownFlag*, which is set when one of the mouse buttons is pressed, and *m_pntPrevLoc*, which contains the previous mouse location (the handlers for the *WM_LBUTTONDOWN* and *WM_RBUTTONDOWN* messages were added with the ClassWizard):

```
// Prog3vw.h : interface of the CProg3_1cView class
//
/////////////////////////////////////////////////////////

class CProg3_1cView : public CView
{
protected:
    // the current location of the mouse
    CPoint m_pntMouseLoc;

    // the previous location of the mouse
    CPoint m_pntPrevLoc;

    // the mouse flags
    UINT   m_nMouseFlags;
    UINT   m_bButtonDown;   // if this is set, then a
                            // mouse button was just pushed

    // ...remainder of include file same as before...
```

The Prog3vw.cpp for Prog3_1c is substantially changed, however:

```
// Prog3vw.cpp : implementation of CProg3_1cView class
//
```

```
#include "stdafx.h"
#include "Prog3_1c.h"

#include "Prog3doc.h"
#include "Prog3vw.h"

/////////////////////////////////////////////////////////
// CProg3_1cView

IMPLEMENT_DYNCREATE(CProg3_1cView, CView)

BEGIN_MESSAGE_MAP(CProg3_1cView, CView)
    //{{AFX_MSG_MAP(CProg3_1cView)
    ON_WM_LBUTTONDOWN()
    ON_WM_RBUTTONDOWN()
    ON_WM_MOUSEMOVE()
    //}}AFX_MSG_MAP
END_MESSAGE_MAP()

/////////////////////////////////////////////////////////
// CProg3_1cView construction/destruction

CProg3_1cView::CProg3_1cView()
{
    // initialize the current mouse location to null
    m_pntMouseLoc = m_pntPrevLoc = CPoint(0, 0);
    m_nMouseFlags = 0;
    m_bButtonDown = FALSE;
}

CProg3_1cView::~CProg3_1cView()
{
}

/////////////////////////////////////////////////////////
// CProg3_1cView drawing

void CProg3_1cView::OnDraw(CDC* pDC)
{
    // If the no button is down, select black...
    COLORREF nColor = RGB(0, 0, 0);
    if (m_nMouseFlags & MK_RBUTTON)
    {
        // ...if the right button is down, red
        nColor = RGB(0xff, 0, 0);
    }

    // Now put a dot there if either left or
```

```
        // right button is down
        if (m_nMouseFlags & (MK_LBUTTON | MK_RBUTTON))
        {
            pDC->SetPixelV(m_pntMouseLoc, nColor);

            // If this is not a button press...
            if (!m_bButtonDown)
            {
                // ...draw a line from the previous location
                // to the new mouse location — create a pen
                // of the proper color
                CPen penStroke(PS_SOLID, 1, nColor);

                // Select it into the device context
                CPen *ppenPrevious =
                            pDC->SelectObject(&penStroke);

                // Now draw with it
                pDC->MoveTo(m_pntPrevLoc);
                pDC->LineTo(m_pntMouseLoc);

                // Make the current location the
                // previous location next time you
                // get a mouse-move message
                m_pntPrevLoc = m_pntMouseLoc;

                // Put the old pen back
                pDC->SelectObject(ppenPrevious);
            }
        }
}

/////////////////////////////////////////////////////////
// CProg3_1cView message handlers

void CProg3_1cView::OnLButtonDown(UINT nFlags,
                                  CPoint point)
{
    // Save the mouse location and flags
    m_pntPrevLoc = m_pntMouseLoc = point;
    m_nMouseFlags = nFlags;

    // Note that this is a button press
    m_bButtonDown = TRUE;

    // Cause the pixel to be drawn
    Invalidate(FALSE);
```

```
    }

    void CProg3_1cView::OnRButtonDown(UINT nFlags,
                                          CPoint point)
    {
        // Save the mouse location and flags
        m_pntPrevLoc = m_pntMouseLoc = point;
        m_nMouseFlags = nFlags;

        // Note that this is a button press
        m_bButtonDown = TRUE;

        // Cause the pixel to be drawn
        Invalidate(FALSE);
    }

    void CProg3_1cView::OnMouseMove(UINT nFlags, CPoint point)
    {
        // Save the mouse location and flags
        m_pntMouseLoc = point;
        m_nMouseFlags = nFlags;

        // Note that this is NOT a button press
        m_bButtonDown = FALSE;

        // Cause the pixel to be drawn
        Invalidate(FALSE);
    }
```

Skipping ahead, you can see that *OnLButtonDown( )* and *OnRButtonDown( )* do nothing more than save the current mouse position in both *m_pntPrevLoc* and *m_pntMouseLoc*. Before causing *OnDraw( )* to be called, they set the *m_bButton-Down* flag to *TRUE*. If the *m_bButtonDown* flag is *TRUE*, *OnDraw( )* sets the current pixel position, but it doesn't attempt to draw a line — the mouse hasn't moved anywhere yet.

The *OnMouseMove( )* function saves the same mouse location as it did earlier, but it sets the *m_bButtonDown* flag to *FALSE*, indicating that this is not a button-press. When the *m_bButtonDown* flag is *FALSE*, *OnDraw( )* draws a line from the preceding location to the current location.

To draw a line segment, *OnDraw( )* first must create one of those imaginary pens described by the class *CPen*. The first argument to the constructor is the type of pen. Unlike real pens, imaginary pens can be dashed or dotted as well as solid. The next argument is the width in physical units. A 1-pixel pen is the computer version of a Mont Blanc fine. The final argument is the color.

Next, the program must "pick up" the pen, by selecting the pen into the device context by using the *SelectObject( )* function. The return from this function is the preceding pen, which you have to save in order to put it back after you finish drawing.

Finally, you move the pen to the preceding location, *m_pntPrevLoc*, and then draw to the present location, *m_pntMouseLoc*. Saving the current location into the preceding location makes it the preceding location the next time.

The result of executing this program is much more satisfactory, as shown in Figure 10-5.

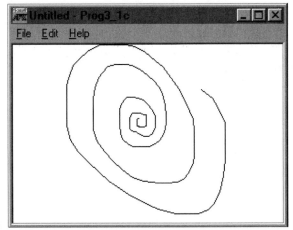

Figure 10-5:
This spiral is much more satisfactory (except for the author's awful penmanship).

As the mouse moves faster, notice that the screen display gets a minor case of the "jaggies"; the human eye doesn't object much, however, as long as there are no noticeable breaks.

Conclusion

Before you get excited and pat yourself on the back, I should point out that this program is still not what anyone would consider a serious drawing application. To see the problem, resize the window. Poof! The Etch-A-Sketch is flipped over, and the entire display is gone.

Gee, that's disappointing. What you really want is for the drawing to stay visible even if the window is resized, minimized — whatever — until the user decides to clear it. In other words, "It ain't cleared until I say it's cleared." The next chapter explains ways you can make the information stick around.

Chapter 11

A Rodent Recorder

● ●

In This Chapter

▶ Mouse droppings: Recording mouse activity

▶ Minimizing the number of mouse segments to repaint

● ●

*T*he results of improving the mouse-drawing program in Chapter 10 were close, but no cigar. The problem with Prog3_1 as it stands is that after you spend hours creating the perfect drawing, you lose the drawing as soon as the window is resized.

If you look carefully, you can see the problem: The drawing information isn't stored anywhere except on the screen. Thus, when the window is erased as part of the resize operation, the painstakingly generated information is gone (in the case of my drawings, it was more painful than painstaking).

To solve this problem, you need to record the window information in a form apart from the window itself. Then, when the window is erased, either accidentally or maliciously, the program can spring into action and replace any lost or stolen information by using the *OnDraw( )* function — (it's sort of the Windows version of the FDIC).

Saving the Screen: Prog3_2

Okay, so you want to "record the window information." What does that mean? Your initial reaction might be to save the contents of the window in a separate data structure that looks exactly like the window. (This type of structure is called a *bitmap,* (or *BMP,* for short) because every bit in the structure maps to a pixel on the screen.) The bitmap represents a sort of virtual window — a window that doesn't get overwritten or hidden.

This type of program would work something like this. Every time the program received a *WM_MOUSEMOVE* message, it would draw on the bitmap in

the same way the *OnDraw( )* function works. It then would generate a
WM_PAINT message. The *OnDraw( )* function would transfer the affected portions from the virtual, bitmap window to the displayed, physical window. If
the physical window needs updating, the relevant portions of the bitmap
stand ready to be transferred.

This approach has a few problems, however. First, you must choose a size in
memory for this virtual bitmap window. What do you do when the window
exceeds that size? It isn't easy to increase the size of the bitmap window.

Microsoft Paint solves this problem by making the bitmap window size equal
to the size of the entire screen. (The reasoning is that the current window
can never be greater than the size of the screen).

Second (and much worse), it turns out that a bitmap screen can be a large
data structure. A full-screen window on a 256-color, 800×600 monitor, which
is modest by today's standards, consumes almost 500K of memory. More typical screens consume as much as 2MB. This amount of memory is very large
for a silly drawing program to consume.

Third, manipulating this much memory takes time. Any program built on the
presumption of manipulating and transferring 2MB of memory at a time will
not be very fast.

A better approach might be to store the data that is necessary to create the
window (in this case, the mouse input) rather than a virtual bitmapped pho-
tograph of the window in memory.

This approach offers a couple of advantages. First, there's much less data to
store. You can store a large number of mouse movements in 500 kilobytes.
(You learn about the memory usage of this approach later in this chapter.)
Second, re-creating the window from the stored input data is much easier to
do. Prog3_1 already had the capability to convert *WM_MOUSEMOVE* events
into Etch-a-Sketch marks in the window. All you have to do to be able to re-
create the window is to save the mouse-reported locations in a buffer, as
shown in Figure 11-1. When the window is repainted, the program reads from

Figure 11-1:
Mouse
events get
stored in a
buffer with
which the
window can
be
repainted as
necessary.

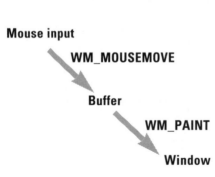

Mouse input

WM_MOUSEMOVE

Buffer

WM_PAINT

Window

the buffer to re-create the window as though the user were rapidly redrawing everything from scratch.

Saving mouse input

To save the mouse activity, you have to store the *CPoints* that get reported as the mouse moves around the screen. This process is fundamentally straight-forward, but the details are somewhat cumbersome. Before you take on the job of generating a recording version of the Prog3_1 drawing program, let's solve a slightly simpler problem.

Rather than record all the mouse locations that are reported as the user navigates the pointer around the screen, let's just record the screen locations that are reported when the left mouse button is pressed. You can generate an interesting display like the one shown in Figure 11-2 by drawing line segments between all the combinations of mouse positions that are reported (at least I thought that it was interesting).

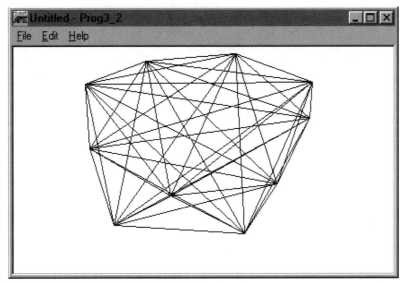

Figure 11-2:
The output of Prog3_2's version of connect-the-dots.

Here are some of the basics of this new Prog3_2 program. Prog3_2 maintains a list of mouse locations. A new mouse location is added to the list every time the left button is pressed. Every time a new member is added, line segments are drawn between each combination of locations. The right mouse button is used to clear the list.

Use the AppWizard to create the standard basic application framework for Prog3_2. Use the same options for this program as you used for Prog3_1 (that is, with all fancy features turned off). Leave the default names for all the classes. Use the ClassWizard to add to CProg3_2View a message handler for the *WM_LBUTTONDOWN* and *WM_RBUTTONDOWN* messages.

Viewing the View include file

The work for Prog3_2 is performed in the View class. Edit the *include* file Prog3vw.h by adding the grayed sections shown here:

```
// Prog3vw.h : interface of the CProg3_2View class
//
/////////////////////////////////////////////////////////////

class CProg3_2View : public CView
{
protected:
    // An array of CPoints where left button
    // was pressed. Program connects these
    // with line segments to make pictures.
    CPtrArray  m_MousePositions;

    // The following function clears the
    // m_MousePositions array
    void ClearList();

protected: // create from serialization only
    CProg3_2View();
    DECLARE_DYNCREATE(CProg3_2View)

// Attributes
public:
    CProg3_2Doc* GetDocument();

// Operations
public:

// Overrides
    // ClassWizard generated virtual function overrides
    //{{AFX_VIRTUAL(CProg3_2View)
    public:
    virtual void OnDraw(CDC* pDC);
```

```
        protected:
        //}}AFX_VIRTUAL

// Implementation
public:
        virtual ~CProg3_2View();

// Generated message map functions
protected:
        //{{AFX_MSG(CProg3_2View)
        afx_msg void OnLButtonDown(UINT nFlags, CPoint point);
        afx_msg void OnRButtonDown(UINT nFlags, CPoint point);
        //}}AFX_MSG
        DECLARE_MESSAGE_MAP()
};
```

The message map includes the *OnLButtonDown* and *OnRButtonDown* member functions that are added by the ClassWizard to handle the *WM_LBUTTON-DOWN* and *WM_RBUTTONDOWN* messages, respectively.

The data member *m_MousePositions* at the beginning of the class has been added to store the list of reported mouse positions. It is of type *CPtrArray* (see the following section).

C...arrays; C...arrays run; run, arrays, run!

In C++ (as in most other compiled languages), an array is an efficient structure for handling large numbers of uniform objects. The only problem is that arrays have a fixed length. When the program starts, the programmer must know how many entries will be in the array and then allocate space for the entire array at that time. Unfortunately, it's not always possible to know how many entries are needed.

In older programming languages, the only solution to this problem was to allocate memory for the absolute maximum number of objects all at one time. The trouble with this approach was that the memory was consumed even if the program happened to be storing only a few objects. And what if the program needed more than the preallocated number? The program had no other choice than to terminate, even though some memory may have remained. It's better to allocate memory dynamically, which enables the array to grow or shrink as necessary.

This capability is similar to the one provided by the *ReDim Preserve* declaration, which is used to redeclare the size of a previously declared and allocated array. ■

The *C...Array* classes are a set of MFC classes that provide this capability to grow and shrink as necessary. Each class is designed to store a different type of object. For example, *CByteArray* provides for a dynamic array of bytes.

Unfortunately, there is no *CCPointArray* class to handle arrays of *CPoints*.

A *CArray* template class is available, of course, that would enable a C++ expert to easily create a *CCPointArray* class. But this book discusses primarily Windows programming and not C++, I don't want to get too deep into the C++ tricks of the trade. ■

Fortunately, you don't need a *CCPointArray* class — you can just use the *CPtrArray* class, which creates a dynamic array of pointers that you can let point to *CPoint* objects.

The constructor for *CPtrArray* creates an empty array. An element is added to the list by using the *CPtrArray::Add(void*)* member function. The argument to *Add( )* is of type *void** (or "pointer to nothing") because *Add( )* has no idea which type of pointer it's about to receive.

The *CPtrArray* class overloads the index operator, *operator[ ]*, so that it can be used to access elements from the *CPtrArray* object exactly as though it were a real array.

Whenever you get the urge to see how the MFC classes (such as *CPtrArray*) work, you have two choices: You can stay firmly planted on your couch and wait until the urge passes, or you can single-step into the *CPtrArray* call. The source code for the MFC Library is on the Visual C++ CD-ROM, in the directory \msvc20\mfc\src. ■

The following nonsensical code segment creates an empty pointer array, adds ten *null* pointers to the list, and then stores the address of *localVar* in the fifth element of the array:

```
CPtrArray ptrArray;              // create an empty array

int i;
for (i = 0; i < 10; i++)
{
    ptrArray.Add((void*)0);      // add a NULL pointer
```

```
    }

    int nLocalVar;
    ptrArray[5] = (void*)&nLocalVar;    // store in fifth element
```

The following section explains how CProg3_2View uses *CPtrArray* to save mouse locations.

Finding the source of the source code

Edit Prog3vw.cpp by adding the following grayed sections:

```
// Prog3vw.cpp : implementation of the CProg3_2View class
//

#include "stdafx.h"
#include "Prog3_2.h"

#include "Prog3doc.h"
#include "Prog3vw.h"

/////////////////////////////////////////////////////////
// CProg3_2View

IMPLEMENT_DYNCREATE(CProg3_2View, CView)

BEGIN_MESSAGE_MAP(CProg3_2View, CView)
    //{{AFX_MSG_MAP(CProg3_2View)
    ON_WM_LBUTTONDOWN()
    ON_WM_RBUTTONDOWN()
    //}}AFX_MSG_MAP
END_MESSAGE_MAP()

/////////////////////////////////////////////////////////
// CProg3_2View construction/destruction

CProg3_2View::CProg3_2View()
{
    // Set the size of the m_MousePositions array
    // so that it will grow by 100 CPoints
    // every time it needs to
    m_MousePositions.SetSize(0, 100);
}

CProg3_2View::~CProg3_2View()
{
```

```
        ClearList();
}


//////////////////////////////////////////////////////
// CProg3_2View drawing

void CProg3_2View::OnDraw(CDC* pDC)
{
    // Loop through the mouse positions stored
    // in 'm_MousePositions'
    int i, j;
    int nPositions = m_MousePositions.GetSize();
    CPoint *pPointFrom;
    CPoint *pPointTo;
    for (i = 0; i < nPositions; i++)
    {
        // Put a dot at each point
        pPointFrom = (CPoint*)m_MousePositions[i];
        pDC->SetPixelV(*pPointFrom, RGB(0, 0, 0));

        // Now draw a line from this point
        // to every subsequent mouse position
        for (j = i + 1; j < nPositions; j++)
        {
            pPointTo = (CPoint*)m_MousePositions[j];

            // Draw a line from pPointFrom to pPointTo
            pDC->MoveTo(*pPointFrom);
            pDC->LineTo(*pPointTo);
        }
    }
}


//////////////////////////////////////////////////////
// CProg3_2View message handlers

void CProg3_2View::OnLButtonDown(UINT nFlags,
                                 CPoint point)
{
    // Add the current mouse position to the list
    // stored in m_MousePositions

    // Get the memory to hold the mouse location
    // off the heap.
    CPoint *pNewPoint = new CPoint(point);

    // Now add it to the list
```

```
        m_MousePositions.Add((void*)pNewPoint);

        // Force a repaint to see the effect
        Invalidate();
}

void CProg3_2View::OnRButtonDown(UINT nFlags,
                                  CPoint point)
{
        // On right-button clicks, clear the entire mouse
        // point list
        ClearList();

        // Force a repaint with the empty list
        Invalidate();
}

//ClearList — clear out the m_MousePositions list,
//                  returning all memory to the heap
void CProg3_2View::ClearList()
{
        // First delete each CPoint in the list
        int i;
        CPoint *pPoint;
        for (i = 0; i < m_MousePositions.GetSize(); i++)
        {
             pPoint = (CPoint*)m_MousePositions[i];
             delete pPoint;
        }

        // Now clear the list itself of all entries
        m_MousePositions.RemoveAll();
}
```

Understanding this program is crucial to understanding the information presented in the remainder of Part III.

Recording mouse events

Mouse events are recorded in the *OnLButtonDown( )* member function.

As always, mouse locations are reported to *OnLButtonDown( )* in the form of a *CPoint* object argument. The *m_MousePositions* array is the member that is created to store the mouse locations. You might be tempted to try something like the following:

```
m_MousePositions.Add((void*)&point); // Won't work!!
```

The problem is that an argument to a function is considered to be local to that function. As soon as control exits from *OnLButtonDown( )*, the object *point* ceases to exist. As soon as that happens, the address added to *m_Mouse-Positions* no longer points to a valid *CPoint* object.

 Storing the address of a local object and then using it after the object has been destructed is a common and difficult pointer error. Because a statement like the preceding one is syntactically correct, the C++ compiler gives you no help in finding this type of problem either. You must constantly guard against this type of error. ■

What you need is a way to allocate a piece of memory that doesn't go away when the function exits. The best place to get this type of memory is from the *free memory pool,* otherwise known affectionately to C and C++ programmers worldwide as the heap.

The *heap* consists of all the memory that's not otherwise in use. When a program wants some of this memory, it just asks for it. In C++, one way to get some heap memory is through the C++ *new* operator:

```
CPoint *pHeapPoint;
pHeapPoint = new CPoint(0, 0);  // allocate a CPoint
// ...program continues...
delete pHeapPoint;              // now return it
```

The reserved word *new* allocates enough memory to store a *CPoint* object (in this case). It then uses the *CPoint* constructor to initialize that memory and returns the address, where it is stored in the pointer *pHeapPoint*. If no more heap memory is available, it returns a *NULL*.

The reserved word *delete* calls the destructor to destroy the object and then returns the memory to the heap.

 The program must return any memory allocated from the heap after it is no longer needed; this process is not done automatically.

(When a program terminates, any memory it has allocated from the heap is returned automatically; relying on this return is considered bad form, however, and Visual C++ complains about such childish behavior.) ■

The following statement is taken from the *OnLButtonDown( )* function:

```
CPoint *pNewPoint = new CPoint(point);
```

This statement allocates a new *CPoint* object with the same location information as is already contained in *point* off the heap (it sort of resembles a *CPoint* photocopy machine).

The address of this new object is added to the *m_MousePositions* list. Calling *Invalidate( )* forces the screen to be repainted with the new information.

Repainting

Now turn your attention to the *OnDraw( )* function. The call to *GetSize( )* returns the number of members in the *m_MousePositions* list. The outer loop gets each *CPoint* object and then sets the pixel at that window location.

Notice that the (*CPoint**) cast is necessary because *m_MousePositions[i]* returns a pointer of type *void**.

The inner *for* loop draws a line from the current mouse location to each subsequent location in the list. Suppose that four mouse locations are in the list (that is, *GetSize( )* returns a 4). The first pass through the outer loop draws a line from location 0 to locations 1, 2, and 3; the next pass, from location 1 to 2 and 3; and the final pass, from 2 to 3.

Clearing the screen

The screen is cleared in function *ClearList( )* by removing all elements from the list and then repainting the screen with an empty list.

ClearList( ) first loops through the list of mouse locations stored in *m_Mouse-Positions* and deletes each one by using the *delete* operator. This process is necessary because each *CPoint* object was allocated off the heap by using the *new* operator. After all the objects pointed to by the pointers in *m_MousePositions* have been returned, the array is emptied by calling *RemoveAll( )*.

Looking at other stuff

The only tasks that remain in order to make this program complete are performed by the constructor and destructor. The destructor calls *ClearList( )* to clear the list of any mouse locations. This call handles the (most likely) case in which a user terminates the program without first clearing the list with the right mouse button.

The constructor contains a single call, *SetSize(0, 100)*, which is best explained by using an analogy (so what else is new?).

When you're cooking and you run out of eggs, it's doubtful that you would ever send your son to the store to buy just one egg. If he's anything like my son, he would just look at you as though he had suddenly lost the ability to understand the English language. In addition, if he goes to the trouble of driving down to the store, it's better to have him buy one or two dozen eggs at a time. You'll almost surely use them all eventually (to the certain detriment of your cardiovascular system).

The same concept applies to *CPtrArray*. As noted, the attraction of *CPtrArray* was that it could grow as necessary to fit the application's requirements. *CPtrArray* grows by allocating memory off the heap (just like you did). Normally, every time it needs to grow, *CPtrArray* allocates enough memory for one more element. This process is about as efficient as buying only one egg. The call to *SetSize( )* sets the initial size to 0 (empty) and tells *CPtrArray* to allocate room for 100 new elements every time it needs more memory. This method reduces by 100 the number of times the *CPtrArray* object must undergo the relatively painful process of shedding its skin and molting into a larger array.

Voilà!

Let's quickly review Prog3_3. Try executing the program and clicking the mouse at different positions in the drawing window. The program not only generates some really neat-looking screens, but it's also free of the problems of Prog3_1: With Prog3_2, you can hide the window and then unhide it, and your carefully (or even haphazardly) generated drawing is still displayed.

Fixing the Draw Program: Prog3_1d

Let's apply this newfound knowledge to fix the drawing program, Prog3_1. All you have to do is save the mouse locations that result from the *WM_MOUSE-MOVE* and *WM_LBUTTONDOWN* messages. Because the window no longer unexpectedly erases itself, you need a way to erase the window; use the *WM_RBUTTONDOWN* message for that function, just as you did in Prog3_2. You won't be able to draw in color anymore, but you've already seen how that process works, anyway.

The changes to the View *include* file for Prog3_1d appear as follows (if you're following my suggestion, remember that your class is called *CProg3_1View*, without the minor version letter):

```
// Prog3vw.h : interface of the CProg3_1dView class
//
```

```
/////////////////////////////////////////////////////

class CProg3_1dView : public CView
{
protected:
    // An array of CPoints containing the
    // location of the mouse recorded as the
    // mouse moved with the button down
    CPtrArray  m_MousePositions;

    // The same thing containing a TRUE if
    // the corresponding location represents
    // a mouse button and a FALSE if a
    // mouse-move location
    CWordArray m_MouseButtons;

    // The following functions manipulate
    // the lists
    void ClearList();
    void AddList(CPoint&, UINT nButtonFlag);
```

```
// ...from here on, the same as before...
```

As in Prog3_2, the member *m_MousePositions* is used to store the location of the mouse. In addition to this list, however, is a *CWordArray*, *m_MouseButtons*. This *CWordArray* is used to record the button-status information.

The code to implement this View class appears as follows:

```
// Prog3vw.cpp : implementation of the CProg3_1dView
//              class

#include "stdafx.h"
#include "Prog3_1d.h"

#include "Prog3doc.h"
#include "Prog3vw.h"

/////////////////////////////////////////////////////
// CProg3_1dView

IMPLEMENT_DYNCREATE(CProg3_1dView, CView)

BEGIN_MESSAGE_MAP(CProg3_1dView, CView)
    //{{AFX_MSG_MAP(CProg3_1dView)
    ON_WM_MOUSEMOVE()
    ON_WM_RBUTTONDOWN()
```

```
        ON_WM_LBUTTONDOWN()
        //}}AFX_MSG_MAP
END_MESSAGE_MAP()


/////////////////////////////////////////////////////
// CProg3_1dView construction/destruction

CProg3_1dView::CProg3_1dView()
{
    // Set the size of the m_MousePositions and
    // m_MouseButtons arrays so that they are
    // empty but will allocate enough room
    // for 100 entries every time they need
    // to (this number is arbitrary)
    m_MousePositions.SetSize(0, 100);
    m_MouseButtons.SetSize(0, 100);
}


CProg3_1dView::~CProg3_1dView()
{
    ClearList();
}


/////////////////////////////////////////////////////
// CProg3_1dView drawing

void CProg3_1dView::OnDraw(CDC* pDC)
{
    // Loop through the mouse positions stored
    // off - if there aren't any, then there's
    // nothing to do
    CPoint *pPoint;
    UINT i;
    UINT nPositions = m_MousePositions.GetSize();
    for (i = 0; i < nPositions; i++)
    {
        // For each mouse location, if it's a
        // button click...
        pPoint = (CPoint*)m_MousePositions[i];
        if (m_MouseButtons[i])
        {
            // ...then just position the mouse and
            // set the pixel; otherwise,...
            pDC->MoveTo(*pPoint);
            pDC->SetPixelV(*pPoint, RGB(0, 0, 0));
        }
        else
```

```
        {
            // ...draw a line from the previous
            // mouse location to the current
            // location
            pDC->LineTo(*pPoint);
        }
    }
}


///////////////////////////////////////////////////////////
// CProg3_1dView message handlers

void CProg3_1dView::OnLButtonDown(UINT nFlags,
                                  CPoint point)
{
    // Add the current mouse position to the list
    // stored in m_MousePositions
    AddList(point, TRUE);

    // Force a repaint to see the effect
    Invalidate(FALSE);
}

void CProg3_1dView::OnMouseMove(UINT nFlags,
                                CPoint point)
{
    // If the left mouse button is not pressed,
    // don't do anything
    if (nFlags & MK_LBUTTON)
    {
        // Otherwise, handle like a left-button press
        // except set flag to FALSE
        AddList(point, FALSE);
        Invalidate(FALSE);
    }
}

void CProg3_1dView::OnRButtonDown(UINT nFlags,
                                  CPoint point)
{
    // On right-button clicks, clear the list
    ClearList();

    // Force a repaint with the empty list
    Invalidate(TRUE);
}
```

```
//ClearList — clear out the m_MousePositions list,
//              returning all memory to the heap
void CProg3_1dView::ClearList()
{
    // First delete each CPoint in the list
    int i;
    CPoint *pPoint;
    int n_Size = m_MousePositions.GetSize();
    for (i = 0; i < n_Size; i++)
    {
        pPoint = (CPoint*)m_MousePositions[i];
        delete pPoint;
    }

    // Now clear the lists themselves of all entries
    m_MousePositions.RemoveAll();
    m_MouseButtons.RemoveAll();
}

void CProg3_1dView::AddList(CPoint &point, UINT nButton)
{
    // Construct a CPoint object off the
    // heap with the mouse location in it
    CPoint *pNewPoint = new CPoint(point);

    // Now add it to the list
    m_MousePositions.Add((void*)pNewPoint);

    // Record whether this was a button event
    // or a mouse-move event
    m_MouseButtons.Add(nButton);
}
```

The *OnLButtonDown( )* and *OnRButtonDown( )* member functions work just like their Prog3_2 counterparts. *OnMouseMove( )* adds mouse locations to the list just like *OnLButtonDown( )* does — the only difference is the value of the button-state flag, *nButton*, passed to *AddList( )*. The remainder of the program also works the same, except for the *OnDraw( )* function.

OnDraw( ) starts in the same way, looping through each mouse location in the list; rather than connect each location with every other mouse location in the list, however, *OnDraw( )* does one of two things:

- ✔ If this location was a button press, it moves to the current location, *pDC->MoveTo( )*, and sets the pixel, *pDC->SetPixelV( )*.

- ✔ If this location was a mouse move, it draws a line from the preceding location to the current location, *pDC->LineTo( )*.

The output from this program appears the same as the output from its predecessor, Prog3_1c; when this window is hidden and then redisplayed, however (drum roll, please), the drawing reappears in its full glory.

Was It Worth It?

The beginning of this chapter states that less memory is used to save the mouse locations and re-create the screen than to save the window information. To check out this assertion, I set a breakpoint in the *ClearList( )* function to find the value returned from *GetSize( )*. I then started the program and scribbled for a long time, until the screen was almost black. When I cleared the screen, the value returned from *GetSize( )* was 1092, or roughly 1K. Each pointer within *CPtrArray* is 4 bytes. In addition, each *CPoint* object is 48 bytes. The total memory consumption was therefore 52K. That's a large amount, but it's still nothing compared to the more than 500K required in the approach in which you maintain a bitmapped virtual window, as described at the beginning of this chapter.

I could have saved even more if I hadn't used *CPoint* to store the mouse locations. Instead, I could have packed the *x* and *y* locations into a double word and used the *CDWordArray* class. This method would have reduced memory consumption to a Spartan amount of between 4 and 8 kilobytes. ■

Drawing to a Close

You're almost, but not quite, finished. If you draw with Prog3_1d for a long time, you might notice that, as the amount of displayed data increases, the program seems to fall a little behind the mouse pointer.

To see what I mean, start the program. Run the mouse pointer back and forth across the top of the window 50 to 100 times. Don't worry that the screen turns jet-black after the first 20 or 30 passes — the ink won't bleed through the screen and onto your shirt.

Move the mouse pointer to the bottom of the window where you can still see what's going on, and move the mouse at a steady, slow pace across the screen. A noticeable gap opens between the mouse and the line that follows along behind it. As soon as the mouse stops moving, the line catches up, and the gap is closed.

What's going on here?

The answer is back in the *OnDraw( )* routine. Notice that the loop redraws the screen, starting from index 0. That is, it starts with the first element every time. By the time you've been scribbling for a while, there can be numerous elements in the list.

If you think about it, the only time it's necessary to redraw the entire list is when the window is being unhidden. When you add new mouse strokes to the display, you have to draw only the new locations. The old markings are still there.

How can you do that? First, you have to add a member to store the index of the last painted mouse location. Every time you're asked to repaint the window to add mouse strokes, you know that all the mouse activity up to that index is still valid. You have to paint only the strokes that appear after the index. When you're finished, you can then update the index to indicate that these new locations have also been painted.

How, then, do you know when it's time to repaint the entire window, as is the case if the window has been hidden or obscured and is now being unhidden? A message called *WM_ERASEBKGND* is sent whenever the client area is erased. Updates caused by *WM_LBUTTONDOWN* and *WM_MOUSEMOVE* messages don't erase the background (passing a *FALSE* if the call to *Invalidate( )* suppresses the erase step). When this message is received, you know that the entire window must be repainted from scratch.

The *include* file for the View class of your new version, Prog3_1e, appears as follows:

```
// Prog3vw.h : interface of the CProg3_1eView class
//
/////////////////////////////////////////////////////////

class CProg3_1eView : public CView
{
protected:
    // An array of CPoints containing the
    // location of the mouse recorded as the
    // mouse moved with the button down
    UINT m_nPrevIndex;
    CPtrArray  m_MousePositions;
    CWordArray m_MouseButtons;
```

```
// ...the same from here on out...
```

The new member *m_nPrevIndex* is set to the index of the previously drawn *m_MousePositions*. Put another way, all the *m_MousePositions* up to *m_nPrevIndex* have already been drawn.

The View code for Prog3_1e appears as follows (for brevity, all functions that did not change from the Prog3_1d versions have been removed):

```
// Prog3vw.cpp : implementation of the CProg3_1eView
// class

#include "stdafx.h"
#include "Prog3_1e.h"

#include "Prog3doc.h"
#include "Prog3vw.h"


/////////////////////////////////////////////////////
// CProg3_1eView

IMPLEMENT_DYNCREATE(CProg3_1eView, CView)

BEGIN_MESSAGE_MAP(CProg3_1eView, CView)
    //{{AFX_MSG_MAP(CProg3_1eView)
    ON_WM_MOUSEMOVE()
    ON_WM_RBUTTONDOWN()
    ON_WM_LBUTTONDOWN()
    ON_WM_ERASEBKGND()
    //}}AFX_MSG_MAP
END_MESSAGE_MAP()


/////////////////////////////////////////////////////////////////
          //////////
// CProg3_1eView construction/destruction

CProg3_1eView::CProg3_1eView()
{
    // Set the size of the m_MousePositions array
    // so that it will grow by 100 CPoints
    // every time it needs to
    m_nPrevIndex = 0;
    m_MousePositions.SetSize(0, 100);
    m_MouseButtons.SetSize(0, 100);
}

CProg3_1eView::~CProg3_1eView()
```

```
{
    ClearList();
}


/////////////////////////////////////////////////////////
// CProg3_1eView drawing

void CProg3_1eView::OnDraw(CDC* pDC)
{
    // Loop through the mouse positions stored
    // off — if there aren't any, then there's
    // nothing to do, so quit
    UINT nPositions = m_MousePositions.GetSize();
    if (nPositions <= m_nPrevIndex)
    {
        return;
    }

    CPoint *pPoint;
    pPoint = (CPoint*)m_MousePositions[m_nPrevIndex];
    pDC->MoveTo(*pPoint);

    UINT i;
    for (i = m_nPrevIndex; i < nPositions; i++)
    {
        pPoint = (CPoint*)m_MousePositions[i];
        if (m_MouseButtons[i])
        {
            pDC->MoveTo(*pPoint);
            pDC->SetPixelV(*pPoint, RGB(0, 0, 0));
        }
        else
        {
            pDC->LineTo(*pPoint);
        }
    }
    m_nPrevIndex = nPositions - 1;
}


/////////////////////////////////////////////////////////
// CProg3_1eView message handlers

// ...other message-handling functions
//     same as before...

BOOL CProg3_1eView::OnEraseBkgnd(CDC* pDC)
{
```

```
    // When asked to perform a "real redraw,"
    // redraw the entire list
    m_nPrevIndex = 0;
        return CView::OnEraseBkgnd(pDC);
}

// ClearList — clear out the m_MousePositions list,
//              returning all memory to the heap
void CProg3_1eView::ClearList()
{
    // First delete each CPoint in the list
    int i;
    CPoint *pPoint;
    int n_Size = m_MousePositions.GetSize();
    for (i = 0; i < n_Size; i++)
    {
        pPoint = (CPoint*)m_MousePositions[i];
        delete pPoint;
    }

    // Now clear the list itself of all entries
    m_nPrevIndex = 0;
    m_MousePositions.RemoveAll();
    m_MouseButtons.RemoveAll();
}
```

m_nPrevIndex is zeroed when the *WM_ERASEBKGND* message is received.
Clearly, *m_nPrevIndex* must also be zeroed whenever the list is cleared. You
see *m_nPrevIndex* in operation in the *OnDraw( )* member function.

OnDraw( ) first moves the current draw location to the location where it left
off: *m_MousePositions[m_nPrevIndex]*. It then progresses from there to the end of
the list, just as it does in Prog3_1d. Finally, after *OnDraw( )* finishes the loop, it
stores the index of the last entry processed into *m_nPrevIndex*.

How much time does this process save? If you repeat the preceding experiment, you notice that the line never lags appreciably behind the mouse
pointer. The reason is that, no matter how many items are in the list, the program doesn't redraw more than the last few entries (except when the window
is unhidden).

To quantify the savings, make the following trivial change to *OnDraw( )*:

```
/////////////////////////////////////////////////////////
// CProg3_1eView drawing
```

```
void CProg3_1eView::OnDraw(CDC* pDC)
{
    // Loop through the mouse positions stored
    // off — if there aren't any, then there's
    // nothing to do, so quit
    UINT nPositions = m_MousePositions.GetSize();
    if (nPositions <= m_nPrevIndex)
    {
        return;
    }

    TRACE(
      "Total = %3d, Already done = %3d, Delta = %3d\n",
      nPositions,
      (m_nPrevIndex + 1),
      nPositions - (m_nPrevIndex + 1));

    CPoint *pPoint;
    pPoint = (CPoint*)m_MousePositions[m_nPrevIndex];
    pDC->MoveTo(*pPoint);

    UINT i;
    for (i = m_nPrevIndex; i < nPositions; i++)
    {
        pPoint = (CPoint*)m_MousePositions[i];
        if (m_MouseButtons[i])
        {
            pDC->MoveTo(*pPoint);
            pDC->SetPixelV(*pPoint, RGB(0, 0, 0));
        }
        else
        {
            pDC->LineTo(*pPoint);
        }
    }
    m_nPrevIndex = nPositions - 1;
}
```

When the program is built in Debug mode, the macro *TRACE( )* prints to the output window of the debugger: You choose Toolbar Go or Menu|Debug|Go from the menu or press F5. (TRACE is discussed in detail in Chapter 14.)

The debugger window output from executing the program is shown in Figure 11-3.

```
Total = 282, Already done = 281, Delta =    1
Total = 283, Already done = 282, Delta =    1
Total = 284, Already done = 283, Delta =    1
Total = 286, Already done = 284, Delta =    2
Total = 287, Already done = 286, Delta =    1
Total = 288, Already done = 287, Delta =    1
Total = 288, Already done =   1, Delta = 287
```

```
Build \ Debug / Find in Files / Profile /
Ready                              Ln 66, Col 1    REC COL OVR RI
```

Figure 11-3:
The debug
results from
executing
Prog3_1e
with TRACE.

As I moved the mouse around, the *OnDraw( )* repaint efforts never got more
than a couple of mouse locations behind. In the last output line, I minimized
and then redisplayed the window, which forced the program to redraw the
full list of 288 mouse locations.

Conclusion

One of the problems with the Etch-a-Sketch program has been solved. By saving the string of mouse events that created your masterpiece, Prog3_1e can
re-create the sketch on demand. Every time you resize the window, you no
longer shake the picture into oblivion.

Most WinApps can save their data to disk, however — a capability your program still lacks. In the next chapter, you learn how to create a document to
save your mouse strokes.

Chapter 12

Viewing a Document (or Is It Documenting a View?)

● ●

In This Chapter

▶ Introducing the *CDocument* class

▶ Separating the document from the view

▶ Storing mouse activity in a document

▶ Saving a document to disk

▶ Registering your document for the draft

▶ Registering a file type

▶ Introducing .INI files

● ●

*I*n Chapter 11, "A Rodent Recorder," you learned how to successfully save your drawings from being obliterated the first time the window was repainted, by storing the mouse strokes in a data structure. This data structure was kept in RAM, however. Your drawings aren't really safe until you can store them on disk, where they can be recalled and admired for generations.

MFC provides a great deal of support for disk-save and -restore operations, by using the *CDocument* and *CArchive* classes. This chapter investigates the *CDocument* class and its relationship to a concept known as the Document-View model. You then add the *CArchive* class to effect disk storage and retrieval.

The Document-View Model

If you think about it, the code you've written so far to implement your sketch program comes in two distinctly different flavors:

✔ The *view:* The code that interacts with users by collecting mouse events and displaying the drawing in the client area

✔ The *document:* The part of the code that stores and retrieves mouse strokes

In this *Document-View Model* of the world, these two operations are split into two separate classes. The View class is assigned the role of interacting with users, including receiving mouse clicks and keystrokes; this class handles any information that is displayed to users. The Document class is assigned the role of maintaining the data, including saving the data to disk and reading it from disk.

In a word-processing program, when a user clicks the mouse in the edit window, she is interacting with the view. When she types, the view passes her keystrokes on to the document for storage. When the view needs information in order to redraw the window, it can simply ask for it.

Why bother?

Before you see how to implement the Document-View Model, it's worthwhile to pose the question, "Why bother with this separation of church and state?" After all, not everything that can be done is worth doing. This list shows a few of the advantages of this model:

✔ Separating the document from the view makes both classes easier to use. In theory, you can graft the same view code onto brand-new document code or vice versa to generate entirely new applications in less time and with less work.

✔ Separating the document from the view makes both classes simpler. There's much to be said for not putting too much capability into a single class. Limiting the scope of the Document class to just maintaining the data while letting the View class worry only about displaying it makes both classes easier to code, debug, and maintain.

✔ The view generally is concerned with only the data users can see. This data may be only a small subset of the data contained within a document. When a user edits a large file, for example, he can see, at most, only 50 lines at a time. The view concerns itself only with displaying those 50 lines. The document must concern itself with the entire file.

✔ By the same token, it's also possible that some filter is at work. Consider what you see, for example, when you switch your editor into outline mode. The document is still there in its entirety, even though all you see are the level heads. The view filters out everything except the data it wants you to see.

✔ Finally, it's possible for a single document to have more than one view — it happens all the time. While you're scratching your head and trying to make sense of the rows and columns of data in an Excel spreadsheet, for example, you're looking at just one view of the data. After all, the "real data" is just a bunch of ones and zeroes stored in semiconductor memory somewhere. A bar chart is another interpretation, or view, of the same data; a scatter graph, a third; and so on.

If you have a window open that shows the spreadsheet and a second window with a bar chart while you simultaneously edit the formula in a given cell, you have three different views of the single document.

MFC's version of the Document-View Model

The Document-View Model explains why the class that controls the client area is called *CView* and not something clever, such as *CClientArea* (not to mention that *CView* is much shorter). The *CView* class and its subclasses describe the operations necessary to maintain the user's view of the data. By subclassing *CView* in different ways, you create your unique view of the data.

In a similar manner, the *CDocument* class provides the document operations you can inherit.

Separating the Document from the View

Let's look at a version of the Etch-A-Sketch program that separates the document-related code from the view. Although *CView*-polygamy is possible, limit yourself for now to documents that maintain only a single view at a time.

The document

CProg3_3a was created in what has become the conventional method of turning off all options. The document *include* file Prog3doc.h appears as follows:

```
// Prog3doc.h : interface of the CProg3_3aDoc class
//
/////////////////////////////////////////////////////

class CProg3_3aDoc : public CDocument
{
// Attributes
```

```
protected:
    // An array of CPoints containing the
    // location of the mouse recorded as the
    // mouse moved with the button down
    CPtrArray  m_MousePositions;
    CWordArray m_MouseButtons;c

    // The following flag is necessary
    // to correct what appears to be a
    // bug -- when an entry in the File Selection
    // box is double-clicked, the view
    // gets a WM_MOUSEMOVE message. This
    // flag is set to TRUE when you are expecting
    // this message and want to ignore it.
    int m_bNoUpdate;

// Operations
public:
    // The following functions clear or
    // add to the m_Mouse... arrays
    void ClearList();
    void AddList(CPoint&, UINT);

    // Clear the update disable flag
    void EnableUpdate();

    // The following two functions access
    // the m_Mouse... arrays
    UINT    GetSize();
    CPoint* GetMPosition(UINT index);
    int     GetMButton(UINT index);
```

```
protected: // create from serialization only
    CProg3_3aDoc();
    DECLARE_DYNCREATE(CProg3_3aDoc)

// Overrides
    // ClassWizard generated virtual function overrides
    //{{AFX_VIRTUAL(CProg3_3aDoc)
    public:
    virtual BOOL OnNewDocument();
    //}}AFX_VIRTUAL

// Implementation
public:
    virtual ~CProg3_3aDoc();
```

```
         virtual void Serialize(CArchive& ar);

// Generated message map functions
protected:
     //{{AFX_MSG(CProg3_3aDoc)
     // NOTE: the ClassWizard will add and remove
     // member functions here.
     //      DO NOT EDIT what you see in these blocks
     //      of generated code!
     //}}AFX_MSG
     DECLARE_MESSAGE_MAP()
};


/////////////////////////////////////////////////////////
```

The *m_MousePositions* and *m_MouseButtons* that were previously resident in the View class are now members of *CProg3_3aDoc*. They have been declared *protected* because you don't want other classes to mess with them without the class's knowledge and permission.

Because *m_MousePositions* and *m_MouseButtons* are protected, the two access functions *GetMPosition( )* and *GetMButton( )* have been provided to enable the view to read the two lists. The member function *GetSize( )* returns the number of elements in both lists.

Finally, the *ClearList( )* and *AddList( )* member functions are the same as their earlier *CView* equivalents — they've just emigrated to the other side of the Document-View border.

The *m_bNoUpdate* flag and the *EnableUpdate( )* member function have been added to solve an apparent bug (described later in this chapter).

The remainder of the *include* file is unchanged from the one generated by AppWizard.

The implementation for class *CProg3_3aDoc* appears in Prog3doc.cpp:

```
// Prog3doc.cpp : implementation of the CProg3_3aDoc
//                class
//

#include "stdafx.h"
#include "Prog3_3a.h"

#include "Prog3doc.h"

/////////////////////////////////////////////////////////
```

```
// CProg3_3aDoc

IMPLEMENT_DYNCREATE(CProg3_3aDoc, CDocument)

BEGIN_MESSAGE_MAP(CProg3_3aDoc, CDocument)
    //{{AFX_MSG_MAP(CProg3_3aDoc)
    // NOTE: The ClassWizard will add and remove
    // mapping macros here.
    //      DO NOT EDIT what you see in these blocks
    //      of generated code!
    //}}AFX_MSG_MAP
END_MESSAGE_MAP()

/////////////////////////////////////////////////////
// CProg3_3aDoc construction/destruction

CProg3_3aDoc::CProg3_3aDoc()
{
    m_MousePositions.SetSize(0, 100);
    m_MouseButtons.SetSize(0, 100);
    m_bNoUpdate = FALSE;
}

CProg3_3aDoc::~CProg3_3aDoc()
{
    ClearList();
}

BOOL CProg3_3aDoc::OnNewDocument()
{
    if (!CDocument::OnNewDocument())
                    return FALSE;

    ClearList();
    return TRUE;
}

/////////////////////////////////////////////////////
// CProg3_3aDoc serialization

void CProg3_3aDoc::Serialize(CArchive& ar)
{
    if (ar.IsStoring())
    {
                    // TODO: add storing code here
    }
    else
```

```
                    {
                                        // TODO: add loading code here
                    }
    }


    /////////////////////////////////////////////////////
    // CProg3_3aDoc commands
```

```
// GetSize, GetMPosition, GetMButton -- access functions
UINT CProg3_3aDoc::GetSize()
{
    return m_MousePositions.GetSize();
}

CPoint* CProg3_3aDoc::GetMPosition(UINT index)
{
    return (CPoint*)m_MousePositions[index];
}

int CProg3_3aDoc::GetMButton(UINT index)
{
    return (int)m_MouseButtons[index];
}

// ClearList -- clear out the m_MousePositions list,
//              returning all memory to the heap
void CProg3_3aDoc::ClearList()
{
    // First delete each CPoint in the list
    int i;
    CPoint *pPoint;
    int n_Size = m_MousePositions.GetSize();
    for (i = 0; i < n_Size; i++)
    {
        pPoint = (CPoint*)m_MousePositions[i];
        delete pPoint;
    }

    // Now clear the list itself of all entries
    m_MousePositions.RemoveAll();
    m_MouseButtons.RemoveAll();
}

void CProg3_3aDoc::AddList(CPoint &point, UINT nButton)
{
    // If update is disabled, ignore the request
    if (m_bNoUpdate)
```

```
    {
        return;
    }

    // Get the memory to hold the mouse location
    // off the heap
    CPoint *pNewPoint = new CPoint(point);

    // Now add it to the list
    m_MousePositions.Add((void*)pNewPoint);

    // Record whether this was a button event
    // or a mouse-move event
    m_MouseButtons.Add(nButton);

    // Flag the document as changed
    SetModifiedFlag();
}

void CProg3_3aDoc::EnableUpdate()
{
    m_bNoUpdate = FALSE;
}
```

As you would expect, the majority of the code that appears in this class is identical to the *m_MousePositions-* and *m_MouseButtons*-related code previously contained in the View class. The only real change is the call to *SetModified-Flag( )* at the end of the *AddList( )* function. This call sets a member flag inherited as part of the *CDocument* class to indicate that the document has changed since it was last saved to disk.

The extra member functions *GetSize( )*, *GetMPosition( )*, and *GetMButton( )* are implemented as "one-liners" to access the protected data members previously contained within the View class.

The view

The View class, CProg3_3aView, is reduced to only the elements necessary to manipulate the client area of the user's window. You notice these elements first in the *include* file. (As always, the ClassWizard was used to add the message handlers, which accounts for their appearance in the dispatch table in the class definition.)

```
// Prog3vw.h : interface of the CProg3_3aView class
//
///////////////////////////////////////////////////////////
```

```
class CProg3_3aView : public CView
{
protected:
    // The most recently updated location
    UINT m_nPrevIndex;

protected: // create from serialization only
      CProg3_3aView();
       DECLARE_DYNCREATE(CProg3_3aView)

// Attributes
public:
      CProg3_3aDoc* GetDocument();

// Operations
public:

// Overrides
      // ClassWizard generated virtual function overrides
      //{{AFX_VIRTUAL(CProg3_3aView)
      public:
      virtual void OnDraw(CDC* pDC);
      protected:
      //}}AFX_VIRTUAL

// Implementation
public:
      virtual ~CProg3_3aView();

// Generated message map functions
protected:
      //{{AFX_MSG(CProg3_3aView)
      afx_msg void OnLButtonDown(UINT nFlags, CPoint point);
      afx_msg void OnMouseMove(UINT nFlags, CPoint point);
      afx_msg void OnRButtonDown(UINT nFlags, CPoint point);
      afx_msg BOOL OnEraseBkgnd(CDC* pDC);
      //}}AFX_MSG
      DECLARE_MESSAGE_MAP()
};
//////////////////////////////////////////////////////////
```

All the message handlers are still present. The mouse messages still come through the view, even though their data is being stored in the document.

The only user-defined data member left behind in the View class is *m_nPrev-Index*. I can almost hear you asking, "If you transferred *m_MousePositions* and *m_MouseButtons* over to the document department, why did you leave this member behind the view counter?" The reason is that the index of the most recently painted mouse stroke is a function of the view and not of the document.

Ask yourself the following question: "Can I describe fully what the data member does without referencing the act of repainting or the appearance of the client window?" If not, the object is a property of the view. ■

The member function *GetDocument( )* returns a pointer to the document object associated with this view. This pointer is the link from the view to the document.

The source file Prog3vw.cpp contains the implementation of the *CProg3_3a-View* class (the grayed areas represent the areas that have changed relative to the view-only version, *CProg3_1e*):

```
// Prog3vw.cpp : implementation of the CProg3_3aView
//               class
//

#include "stdafx.h"
#include "Prog3_3a.h"

#include "Prog3doc.h"
#include "Prog3vw.h"

/////////////////////////////////////////////////////////
// CProg3_3aView

IMPLEMENT_DYNCREATE(CProg3_3aView, CView)

BEGIN_MESSAGE_MAP(CProg3_3aView, CView)
    //{{AFX_MSG_MAP(CProg3_3aView)
    ON_WM_LBUTTONDOWN()
    ON_WM_MOUSEMOVE()
    ON_WM_RBUTTONDOWN()
    ON_WM_ERASEBKGND()
    //}}AFX_MSG_MAP
END_MESSAGE_MAP()

/////////////////////////////////////////////////////////
// CProg3_3aView construction/destruction

CProg3_3aView::CProg3_3aView()
{
```

```
    m_nPrevIndex = 0;
}


CProg3_3aView::~CProg3_3aView()
{
}


/////////////////////////////////////////////////////
// CProg3_3aView drawing

void CProg3_3aView::OnDraw(CDC* pDC)
{
    CProg3_3aDoc* pDoc = GetDocument();
    ASSERT_VALID(pDoc);

    // Loop through the mouse positions stored
    // off -- if there aren't any, then there's
    // nothing to do, so quit
    UINT nPositions = pDoc->GetSize();
    if (nPositions <= m_nPrevIndex)
    {
        return;
    }

    CPoint *pPoint;
    pPoint = pDoc->GetMPosition(m_nPrevIndex);
    pDC->MoveTo(*pPoint);

    UINT i;
    for (i = m_nPrevIndex; i < nPositions; i++)
    {
        pPoint = pDoc->GetMPosition(i);
        if (pDoc->GetMButton(i))
        {
            pDC->MoveTo(*pPoint);
            pDC->SetPixelV(*pPoint, RGB(0, 0, 0));
        }
        else
        {
            pDC->LineTo(*pPoint);
        }
    }

    m_nPrevIndex = nPositions - 1;

    // Enable document updates from now on
    pDoc->EnableUpdate();
```

```
    }

CProg3_3aDoc* CProg3_3aView::GetDocument()
{
     return (CProg3_3aDoc*)m_pDocument;
}

/////////////////////////////////////////////////////////
// CProg3_3aView message handlers

void CProg3_3aView::OnLButtonDown(UINT nFlags,
                                     CPoint point)
{
    CProg3_3aDoc* pDoc = GetDocument();
    ASSERT_VALID(pDoc);

    // Add the current mouse position to the list
    // stored in m_MousePositions
    pDoc->AddList(point, TRUE);

    // Force a repaint to see the effect
    Invalidate(FALSE);
}

void CProg3_3aView::OnMouseMove(UINT nFlags,
                                  CPoint point)
{
    // If the left mouse button is not pressed,
    // don't do anything
    if (!(nFlags & MK_LBUTTON))
    {
        return;
    }

    // Otherwise, handle like a left-button press
    CProg3_3aDoc* pDoc = GetDocument();
    ASSERT_VALID(pDoc);
    pDoc->AddList(point, FALSE);

    Invalidate(FALSE);
}

void CProg3_3aView::OnRButtonDown(UINT nFlags,
                                    CPoint point)
{
    // On right-button clicks, clear the entire mouse
    // point list
```

```
      CProg3_3aDoc* pDoc = GetDocument();
      ASSERT_VALID(pDoc);
      pDoc->ClearList();

      // Force a repaint with the empty list
      m_nPrevIndex = 0;
      Invalidate(TRUE);
  }


  BOOL CProg3_3aView::OnEraseBkgnd(CDC* pDC)
  {
      // When asked to perform a "real redraw,"
      // redraw the entire list
      m_nPrevIndex = 0;
      return CView::OnEraseBkgnd(pDC);
  }
```

The constructor for *CProg3_3aView* has nothing left to initialize except the *m_nPrevIndex* data member.

The *OnDraw( )* member function works as it did earlier except that it first must get a pointer to the document object by using the *GetDocument( )* function. *OnDraw( )* relies on this object for the size information (*GetSize( )*), the mouse position (*GetMPosition( )*), and the mouse button (*GetMButton( )*) information. (The call to *EnableUpdate( )* at the end of the function is there to solve a bug that is explained later in this chapter.)

Each of the message-handling functions appears almost unchanged from its previous all-view version except that it adds to or clears a list contained in the document (*pDoc->AddList( )* or *pDoc->ClearList( )*) rather than in the view.

Executing the program by lethal injection

Compiling and executing program Prog3_3a reveals a surprising and intriguing result: Nothing has changed. The characteristics and output of this program appear identical to those of its predecessor.

This result should hardly be surprising because you haven't added anything. All you've done is separate the document code from the view code. In doing so, however, you've positioned yourself to solve the real problem, to paraphrase JFK, "of sending a sketch to the disk and returning it to the window successfully in our lifetime."

Save the Documents!

If you look back at the *CProg3_3aDoc* class, you see a curious function I have yet to explain: *Serialize(CArchive&)*. This default serialize function provided by the AppWizard contains only the curious admonitions to "add storing code here" and "add loading code there":

```
void CProg3_3aDoc::Serialize(CArchive& ar)
{
      if (ar.IsStoring())
      {
                  // TODO: add storing code here
      }
      else
      {
                  // TODO: add loading code here
      }
}
```

What could these admonitions possibly mean?

The *Serialize( )* function is called when MFC wants your Document class to either store itself to disk or read itself from disk. This section explains how this function works.

When you choose Save from the File menu, MFC opens the file and attaches it to a newly created object of class *CArchive*. MFC sets an internal data member flag *m_nMode* to the state *Storing* to indicate that the program is saving information to disk. It then calls the virtual member function *CDocument::Serialize( )* and passes it the *CArchive* object that was just created. This is your class's opportunity to save any information it wants by passing it to the *CArchive* object for safekeeping.

When it's time to read the information back from disk, the program repeats the same steps except that it sets the *m_nMode* flag to *Loading* before calling the *Serialize( )* function. When this flag is set, it tips off your program that it's time to read the data.

The call to *CArchive::IsStoring( )* returns a *TRUE* if *m_nMode* is set to *Storing*, and a *FALSE* if it is set to *Loading*.

All you really have to do to give your next version of the sketch program, Prog3_3b, the capability to read and write to disk is to fill in the sections indicated in the *Serialize( )* function.

Adding serial filler

To implement the save-and-restore capability, I added two member functions — cleverly named *Save( )* and *Restore( )* — to the Prog3doc.h *include* file:

```
class CProg3_3bDoc : public CDocument
{
// Operations
protected:
    void Save(CArchive& ar);
    void Restore(CArchive& ar);

    // ...the remainder of the class unchanged...
```

I then modified *Serialize( )* in Prog3doc.cpp to call one of these functions according to the returned value from *IsStoring( )*:

```
/////////////////////////////////////////////////////
// CProg3_3bDoc serialization

void CProg3_3bDoc::Serialize(CArchive& ar)
{
    if (ar.IsStoring())
    {
                        Save(ar);
    }
    else
    {
                        Restore(ar);
    }
}

void CProg3_3bDoc::Save(CArchive& ar)
{
    // First save the size of the list
    WORD nPositions;
    nPositions = GetSize();
    ar << nPositions;

    // Now save mouse movement in list
    WORD i;
    WORD wTemp;
    CPoint *pPoint;
    for (i = 0; i < nPositions; i++)
    {
        wTemp = (WORD)GetMButton(i);
```

```
        ar << wTemp;

        pPoint = GetMPosition(i);
        wTemp = (WORD)pPoint->x;
        ar << wTemp;
        wTemp = (WORD)pPoint->y;
        ar << wTemp;
    }
}

void CProg3_3bDoc::Restore(CArchive& ar)
{
    // Remove whatever is already in the list
    ClearList();

    // First save the size of the list
    WORD nPositions;
    ar >> nPositions;

    // Now save mouse movement in list
    WORD i;
    WORD wButton, wX, wY;
    for (i = 0; i < nPositions; i++)
    {
        // Read up the button, x & y locations
        ar >> wButton;
        ar >> wX;
        ar >> wY;

        // Now add them to the list
        AddList(CPoint(wX, wY), wButton);
    }

    m_bNoUpdate = TRUE;
}
```

So far, so good. The member functions require a good bit of explanation.
First, let's review exactly what you have to do. You have a list of mouse locations and mouse buttons in memory. Your task is to save this list to a disk file
in a format of your choosing in such a way that you can read that file later to
re-create the list.

Save( ) begins by saving the length of the list. That information is useful when
it's time to perform the read operation, because it tells you how many
objects to read from the file. To save the number of positions in the list,
Save( ) calls *GetSize( )* and stores the result in an object of type *WORD*. It then
inserts this *WORD* into the *CArchive* object.

C++ commonly overloads the left-shift and right-shift operators to perform output and input, respectively. When overloaded, the left-shift operator is called the *inserter,* and the right shift is called the *extractor.* ■

The class *CArchive* defines inserters for types such as *BYTE, WORD,* and *DWORD.* The following statement taken from *Save( )* writes to the *CArchive* object the *WORD nPositions* that contain the number of mouse locations in the list:

```
WORD nPositions;
nPositions = GetSize();
ar << nPositions;
```

MFC doesn't define an inserter for type *int,* however, because this type isn't the same size in all versions of Windows. In this way, MFC forces applications programmers to write functions in a Windows version-independent way.

Having saved the number of entries, the *Save( )* function then must save the list of mouse-button flags and mouse locations. The function begins by looping through the list of mouse stopping points. For each location, it stores the mouse flag by using the *WORD* inserter:

```
wTemp = (WORD)GetMButton(i);
ar << wTemp;
```

Unfortunately, no inserter exists for a *CPoint* object. That is, it's not possible to write the following:

```
ar << GetMPosition(i);
```

The alternative is to store the *x* and *y* components, which together make up a *CPoint*:

```
pPoint = GetMPosition(i);
wTemp = (WORD)pPoint->x;
ar << wTemp;
wTemp = (WORD)pPoint->y;
ar << wTemp;
```

You might wonder why it's necessary to loop through the members of the *CPtrList* individually. Why not insert the entire list at one time, as follows:

```
ar << m_MousePositions;
```

Even if you assume for a minute that an inserter exists for the *CPtrList* class, this inserter could not possibly work for your application. Although it might be able to save the addresses, without knowing what these addresses point to, it couldn't possibly save the *CPoint* data in a reasonable manner. The *WORD* inserter works for the mouse buttons. ▪

The *Restore( )* function follows the same pattern in the reverse direction. First, it calls *ClearList( )* to make sure that the list is free of any previous drawing information (otherwise, the data in the file would be added to whatever was in the document object).

Restore( ) then reads *nPositions* number of mouse-button and mouse-location values from the file referenced by the *CArchive* object. Of course, it must convert the *x* and *y* values back into a *CPoint* object. Having done so, the *AddList( )* function is the perfect mechanism to add them to the list.

The expression *CPoint(x, y)* calls the constructor *CPoint::CPoint(int, int)* to build a temporary *CPoint* object that is then passed to *AddList( )*. ▪

Check it out!

Now you're ready. Execute the program and draw something. Give it your best shot — this one will be saved for posterity. Choose Save from the File menu. The Save File Selection dialog box, similar to the one shown in Figure 12-1, should be displayed.

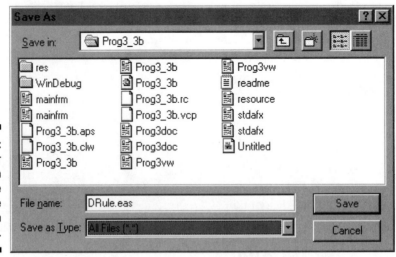

Figure 12-1:
Make your
choices in
the Save
File
Selection
dialog box.

Enter the name of a file, and then click Save. The disk light comes on, the dialog box disappears, and — voilà! — the file is saved.

To prove it, clear the window by choosing New and then Open from the File menu.

Double-click the file you chose earlier from the list of filenames; your drawing reappears, looking just like it did when you left it.

MFC provides a large amount of functionality. Try drawing something in the window and then reading another file. Before MFC reads the new file, it notices that the current document has been changed and was not saved. It provides a warning box that gives users the opportunity to save the current drawing before reading the new one.

How did MFC know that the document had changed? You told it, by calling *SetModifiedFlag( )* in the *AddList( )* member function. MFC clears this flag after the document has been saved to disk.

The remainder of the File menu operations also now work (choosing New clears the current document, for example, and choosing Save As saves the document under a different name). The File menu even has a list of the *most recently used* filenames (called the *MRU list*). You specified the number of entries in the MRU list when you built the framework with the AppWizard.

Registering a file type

As neat as serialization is, the filter *.* displays all files in the current directory. Most programs stake out a particular file extension as their file type and list only files of that type (for example, Word uses .DOC, and Write uses .WRI). I decided on the extension .eas for my drawings (it stands for Etch-A-Sketch). Having chosen this extension, I want the File-Selection dialog box to list only .eas files.

This is best handled from AppWizard when you build the application framework. Choose the Advanced options from the window labeled Step 4 of 6. In the File Extension field, fill in a three-letter file extension. You can also provide a suitable description of the file type in the Filter Name field.

Learning about that "no update" stuff

One question remains. What is the significance of the *m_bNoUpdate* flag in the document? The addition of this flag hides an apparent bug. Under some circumstances, when you choose a filename to read from the File Selection dia-

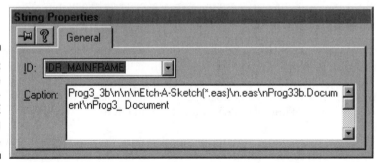

Figure 12-2:
Editing the
IDR_MAIN-
FRAME
string
resource.

log box, an extra *WM_MOUSEMOVE* message is sent to the application. The program interprets this message as though the user had rapidly moved the mouse to some new location. This message causes an extra drawing segment to be added to the end of the image that was just read from disk.

Setting *m_bNoUpdate* to *TRUE* causes the Document class to ignore attempts to add mouse-move events to the list. This flag is set when the document is read, and it is cleared after the window has been repainted in the *OnDraw( )* function.

What?! You forgot to register a file type?

It is easy to fail to register a file type when you execute the AppWizard. At that point in the development of a program, you may not even know whether you'll need a file type. It's possible, with a simple edit to one of the program's resources, to register a file type after the application is already written. One of the string resources, *IDR_MAINFRAME*, contains a list of seven strings separated by the \n newline character. The fifth field, which defaults to *NULL*, is the file type for this program (in this case, .eas). The field immediately in front of the fifth field is the *Filter name*. This string appears in the Save as Type window in the File Save dialog box.

Both the filter name and the file extension default to *NULL*. Notice that the filter name All

Files (*.*) and the corresponding file extension (.*) are appended to whatever you provide.

Edit the string by double-clicking the Prog3_3.rc file, choosing String Table, and then double-clicking *IDR_MAINFRAME*. When you finish, the string should look like the one in Figure 12-2.

When the program is rebuilt and executed, the File Open selection box defaults to showing only files that end in .eas. When you save your drawing, the .eas extension is automatically appended to the filename you provide. (You can choose other file types, of course, by clicking the down arrow in the Save as Type window.)

The *WM_PAINT* message is the lowest-priority message in the system. By the time the *WM_PAINT* message has been processed, the extraneous *WM_MOUSEMOVE* (and any other mouse-move or mouse-button messages that result from the File Selection dialog box) will have already been processed, and the proverbial coast will be clear. ∎

Revisiting Prog3_3b.cpp

Although all your attention so far has been directed to the Document and View classes, a few tricks remain to be played in the main file, Prog3_3b.cpp. As you'll recall from Chapter 7, this file contains the function *InitInstance( )*, which is called when the application starts. *InitInstance( )* creates the other classes and generally gets things started.

You can add several capabilities to *InitInstance( )* — what's already there as part of the application framework.

The contents of the file Prog3_3b.cpp appear as follows (my additions to the default application framework are marked in gray):

```
// Prog3_3b.cpp : Defines the class behaviors for the
//                application

#include "stdafx.h"
#include "Prog3_3b.h"

#include "mainfrm.h"
#include "Prog3doc.h"
#include "Prog3vw.h"


/////////////////////////////////////////////////////////
// CProg3_3bApp

BEGIN_MESSAGE_MAP(CProg3_3bApp, CWinApp)
    //{{AFX_MSG_MAP(CProg3_3bApp)
    ON_COMMAND(ID_APP_ABOUT, OnAppAbout)
    // NOTE: the ClassWizard will add and remove
    // mapping macros here.
    //      DO NOT EDIT what you see in these blocks of
    //      generated code!
    //}}AFX_MSG_MAP
    // Standard file-based document commands
    ON_COMMAND(ID_FILE_NEW, CWinApp::OnFileNew)
    ON_COMMAND(ID_FILE_OPEN, CWinApp::OnFileOpen)
```

```
END_MESSAGE_MAP()

/////////////////////////////////////////////////////
// CProg3_3bApp construction

CProg3_3bApp::CProg3_3bApp()
{
    // TODO: add construction code here
    // Place all significant initialization in InitInstance
}

/////////////////////////////////////////////////////
// The one and only CProg3_3bApp object

CProg3_3bApp theApp;

/////////////////////////////////////////////////////
// CProg3_3bApp initialization

BOOL CProg3_3bApp::InitInstance()
{
    // Standard initialization
    // If you are not using these features and want to
    // reduce the size of your final executable, you
    // should remove from the following the specific
    // initialization routines you do not need.

    LoadStdProfileSettings();  // Load standard INI file
                               // options (including MRU)

    // Register the application's document templates.
    // Document templates serve as the connection between
    // documents, frame windows, and views.

    CSingleDocTemplate* pDocTemplate;
    pDocTemplate = new CSingleDocTemplate(
                    IDR_MAINFRAME,
                    RUNTIME_CLASS(CProg3_3bDoc),
                    RUNTIME_CLASS(CMainFrame),
                    RUNTIME_CLASS(CProg3_3bView));
    AddDocTemplate(pDocTemplate);

    // Register Etch-A-Sketch files
    // with Windows so that you can double-click
    // from now on
    RegisterShellFileTypes();

    // create a new (empty) document
```

```
    OnFileNew();

    if (m_lpCmdLine[0] != '\0')
    {
        // If a document name is provided,
        // open it up
        OpenDocumentFile(m_lpCmdLine);
    }

    return TRUE;
}


//////////////////////////////////////////////////////////
// CAboutDlg dialog used for App About

    // ...the remainder of the file dedicated to the
    // About dialog box, which is covered later...
```

As noted, the application is described by the *CProg3_3bApp* class. As soon as the application starts, the object *theApp* is created, which causes the constructor for *CProg3_3bApp* to be invoked. The constructor should limit itself to initializing any data members you have added to the class. The real work of starting up the program — registering windows and opening documents — doesn't begin until the *InitInstance( )* member function is invoked by MFC.

The call to *LoadStdProfileSettings( )* enables MFC to read any information it might have saved in the .INI file (which is discussed in the following section).

What's an .INI file?

An .INI file is a simple text file that stores information for use by the program. The .INI file usually carries the same name as the program with the extension .INI (pronounced either "inny" or "dot-eye-in-eye").

You've seen these files many times. They usually reside in the Windows directory and clutter it up so that it's virtually impossible to find anything.

.INI files exist to enable a program to save state information easily, such as preferences or settings from one execution of a program to another. For example, MFC saves a program's MRU list in the .INI file.

This saving of state information is easy to demonstrate. First, execute the Prog3_3b program. Create and save a few drawings under different names, and then exit from the program. When you go into the Windows directory and look at the file Prog3_3b.ini, you find the names of the files you just saved.

You can save and read settings from the .INI file as well. The member function *CWinApp::WriteProfileString( )* writes a string to the .INI file, whereas the function *CWinApp::WriteProfileInt( )* can be used to write integer values. The *CWinApp* member functions *GetProfileString( )* and *GetProfileInt( )* read these values back:

```
void Save(CString &csValue, int nValue)
{
    // Get a pointer to the current application
    CWinApp *pWinApp = AfxGetApp();

    // Save the string into 'My Section' under
    // the heading 'String value'
    pWinApp->WriteProfileString("My Section",
                                "String value",
                                 csValue);

    // Same for the integer value
    pWinApp->WriteProfileInt("My Section",
                             "Int value",
                             nValue);
}

void Recover(CString &csValue, int &nValue;)
{
    CWinApp *pWinApp = AfxGetApp();

    // Recover the string into a CString --
    // if you can't find it, return a CString object
    // containing the value "default string"
    csValue = pWinApp->GetProfileString("My Section",
                                        "String value",
                                        "default string");

    // Read the int -- if you can't find it, return 0
    nValue = pWinApp->GetProfileInt("My Section",
                                    "Int value", 0);
}
```

Executing *Save( )* and passing it the filename DRule.eas and the value 32 results in the addition of the following lines to the .INI file:

```
[My Section]
String value=DRule.eas
Int value=32
```

Calling *Recover( )* reads the two values from the .INI file and returns them to the caller.

What's next?

After the profile has been read, the main program continues by creating the document template. Without going into a great deal of detail, this process establishes the relationship between the document, the frame, and the view.

The call to *RegisterShellFileTypes( )* registers the program's file type (the extension of the type of file the application handles) with Windows. After this registration has been performed, a user can simply double-click a file of type .eas and Windows automatically executes the program. Because this registration is more or less permanent, this call really has an effect only the first time the program is executed; every subsequent time, the type has already been registered.

This call is added automatically by AppWizard if you provide it a file type from the window labeled Step 4 of 6, as noted earlier in this chapter. ▪

The call to *RegisterShellFileTypes( )* is followed by a call to *OnFileNew( )*. It's the *OnFileNew( )* function's job to empty out the document. This function is also called when the operator chooses New from the File menu.

The program then checks to see whether a filename was passed as an argument to the program. For example, the pointer *m_lpCmdLine* points to the string *"drule.eas"* if a user does any one of these four things:

- ✔ Chooses Run from the Start menu and enters *drule.eas* as the argument. There's not much chance of that, however, because hardly anyone uses the Run option anymore.

- ✔ Enters *prog3_3b drule.eas* from the MS-DOS command-line prompt. The DOS window under Windows 95 is smart enough to recognize a WinApp and pass the application to Windows for execution.

- ✔ Grabs the drule.eas icon or filename and drops it on top of the Prog3_3b icon or filename. (This process is called *drag-and-drop,* for obvious reasons.)

- ✔ Double-clicks the DRule.eas icon or filename after the type .eas has been registered with Windows by having executed Prog3_3b earlier.

If *m_lpCmdLine* points to a *NULL* character, the program was not executed in one of these four ways and, therefore, there's no file to open on start-up.

There is one other possible way to execute the program, which you don't handle in this program: *m_lpCmdLine* can point to *-e* or */e*, which indicates that another program is attempting to establish an OLE connection. (OLE is not covered in this book. Let's dodge that bullet for now — Olé!) ▮

Conclusion

Neat. Now you can save your drawings to disk and restore them later. You can even edit them some more and save the modifications to disk. The next chapter investigates scrolling, which handles those large drawings you might create.

Chapter 13

Scrolling the Window

● ●

In This Chapter

▶ The *CScrollView* class

▶ Letting the view scroll by your window

▶ Training your mouse to scroll

● ●

*Y*our drawing program is beginning to look reasonably complete. Mac-Draw it's not, but, hey, it's not bad for just a few lines of C++. You can add one more cheap and frivolous feature with little investment in time, either yours or mine: the ability to scroll the drawing in the window. For small documents, MFC reduces this process to a trivial exercise you will want to add to all your applications.

Scrolling

Part of the Windows metaphor is that, if an application has a document open, the entire document — no matter how large — is available to be displayed through the client area window, no matter how small that window might be. This capability is added through scrolling.

Figure 13-1 shows that the physical client area represents a view port into the logical window containing the document in its entirety.

Scrolling moves the physical window around on the logical window. In this way, you can use a small physical window to view a much larger logical window.

Windows supports scrolling through the *WM_VSCROLL* and *WM_HSCROLL* messages. It is possible to add these messages to the view's message dispatch table via the ClassWizard; it isn't necessary, however. MFC allows users to override a member function called *CView::OnScroll( )*, which is invoked automatically whenever one of these messages is received.

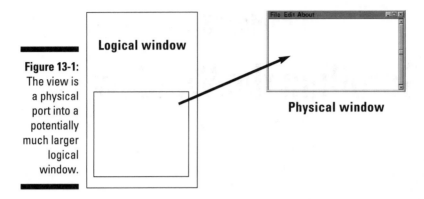

Figure 13-1:
The view is
a physical
port into a
potentially
much larger
logical
window.

For documents small enough to fit entirely in memory, even this isn't necessary. The *CScrollView* class handles the scroll messages automatically. *CScrollView* is a subclass of *CView*. It has all the capabilities of a *CView* except that it adds the ability to scroll. Inheriting from *CScrollView* rather than from the *CView* class adds this scrolling capability to your program with almost no additional effort on your part.

Let's Do It

There are two ways to modify *CProg3_3View* so that it's based on the scrolling *CScrollView*. When you first build a program, the easiest way is to let the AppWizard handle it. When you get to step 6 in the AppWizard, choose the Advanced options, and then choose *CProg3_3View* from the list of classes that AppWizard is about to create. In the lower-left corner, choose *CScrollView* rather than *CView* as the base class, as shown in Figure 13-2.

When you modify an existing program, the AppWizard is not much help — it can't go back and change decisions that were made earlier. Fortunately, it isn't difficult in this case to make the changes by hand. Simply open the CProg3vw.cpp and CProg3vw.h source files, and change every occurrence of *CView* to *CScrollView*.

The implementation for the new CProg3vw.cpp is as follows (notice the changes with respect to Prog3_3b, which have been flagged in gray):

```
// Prog3vw.cpp : implementation of the CProg3_3cView
//               class
//

#include "stdafx.h"
#include "Prog3_3c.h"
```

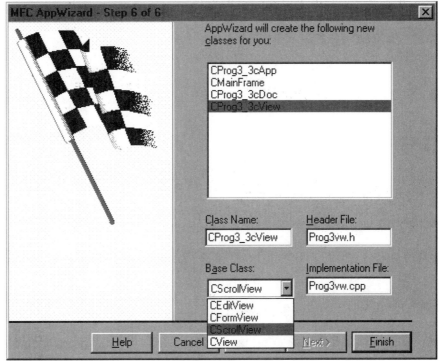

Figure 13-2:
Inheriting
from
CScrollView
rather than
from the
default
CView.

```
#include "Prog3doc.h"
#include "Prog3vw.h"


/////////////////////////////////////////////////////
// CProg3_3cView

IMPLEMENT_DYNCREATE(CProg3_3cView, CScrollView)

BEGIN_MESSAGE_MAP(CProg3_3cView, CScrollView)
   //{{AFX_MSG_MAP(CProg3_3cView)
   ON_WM_LBUTTONDOWN()
   ON_WM_MOUSEMOVE()
   ON_WM_RBUTTONDOWN()
   ON_WM_ERASEBKGND()
   //}}AFX_MSG_MAP
END_MESSAGE_MAP()


/////////////////////////////////////////////////////
// CProg3_3cView construction/destruction
```

```
CProg3_3cView::CProg3_3cView()
{
    m_nPrevIndex = 0;
}

CProg3_3cView::~CProg3_3cView()
{
}

//////////////////////////////////////////////////////
// CProg3_3cView drawing

void CProg3_3cView::OnDraw(CDC* pDC)
{
    // ...same as before...
}

void CProg3_3cView::OnInitialUpdate()
{
    CScrollView::OnInitialUpdate();

    // Set the scroll size based on
    // the size of the initial window
    RECT rectClientArea;
    GetClientRect(&rectClientArea);

    CSize sizeTotal(rectClientArea.right,
                    rectClientArea.bottom);

    SetScrollSizes(MM_TEXT, sizeTotal);
}

//////////////////////////////////////////////////////
// CProg3_3cView message handlers

void CProg3_3cView::OnLButtonDown(UINT nFlags,
                                  CPoint point)
{
    CProg3_3cDoc* pDoc = GetDocument();
    ASSERT_VALID(pDoc);

    // Offset the mouse position by the scroll
    // position within the logical window
    point += CSize(GetDeviceScrollPosition());

    // Add the current mouse position to the list
    // stored in m_MousePositions
```

```
        pDoc->AddList(point, TRUE);

        // Force a repaint to see the effect
        Invalidate(FALSE);
    }

    void CProg3_3cView::OnMouseMove(UINT nFlags,
                                    CPoint point)
    {
        // If the left mouse button is not pressed,
        // don't do anything
        if (!(nFlags & MK_LBUTTON))
        {
            return;
        }

        // Offset the mouse position by the scroll
        // position within the logical window
        point += CSize(GetDeviceScrollPosition());

        // Otherwise, handle like a left-button press
        CProg3_3cDoc* pDoc = GetDocument();
        ASSERT_VALID(pDoc);
        pDoc->AddList(point, FALSE);
        Invalidate(FALSE);
    }

    // ...the rest of the module the same as before...
```

The first change is the addition of the *OnInitialUpdate( )* function to the
CProg3_3cView class. The AppWizard adds this empty function to
CProg3vw.cpp if you base your view class on *CScrollView* as a hint that you
probably want to add something here. If you manually replaced *CView* with
CScrollView, you must add the *OnInitialUpdate( )* function with ClassWizard.

OnInitialUpdate( ) begins life as a virtual function of the class *CView( )*. A
related function, *CView::OnUpdate( )*, is called by MFC whenever the document changes. This function enables the view to update itself based on
changes to the document.

The *OnInitialUpdate( )* function is called immediately after the view has been
attached to the document or whenever *CDocument::OnNewDocument( )* is
called to create a new document. In effect, *OnInitialUpdate( )* is called in place
of the first *OnUpdate( )* call.

A programmer normally overloads *OnInitialUpdate( )* to calculate some static
value the view needs based on the document. If the size of the document is

fixed, for example, this would be a good place to retrieve and save that information. In this case, the size of the logical drawing area is a good value to save.

CScrollView doesn't know how big the document is until you tell it. You do this by calling *SetScrollSize( )* and passing the width and height of the logical window. As long as the physical window is as large as (or larger than) the logical window, no scroll bars appear — there's no need for them because the entire logical window is visible. As soon as a user shrinks the physical window so that it's smaller than the logical window, scroll bars appear to allow her to move around the logical window.

What would be a good value for the size of the logical window? I simply chose the initial size of the window as the logical window. The function therefore gets the size of the client area by calling *GetClientRect( )*, stores this in a *CSize* object, and passes this object to *SetScrollSizes( )*.

The second change to Prog3vw.cpp relates to the two mouse functions *OnLButtonDown( )* and *OnMouseMove( )*. The location reported to these functions is the address of the mouse measured in pixels from the upper-left corner of the client area — that is, the physical window. The document is planted firmly in the logical window, however. No problem occurred when the physical and logical window were coincident, which is always the case when scrolling is not enabled.

Problems do occur, however, when the view is allowed to move around within the logical window. As shown in Figure 13-3, the mouse location reported in the *WM_MOUSEMOVE* message and others must be adjusted by the offset of the view from the upper-left corner of the logical window. This offset is reported by the function *CScrollView::GetDeviceScrollPosition( )*.

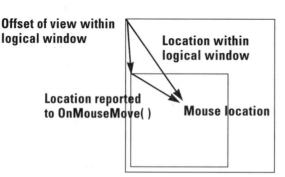

Figure 13-3:
Calculating
the location
of the
mouse in
the logical
window.

This correction is handled by the marked lines added to both the *OnLButtonDown( )* and *OnMouseMove( )* functions.

Executing the Program at Dawn

When you first execute this program, there seems to be no difference compared to the earlier versions of the application. As soon as you resize the window to make it smaller than the original window, however, scroll bars appear along the right and bottom edges.

To test this new version, read in one of your previously saved images to a small window. You should be able to scroll back and forth across your image by grabbing hold of the slider bars or clicking the scroll bar gadgets. (An example is shown in Figure 13-4.) Finally, draw the window to make sure that the lines appear where the mouse points.

Figure 13-4:
Scrolling
the view
within the
DRule.eas
document.

Conclusion

The Etch-A-Sketch program is now complete (at least for the purposes of this book). It can do the following:

- ✔ Draw
- ✔ Resize and iconify without losing any data
- ✔ Scroll when necessary
- ✔ Save drawings to disk
- ✔ Restore previously saved drawings from disk

You have only one more topic to look at in Part III; diagnostic code. Then, in Part IV, you get to work on a totally new sample program.

Chapter 14

Debugging de Code

· ·

In This Chapter

▶ Using *TRACE*

▶ Understanding MFC automatic checks and balances

▶ Enhancing *AssertValid( )* and *Dump( )*

· ·

*I*f you're like me, you're beginning to get tired of this silly drawing program. There's one final subject I want to look at, however, before moving on to a new Windows application: diagnostic code.

Diagnostic code includes checks put in a program for the sole purpose of detecting bugs that otherwise might be overlooked.

The programs in this book (and any other book you're likely to find) have been presented as though I just sat down and whipped them out the way you see them in print. (If only it were so. My programs have about as much chance of working the first time I run them as a balanced budget has of making it through Congress.)

After all the compile errors have been corrected, like an apprehensive father watching his kid take off on his first bicycle ride, I invariably set my program off to execute — and my program usually gets just about as far as that kid on his first ride before ending up in a ditch. I'm continually amazed at the myriad ways my programs find to screw up.

The problem is not with the program, of course — it's with me. Humans (even programmers) are fallible. We recognize this in almost every other human activity: We wear seat belts when we drive, we execute spell-checkers on our letters, and we double-check our arithmetic before sending in our 1040 forms (I have, ever since that unfortunate incident back in 1981).

We admit imperfection in every other aspect of the human existence except for programming.

Our lives would be much simpler if we would just admit that we probably will make a mistake or two (or ten) in a program when we first write it. Including diagnostic code in your program when you first write it is similar to putting training wheels on your kid's bike for his first few rides: After the program has proven itself capable of running without ending up in a ditch, you can think about removing the diagnostic training wheels. For those first few rides, however, "don't leave home without it."

Fortunately, MFC provides a suite of powerful diagnostic functions designed to detect some of the most common and difficult-to-find errors. This chapter examines a few of these functions.

Operator, "TRACE This Call and Tell Me Where I Am!"

The simplest of the MFC diagnostic functions is *TRACE( )*. It isn't exactly a diagnostic function in the normal sense of the word. *TRACE( )* doesn't check anything — it just enables you to display information at runtime so that you can see what's happening at certain key moments in your program's execution.

When *TRACE( )* calls are compiled in WinDebug mode, *TRACE( )* sends its output to the Output window of the debugger. When *TRACE( )* calls are compiled in Release mode, they have no effect. The syntax of *TRACE( )* is the same as that of *printf( )*.

TRACE( ) looks and acts much like *Debug.Print( )*. ■

WinWhat mode?

Remember that Visual C++ generates WinApps in one of two modes: WinDebug mode and Release mode. In WinDebug mode, Visual C++ does the following:

- ✔ *Defines the preprocessor symbol _DEBUG.* Your code then can check the _DEBUG flag to determine whether it's being compiled in WinDebug mode. You'll see an example in action later in this chapter.

- ✔ *Links with the WinDebug MFC libraries.* These versions of the MFC libraries were compiled and built with the _DEBUG flag defined, which means that these functions include a considerable amount of diagnostic code.

- ✔ *Disables compiler optimizations so that the debugger doesn't get confused.*

> ✔ *Includes symbol information in the .EXE executable file.* This capability makes the executable file much larger, but the debugger needs this information in order to set breakpoints and examine variables.

Having two modes enables you to "remove the training wheels" by just rebuilding your program in Release mode. The checks are still in the source code — they just don't have any effect anymore. If a problem occurs, slapping the training wheels back on is just a matter of rebuilding the program.

Applying a TRACE

Interestingly, if you've executed the programs in this book, you've probably already seen *TRACE( )* at work. For example, execute Prog3_3c under the debugger and draw something. Then choose New from the File menu. When the program asks you whether you want to save your drawing, click the No button. The following message appears in the debug output window:

```
Warning: OnNewDocument replaces an unsaved document.
```

This message was generated by a call to *TRACE( )* from within the MFC library. This is just the type of output for which *TRACE( )* is most useful: to alert you, the programmer, that certain conditions have occurred.

Use the following example to add *TRACE( )* calls to your application:

```
void MyFun()
{
    static int nCnt = 0;
    TRACE("Entering MyFun() for the %dth time", ++nCnt);
    // ...remainder of the function like normal...
}
```

Notice that the format controls, such as *%d*, are the same as those used with *printf( )*.

TRACE( ) calls can be placed anywhere you want within your program; be careful, however . Don't place them in sections of code that are likely to be called frequently. For example, the *for* loop within the *OnDraw( )* function might not be the best choice.

Interestingly enough, *TRACE( )* calls don't slow the program much. The output is buffered to the debugger window. Your program continues without waiting for the *TRACE( )* information to be displayed. If *TRACE( )* is called frequently, however, the amount of output can become staggering.

The first time you try to use *TRACE( )*, it might not produce any output. Not to worry: Output to the debugger output window can be disabled by way of the MfcTracer utility. This program enables users to enable or disable various types of debugger output. To enable *TRACE( )* output, execute the MfcTracer utility and choose Enable Tracing before your program begins execution. ■

This particular example function shows a common technique for counting the number of times a function has been called. Static variables are initialized only the first time they are declared and retain their value thereafter. Thus, *nCnt* begins life with the value 0, but is quickly incremented to 1 before being printed. Because static variables retain their value, the next time the function is called, *nCnt* has the value 1 and is incremented to 2. This process repeats itself each time the function is called so that *nCnt* contains a count of the number of times *MyFun( )* has been invoked. ■

The Diagnostic Framework

MFC has other diagnostic functions in addition to *TRACE*. AppWizard automatically includes several of them in the application framework it creates for you.

Until now, I've removed the diagnostic sections from the listings shown in this book because they tend to clutter up the listings and because they weren't relevant until now. ■

Consider, for example, the default diagnostic framework for the document class: the diagnostic framework for the other classes are similar (remember that the nondiagnostic sections have been removed from the code):

```
// Pattdoc.cpp : implementation of the CPatternDoc class
//

#include "stdafx.h"
#include "Pattern.h"

#include "Pattdoc.h"

#ifdef _DEBUG
#undef THIS_FILE
static char BASED_CODE THIS_FILE[] = __FILE__;
#endif

/////////////////////////////////////////////////////////
// CPatternDoc
```

```
// ...the message map, construction/destruction, and
// serialization sections appear here as always...
```

```
/////////////////////////////////////////////////////////
// CPatternDoc diagnostics

#ifdef _DEBUG
void CPatternDoc::AssertValid() const
{
      CDocument::AssertValid();
}

void CPatternDoc::Dump(CDumpContext& dc) const
{
      CDocument::Dump(dc);
}
#endif //_DEBUG
```

After a breakfast of the normal *include* files, Pattdoc.cpp contains the following code:

```
#ifdef _DEBUG
#undef THIS_FILE
static char BASED_CODE THIS_FILE[] = __FILE__;
#endif
```

C statements that begin with a # in column 1 are directives to the preprocessor. This preprocessor is executed before the compiler at compile-time. The *#if expression* says that if *expression* evaluates to 0, all the statements up to the corresponding *#endif* should be ignored. Similarly, *#ifdef label* ignores all statements if *label* is not defined.

This decision isn't made at runtime, like a normal *if* statement is, but rather at compile-time. ∎

Remember that *_DEBUG* is defined automatically by Visual C++ when the program is compiled in WinDebug mode. In Release mode, therefore, the compiler ignores these statements as though they weren't even there.

Visual C++ defines *_DEBUG* by including the statement *-D_DEBUG* on the command line when you choose WinDebug mode. You can define your own symbols in the same way (for example, *-DMYSYM*), or you can include the statement *#define MYSYM* within the source code. ∎

The next statement, *#undef THIS_FILE*, undefines the symbol *THIS_FILE* just in case it has already been *#define*d somewhere.

The declaration defines *THIS_FILE* to be a character string containing the name of the current source file (in this case, "Pattdoc.cpp").

You might ask, "Where did that come from? All I see is _ _FILE_ _." C and C++ automatically define a few preprocessor labels, including two symbols of particular interest in writing diagnostic code: _ _FILE_ _ is defined as the name of the current source file, and _ _LINE_ _ contains the current line number. ■

If you continue a little farther, you see the source listing's two member functions, *AssertValid( )* and *Dump( )*. Both member functions are included in the default framework but do nothing more than invoke the corresponding function from the parent class.

AssertValid( ): Calling the role in class

AssertValid( ) is a virtual member function which checks to see that the object passed to it is a valid "whatever" object — in this case, a valid *CPatternDoc* object — by checking each member in the class. Because the framework has no idea what you might add to your *CPatternDoc* class, about all it can do is allow the *CDocument* portion to check itself.

For example, a programmer might do something like the following (this is not the best way to invoke *AssertValid( )*, as you'll see in just a moment):

```
void MyFun(CPatternDoc &doc)
{
    // Check to make sure that doc is valid
    doc.AssertValid();  // Don't do this

    // From here on out, you know that pDoc points
    // to a valid CPatternDoc object
```

The function accepts as its argument a *CPatternDoc* object; rather than just accept any ole object, however, the function checks first that the object passed has been accredited by the *CPatternDoc* board of good health.

There are two problems with accessing *AssertValid( )* directly. One problem is that the *AssertValid( )* function exists only if _DEBUG is defined. This problem can be solved easily by enclosing all calls as follows:

```
void MyFun(CPatternDoc *pDoc)
{
    // Check to make sure that doc is valid
#ifdef _DEBUG
    pDoc->AssertValid();  // Don't do this
#endif
```

Defensive programming, or don't trust yourself

I prefer to call the use of *AssertValid( )* functions "defensive programming." With this technique, you shouldn't trust the other guy, even if the other guy is you. Even though the function may say that it takes a pointer to a particular type of object, don't believe it. Programmers have the best intentions, but slap those seat belts on anyway (programmers don't make good drivers either).

"But that's what strong typing is for!" I can hear you say. Not so. Strong typing catches the following problem:

```
void AFun(UrObject *puObject);
void Sample(MyObject *pmObject)
{
    AFun(puObject);  // types
                     // don't match
```

The function *AFun( )* is declared to take a pointer to a *UrObject*, but you are trying to pass it the address of *MyObject*. Assuming that one doesn't inherit from the other, this can't possibly be correct and, because of strong typing, the compiler knows it.

The problem here is different, however. Consider the following, admittedly simplistic, code snippet:

```
void Sample()
{
    UrObject *puObject;
    AFun(puObject);
```

This example calls *AFun( )* and passes it an address of type *UrObject**, but the pointer is completely bogus—it doesn't point to anything. This problem is often a difficult one to find. It may just so happen that *puObject* points to real memory somewhere. If *AFun( )* reads from that location, it surely will get garbage. It's when *AFun( )* begins writing to the location that things get interesting. These types of writes may not even be fatal—for a while. They can turn into a ticking time bomb that causes the program to blow up somewhere else in the code.

Without special diagnostic code, problems like this one are about as easy to find as a duck in winter.

Strong type-checking doesn't catch this type of problem—*AssertValid( )* does.

A more serious problem stems from the fact that *AssertValid( )* is a virtual member function of *CPatternDoc*. For reasons you don't want me to get into, invoking a virtual member function with an invalid pointer is always fatal. Stated another way, if *pDoc* doesn't actually point to a *CPatternDoc* of some type, the call to *AssertValid( )* jumps off the end of the world.

Fortunately, this problem has also been addressed. MFC provides a macro, *ASSERT_VALID( )*, with which to invoke the *AssertValid( )* member function. In use, it looks like this:

```
void MyFun(CPatternDoc *pDoc)
{
    // Check to make sure that doc is valid
    ASSERT_VALID(pDoc);
```

If _DEBUG isn't defined, ASSERT_VALID( ) converts into nothing. Poof! It just goes away. If _DEBUG is defined, ASSERT_VALID( ) invokes a function that first checks to make sure that the pointer actually points to a valid CObject of some type. If it does, this function invokes the AssertValid( ) member function to make sure that the members of the object are valid.

Dumping an object

Another of the built-in MFC diagnostic functions is Dump( ). This function is invoked by MFC when an object is found to be in error, to give the programmer as much information as possible (sometimes, almost too much information, as you'll see later). You're free to include a call to Dump( ) whenever you want, but be prepared for the output. MFC spits out just about everything it knows or ever knew about the object in question. The output from a single object can consume several dozen lines of output.

Diagnosing Yourself

To get a feel for how to use these functions, let's see the drawing classes outfitted with customized AssertValid( ) and Dump( ) member functions, first for the view class CProg3_3dView contained in CProg3vw.cpp:

```
// Prog3vw.cpp : implementation of the CProg3_3dView
//                class
//

#include "stdafx.h"
#include "Prog3_3d.h"

#include "Prog3doc.h"
#include "Prog3vw.h"

#ifdef _DEBUG
#undef THIS_FILE
static char BASED_CODE THIS_FILE[] = __FILE__;
#endif


/////////////////////////////////////////////////////////
// CProg3_3dView

IMPLEMENT_DYNCREATE(CProg3_3dView, CScrollView)

BEGIN_MESSAGE_MAP(CProg3_3dView, CScrollView)
    //{{AFX_MSG_MAP(CProg3_3dView)
```

```
        ON_WM_LBUTTONDOWN()
        ON_WM_MOUSEMOVE()
        ON_WM_RBUTTONDOWN()
        ON_WM_ERASEBKGND()
        //}}AFX_MSG_MAP
END_MESSAGE_MAP()


/////////////////////////////////////////////////////////
// CProg3_3dView construction/destruction

CProg3_3dView::CProg3_3dView()
{
    m_nPrevIndex = 0;
}


CProg3_3dView::~CProg3_3dView()
{
}


/////////////////////////////////////////////////////////
// CProg3_3dView drawing

void CProg3_3dView::OnDraw(CDC* pDC)
{
    // Loop through the mouse positions stored --
    // if there aren't any, then there's
    // nothing to do, so quit
    CProg3_3dDoc* pDoc = GetDocument();
    ASSERT_VALID(pDoc);

    // ...same as in version 3_3c...
}


void CProg3_3dView::OnInitialUpdate()
{
    // ...same as in version 3_3c...
}


/////////////////////////////////////////////////////////
// CProg3_3dView diagnostics

#ifdef _DEBUG
void CProg3_3dView::AssertValid() const
{
    // Check the CScrollView parts of
    // the object first
    CScrollView::AssertValid();
```

```
    // Check the m_nPrevIndex field --
    // there's no way it could be larger
    // than a few thousand
    ASSERT(m_nPrevIndex < (UINT)100000L);
}

void CProg3_3dView::Dump(CDumpContext& dc) const
{
    dc << "\n\nDump of CProg3_3dView follows:\n";
    CScrollView::Dump(dc);

    // Not much to output from the view
    dc << "m_nPrevIndex = " << m_nPrevIndex << "\n";
}

CProg3_3dDoc* CProg3_3dView::GetDocument() const
{
    ASSERT(m_pDocument->IsKindOf(
                    RUNTIME_CLASS(CProg3_3dDoc)));
    return (CProg3_3dDoc*)m_pDocument;
}
#endif //_DEBUG

//////////////////////////////////////////////////////
// CProg3_3dView message handlers

void CProg3_3dView::OnLButtonDown(UINT nFlags,
                                  CPoint point)
{
    CProg3_3dDoc* pDoc = GetDocument();
    ASSERT_VALID(pDoc);

    // ...from here on, the same as 3_3c...
```

The *AssertValid( )* function for *CProg3_3dView* first calls *CScrollView::AssertValid( )* to check the data members inherited from *CScrollView*. If these members pass muster, the function then begins checking its own data members. The only member that's unique to *CProg3_3dView* is *m_nPrevIndex*, the index of the last document item that was painted.

One thing you can say for sure about *m_nPrevIndex* is that it's greater than 0. There's no way that *m_nPrevIndex* could be larger than a few thousand either, but you want to be really careful about setting such arbitrary limits — you're just trying to set limits to detect errors.

The preprocessor directive _ASSERT(m_nPrevIndex < (UNIT)100000L)_ asserts that the condition within the parentheses is true (that is, that _m_nPrevIndex_ is less than 100,000). If it isn't true, the program stops with the message "Assert failed on line" followed by the filename and line number. Again, when _ASSERT( )_ is compiled in Release mode, it converts to nothing.

To check _m_nPrevIndex_ against the size of the document, you first have to get a pointer to the document. Getting this pointer is a little tricky because when the view is first created, it doesn't have a document. At this time, the document pointer, _m_pDocument_, is 0.

If you intend to place a validity check involving the document in your view's _AssertValid( )_ function, remember these points:

- When the view is first created, the document pointer is _NULL_, so you must include a check equal to 0 for _m_pDocument_.

- Don't check the document pointer to see whether it's valid, because the default validity check for _CDocument_ calls the view's _AssertValid( )_ function. To do so would generate an infinite loop. ■

The _Dump( )_ function also relies on _CScrollView::Dump( )_ to display the majority of the data members of the class. Only the _m_nPrevIndex_ must be displayed specifically in this member function.

The actual output is performed by inserting the argument to _Dump( )_ in much the same way a C++ programmer inserts output to the standard output object, _cout_. This argument is of class _CDumpContext_, which overloads the inserter to provide output for a variety of different object types.

The remainder of CProg3vw.cpp is the same as before; you might want to take another look at the calls to _ASSERT_VALID(pDoc)_, however, after each call to _GetDocument( )_. Each of these calls is to check that the document object returned from _GetDocument( )_ is valid before messing with it.

The diagnostic functions for the document class are considerably more involved because there are more data members to be checked:

```
//////////////////////////////////////////////////////
// CProg3_3dDoc diagnostics

#ifdef _DEBUG
void CProg3_3dDoc::AssertValid() const
{
    // Start by checking the base document
    CDocument::AssertValid();
```

```
      // Both lists must be valid
      ASSERT_VALID(&m_MousePositions);
      ASSERT_VALID(&m_MouseButtons);

      // There must be the same number of buttons
      // as mouse positions stored
      ASSERT(m_MousePositions.GetSize() ==
              m_MouseButtons.GetSize());

      // The locations stored within the
      // two data members cannot be "wild"
      int i;
      int nSize = GetSize();
      CPoint *pcpTest;
      int nTest;
      for (i = 0; i < nSize; i++)
      {
          pcpTest = GetMPosition(i);
          ASSERT(pcpTest->x >= 0 && pcpTest->x < 1500);
          ASSERT(pcpTest->y >= 0 && pcpTest->y < 1500);

          nTest = GetMButton(i);
          ASSERT(nTest == 0 || nTest == 1);
      }
  }
```

```
void CProg3_3dDoc::Dump(CDumpContext& dc) const
{
    CDocument::Dump(dc);
```

```
    dc << "No update = "
        << (m_bNoUpdate ? "TRUE" : "FALSE")
        << "\n";
    dc << GetSize() << " positions in list\n";
}
#endif //_DEBUG
```

The *CProg3_3dDoc* begins by calling *CDocument::AssertValid( )* to check the inherited members. This function also checks any attached views for validity. It then checks the *m_MousePositions* and *m_MouseButtons* lists via the call to *ASSERT_VALID*. Because they inherit from *CObject*, both the *CWordArray* and *CPtrArray* have an *AssertValid( )* member function of their own.

Of course, the *C...Array::AssertValid( )* functions cannot test the validity of the data. You have to do that for yourself by looping through the members of the array and checking each one individually. In this case, each of the members of *m_MouseButtons* must be either 0 or 1, and each *m_MousePositions* must be less than 1500 or so.

The *CProg3_3dDoc::Dump( )* function displays the document information in the same way as the view did.

In use, calls to *ASSERT_VALID( )* within the document class are the same as within the view class. For example, consider the slightly modified *Serialize( )* member function:

```
void CProg3_3dDoc::Serialize(CArchive& ar)
{
    // Check the document once and then disable checking
    // so that you don't end up rechecking it after
    // adding each data point
    ASSERT_VALID(this);

    if (ar.IsStoring())
    {
        Save(ar);
    }
    else
    {
        Restore(ar);
    }

    // Now check to make sure that it's still okay
    ASSERT_VALID(this);
}
```

The function first checks the document before beginning the *Save( )* or *Restore( )* operations — if the document has a problem, you don't want to overwrite the file on disk with invalid information. Just as important, however, the document is checked after the *Save( )* or *Restore( )* operation. This check primarily makes sure that the object created by the *Restore( )* operation is valid before letting it loose on the world.

Notice that in a member function the current object is pointed to by the keyword *this*. Thus, to check the current object with the *ASSERT_VALID( )* macro, the call is *ASSERT_VALID(this)*. ■

Does It Work?

You're probably wondering whether all this diagnostic stuff is really worth the trouble. I can't prove that diagnostic code is valuable, but I *can* demonstrate the type of errors it catches.

Let's begin with the case of the wild pointer — that is, a pointer that's declared properly but that doesn't point to a valid object. I added the following function, which I called from the *OnRButtonDown( )* function:

```
void TestFn(CProg3_3dDoc *pDoc)
{
    // Don't trust that your arguments are valid
    ASSERT_VALID(pDoc);
}

void CProg3_3dView::OnRButtonDown(UINT nFlags, CPoint point)
{
    // Test the ASSERT_VALID function
    CProg3_3dDoc *pD;   // Forget to initialize...
    TestFn(pD);         // ...and pass it to the function
    // ...and so on as before...
```

Execute the program from the Visual C++ environment. As soon as the right mouse button is pressed, the window in Figure 14-1 pops up.

Line 167 is the call to *ASSERT_VALID( )* within *TestFn( )*. The exact nature of the problem that is detected is displayed in the output window of the debugger:

```
ASSERT_VALID fails with illegal vtable pointer.
```

This error message may seem somewhat cryptic, but you'll eventually recognize it as a sure indication that the pointer was bogus (or, at least, that it didn't point to a valid class object).

"Okay, but that's too easy," you may say. "Try something a little more subtle, like an invalid member of an otherwise valid object."

Fair enough. To test this, I removed the code in the constructor where *m_nPrevIndex* is initialized to 0. You have to admit that forgetting to initialize a variable in the constructor is an easy thing to do. (Heck, I've been known to do it twice just on the way to the refrigerator.) In this case, the oversight is caught as soon as the program starts. You see the same message box as shown in Figure 14-1, this time indicating line 107 as the incorrect assertion (line 107 is the test for less than 100,000).

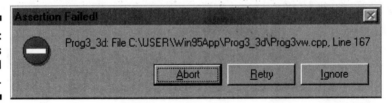

Assertion Failed!

Prog3_3d: File C:\USER\Win95App\Prog3_3d\Prog3vw.cpp, Line 167

Abort   Retry   Ignore

Dumping Out an Object

The *Dump( )* member function is used to display the contents of the object in question in a meaningful way (that is, other than a difficult-to-decipher hex dump). Calling the *Dump( )* function in response to a particular user-controlled event gives the programmer a chance to take a peek at the state of critical objects within the program. For example, I added the following to cause the view object to be displayed when the right mouse button is pressed:

```
void CProg3_3dView::OnRButtonDown(UINT nFlags,
                                  CPoint point)
{
    // Use this opportunity to dump out the view
    // object
    Dump(afxDump);

    // ...continues as before...
```

Remember that *Dump( )* displays to an object of class *CDumpContext*. A *CDump-Context* is like a device context: a device-independent description of the debug output device. The global object *afxDump* refers to the output window of the debugger.

After rebuilding the program and executing it from within the Visual C++ environment, clicking the right mouse button generates the following output:

```
Dump of CProg3_3dView follows:
a CProg3_3dView at $6E0BA0

m_hWnd = 0x550 (permanent window)
caption = ""
class name = "AfxFrameOrView"
rect = (L 91, T 129, R 685, B 517)
parent CWnd* = $6E08D4
style = $50800000
id = 0xE900
with document: a CProg3_3dDoc at $6E07FC
m_strTitle = DRule.eas
m_strPathName = C:\USER\Win95App\DRule.eas
m_bModified = 0
m_pDocTemplate = $6E0654
No update = FALSE
0x1F0 positions in list
m_totalLog = (588 x 382)
m_totalDev = (588 x 382)
m_pageDev = (58 x 38)
```

```
m_lineDev = (5 x 3)
m_bCenter = 0
m_bInsideUpdate = 0
m_nMapMode = MM_TEXT
m_nPrevIndex = 0x1EF
```

Notice that the view also dumped the attached document. The document part of the output has been highlighted.

This may be more information than you really want. But better too much than too little, I always say; there is a limit, however, to what decorum will accept. To reduce the amount of output, just don't call the base class *CScroll-View::Dump( )* function. For example, I made the following change:

```
void CProg3_3dView::Dump(CDumpContext& dc) const
{
    // Just output the view's address
    dc << "\nDump of CProg3_3dView @"
        << (void*)this
        << "\n";

    // Dump the document
    CDocument *pDoc = GetDocument();
    pDoc->Dump(dc);

    // Not much to output from the view
    dc << "m_nPrevIndex = " << m_nPrevIndex << "\n";
}
```

(Notice the absence of the call to *CScrollView::Dump( )*.) The preceding *Dump( )* function generates considerably less output:

```
Dump of CProg3_3dView @$6E0BA0
a CProg3_3dDoc at $6E07FC
m_strTitle = DRule.eas
m_strPathName = C:\USER\Win95App\DRule.eas
m_bModified = 0
m_pDocTemplate = $6E0654
No update = FALSE
0x1F0 positions in list
m_nPrevIndex = 0x1EF
```

If this is still too much information for you, you can rewrite the document's *Dump( )* member function as well.

Going Through Heaps of Memory

Like a good drink, memory leaks are hard to find. (Why hasn't some country singer been able to make a hit out of that line? Go figure.)

A memory leak occurs when the program allocates memory from the heap and then forgets to put it back. The program slowly (or not so slowly) consumes more and more memory until the system no longer can honor the requests and the program crashes (if you're lucky). ■

The thing that makes memory leaks so hard to find is that it may take hours for the faulty program to consume enough memory to cause the system to crash. Because the user can do quite a few things in an hour, it becomes very difficult to know exactly which command has the leak. This difficulty in detecting memory leaks makes memory-leak diagnostic code important.

Luckily, MFC contains considerable support for detecting memory leaks. To test this support, let's introduce a leak and see what happens.

Suppose that I had forgotten to release the list of mouse locations in the destructor. Because these mouse locations are contained in *CPoint* objects that are allocated off the heap, this would represent a form of memory leak (admittedly, a rather benign memory leak because the program is about to terminate anyway). I simulated this leak by commenting out the call to *ClearList( )* in the destructor:

```
CProg3_3dDoc::~CProg3_3dDoc()
{
    // ClearList();
}
```

I then rebuilt and executed the program from the Visual C++ environment. Everything worked normally, except that when I told the program to exit, I received the following list of error messages:

```
Detected memory leaks!
Dumping objects ->
{36} non-object block at $006E1664, 8 bytes long
{35} non-object block at $006E1634, 8 bytes long
{34} non-object block at $006E1604, 8 bytes long
{33} non-object block at $006E15D4, 8 bytes long
// ...list continues...
```

These messages indicate that a series of 8-byte objects were allocated off the heap and not released. The description "non-object" means that the blocks weren't a subclass of *CObject* (*CDocument*, *CView*, and so on are all subclasses of *CObject*, but *CPoint* is not). The hex number indicates the address of these blocks, which isn't very useful information. The number to the left indicates the order in which these blocks were allocated. In other words, the blocks shown here were the 36th, 35th, 34th, and so on to be allocated off the heap.

It would be more helpful, however, to know *where* these blocks were allocated. MFC provides a means to record this information as well: Replace all calls to *new* with calls to the MFC macro *DEBUG_NEW*. Thus, you would change *AddList( )* to allocate memory off the heap:

```
// Get the memory to hold the mouse location
// off the heap
CPoint *pNewPoint = DEBUG_NEW CPoint(point);
```

In Release mode, *DEBUG_NEW* reduces to *new*; in WinDebug mode, however, *DEBUG_NEW* passes diagnostic information to a special version of *new* that records this information for display in the event that the blocks aren't returned properly.

Now when you execute the program from Visual C++, you get the following output:

```
Detected memory leaks!
Dumping objects ->
{52} C:\USER\Win95App\Prog3_3d\Prog3doc.cpp(236) :
          non-object block at $006E1964, 8 bytes long
{51} C:\USER\Win95App\Prog3_3d\Prog3doc.cpp(236) :
          non-object block at $006E1934, 8 bytes long
{50} C:\USER\Win95App\Prog3_3d\Prog3doc.cpp(236) :
          non-object block at $006E1904, 8 bytes long
// ...and so on for 50 more blocks...
```

The message now indicates that the blocks were allocated in the file Prog3doc.cpp at line 236, which is in *AddList( )*. Clearly, the *CPoint* objects are not being returned to the heap.

What would the output be if the object were a *CObject* of some kind? To test this, I modified the *OnInitialUpdate( )* member function to allocate a dummy *CProg3_3dView*, which I conveniently forgot to delete before the program terminated. When I chose File|Exit, MFC dutifully displayed the following:

```
Detected memory leaks!
Dumping objects ->
{23} C:\USER\Win95App\Prog3_3d\Prog3vw.cpp(97) :

Dump of CProg3_3dView follows:
```

```
a CProg3_3dView at $6E0E80

m_hWnd = 0x0with no document
m_totalLog = (0 x 0)
m_totalDev = (0 x 0)
m_pageDev = (0 x 0)
m_lineDev = (0 x 0)
m_bCenter = 0
m_bInsideUpdate = 0
m_nMapMode = MM_NONE
m_nPrevIndex = 0x0

Object dump complete.
```

The first line indicates the filename and line number where the object was allocated, just as it did earlier. This time, however, because the object is a type of *CObject*, MFC uses the *Dump( )* member function to display some truly useful information about the object in question rather than just the object's address and length. (It would have been more useful if the object had actually been used for something and if the fields had been set to something other than 0.)

If you don't want to wait until the program terminates to get a view of all the objects that are allocated, you can invoke the member function *CMemory-State::DumpAllObjectsSince( )*:

```
CMemoryState msObject;
msObject.DumpAllObjectsSince();
```

This can be quite a list if you have a large number of objects outstanding. If you want to see just those objects since a certain point, you can update the *msObject*:

```
CMemoryState msObject;
//...code continues...
msObject.CheckPoint(); // update the msObject
// ...keep on truckin'...
msObject.DumpAllObjectsSince();
```

The dump is now limited to those objects allocated since the call to *Check-Point( )*. It is also possible, via the *Difference( )* member function, to look at just the difference between two previously checkpointed *CMemoryState* objects.

Conclusion

In this chapter, you've learned how to do the following:

✔ Add message handlers

✔ Separate the document from the view, like all good MFC programmers do

✔ Use MFC to quickly and easily save and restore the document to and from disk

✔ Use the *CScrollView* class to implement scrolling with practically no effort on your part

✔ Use the diagnostic code the AppWizard includes in the application framework to simplify your programming job

That's it — enough with the drawing program already. It's been nice.

Still, I'm getting a little tired of drawing lines. Let's move on to Part IV. It discusses the next WinApp, which is just full of neat toolbars, dialog boxes, buttons, and switches.

20-Minute Workout

Questions

1 The prototype for the *WM_MOUSEMOVE* message handler is as follows:

```
void CProg3_1View::OnMouseMove(UINT nFlags,
                               CPoint point)
```

The *nFlags* argument contains the state of the mouse buttons, and *point* contains the location of the mouse pointer on the screen. Where did this data come from?

2 The first attempt at a drawing program simply set a pixel at each mouse location reported by the *WM_MOUSEMOVE* messages. Why were the results completely unacceptable? (**Hint:** There are actually two reasons.)

3 The code to save the reported mouse locations in Prog3vw.cpp appears as follows:

```
void CProg3_2View::OnLButtonDown(UINT nFlags,
                                 CPoint point)
{
    // Add the current mouse position to the list
    // stored in m_MousePositions

    // Get the memory to hold the mouse location
    // off of the heap.
    CPoint *pNewPoint = new CPoint(point);

    // Now add it to the list
    m_MousePositions.Add((void*)pNewPoint);

    // Force a repaint to see the effect
    Invalidate();
}
```

Even though it complies just fine, what's wrong with the following code snippet?

```
void CProg3_2View::OnLButtonDown(UINT nFlags,
                                 CPoint point)
{
    // Add the mouse location to the list
    m_MousePositions.Add((void*)&point);
    // Force a repaint to see the effect
    Invalidate();
}
```

Explain, as succinctly as possible, the role of each of the following:

A. The document

B. The view

C. The mainframe

What is WinDebug mode? Why does the compiler include the compiler directive *-D_DEBUG* when it performs a make in WinDebug mode?

Why are MFC programmers encouraged to use the *ASSERT_VALID( )* macro to test the validity of an object pointer rather than call *AssertValid( )* directly? Notice that *ASSERT_VALID( )* eventually calls *AssertValid( )*.

Answers

All messages have the same format: message ID, *wparam*, and *lparam*. The meaning of the *wparam* and *lparam* parameters depends on the message ID. The MFC message dispatcher passes the *wparam* and *lparam* parameters in the arguments to the message-handling function and assigns them meaningful variable names in the process. Thus, *nFlags* and *point* come from the *wparam* and *lparam* parameters in the original message.

A. As the mouse moves, Windows reports mouse locations as fast as it can, but Windows doesn't guarantee that it reports every pixel location of the mouse.

B. Multiple *WM_PAINT* messages can be combined if something else is in the queue, such as another *WM_MOUSEMOVE* message. This results in some mouse locations not getting reported and painted.

The memory for the variable point is allocated off *OnLButtonDown( )*'s stack. This memory is de-allocated as soon as the function exits. This memory cannot be added to a list such as the one contained in *m_MousePositions*, which lasts longer than the variable.

A. The document stores the application's data.

B. The view enables the user to see the data.

C. The mainframe handles the window dressing, such as the scroll bar and the title bar.

WinDebug mode is used by the compiler to generate an executable file suitable for debugging. This executable contains symbol information for both the code and the data. The compiler directive *-D_DEBUG* defines the preprocessor symbol *_DEBUG*. The user can include preprocessor checks by using the *#ifdef* preprocessor directive to include diagnostic tests in *WinDebug* mode.

AssertValid( ) is a virtual function. Invoking a virtual function with an invalid object address is fatal (not to the programmer, thank goodness!). *ASSERT_VALID( )* first makes sure that the object address is valid so that at least the call to *AssertValid( )* will be successful before attempting the call.

Part IV

App2: The Personal Scheduler

The 5th Wave   By Rich Tennant

Re·al Pro·gram·mers

Real Programmers never laugh at science fiction movies regardless of how dumb they are.

In this Part...

This, the second of three applications presented in this book, is a personal-scheduler application designed to keep you from being late all the time. This application teaches you how to manipulate menus and toolbar icons and explains the ins and outs of printing and print preview. Finally, you learn how to set timers and use the idle loop to get work done in the background.

Chapter 15

Breaking the Ice:
Opening a Dialog Box

*T*he Etch-A-Sketch program handled its own input by snagging the mouse-move messages that Windows sends the application every time the mouse pointer sweeps across the program's view window.

For the simple mouse input of a drawing program, this program worked fine. If the input window got complicated, however — with lots of different types of input, such as mouse clicks, keyboard input, buttons, and check boxes — it could quickly become a real pain to interpret all the different types of input an operator can make.

Fortunately, MFC contains extensive support for that master of input, the dialog box.

The dialog box is a pop-up window with fields and buttons and stuff a user can manipulate, type, and click. When a user clicks the OK button, MFC closes the dialog box, reads the fields, and returns that data to the application program.

As a programmer, all you have to do is build the dialog box with the App-Studio resource file editor, display it, and wait for your data to rain down on you.

In the mode just described, user input is restricted to the dialog box as long as the box is visible. That is, a user can't do anything else within the program except respond to the dialog box. To be able to go off and do something else, a user first must exit from the dialog box. (This type of dialog box is called a *modal* dialog box.)

A modal dialog box may also be system modal (that's really severe). In *system modal* mode, users can't access other fields within the program, and they can't even switch to a different program until the dialog box is closed. In Windows 95, with its advanced multiprogramming support, this is too restrictive for all but the most draconian programs.

By comparison, a *modeless* dialog box enables a user to sneak around behind the box and do other things in the program while the dialog box is displayed.

MFC supports all three types of dialog boxes. Modal dialog boxes, however, are easier to program than modeless ones are. Maybe that's why (or maybe there's another reason I haven't thought of) most dialog boxes are modal. This book sticks with simple modal dialog boxes. ■

The Scheduler Application

The personal-scheduler Windows application is a simple personal scheduler. By the time you're finished, it will have the following impressive list of capabilities:

- A user can pop up a dialog box to expose an entry form for each new schedule entry. The user enters a date and time, to the nearest minute, in addition to any text to be displayed with the schedule entry. When the dialog box is closed, a new schedule entry is constructed from the information entered in the dialog box.

- The current list of schedule entries can be viewed in a main view window.

- Schedule entries can be added, edited, and deleted.

- Entries can be enabled and disabled: Enabled schedule entries appear dark in the main view, and disabled entries appear grayed out in the list.

- Entries can be printed and print-previewed.

- Whenever an enabled schedule entry "comes due," the program pops a message on the screen, with a portion of the text in it.

That may seem like a great deal to expect when your only Windows experience consists of an Etch-A-Sketch program, but take heart: It isn't so difficult if you take it one concept at a time.

Building Prog4

As always, you begin with the AppWizard to build a new WinApp, Prog4.

Notice the absence of a minor version number. This part of the book steers you toward a single, complete application using several tools, such as Class-Wizard and AppStudio, that weren't written specifically for writing books. Changing minor version numbers generates more confusion than it avoids. ■

This time, choose MDI (Multiple Document Interface) in step 1 of the App-Wizard build process. In addition, keep all the default features (such as dockable toolbars, initial status bar, printing, and 3-D buttons) enabled in step 4.

Also from within step 4, display the Advanced window and register a file type by entering the proper three-letter extension in the File Extension field. I chose the file type .skd (which is supposed to stand for "skedule"). Visual C++ responds by entering *Prog4 Files (*.skd)* in the Filter Name field. You can leave this field as is or you can change it to whatever you want; you should leave the extension *(*.skd)* at the end, however, to prompt users for the proper file extension.

In step 6, base *CProg4View* on the *CScrollView* class. Click *CProg4View* in the list of classes in the upper window. *CView* should appear as the base class in the lower-left field. Click the down arrow and choose *CScrollView* from the list.

When your project-information synopsis matches what's shown in Figure 15-1, "let it fly" to create the new application framework.

Something Old: The About Box

The first order of business is to build and code up the dialog box that will accept user input. Thankfully, you already have a ready-made example of how dialog boxes work. Every program you've built with the AppWizard has a dialog box already associated with it — the About box. Admittedly, the About box doesn't do much, but let's see what you can learn from it anyway.

How "About" an example dialog box?

The About box is displayed whenever a user chooses About from the Help menu. All it does is open a dialog box that lists the name of the program, the program's icon, and the current version number. (Try it: Build the current Prog4, execute it, and choose Menu|Help|About Prog4.)

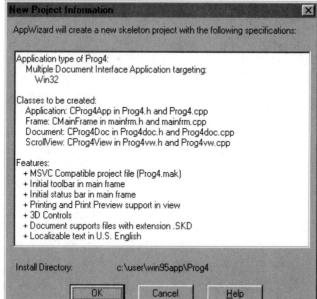

New Project Information

AppWizard will create a new skeleton project with the following specifications:

Application type of Prog4:
    Multiple Document Interface Application targeting:
       Win32

Classes to be created:
    Application: CProg4App in Prog4.h and Prog4.cpp
    Frame: CMainFrame in mainfrm.h and mainfrm.cpp
    Document: CProg4Doc in Prog4doc.h and Prog4doc.cpp
    ScrollView: CProg4View in Prog4vw.h and Prog4vw.cpp

Features:
    + MSVC Compatible project file (Prog4.mak)
    + Initial toolbar in main frame
    + Initial status bar in main frame
    + Printing and Print Preview support in view
    + 3D Controls
    + Document supports files with extension .SKD
    + Localizable text in U.S. English

Install Directory: c:\user\win95app\Prog4

[OK]   [Cancel]   [Help]

Figure 15-1:
The New
Project
Information
window for
the new
WinApp,
Prog4.

The code to open the About dialog box appears in the application's source module, Prog4.cpp:

```cpp
// Prog4.cpp : Defines the class behaviors for the
//             application.
//

#include "stdafx.h"
#include "Prog4.h"

#include "mainfrm.h"
#include "Prog4doc.h"
#include "Prog4vw.h"

#ifdef _DEBUG
#undef THIS_FILE
static char BASED_CODE THIS_FILE[] = __FILE__;
#endif

/////////////////////////////////////////////////////////
// CProg4App

BEGIN_MESSAGE_MAP(CProg4App, CWinApp)
    //{{AFX_MSG_MAP(CProg4App)
```

```
    ON_COMMAND(ID_APP_ABOUT, OnAppAbout)
    // NOTE: The ClassWizard will add and remove
    //       mapping macros here.
    //    DO NOT EDIT what you see in these blocks
    //    of generated code!
    //}}AFX_MSG_MAP
    // Standard file-based document commands
    ON_COMMAND(ID_FILE_NEW, CWinApp::OnFileNew)
    ON_COMMAND(ID_FILE_OPEN, CWinApp::OnFileOpen)
    // Standard print setup command
    ON_COMMAND(ID_FILE_PRINT_SETUP,
                    CWinApp::OnFilePrintSetup)
END_MESSAGE_MAP()

/////////////////////////////////////////////////////
// CProg4App
//
//    ...the application code like normal...

/////////////////////////////////////////////////////
// CAboutDlg dialog used for App About

class CAboutDlg : public CDialog
{
public:
    CAboutDlg();

// Dialog Data
    //{{AFX_DATA(CAboutDlg)
    enum { IDD = IDD_ABOUTBOX };
    //}}AFX_DATA

// Implementation
protected:
        virtual void DoDataExchange(CDataExchange* pDX);
    //{{AFX_MSG(CAboutDlg)
    // No message handlers
    //}}AFX_MSG
    DECLARE_MESSAGE_MAP()
};

CAboutDlg::CAboutDlg() : CDialog(CAboutDlg::IDD)
{
    //{{AFX_DATA_INIT(CAboutDlg)
    //}}AFX_DATA_INIT
}
```

```
void CAboutDlg::DoDataExchange(CDataExchange* pDX)
{
    CDialog::DoDataExchange(pDX);
    //{{AFX_DATA_MAP(CAboutDlg)
    //}}AFX_DATA_MAP
}

BEGIN_MESSAGE_MAP(CAboutDlg, CDialog)
    //{{AFX_MSG_MAP(CAboutDlg)
    // No message handlers
    //}}AFX_MSG_MAP
END_MESSAGE_MAP()
```

```
// App command to run the dialog
void CProg4App::OnAppAbout()
{
    CAboutDlg aboutDlg;
    aboutDlg.DoModal();
}
```

First notice the message map for the *CProg4App* class. Until now, all your message handlers have been of the *ON_WM_MOUSEMOVE( )* variety. The *ON_COMMAND( )* macro establishes a handler for a menu command message. The first argument to the *ON_COMMAND( )* macro is the ID of the command message, and the second is the address of the member function that will handle that command message. Thus, *ON_COMMAND(ID_APP_ABOUT, OnAppAbout)* assigns the *ID_APP_ABOUT* message to function *OnAppAbout( )*.

All menu items generate the same *WM_COMMAND* message. The menu item ID contained in the *WPARAM* entry of the message is the one which identifies the menu item that generated the request. The AppStudio assigns each menu item a unique ID as it is created. For example, the About menu item is assigned the identifier *ID_APP_ABOUT*.

These IDs are defined for your code in the *include* file resource.h. You should never edit this file directly. Instead, as you edit the menu, AppStudio updates resource.h. ■

The AppWizard creates the class *CAboutDlg* to describe the About dialog box. This class inherits almost all its functionality from *CDialog* — the application does almost nothing on its own (sounds like my kind of programming!).

To open the dialog box, *OnAppAbout( )* creates an object of class *CAboutDlg*. It then calls *DoModal( )* with that object. *DoModal( )* displays the dialog box associated with the *CDialog* object passed to it. *DoModal( )* doesn't return until the user has closed the dialog box. *DoModal( )* returns a *TRUE* if the user closes the box by clicking OK and a *FALSE* if the user chooses Cancel.

Editing the About box

Before you build a dialog box of your own, try playing with the one you have. Use the AppStudio to edit the resource file, Prog4.rc.

The easiest way to do this is just to double-click the .rc file in the project list that appears in the .mak file. ▪

Double-click the folder marked Dialog to display the existing dialog boxes. There should be only one: *IDD_ABOUTBOX*. Double-click the *IDD_ABOUTBOX* label to edit it. A window that resembles Figure 15-2 should appear.

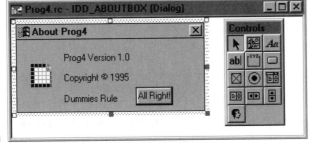

Figure 15-2:
Editing the
About
dialog box.

To edit any of the existing objects, double-click the object and edit the properties window that appears. Double-click the box to edit the properties of the dialog box itself.

To add an extra string, click the Static Text box on the tool menu (it's normally in the first row, but be careful — it looks much like the EditBox tool). Position the pointer where you want the text, and then click and drag to the width and height you want.

Don't worry if you get it wrong: You can move and resize the field all you want.

When the dialog box looks the way you want, close the dialog editor window and rebuild the program. Notice that only the resource compiler and linker are executed, because the code hasn't changed. Execute the program and choose About to see your new and improved dialog box.

Something New: Building a New Dialog Box

Okay, you're ready for the big leagues. You'll build a data-entry dialog box that looks like the one in Figure 15-3. In this section, I've provided help for each of the different field types (use Figure 15-3 as a guide).

First create a new dialog box. You can do this from the Resource menu, but the quickest way is to point your mouse at the Dialog folder and click the right mouse button. Choose New, and then choose Dialog (the default) as the resource type.

Change the title of the dialog box to New/Edit Schedule Entry, by double-clicking the title to get the Dialog Properties window and changing the Caption field.

While the property window for the dialog box is displayed, change the box's ID from the meaningless *IDD_DIALOG1* to *IDD_DIALOG_NSE* (NSE stands for *n*ew *s*chedule *e*ntry).

1a Pointer	**2a Text**	**3a Check box**	**4a List**
1b Bitmap	**2b Group**	**3b Radio button**	**4b Horizontal scroll bar**
1c Static text	**2c Pushbutton**	**3c Combo box**	**4c Vertical scroll bar**
			5a User-defined

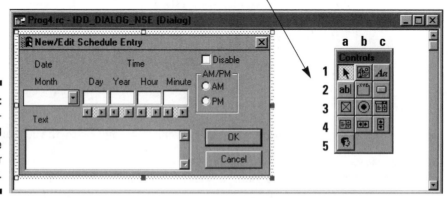

Figure 15-3:
The data-entry dialog box for the Scheduler program.

Enter the static text field labeled Date (click the Static Text control, the upper-right control in the control box). Create room for the control: Place the cross hair in one corner, and then click and drag it to the opposite corner of the area to contain the static text "Date." Having made room, change the text by double-clicking the field and editing the caption to read "Date." Resize the field so that the box provides just enough room for its contents, and position it roughly where it needs to go; you have to adjust the position as the dialog box grows.

Repeat this process, in any order, for the Time, Month, Day, Year, Hour, Minute, and Text labels.

Add a combo box underneath the Month label. You use this box to choose the names of the months from a drop-down list. Click the ComboBox icon, and create a field with enough room to hold the month with the longest name. After the box has been sized and positioned, double-click the box to see the ComboBox Properties window. Change the ID to *IDC_COMBO_MONTH*. (The new names are not only more meaningful, but assigning the same names also ensures that your code matches what's in this book.)

Set the style of the combo box to Drop List, and enter the names of the months in the List of Choices field.

Separate the names of the months by pressing Ctrl+Enter. Pressing Enter closes the ComboBox Properties window. Notice that you must deselect the Sort option in the Style section of the ComboBox Properties window unless you want the months to appear in alphabetical rather than in calendar order (ick!). ■

Finally, set the *TabStop* general property. This setting causes the cursor to start out in this field and to be included in the tab group. Every time a user presses the Tab key, the cursor moves to the next field with the *TabStop* property set in the order in which the fields were created. After the cursor gets to the last field in the dialog box, pressing Tab one more time brings the tab around to the first field again.

Now add an edit box underneath each remaining time label, moving from left to right. Use the same procedure as you did for creating a static text field. All the boxes should be as close as possible to the same size, and they all should be large enough to accommodate a two-digit number. Make sure that the *TabStop* property is set for these fields as well.

It's important that you create these fields in order from left to right. The reason is that, when you press Tab to move from one field to the next, the succession order is the same as the order in which the fields were created and has nothing to do with the physical layout of the fields.

For each edit box, open the EditBox Properties window by double-clicking the box and changing the ID. Name the boxes *IDC_EDIT_DAY*, *IDC_EDIT_YEAR*, *IDC_EDIT_HOUR*, and *IDC_EDIT_MINUTE*.

To align the edit boxes, select each one (click the first one, and Shift+click the rest), click the group with the right mouse button, and choose Align Top Edges or use Align Top from the toolbar at the bottom of AppStudio. ▪

Make the final edit box, the text EditBox, considerably larger than the others. In addition, mark this edit box as Multiline and choose *VertScroll* to give it vertical scroll bars (these properties are in the Style section of the Edit Properties window). Name this box *IDC_EDIT_TEXT*.

Now would be a good time to test what you have: Click the icon that looks like a wall switch in the lower-left corner. The dialog box should now appear functional. Choose OK to stop the simulation.

If you have any clipping (if any of the fields seems to be cut off), it may be that the field next to it is too large. It is particularly easy to overlook static fields. Selecting the field reveals its dimensions. To shrink the field, grab one of the dots around the edges of the field box with your mouse, and drag it so that the box is just large enough to hold the static text. ▪

Underneath the Day, Year, Hour, and Minute edit fields, place horizontal scroll bars sized to the same width as the edit fields. Name these fields *IDC_SCROLLBAR_DAY*, *IDC_SCROLLBAR_YEAR*, *IDC_SCROLLBAR_HOUR* and *IDC_SCROLLBAR_MINUTE*. (I'll let you figure out which name goes with which field).

Next, create the AM and PM radio buttons. First choose the GroupBox tool and construct a box to contain the buttons. Give the group box the caption "AM/PM," and set the ID to *IDC_AMPM*. (It isn't absolutely necessary to put the radio buttons in a box, but I think that it looks better that way.)

Choose the RadioButton tool and click it where you want the AM radio button to go within the box. In this radio button, set the *Group* property and change the caption to "AM." Set the ID to *IDC_RADIO1*. Then place the PM radio button underneath it. Do not set the *Group* property for this button. Set the caption to "PM" and the ID to *IDC_RADIO2*.

You can set the ID of these two fields if you want. This isn't necessary, however, because these fields are considered to be members of a list, in the same way that the days of the month are members of the list associated with the combo box.

Also note that the Group property tells MFC that the flagged radio button is the first in a group of radio buttons. The group ends either when the list of objects in the dialog box is exhausted or when another object with the group flag is encountered. When any one of the radio buttons in a group is selected, MFC automatically deselects the other radio buttons in the group. ■

Finally, add a check box in the same way as you would add an edit box. Set its caption to "Disable," and name it *IDC_CHECK_DISABLE*. Set the *Group* property in this object to tell MFC that this object is not to be included in the group of radio buttons that precede it.

Building a dialog interface class

The next step is to build a class to represent the new dialog box to your program; the class *CAboutDlg* plays this role for the About dialog box. To create a dialog class, use the ClassWizard (you can do it by hand if you're really masochistic).

Don't create the dialog class until the dialog box looks like what you want. After you've created a class, it can be tricky to change the dialog box and keep the class in synch. ■

With the Dialog edit window still displayed, enter the ClassWizard. The Class-Wizard senses that you must want to add a class to describe that dialog box, so it immediately enters the *Add Class* mode and fills in as much as it can. Fill in the class name *CProg4Dialog* and click *Create Class*.

The name *CProg4Dialog* was chosen more as a way to be consistent with the AppWizard-generated class names than to be descriptive. In addition, when you use this class name, the ClassWizard-generated filenames CProg4Dia.cpp and CProg4Dia.h are similarly consistent with the other filenames. (Besides, it just seemed like a neat thing to do at the time.) ■

Take a minute to examine the class that the ClassWizard so graciously created for you. If you aren't already in the ClassWizard, enter it and choose the *CProg4Dialog* class to produce a screen like the one shown in Figure 15-4.

Underneath the class name, you see a list of the object IDs that appear in the dialog box.

Open CProg4Dia.h to see how the class is defined in C++. You might be surprised to find out that the class has no data members because you have yet to define these members. The dialog box you built in the AppStudio is the Windows 95 window and not the *CDialog* object. You still have to add the data members to the class.

You can add the data members either from the AppWizard directly or from the Dialog edit window in AppStudio (the results are the same). Try it from the Dialog edit window. To edit the *IDC_EDIT_DAY* EditBox, for example, hold

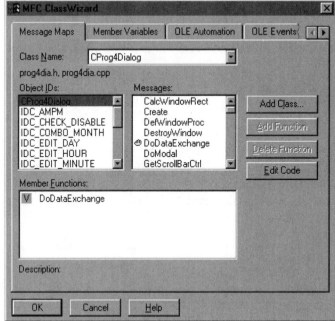

Figure 15-4:
The Class-
Wizard
creates the
CProg4-
Dialog class
to describe
the dialog
box.

down the Ctrl key and double-click the Day field from within the resource editor. The ClassWizard opens an Add Member Variable window.

The variable type for an edit box defaults to *CString*; the day of the month is expressed more conveniently, however, as an unsigned integer. Choose *UINT* from the drop-down list. Enter the name *m_nDay* for this data member. After it's edited, the screen should look like the one shown in Figure 15-5.

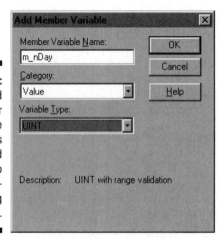

Figure 15-5:
The Add
Member
Variable
window is
used to add
members to
the CProg4-
Dialog
class.

Repeat this process for each of the fields except for the group-box scroll bars, static text, OK button, Cancel button, and PM radio button. (I don't want to stifle your creativity, but it's much easier to follow the rest of this part of the book if you use the same names I've used, as shown in Figure 15-6.)

After you've finished this process, return to the ClassWizard, and choose the *CProg4Dialog* class and the Member Variables sheet.

Your screen should look something like the one shown in Figure 15-6.

If you look back at the definition of the *CProg4Dialog* class in CProg4dia.h, you notice that the ClassWizard has added these data members to the class.

In the ClassWizard Member Variable window, you not only can see the name and type of each variable but also, after clicking a variable, you can adjust the legal range for the integer types.

Set the following ranges:

IDC_EDIT_DAY	1–31
IDC_EDIT_HOUR	1–12
IDC_EDIT_MINUTE	0–59
IDC_EDIT_YEAR	1990–2020

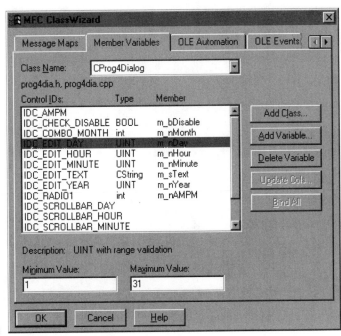

Figure 15-6:
The member variables of the CProg4-Dialog class look like this after all of them have been defined.

Setting the range of days from 1 to 31 is not completely valid because some months have fewer days, but it's not a bad idea. In addition, allowing dates earlier than the current year is pointless, and the upper range of 2020 was selected somewhat arbitrarily.

Displaying and reading the dialog box

Now that you have a dialog box, you need a way for users to display it. For now, just let them double-click in the view window. To do that, just grab the left button's double-click message. Choose the *CProg4View* class in the Class-Wizard, and add a handler for the *WM_LBUTTONDBLCLK* message. Edit it to appear as follows:

```
// Prog4vw.cpp : implementation of the CProg4View class
//

#include "stdafx.h"
#include "Prog4.h"

#include "Prog4ent.h"
#include "Prog4doc.h"
#include "Prog4vw.h"

// include the dialog definitions
#include "Prog4dia.h"

// ...the rest is the same until you get to here...
//////////////////////////////////////////////////////////
// CProg4View message handlers

void CProg4View::OnLButtonDblClk(UINT nFlags,
                                 CPoint point)
{
    // Create the dialog object...
    CProg4Dialog dlgObject;

    // ...now display it
    dlgObject.DoModal();

    // Dump the data just to see whether it worked
    TRACE("Month = %d, day = %d, year = %d\n",
          dlgObject.m_nMonth,
          dlgObject.m_nDay,
          dlgObject.m_nYear);
    TRACE("Hour = %d, Minute = %d, Disabled = %d\n",
          dlgObject.m_nHour,
```

```
            dlgObject.m_nMinute,
            dlgObject.m_bDisable);
    TRACE("AM/PM = %d\n",
            dlgObject.m_nAMPM);
}
```

The function creates a *CProg4Dialog* object and then invokes *DoModal( )* on it. The *DoModal( )* call does the following:

✔ Loads the value of each member variable from the *dlgObject* into the dialog box

✔ Displays the dialog box

✔ Processes a user's input

✔ Removes the window when a user clicks the OK or Cancel buttons

✔ Updates *dlgObject* with the values from the dialog box if a user clicked OK

The return from *DoModal( )* is zero if the command failed, *IDOK* if the user exits from the dialog box by clicking OK, and *IDCANCEL* if the user exits by clicking the Cancel button or pressing Esc from the keyboard.

That's quite a bit (or is it byte?) for one function to do, and it makes your job amazingly simple. In fact, the entire dialog-box open and read code consists of just the one declaration and the *DoModal( )* call. The calls to *TRACE* are just there to display the results during debugging.

Build and execute the program by using the Visual C++ debugger (choose Menu|Debug|Go or click the Go button on the toolbar).

Double-click in the otherwise empty view to display the dialog box. The dialog box looks just like it did from within the AppStudio editor (it had better!).

The dialog box starts out with zeroes in the edit boxes. You cannot exit from the dialog box with an OK until you have replaced those vile zeroes with valid numbers in the Day and Year EditBoxes. (Why? Because MFC doesn't let you exit until the data entered is within the range specified in the Class-Wizard — zero is not a legal day or year.)

Notice, however, that you can click Cancel to get out of the dialog box regardless of whether the values in the edit boxes are valid. The reason is that no data transfer — and, therefore, no data validation — takes place when you cancel out of a dialog box.

As the program exits from the dialog box, the values that are entered are displayed in the Output window of the debugger. If a user chooses the month of

January, notice that the dialog box returns a 0. Similarly, a 1 is returned for February, a 2 for March, and so on. The dialog box returns –1 if no month is selected.

Something Borrowed: M(u)DI Waters

This WinApp is the first one you've written that makes use of the *Multiple Document Interface,* or *MDI.* Until now, you've used what Microsoft calls *Single Document Interface,* or *SDI.* In SDI mode, the application can have only a single document open, and that document can have only one view at a time.

In MDI mode, the application can open multiple documents simultaneously, and each document can have multiple view windows open. You'll notice this when you execute the program. A Window I New Window menu command enables you to open a new view of an existing document. In addition, opening a new document doesn't force the preceding document to be closed, as it does in an SDI environment.

Opening a new view causes that view to share the same document with other views. The document isn't closed until the last view attached to that document is closed.

Each MDI view is assigned its own child frame. It is also clipped to fit within the confines of a mother window: the mainframe. In an SDI application, there is no child frame — the view's frame is the mainframe.

 The designers of Windows 95 discourage the use of MDI because studies have shown that the clipping of inferior windows to fit within the parent window is not obvious to inexperienced users. They suggest instead that child windows be independent in the sense that users should be able to place them anywhere they want on the desktop. Note however, that MFC does not yet support independent, children windows. ■

Something Blue (Just Joking): Conclusion

Great. You've already opened a dialog box and transferred data in both directions. But you still don't have much of a feel for how this data transfer took place. In addition, the scroll bars don't do anything, and the program starts out with an illegal and patently ridiculous time displayed. In short, the data transfer still needs some work, so Chapter 16 looks into that subject.

Chapter 16

Dialog Box Dialogue

● ●

In This Chapter

▶ Interfacing with a dialog box

▶ Initializing the dialog-box information

▶ Reading lists and buttons

▶ Handling dialog-box scroll bars

▶ Custom data exchange and validation

● ●

*I*n Chapter 15, you managed to get the dialog box for your new personal-scheduler application built and displayed. You even took it out on the screen for a trial run. You're far from finished with your dialog box, however. You saw the data get transferred from the dialog box into your program, but you probably have only a vague idea (you're probably clueless) about how that occurred. In addition, you'll probably notice that the scroll bars don't do anything. And finally, the limit checks allow certain illegal dates (such as my personal favorite, February 30). These concerns must be addressed before you can move on.

Object Futures on the DataExchange

The information necessary to display the dialog box was placed in the resource file by the AppStudio. This information was read by MFC as a result of the *DoModal( )* call to display the dialog box just as you drew it. Okay, but how did the data get from the dialog box back into your *CProg4Dialog* object?

The critical piece of code is in CProg4Dia.cpp:

```
void CProg4Dialog::DoDataExchange(CDataExchange* pDX)
{
    // First read the dialog box
    CDialog::DoDataExchange(pDX);
```

```
// Now transfer and validate the results

//{{AFX_DATA_MAP(CProg4Dialog)
DDX_Radio(pDX, IDC_RADIO1, m_nAMPM);
DDX_Check(pDX, IDC_CHECK_DISABLE, m_bDisable);
DDX_CBIndex(pDX, IDC_COMBO_MONTH, m_nMonth);
DDX_Text(pDX, IDC_EDIT_DAY, m_nDay);
DDV_MinMaxUInt(pDX, m_nDay, 1, 31);
DDX_Text(pDX, IDC_EDIT_HOUR, m_nHour);
DDV_MinMaxUInt(pDX, m_nHour, 1, 12);
DDX_Text(pDX, IDC_EDIT_MINUTE, m_nMinute);
DDV_MinMaxUInt(pDX, m_nMinute, 0, 59);
DDX_Text(pDX, IDC_EDIT_TEXT, m_sText);
DDX_Text(pDX, IDC_EDIT_YEAR, m_nYear);
DDV_MinMaxUInt(pDX, m_nYear, 1990, 2020);
//}}AFX_DATA_MAP
}
```

The virtual function *DoDataExchange( )* is called when a user clicks the OK button to close the dialog box (it's also called when the dialog box opens, as you'll see later). It is the job of *DoDataExchange( )* to read the information from the dialog box and transfer it into the appropriate members of the *CProg4Dialog* class object.

To see how this process works, consider the last two function calls in the preceding code. The call to *DDX_Text( )* reads the *IDC_EDIT_YEAR* edit-box field from the dialog box and stores it in the *m_nYear* data member of the current *CProg4Dialog* object (the one pointed to by *this*). The call to *DDV_MinMaxUInt( )* that follows checks that the value stored in *m_nYear* is between 1990 and 2020, the legal range you specified in ClassWizard. Had you not specified a legal range in ClassWizard, the call to the *DDV_* routine would not be present. It's important to note that the *DDV_* routine must immediately follow the call to the *DDX_* routine that stores the value it checks.

All the function calls generated earlier were put there by the ClassWizard, as indicated by the funny comments in brackets beside them. As always, don't remove these comments or mess with any of the function calls within these comments, lest you confuse the ClassWizard. You're free, however, to add code both before and after the ClassWizard block. ∎

Initializing the dialog box

An interesting question comes up when you first look at the dialog box: Where did it get its initial data of all zeros? I mean, zeroes and such things aren't very interesting, and they could have come from almost anywhere. Where *did* they come from, though, and (more to the point) can you change the initial dialog box to something more reasonable, such as the current date and time?

The *DoDataExchange( )* is bidirectional: It transfers data not only from the dialog box to the user's object but also from the object to the dialog box. This section explains how it works.

After the dialog box has been created but before it is displayed, *OnInitDialog( )* calls *UpdateData(FALSE)*, which in turn calls *DoDataExchange( )*. The *FALSE* passed in the argument is stored in a data member within **pDX*, called *m_bSaveAndValidate*. This tells *DoDataExchange( )* to transfer the data from the object to the dialog box rather than the other way around.

Each of the *DDX_* calls checks the *m_bSaveAndValidate* flag to determine the direction of transfer. Even though the *DDV_* routines perform error-checking, a range error that is detected when data is being transferred to the dialog box results in only a *TRACE( )* slap-on-the-wrist warning rather than a kick-in-the-butt error message.

After *DoDataExchange( )* has worked its magic, the dialog box is displayed in its full glory, with all its initial data in place.

If a user closes the dialog box by choosing OK, *DoModal( )* calls *UpdateData (TRUE)*.

This step invokes *DoDataExchange( )* with the *m_bSaveAndValidate* member set to *TRUE*, which directs the flow of data in the other direction, from the dialog box to the *CProg4Dialog* object.

Can we cut to the chase here?

To make a long story short, all you really have to do to initialize the dialog box to the current time is store the current time into the dialog object before calling *DoModal( )*.

Initializing the object to the current time is best handled in the constructor for *CProg4Dialog*.

You could leave the *CProg4Dialog* constructor as it is, initializing the object to *NULL* values, and then store the current time in the object before the *DoModal( )* call. Leaving it as is, however, is a bad thing to do, for two reasons:

- ✔ It forces the user function to worry about such details as properly initializing the dialog box. These types of concerns should be limited to the dialog class if at all possible.

- ✔ It forces the dialog class to expose a large number of otherwise protected data members so that the user function can initialize them. ∎

The following change to the *CProg4Dialog* constructor does the trick:

```
// prog4dia.cpp : implementation file
//

#include "stdafx.h"
#include "Prog4.h"
#include "prog4dia.h"

#ifdef _DEBUG
#undef THIS_FILE
static char BASED_CODE THIS_FILE[] = __FILE__;
#endif


/////////////////////////////////////////////////////////
// CProg4Dialog dialog


CProg4Dialog::CProg4Dialog(CWnd* pParent /*=NULL*/)
        : CDialog(CProg4Dialog::IDD, pParent)
{
    // Leave the following alone because the ClassWizard
    // created it

    //{{AFX_DATA_INIT(CProg4Dialog)
    m_nAMPM = -1;
    m_bDisable = FALSE;
    m_nMonth = -1;
    m_nDay = 0;
    m_nHour = 0;
    m_nMinute = 0;
    m_sText = _T("");
    m_nYear = 0;
    //}}AFX_DATA_INIT

    // Now set the time to what it really is currently

    // Start with the current system time
    time_t ttCurrent;
    time(&ttCurrent);

    // Convert that to a CTime object...
    CTime tCurrent(ttCurrent);

    // ...and then read the members out of that object
    m_nMonth = tCurrent.GetMonth() - 1;
    m_nDay   = tCurrent.GetDay();
```

```
    m_nYear   = tCurrent.GetYear();
    m_nHour   = tCurrent.GetHour();
    m_nMinute = tCurrent.GetMinute();
}


void CProg4Dialog::DoDataExchange(CDataExchange* pDX)
{
    // Put conversion routines from class object
    // to dialog box on this side
    if (!pDX->m_bSaveAndValidate)
    {
        // Going from object to dialog box:
        // convert from 24 to 12
        if (m_nHour < 12)    // Set AM/PM flag
        {
            m_nAMPM = 0;
        }
        else
        {
            m_nAMPM = 1;
        }
        m_nHour %= 12;       // Now round off to 12
        if (m_nHour == 0)    // Convert 0s to 12
        {
            m_nHour = 12;
        }
    }

    // Now exchange data with the display
    CDialog::DoDataExchange(pDX);
    //{{AFX_DATA_MAP(CProg4Dialog)
    DDX_Radio(pDX, IDC_RADIO1, m_nAMPM);
    DDX_Check(pDX, IDC_CHECK_DISABLE, m_bDisable);
    DDX_CBIndex(pDX, IDC_COMBO_MONTH, m_nMonth);
    DDX_Text(pDX, IDC_EDIT_DAY, m_nDay);
    DDV_MinMaxUInt(pDX, m_nDay, 1, 31);
    DDX_Text(pDX, IDC_EDIT_HOUR, m_nHour);
    DDV_MinMaxUInt(pDX, m_nHour, 1, 12);
    DDX_Text(pDX, IDC_EDIT_MINUTE, m_nMinute);
    DDV_MinMaxUInt(pDX, m_nMinute, 0, 59);
    DDX_Text(pDX, IDC_EDIT_TEXT, m_sText);
    DDX_Text(pDX, IDC_EDIT_YEAR, m_nYear);
    DDV_MinMaxUInt(pDX, m_nYear, 1990, 2020);
    //}}AFX_DATA_MAP
```

```
        // Put conversion routines from dialog to
        // class object on this side
        if (pDX->m_bSaveAndValidate)
        {
            // Going from dialog box to object;
            // convert from 12 to 24
            if (m_nHour == 12)   // Convert 12s to 0s
            {
                m_nHour = 0;
            }
            if (m_nAMPM)         // Now offset for PM
            {
                m_nHour += 12;
            }
        }
}
```

```
BEGIN_MESSAGE_MAP(CProg4Dialog, CDialog)
    //{{AFX_MSG_MAP(CProg4Dialog)
    //}}AFX_MSG_MAP
END_MESSAGE_MAP()


/////////////////////////////////////////////////////////
// CProg4Dialog message handlers
//
//    Nothing here (yet)
```

The code originally put in the constructor to initialize the data members to *NULL* values has been left in order not to confuse *ClassWizard*.

The additional code first reads the current time into an object of type *time_t*. This object can hold any time between 1970 to 2038 at a one-second resolution.

For the purposes of this discussion, that's fine (one-second resolution is good enough, and I'm sure that you won't be using anything called Windows 95 in the year 2038).

The program then uses the *time_t* time to create an object of *CTime*, one of the MFC classes. The *CTime* object is then queried for the minute, hour, day, month, and year.

This time conversion has two minor problems, both of which must be addressed. One problem is that the month returned by *CTime.GetMonth( )* is relative to one (that is, January is assumed to be 1, February is assumed to be 2, and so on), but the month *ListBox* is relative to zero (January is 0, February is 1, and so on).

Simple subtraction clears up that problem.

The second problem is not as easy to solve. *CTime* uses a 24-hour clock, whereas a more user-friendly 12-hour clock has been chosen. You could convert the 24-hour time returned from *GetHour( )* into a 12-hour time here and then use 12-hour time from now on; because most time functions use the 24-hour format, however, this alternative is not the most convenient one.

Instead, let's keep the time in 24-hour format and convert it to 12-hour format only for display.

The following list explains the additions to *DoDataExchange( )* when the dialog box is being displayed:

- ✔ *DoDataExchange( )* is called with *pDX->m_bSaveAndValidate* set to *FALSE*.
- ✔ The first block of code converts the time stored in the object from 24-hour format into 12-hour format.
- ✔ The *DDX_* calls then transfer the time data from the *CProg4Dialog* object into the *CDataExchange* object for display in the dialog box.
- ✔ The second block of code is skipped.

When a user closes the dialog box by choosing OK, the following things happen:

- ✔ *DoDataExchange( )* is called with *pDX->m_bSaveAndValidate* set to *TRUE*.
- ✔ The 24- to 12-hour conversion is skipped.
- ✔ The *DDX_* functions are called to load the data, in 12-hour format, from the *CDataExchange* object into the *CProg4Dialog* object.
- ✔ The second block of code then converts the time stored in the object from 12-hour format into 24-hour format.

The resulting program displays the current date and time rather than some apocalyptic time of 0.

Reading lists and radio buttons

How is it that setting the *m_nMonth* to 0 results in a display of January? And why is it that setting *m_nAMPM* to 1 causes PM to be selected?

Reading a combo box or a radio button group returns the zero-relative index of the selected item. If the first item is selected, a 0 is returned; if the second item is selected, a 1 is returned; and so on. If no item is selected, the index returned is –1.

The same is also true in reverse: Setting the value to 0 selects the first item in the list — in this case, January for the combo box, and the AM radio button for the radio button group. Setting the value to –1 deselects everything. That's why ClassWizard initialized both *m_nMonth* and *m_nAMPM* to –1: It wanted to start the application with nothing selected.

Scroll Bars

The scroll bars in this application still don't work properly. MFC isn't much help here because you're using the scroll bars for something other than scrolling a view. In this application, you have to handle the scroll bar work yourself.

Figure 16-1 shows the structure of a horizontal scroll bar. Clicking any of the marked scroll-bar gadgets generates a *WM_HSCROLL* message both when the object is pressed and when it is released. The message indicates which scroll bar generated the message (remember that you have four) and which gadget was clicked or released. The different indications are also flagged in Figure 16-1.

To react to the scroll message, you first must add a handler for the *WM_HSCROLL* message to the *CProg4Dialog* class by using the ClassWizard.

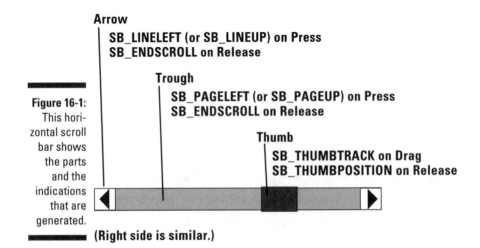

Arrow
SB_LINELEFT (or SB_LINEUP) on Press
SB_ENDSCROLL on Release

Trough
SB_PAGELEFT (or SB_PAGEUP) on Press
SB_ENDSCROLL on Release

Thumb
SB_THUMBTRACK on Drag
SB_THUMBPOSITION on Release

Figure 16-1:
This horizontal scroll bar shows the parts and the indications that are generated.

(Right side is similar.)

You then make the following changes to Prog4Dia.cpp:

```cpp
// prog4dia.cpp : implementation file
//

#include "stdafx.h"
#include "Prog4.h"
#include "prog4dia.h"

#ifdef _DEBUG
#undef THIS_FILE
static char BASED_CODE THIS_FILE[] = __FILE__;
#endif


/////////////////////////////////////////////////////
// CProg4Dialog dialog


CProg4Dialog::CProg4Dialog(CWnd* pParent /*=NULL*/)
      : CDialog(CProg4Dialog::IDD, pParent)
{
    // ...same as before...
}


void CProg4Dialog::DoDataExchange(CDataExchange* pDX)
{
    // Put conversion routines from class object
    // to dialog box on this side
    if (!pDX->m_bSaveAndValidate)
    {
        // Going from object to dialog box;
        // convert from 24 to 12
        if (m_nHour < 12)    // Set AM/PM flag
        {
            m_nAMPM = 0;
        }
        else
        {
            m_nAMPM = 1;
        }
        m_nHour %= 12;       // Now round off to 12
        if (m_nHour == 0)    // Convert 0s to 12s
        {
            m_nHour = 12;
        }
    }
```

```
// When transferring information to the dialog box
if (!pDX->m_bSaveAndValidate)
{
    // Set the range of the horizontal scroll bars
    // before the user gets a chance to see the
    // dialog box
    CScrollBar *psbControl;

    psbControl =
        (CScrollBar*)GetDlgItem(IDC_SCROLLBAR_DAY);
    ASSERT_VALID(psbControl);
    psbControl->SetScrollRange(1, 31, FALSE);
    psbControl->SetScrollPos(m_nDay);

    psbControl =
        (CScrollBar*)GetDlgItem(IDC_SCROLLBAR_YEAR);
    ASSERT_VALID(psbControl);
    psbControl->SetScrollRange(1990, 2020, FALSE);
    psbControl->SetScrollPos(m_nYear);

    psbControl =
        (CScrollBar*)GetDlgItem(IDC_SCROLLBAR_HOUR);
    ASSERT_VALID(psbControl);
    psbControl->SetScrollRange(1, 12, FALSE);
    psbControl->SetScrollPos(m_nHour);

    psbControl =
        (CScrollBar*)GetDlgItem(IDC_SCROLLBAR_MINUTE);
    ASSERT_VALID(psbControl);
    psbControl->SetScrollRange(0, 59, FALSE);
    psbControl->SetScrollPos(m_nMinute);
}
```

```
// Now exchange data with the display
CDialog::DoDataExchange(pDX);
//{{AFX_DATA_MAP(CProg4Dialog)
DDX_Radio(pDX, IDC_RADIO1, m_nAMPM);
DDX_Check(pDX, IDC_CHECK_DISABLE, m_bDisable);
DDX_CBIndex(pDX, IDC_COMBO_MONTH, m_nMonth);
DDX_Text(pDX, IDC_EDIT_DAY, m_nDay);
DDV_MinMaxUInt(pDX, m_nDay, 1, 31);
DDX_Text(pDX, IDC_EDIT_HOUR, m_nHour);
DDV_MinMaxUInt(pDX, m_nHour, 1, 12);
DDX_Text(pDX, IDC_EDIT_MINUTE, m_nMinute);
DDV_MinMaxUInt(pDX, m_nMinute, 0, 59);
DDX_Text(pDX, IDC_EDIT_TEXT, m_sText);
DDX_Text(pDX, IDC_EDIT_YEAR, m_nYear);
```

```
        DDV_MinMaxUInt(pDX, m_nYear, 1990, 2020);
        //}}AFX_DATA_MAP

        // Put conversion routines from dialog to
        // class object on this side
        if (pDX->m_bSaveAndValidate)
        {
            // Going from dialog box to object;
            // convert from 12 to 24
            if (m_nHour == 12)  // Convert  12s to 0s
            {
                m_nHour = 0;
            }
            if (m_nAMPM)            // Now offset for PM
            {
                m_nHour += 12;
            }
        }
    }


BEGIN_MESSAGE_MAP(CProg4Dialog, CDialog)
    //{{AFX_MSG_MAP(CProg4Dialog)
    ON_WM_HSCROLL()
    //}}AFX_MSG_MAP
END_MESSAGE_MAP()


/////////////////////////////////////////////////////
// CProg4Dialog message handlers
```

```
static UINT ScrollBarValue(
    CScrollBar* pScrollBar, // Ptr to scroll bar
    UINT nSBCode, // Slider bar code
    UINT nSBPos)  // Position (if SBCODE thumbtack type)
{
    // Get the current position of the scroll bar...
    int nPos = pScrollBar->GetScrollPos();

    // ...and get the range
    int nMinPos, nMaxPos;
    pScrollBar->GetScrollRange(&nMinPos, &nMaxPos);

    // The sbcode tells you what to do
    switch (nSBCode)
    {
      case SB_LEFT:
        nPos = nMinPos;
        break;
```

```
      case SB_LINELEFT:
        nPos = max(nPos - 1, nMinPos);
        break;

      case SB_LINERIGHT:
        nPos = min(nPos + 1, nMaxPos);
        break;

      case SB_PAGELEFT:
        nPos = max(nPos - 10, nMinPos);
        break;

      case SB_PAGERIGHT:
        nPos = min(nPos + 10, nMaxPos);
        break;

      case SB_RIGHT:
        nPos = nMaxPos;
        break;

      // In these two cases, nSBPos has
      // the current position
      case SB_THUMBPOSITION:
      case SB_THUMBTRACK:
        nSBPos = min((int)nSBPos, nMaxPos);
        nSBPos = max((int)nSBPos, nMinPos);
        nPos   = nSBPos;
        break;

      // Don't do anything with this message
      case SB_ENDSCROLL:
        break;

      default:
        TRACE(
          "Received an nSBCode we didn't understand\n");
    }

    // Update scroll bar
    pScrollBar->SetScrollPos(nPos);

    // Now return the updated position
    return nPos;
}
```

```
void CProg4Dialog::OnHScroll(UINT nSBCode,
```

```
                                   UINT nPos,
                                   CScrollBar* pScrollBar)
{
    // Interpret the scroll bar
    nPos = ScrollBarValue(pScrollBar, nSBCode, nPos);

    // Now update the corresponding edit box:
    // Find who sent the message
    int nSourceID = pScrollBar->GetDlgCtrlID();

    // Convert this to the corresponding text box
    switch(nSourceID)
    {
      case IDC_SCROLLBAR_DAY:
        SetDlgItemInt(IDC_EDIT_DAY, nPos);
        break;

      case IDC_SCROLLBAR_YEAR:
        SetDlgItemInt(IDC_EDIT_YEAR, nPos);
        break;

      case IDC_SCROLLBAR_HOUR:
        SetDlgItemInt(IDC_EDIT_HOUR, nPos);
        break;

      case IDC_SCROLLBAR_MINUTE:
        SetDlgItemInt(IDC_EDIT_MINUTE, nPos);
        break;

      default:
        TRACE(
            "Unrecognized dialog control id received\n");
        return;
    }
}
```

Clicking either the left or right arrow on any of the four horizontal scroll bars sends a *WM_HSCROLL* message that is routed by the message map to the *OnHScroll( )* function. *OnHScroll( )* passes the message data to the local function *ScrollBarValue( )* for initial processing.

The ScrollBarValue( ) Function

The *ScrollBarValue( )* function takes three arguments. The argument *pScrollBar* points to the object corresponding to the scroll bar the user clicked. The indication contained in the argument *nSBCode* is equal to either *SB_LINE_LEFT* or *SB_LINE_RIGHT* for the left and right arrows, respectively. (In the event that the scroll thumb has bumped against the left- or righthand stop, the indicator might be *SB_LEFT* or *SB_RIGHT* instead.)

ScrollBarValue( ) begins by querying the scroll bar for its value and range. Then, depending on the code, it either decrements or increments the scroll bar value, never letting the value get smaller than the minimum value nor larger than the maximum value.

After the new value has been calculated, the scroll position is updated and the new value returned to *OnHScroll( )*.

Setting the scroll-bar range

For the *Scroll Bar Values( )* function to work correctly, all the scroll bars have to know their legal range. How do they know this? That's simple — you tell them.

The best place to set the range of the scroll bars is back in the *DoData-Exchange( )* function. At that point, the dialog box has been created, so the scroll bars exist, but the box has yet to be displayed.

As before, when *pDX->m_bSaveAndValidate* is *FALSE*, data is being transferred to the dialog box. At this point, you can get a pointer to the day scroll bar by calling *CWnd::GetDlgItem( )* and passing the object's ID, *IDC_SCROLLBAR_DAY*. (If you forgot the ID of the edit box, go back with the AppStudio and check the properties box.) After testing that the address is valid, you set the range to be from 1 to 31. Setting the scroll position to the value of *m_nDay* makes sure that the day-of-the-month edit box and its corresponding scroll bar start out in synch. (Remember that the initial value of *m_nDay* can be anything between 1 and 31.)

Repeating this process for the three remaining scroll bars initializes them properly.

Back at the sidebar ranch: OnHScroll( )

After the *ScrollBarValue( )* has calculated the new value, it's time for *OnHScroll( )* to update the corresponding edit box. It does this by first asking the scroll bar for its ID (with the call to *CWnd::GetDlgCtrlID( )* — a *CScrollBar* is a sub-class of *CWnd*).

OnHScroll( ) then maps the returned value to the ID of the corresponding edit box in a switch statement. The call to *CWnd::SetDlgItemInt( )* transfers the newly calculated value to the edit box.

The other sidebar messages

The code is available to handle the *SB_PAGELEFT* and *SB_PAGERIGHT* codes that are generated when a user clicks in the trough to either side of the scroll thumb. In addition, the *SB_THUMB-TRACK* code is also present to handle the message that is generated as the user drags the thumb back and forth across the scroll bar and the *SB_THUMBPOSITION* code when she lets go.

When the scroll bar code is either *SB_THUMBTRACK* or *SB_THUMBPOSITION*, the message also contains a position indicator that contains the current value of the scroll bar. Passing the value keeps you from having to calculate it.

The *SB_ENDSCROLL* code is sent when the user releases the mouse button after clicking any of the controls. Ignore this code.

Scroll messages with the page and track codes are never generated for a scroll bar too small to have a thumb like yours. If you want to see the results of these messages, go into the AppStudio and temporarily lengthen one of the scroll bars until it's large enough to have a thumb with troughs on both sides. When you rebuild the program, you have the following options:

- Increase the value by one by clicking the arrow.

- Increase the value by ten by clicking the trough.

- Increase the value at will by dragging the trough back and forth.

Make the indicated changes and take the new version out for a spin. Double-clicking the open view reveals a dialog box containing the current date and time. Clicking the scroll-bar arrows updates the fields accordingly until the limit of the range is encountered. Holding down either of the scroll-bar arrows increments the field steadily in the proper direction. Nirvana has been reached.

Notice that one problem remains unsolved. If a user types a value in the edit box and then clicks the scroll bar, the value in the box jumps back to the preceding value plus or minus one (depending on which arrow you clicked). The reason for this is that there's nothing to resynch the scroll bar when you type data directly into an edit box.

In practice, this probably never happens. After you've entered the correct value, why would you want to increment it or decrement it? If you do want to solve this problem, however, you can add a message handler for the *WM_CHAR* message to the edit-box fields. This process enables you to update the scroll bars with the modified values of these fields as they are edited. ■

Custom Field Types (DDX / DDV)

Notice that it's still possible to enter an illegal date, such as February 30. This situation that stems from the vagaries of time determination, for which you can blame Pope Gregor. (The French tried to fix it all, as part of the metrification that accompanied the French Revolution. It's about the only part of metrification that didn't get adopted, maybe because of the strange names of the months, such as Fraternity and Sorority.)

To catch these types of errors, you can implement your own checks, by either invoking your own dynamic data validation (*DDV_*) function or including the code directly in the *DoDataExchange( )* function.

Let's take the first route.

The following code shows the minor additions that are made in order to add a custom-built *DDV_* function to compare the number of days against the month.

```
// Prototype required prior to call
void AFXAPI DDV_Time(CDataExchange* pDX,
                     UINT nMonth,
                     UINT nDay);
```

```
void CProg4Dialog::DoDataExchange(CDataExchange* pDX)
{
    // ...same as before...

    //{{AFX_DATA_MAP(CProg4Dialog)
    DDX_Radio(pDX, IDC_RADIO1, m_nAMPM);
    DDX_Check(pDX, IDC_CHECK_DISABLE, m_bDisable);
    DDX_CBIndex(pDX, IDC_COMBO_MONTH, m_nMonth);
    DDX_Text(pDX, IDC_EDIT_DAY, m_nDay);
    DDV_MinMaxUInt(pDX, m_nDay, 1, 31);
    DDX_Text(pDX, IDC_EDIT_HOUR, m_nHour);
    DDV_MinMaxUInt(pDX, m_nHour, 1, 12);
    DDX_Text(pDX, IDC_EDIT_MINUTE, m_nMinute);
    DDV_MinMaxUInt(pDX, m_nMinute, 0, 59);
    DDX_Text(pDX, IDC_EDIT_TEXT, m_sText);
    DDX_Text(pDX, IDC_EDIT_YEAR, m_nYear);
    DDV_MinMaxUInt(pDX, m_nYear, 1990, 2020);
    //}}AFX_DATA_MAP
```

```
    // Add special checks for day
    DDX_Text(pDX, IDC_EDIT_DAY, m_nDay);
    DDV_Time(pDX, m_nMonth, m_nDay);
```

```
                  // ...same here also...
            }

// Custom validation routine
void AFXAPI DDV_Time(CDataExchange* pDX,
                     UINT nMonth,
                     UINT nDay)
{
    // Doesn't work for leap year —
    // the fix is left as an assignment to student
    static UINT nDaysInMonth[]={31, 28, 31, 30, 31, 30,
                                31, 31, 30, 31, 30, 31};
    if (nMonth >= 12 || nDay > nDaysInMonth[nMonth])
    {
        AfxMessageBox("Illegal day/month combination",
                      MB_ICONEXCLAMATION | MB_OK);
        pDX->Fail();
    }
}
```

After the normal set of *DDX_/DDV_* transfers and checks, a call to *DDV_Time( )* has been added to *DoDataExchange( )*. Because the ClassWizard knows nothing about a *DDV_Time( )* check, this call must be placed outside the *AFX_DATA_MAP( )* block. However, the call to *DDV_Time( )* must immediately follow the corresponding *DDX_* transfer routine. This apparent dilemma can be solved by transferring the day of the month twice. That's the reason a second *DDX_Text* is directly in front of the *DDV_Time*.

The test within *DDV_Time( )* is straightforward. If the month isn't in the range of 0 through 11, or if the day isn't within the proper range for that month, the function opens an exclamation message box. After this box is displayed, the function calls *pDX->Fail( )*, which causes the program to return to the dialog box with the *IDC_EDIT_DAY* field highlighted.

In addition to transferring the data, the call to *DDX_Text( )* immediately before the call to *DDV_TIME( )* sets up a pointer within **pDX* so that when *DDV_Time( )* calls *pDX->Fail( )*, MFC highlights the *IDC_EDIT_DAY* field as the culprit. ▪

Message boxes are a particularly simple form of modal dialog box. The arguments to the *AfxMessageBox( )* call are the string to display followed by the type. The *MB_OK* indicates that only an OK button is presented to the user. Other possibilities allow for OK and Cancel or Yes and No buttons. The *MB_ICONEXCLAMATION* puts an exclamation icon on the message box.

A message box is the normal way of reporting errors or other special conditions to users. ▪

Conclusion

In this chapter (and its predecessor), you have learned how to do the following:

- ✔ Build a dialog box
- ✔ Open the dialog box (in modal mode) from within a program
- ✔ Transfer data to the dialog box and get it back
- ✔ Link scroll bars to edit fields
- ✔ Build custom data-validation routines

Of course, the process of opening the dialog box by double-clicking the open view is far from obvious. I chose it only because it was expedient. (You always knew that this "feature" would have to be fixed.) In Chapter 17, you add a new menu to control the dialog box.

Chapter 17

Controlling the Application from the Menu

• •

In This Chapter

▶ Receiving and processing menu messages

▶ Adding a new menu

▶ Adding quick keys

▶ Adding a menu to the toolbar

• •

So far, you've been forced to open the dialog box for your personal-scheduler application by double-clicking in the current view. The reason is that, until now, you didn't know how to add a new menu-processing item to handle this mundane function.

The following section tells you how to fix that blight on an otherwise perfectly decent program.

Editing the Menu

To add a new menu item, you have to complete the following steps:

1. Add the item to the menu.

2. Attach the extra features that users have come to expect, such as keyboard-accelerator keys, a Ready string, and a pop-up "balloon-type" prompt.

3. Add the code to handle the command.

4. For often-used functions, create a toolbar entry and attach it to the menu item. (This step is optional.)

Let's consider each of these steps in turn.

Adding an Item to the Menu

The menu is another one of those helpful resources, such as dialog boxes and toolbars. To modify the menu, double-click the resource file, *Prog4.rc*. From the list of folders, double-click the Menu folder (that's logical enough). Finally, double-click the *IDR_PROG4TYPE* menu.

The other menu, *IDR_MAINFRAME*, is used when no document is open. You don't have to modify this menu for this application because you cannot add, modify, or delete any entries if no document is open. ■

Double-clicking the menu name pops up what looks like a nonfunctional version of the menu that normally appears when *Prog4* is executed with a document.

Across the top of the menu are the generic menu choices File, Edit, View, Window, and Help. Rather than remove any options that are already present, let's add to the end of the Edit menu the new options Add Entry, Del Entry, and Mod Entry.

Click the Edit menu option. Notice that the normal entries appear with an extra, empty box at the bottom, which is where the next menu item is added.

To separate your new entries from the existing ones, the first entry should be a separator bar. This bar serves no function other than to enhance the appearance of the menu. Double-click the box to open the Menu Item Properties window. Click the Separator property, and then close the window by clicking somewhere else on the screen. A separator bar appears in the menu with a new, empty item underneath it. Double-click the empty box again to add the Add Entry menu item. Edit the Menu Item Properties window until it looks like the one shown in Figure 17-1.

Add three more menu items with the following properties:

ID	Caption	Prompt
ID_EDIT_ADD	&Add Entry\tCtrl+A	Add new schedule entry\nAdd entry
ID_EDIT_DELETE	&Del Entry\tCtrl+D	Delete the current schedule entry\nDel entry
ID_EDIT_MODIFY	&Mod Entry\tCtrl+M	Modify current entry\nMod entry

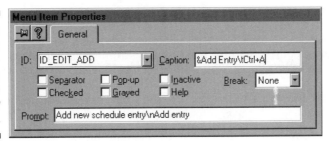

Figure 17-1:
The Menu
Item Prop-
erties dialog
box for the
first new
menu item.

The ID field is the name you use to refer to this menu item from within the program. The caption is the text that appears when the menu is pulled down. As in C++, the \t character represents a tab. The & indicates that the following character can be used to choose this menu option in lieu of the mouse. The ampersand does not appear, but the following character appears underlined.

The prompt consists of two strings separated by a \n character. The first string appears in the Ready window when the menu item is pointed at by the mouse. The second string appears in a yellow balloon whenever the mouse pointer stays motionless over the toolbar item for this menu command for more than a few seconds. This is the pop-up balloon prompt.

If you've done everything right, the menu with the three additions should appear from within the AppStudio resource editor, like the one shown in Figure 17-2.

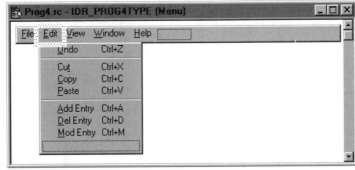

Figure 17-2:
The edited
menu
shows the
new Edit
items.

That's all there is to it! You're finished with the menu. All you have to do is to add the menu controls, and you'll be finished with the resource file as well.

Adding Menu Control Items

Several menu-control features can be added from AppStudio. You've already added the following items from within the Menu Item Properties window:

- ✔ Selection key (the character after the ampersand in the menu caption). This key enables a user to choose a menu item from the keyboard.

- ✔ Ready string (the first string in the menu prompt)

- ✔ Pop-up balloon prompt (the second string in the menu prompt)

The only thing you have left to add is the keyboard-accelerator key. An *accelerator key,* sometimes called a *hot key,* is a Ctrl- or Alt-key combination that enables users to invoke a menu command directly without going through the menu.

It is possible, but not common, to use something other than the Alt or Ctrl keys. Can you imagine how confusing it would be if, for example, every time you pressed the A key, the Add Entry dialog box popped up? ▪

You've already indicated which accelerator key you intend to use for each menu item in the menu text (that was the key after the \t tab); you have yet to "install" the key, however.

To install it, return to the resource editor main menu and double-click the Accelerator folder. Follow this step with a double-click of *IDR_MAINFRAME* to reveal the existing accelerator keys defined for you by AppWizard.

To add a new entry, double-click the empty entry at the bottom of the list. This step opens the Accel Properties window. Enter the name of the menu item, *ID_EDIT_ADD,* and then the accelerator key, A, with the Ctrl box checked. The finished result should look like Figure 17-3. This process installs the Ctrl+A key for the Add menu item.

Figure 17-3:
The Accel
Properties
window for
the Add
Entry menu
item.

Accel Properties

General

ID: ID_EDIT_ADD=32771

Key: A

Next Key Typed

Modifiers
☑ Ctrl ☐ Alt ☐ Shift

Type
○ ASCII ● VirtKey

The number after the ID (32771, in this case), is the numerical value App-Studio has assigned to the constant *ID_EDIT_ADD*. Its actual value is of little interest other than as a note that, yes indeed, the Accel Properties window does know what an *ID_EDIT_ADD* is. This way, you know that you haven't misspelled it.

The number after the ID doesn't appear when you review or modify existing accelerator keys. ▪

Associate Ctrl+D with the *ID_EDIT_DELETE* menu item and Ctrl+M with the *ID_EDIT_MODIFY* menu item. You're finished when your list looks like the one shown in Figure 17-4.

Figure 17-4:
The list of
accelerator
keys is
defined for
Prog4.

ID	Key	Type
ID_EDIT_ADD	Ctrl + A	VIRTKEY
ID_EDIT_COPY	Ctrl + C	VIRTKEY
ID_EDIT_DELETE	Ctrl + D	VIRTKEY
ID_EDIT_MODIFY	Ctrl + M	VIRTKEY
ID_FILE_NEW	Ctrl + N	VIRTKEY
ID_FILE_OPEN	Ctrl + O	VIRTKEY
ID_FILE_PRINT	Ctrl + P	VIRTKEY
ID_FILE_SAVE	Ctrl + S	VIRTKEY
ID_EDIT_PASTE	Ctrl + V	VIRTKEY
ID_EDIT_UNDO	Alt + VK_BACK	VIRTKEY
ID_EDIT_CUT	Shift + VK_DELETE	VIRTKEY
ID_NEXT_PANE	VK_F6	VIRTKEY

Prog4.rc - IDR_MAINFRAME (Accelerator)

The keys are listed in alphabetical order of the key that is entered. This order may seem odd at first, but the reason becomes quickly apparent when you begin searching for the next available accelerator key. (You don't want to define the same accelerator key for two different functions.) ▪

Cuisine Queries: Menu Messages

The next step is to install some message handlers so that your menu options do something.

If you rebuild the program now, you might notice that it does compile and link; when you execute it, however, the Add, Modify, and Delete options are grayed out, indicating that they can't be chosen. It's not just that they're bashful — MFC disables them because it knows that no code is there to handle them if they were to be chosen. ▪

First, you must remove the double-click message handler from the *CProg4View* class. Enter the ClassWizard and choose the *CProg4View* class. Then choose *OnLButtonDblClk* and then *Delete Function*. A message box pops up, warning you that you'll have to remove the code by hand, and asking whether that's okay. (Like you have a choice.) The ClassWizard removes only the message map information plus the declarations within the *include* file. You must remove the function itself from the .cpp source file. Choose Yes and then delete the *OnLButtonDblClk( )* function.

Now you must add handlers for the three functions. Question: To which class should you add the menu-command message handlers? The Add command seems to fit best in the document class. You are adding a new element to the document, irrespective of which view is visible. The Modify and Delete commands are definitely part of the view because some concept of the "current" entry must be in the view.

Choose the class *CProg4Doc* in the ClassWizard. Then choose the ID *ID_EDIT_ADD* on the left. On the right, choose *COMMAND* to indicate that it is the *ID_EDIT_ADD* command message you want to intercept. Finally, press the Add Function button.

The ClassWizard constructs the function name *OnEditAdd( )*, which sounds as good as any, so accept it by clicking OK.

Repeat the process in the class *CProg4View* for the *ID_EDIT_MODIFY* and *ID_EDIT_DELETE* command messages. Notice that these message handlers are to be added to the *CProg4View* class and not to the *CProg4Doc* class.

The *OnEditModify( )* and *OnEditDelete( )* functions can't do much — you don't have a document yet. Let's just insert a call to *TRACE( )* to let you know that control got there okay:

```
// Prog4vw.cpp : implementation of the CProg4View class
//

#include "stdafx.h"
#include "Prog4.h"

#include "Prog4ent.h"
#include "Prog4doc.h"
#include "Prog4vw.h"

// To get access to the dialog definition
#include "Prog4dia.h"

// ...continues the same until the bottom of the file...
```

```
/////////////////////////////////////////////////////
// CProg4View message handlers

void CProg4View::OnEditDelete()

{
    TRACE("Entered OnEditDelete()\n");
}

void CProg4View::OnEditModify()

{
    TRACE("Entered OnEditModify()\n");
}
```

The *CProg4Doc::OnEditAdd( )* function should look like this:

```
// Prog4doc.cpp : implementation of the CProg4Doc class
//

#include "stdafx.h"
#include "Prog4.h"

#include "Prog4ent.h"
#include "Prog4doc.h"

// To get access to the dialog definition
#include "Prog4dia.h"

// ...no changes until the bottom of the file...

/////////////////////////////////////////////////////
// CProg4Doc commands

void CProg4Doc::OnEditAdd()

{
    TRACE("Entered OnEditAdd\n");

    CProg4Dialog dlgObject;
    dlgObject.DoModal();
}
```

If you compile, link, and execute the program now, you see that your new menu items are present, enabled and raring to go. Choose Add, and the dialog box pops up. Press Ctrl+A, and the dialog box appears without going through the menu. If you choose either Delete or Modify, all you get is a silly message in the debugger output window, but, hey, it's a start.

Enabling and Disabling Menu Items: The UI_CMD Msg

If your eyes aren't too blurry from long hours spent entering C++ text from this book, you may have noticed that each menu object ID has something called an *UPDATE_COMMAND_UI* message in addition to *COMMAND* messages. What could this be?

The *COMMAND* message is sent whenever a user chooses a menu item. This message gives the program a chance to implement that menu item. The *UPDATE_COMMAND_UI* message is sent whenever the menu containing the item is opened or whenever the menu item is chosen. This message enables the program to change the menu depending on the internal state of the application.

It doesn't make any sense, for example, to enable either the Modify or Delete menu commands if the document is empty. If there's nothing in the document, there's nothing to modify or delete, so why offer them as an option? The *UPDATE_COMMAND_UI* messages gives you an opportunity to make that determination and disable the menu items if the document is empty.

Try that now. Return to *CProg4View* in the ClassWizard. Choose *ID_EDIT_DELETE* and *UPDATE_COMMAND_UI*, and accept the default name of the function. Repeat the process for the *ID_EDIT_MODIFY* ID. Then edit the functions as follows:

```
void CProg4View::OnUpdateEditDelete(CCmdUI* pCmdUI)

{
    // If the document is empty, deselect the menu item
    TRACE("Entered OnUpdateEditDelete()\n");
    pCmdUI->Enable(TRUE);
}


void CProg4View::OnUpdateEditModify(CCmdUI* pCmdUI)

{
    // If the document is empty, deselect the menu item
    TRACE("Entered OnUpdateEditModify()\n");
    pCmdUI->Enable(FALSE);
}
```

The argument to the *OnUpdate...( )* function is a pointer to an object of class *CCmdUI*. This object is an interface to the menu item. The *CCmdUI* class includes functions such as *Enable( )*, to enable and disable the menu option, and *Check( )*, which puts a small check in front of the menu option.

You don't need a separate *OnUpdate...( )* function for each menu item. For example, the two preceding functions will be identical after the document is in place. The two menus could have shared the same *OnUpdate...( )* function. ▪

If you rebuild and execute the program, you notice, as expected, that the Delete menu item is still enabled because of the call to *pCmdUI->Enable(TRUE)* but that Modify is now disabled because of the call to *pCmdUI->Enable(FALSE)*.

Adding Controls to the Toolbar

The next step in your quest is to add command options to the toolbar. You can add all three, but because I'm lazy, I'll show you how to add only the Add and Delete menu items. A large plus sign should make a good mnemonic icon for the Add function, and a minus sign for Delete.

The toolbar is another one of the resources you get to through AppStudio. This time, choose the *IDR_MAINFRAME* option in the Bitmap folder. A crude paint-type editor should appear with the current toolbar.

To add the plus sign, you must first make room on the toolbar. The easiest place to add the extra icon is on the far right end. Each icon in the toolbar is 16 pixels wide, so expand the bar by 16 pixels by clicking the right side of the bitmap and dragging the bar.

Now you have to lay down the pleasing gray that is behind the other toolbar items. Click the Eye dropper tool, and soak up a pixel of that gray color. Click the Fill bucket tool and pour the color over the new area.

Reselect the pencil tool, and draw a plus sign as best you can. Hold the pointer over a pixel and click the left button to set the pixel to the foreground color, as shown in the box on the right. The right button sets the pixel to the background color. You can click one of the colors shown in the palette to change the foreground or background colors. You can see what the icon will look like by examining the smallish window on the left side of the edit window. Feel free to use whatever artistic ability you may have (you certainly can't do any worse than I did).

When you have a reasonable plus sign, repeat the process for the minus sign: extend the bar another 16 pixels and begin drawing. When you finish with the Add icon, repeat the process for the Delete icon (I used the minus sign). When you finish, close the resource file.

The final step is to link your new edit commands to the new toolbar entries. Edit the static global buttons in mainframe.cpp:

```
// toolbar buttons - IDs are command buttons
static UINT BASED_CODE buttons[] =
{
    // same order as in the bitmap 'toolbar.bmp'
    ID_FILE_NEW,
    ID_FILE_OPEN,
    ID_FILE_SAVE,
        ID_SEPARATOR,
    ID_EDIT_CUT,
    ID_EDIT_COPY,
    ID_EDIT_PASTE,
        ID_SEPARATOR,
    ID_FILE_PRINT,
    ID_APP_ABOUT,
    ID_APP_ABOUT,
        ID_SEPARATOR,
    ID_EDIT_ADD,
    ID_EDIT_DELETE
};
```

This array of menu IDs is associated with the toolbar by mainframe.cpp when the window frame is created at program start-up.

Notice the addition of the extra *ID_APP_ABOUT*. The reason is that MFC thoughtfully provides an extra icon for context-sensitive help. This icon is not displayed when no menu item is assigned to it. Instead of removing it, adding an extra *ID_APP_ABOUT* gives it the same function as the other About button. ■

Rebuild and execute the program. Notice the additional plus and minus signs that appear at the end of the toolbar. Click the plus sign, and the Add/Modify Entry dialog box shows up, as reliably as my son on payday. Hold the mouse pointer on the button for a second or two, and the message *Add entry* appears in a small, yellow balloon.

You may have noticed how the message *Entered OnUpdateEditDelete( )* appears numerous times in the debugger output window as long as the toolbar is visible. The reason is that *UPDATE_COMMAND_UI* messages are sent to the toolbar items whenever the program doesn't have much else to do (that is, when it's in the idle loop). Not to worry — you're about to remove the *TRACE( )* message anyway. ■

Conclusion: All Dressed Up and Nowhere to Go

Your personal scheduler is coming right along. It can pop up a nifty dialog box from either the menu or the toolbar, and it has pop-up support. It supports accelerator keys in case you get tired of using the mouse, and it takes input through a state-of-the-art dialog box. The scheduler validates the data. So far, however, your WinApp is nothing more than a Hollywood facade — a fake. It doesn't do anything with the data it gets.

In Chapter 18, you'll build a document and a view in which to save and display the entries you enter from the dialog box.

Chapter 18

Scheduling a Personal View of the Document

· ·

In This Chapter

▶ Containing multiple entries

▶ Adding, modifying, and deleting entries

▶ Displaying the list of scheduler entries

▶ Choosing an entry to modify or delete

· ·

*I*n this chapter, you take the data created by the dialog box from the previous chapters and save it in a document. You also outfit the program with a view into that document so that you can see previously created scheduler entries. This chapter goes a little faster than other chapters in this book because you're an old hand now at creating documents and views.

Not-so-old hands can refer to Part III for a little more hand-holding in the Document-View department. ■

A Scheduler Entry: The CEntry Class

The first thing you have to do is create a new class designed to hold the data returned from the dialog box. You can use the *CProg4Dialog* class, but it's not a good idea. The *CProg4Dialog* class was created to get data to and from the dialog box. The format of the data in this class is not necessarily the most compact or most convenient for the purpose of this discussion. In addition, trying to use the *CProg4Dialog* class for storage purposes tends to confuse the logic of getting information to and from a dialog box with that of just holding the data. (And you certainly don't need any extra confusion.) By the way, to avoid confusion, add all the changes in this chapter to the program before trying to compile and run it.

To contain the scheduler-entry information, I created a new class *CEntry* in the *include* file Prog4ent.h: ***Note:*** Because all of the code in this chapter is new, none of the new part is shown in gray.

```
// Prog4ent.h : the Time Entry class
//
/////////////////////////////////////////////////////////////

class CEntry
{
// Attributes
protected:
    int     m_bDisabled;
    CTime   m_tTime;
    CString m_sText;

public:
    CEntry();
    CEntry(int nYear,   int nMonth,
           int nDay,    int nHour,
           int nMinute, int bDisabled,
           CString& sText);
    ~CEntry();

    // Access functions
    CTime GetTime();
    CString GetText();
    int    GetDisabled();
    int    SetDisabled(int bNewValue);

    // Serialize functions
    // Return a nonzero on error
    int    Serialize(CArchive& ar);
};
```

The data consists of just three entries: the time, the text, and the disabled flag. The class *CTime* presents the current time (in the range of 1970 to 2038).

The member functions for this class are equally straightforward. Two constructors are necessary, one to create a complete entry and another to create a "null" entry, if necessary. The destructor does nothing in particular — the destructors for *CTime* and *CString* are invoked automatically when a *CEntry* object is destroyed.

The access functions simply return the value of the corresponding data member. The serialize function is necessary when the time comes to save and restore the document to and from disk.

I put the code to implement this class in the new file Prog4ent.cpp:

```
// Prog4ent.cpp : implement the CEntry class
//
///////////////////////////////////////////////////////
#include "stdafx.h"
#include "Prog4.h"

#include "Prog4ent.h"

CEntry::CEntry()
{
    m_bDisabled = FALSE;
}

CEntry::CEntry(int nYear,   int nMonth,
               int nDay,    int nHour,
               int nMinute, int bDisabled,
               CString& sText) :
    m_tTime(nYear, nMonth + 1, nDay, nHour, nMinute, 0),
    m_sText(sText)
{
    m_bDisabled = bDisabled;
}

CEntry::~CEntry()
{
    // Nothing to do here; the destructor for the
    // CTime and CString are invoked automatically
}

// Simple access functions
CTime CEntry::GetTime()
{
    return m_tTime;
}

CString CEntry::GetText()
{
    return m_sText;
}

int CEntry::GetDisabled()
{
    return m_bDisabled;
}
```

```
int CEntry::SetDisabled(int bNewState)
{
    int bOldState = m_bDisabled;
    m_bDisabled = bNewState;
    return bOldState;
}

// Save and restore functions to be called for
// serializing
int CEntry::Serialize(CArchive& ar)
{
    static CString sTestString("Personal_entry:");
    if (ar.IsStoring())
    {
        // Storing:
        // Tag a flag to the beginning of each record
        ar << sTestString;
        ar << m_tTime;
        ar << (WORD)m_bDisabled;
        ar << m_sText;
        return 0;
    }
    else
    {
        // Restoring:
        // Check for the presence of the flag
        CString sTest;
        ar >> sTest;
        if (sTest != sTestString)
        {
            return -1;
        }

        // It's okay — read the data
        ar >> m_tTime;

        WORD bDisabled;
        ar >> bDisabled;
        m_bDisabled = bDisabled;

        ar >> m_sText;

        return 0;
    }
}
```

The default constructor does nothing except set the *m_bDisabled* flag to *FALSE*. The second constructor, however, constructs a complete *CEntry* object by using a full set of time arguments.

Notice how the constructor for *CTime* is invoked on the members *m_tTime* and *m_sText* before the open brace of the constructor:

```
CEntry::CEntry(int nYear,    int nMonth,
               int nDay,     int nHour,
               int nMinute, int bDisabled,
               CString& sText) :
    m_tTime(nYear, nMonth + 1, nDay, nHour, nMinute, 0),
    m_sText(sText)
{
```

This is the proper syntax for constructing data members from the arguments passed to the constructor. (*nMonth* is incremented because in the class *CTime* the months go from 1 to 12, whereas they are returned from the dialog box as 0 through 11.) ■

The access functions are trivial; they simply return the requested data.

The *Serialize( )* function either stores or restores the current *CEntry* object from the *CArchive* object that is provided. When it is storing, it precedes each entry with a flag string. It does this to guard against file corruption on the restore side. In addition, it covers the case of users trying to read nonscheduler files — users are like that. When the *Serialize( )* function restores, it reads the guard string and, if it doesn't match, punches out an error message. Otherwise, it reads the remainder of the object from *CArchive*.

Don't forget to add the file Prog4ent.cpp to the project file, Prog4.mak, by choosing Menu I Project I Files. This step adds the file to the Prog4 program. ■

Saving Entries into a Document

Now you need a document to hold a list of the *CEntry* objects you generate. I added the following members to the *CProg4Doc* class to accommodate this type of list:

```
// Prog4doc.h : interface of the CProg4Doc class
//
//////////////////////////////////////////////////////////

class CProg4Doc : public CDocument
{
```

```
        // User-defined stuff
protected:
    // Use a linked list to store the times
    CPtrList m_lEntry; // list of CEntry*

public:
    // Call GetFirst() the first time. The
    // location of the first element is returned
    // in Index. Subsequent calls update
    // the Index pointer to the next member
    // of the list. CTime* is returned as zero
    // when the list is exhausted.
    CEntry* GetNext(POSITION& Index);
    CEntry* GetFirst(POSITION& Index);

    POSITION Add(CEntry& eNewEntry);
    void Modify(POSITION Index);
    void Delete(POSITION Index);
    void DeleteAll();

    int  GetCount();
```

```
        // ...from here on, the same as that created
        //     by AppWizard and ClassWizard
};
```

In the Etch-A-Sketch program, you used *CPtrArray* to store pointers to mouse locations. The *CPtrArray* class implements a virtual array whose size is determined at runtime and that is subject to change.

In this case, you use the *CPtrList* class instead. This class holds its pointers in a linked list. Functions are provided to add and remove members from either the beginning (called the "head"), end (called the "tail"), or an arbitrary location in the middle (called "an arbitrary location in the middle"). Individual entries in the list are pointed at by an index of class *POSITION*.

The data member *m_lEntry* is a list of pointers to *CEntry* objects. The relationship of the *CPtrList* to the *CEntry* objects is shown in Figure 18-1.

There was really no good reason for me to use *CPtrArray* in Part III and *CPtrList* here. In fact, the *CPtrList* probably would have been the better choice in both cases. I just wanted to use an example of both the *C...Array* and *C...List* classes for your benefit. ■

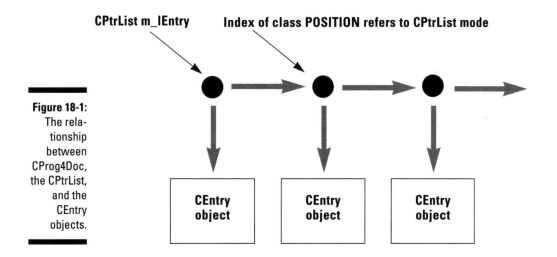

CPtrList m_lEntry   Index of class POSITION refers to CPtrList mode

Figure 18-1:
The rela-
tionship
between
CProg4Doc,
the CPtrList,
and the
CEntry
objects.

CEntry object   CEntry object   CEntry object

The code to implement this class is contained in Prog4doc.cpp:

```
// Prog4doc.cpp : implementation of the CProg4Doc class
//

#include "stdafx.h"
#include "Prog4.h"

#include "Prog4ent.h"
#include "Prog4doc.h"

#include "Prog4dia.h"

#ifdef _DEBUG
#undef THIS_FILE
static char BASED_CODE THIS_FILE[] = __FILE__;
#endif

//////////////////////////////////////////////////////////
// CProg4Doc

IMPLEMENT_DYNCREATE(CProg4Doc, CDocument)

BEGIN_MESSAGE_MAP(CProg4Doc, CDocument)
    //{{AFX_MSG_MAP(CProg4Doc)
    ON_COMMAND(ID_EDIT_ADD, OnEditAdd)
    //}}AFX_MSG_MAP
END_MESSAGE_MAP()
```

```
///////////////////////////////////////////////////////
// CProg4Doc construction/destruction

CProg4Doc::CProg4Doc()
{
}

CProg4Doc::~CProg4Doc()
{
    // Delete all entries from the list
    DeleteAll();
}

BOOL CProg4Doc::OnNewDocument()
{
    if (!CDocument::OnNewDocument())
        return FALSE;

    // Make sure document is empty
    DeleteAll();
    return TRUE;
}


///////////////////////////////////////////////////////
// CProg4Doc serialization

void CProg4Doc::Serialize(CArchive& ar)
{
    if (ar.IsStoring())
    {
    ar << (WORD)GetCount();

        POSITION Index;
        CEntry* pEntry;
        for (pEntry = GetFirst(Index);
            pEntry;
            pEntry = GetNext(Index))
        {
            pEntry->Serialize(ar);
        }
    }
    else
    {
        // Make sure the document is empty
        DeleteAll();

        // Read up the number of entries
```

```
                WORD wCount;
        ar >> wCount;
        while (wCount-)
        {
            // Now read up that many entries
            CEntry eEntry;
            if (eEntry.Serialize(ar))
            {
                // Error on read - abort
                AfxMessageBox(
                        "Error reading sheduler file");
                DeleteAll();
                break;
            }
            Add(eEntry);
        }
    }
    SetModifiedFlag(FALSE);
}


/////////////////////////////////////////////////////
// CProg4Doc diagnostics

#ifdef _DEBUG
void CProg4Doc::AssertValid() const
{
    CDocument::AssertValid();
}

void CProg4Doc::Dump(CDumpContext& dc) const
{
    CDocument::Dump(dc);
}
#endif //_DEBUG


/////////////////////////////////////////////////////
// CProg4Doc commands

void CProg4Doc::OnEditAdd()
{
    CProg4Dialog dlgObject;

    if (dlgObject.DoModal() == IDOK)
    {
        Add(CEntry(dlgObject.m_nYear,
                dlgObject.m_nMonth,
                dlgObject.m_nDay,
```

```
                        dlgObject.m_nHour,
                        dlgObject.m_nMinute,
                        dlgObject.m_bDisable,
                        dlgObject.m_sText));
    }
}

POSITION CProg4Doc::Add(CEntry& eEntry)
{
    // Create a new entry on the heap and add
    // it to the list
    CEntry* peNewEntry = DEBUG_NEW CEntry(eEntry);
    POSITION pNew = m_lEntry.AddTail((void*)peNewEntry);

    // Now mark the doc changed and update all views
    SetModifiedFlag();
    UpdateAllViews(0);
    return pNew;
}


void CProg4Doc::Modify(POSITION Index)
{
    // Get the specified entry
    CEntry* pEntry = (CEntry*)m_lEntry.GetAt(Index);
    if (pEntry == (CEntry*)0)
    {
        // Oops - quit
        return;
    }

    // Create a dialog object with that entry and
    // display it so that the operator can change it
    CProg4Dialog dialog(pEntry);
    if (dialog.DoModal() == IDOK)
    {
        // Delete the old entry
        delete pEntry;

        // Create a new one
        pEntry = DEBUG_NEW CEntry(dialog.m_nYear,
                        dialog.m_nMonth,
                        dialog.m_nDay,
                        dialog.m_nHour,
                        dialog.m_nMinute,
                        dialog.m_bDisable,
                        dialog.m_sText);

        // Store it at the same location in the list
```

```
        m_lEntry.SetAt(Index, pEntry);

        // Update the doc and views
        SetModifiedFlag();
        UpdateAllViews(0);
    }
}

void CProg4Doc::Delete(POSITION Index)
{
    // First return the memory to the heap
    CEntry *pEntry;
    pEntry = (CEntry*)m_lEntry.GetAt(Index);
    delete pEntry;

    // Now delete the entry itself
    m_lEntry.RemoveAt(Index);

    // Update the document and view
    SetModifiedFlag();
    UpdateAllViews(0);
}

void CProg4Doc::DeleteAll()
{
    // Keep deleting the head entry until
    // there aren't any left
    POSITION Index;
    while(GetCount() != 0)
    {
        Index = m_lEntry.GetHeadPosition();
        Delete(Index);
    }
}

CEntry* CProg4Doc::GetFirst(POSITION& Index)
{
    // If there aren't any in the list...
    if (m_lEntry.IsEmpty())
    {
        // ...just let him know
        Index = 0;
        return (CEntry*)0;
    }

    // Otherwise, return the head entry
    Index = m_lEntry.GetHeadPosition();
```

```
        return (CEntry*)m_lEntry.GetAt(Index);
}


CEntry* CProg4Doc::GetNext(POSITION& Index)
{
    // Go to the next entry
    m_lEntry.GetNext(Index);

    // When the list is exhausted, return NULL
    if (Index == (POSITION)0)
    {
        return (CEntry*)0;
    }

    // Otherwise, return that entry
    return (CEntry*)m_lEntry.GetAt(Index);
}


int CProg4Doc::GetCount()
{
    return m_lEntry.GetCount();
}
```

Notice that you must include Prog4ent.h in front of Prog4doc.h to get the definition for the new *CEntry* class. This is true for every .cpp file that includes Prog4doc.h (prog4.cpp, prog4dia.cpp, prog4doc.cpp, and prog4vw.cpp).

Why not just include Prog4ent.h at the beginning of Prog4doc.h? That wouldn't be a bad solution, except for two things:

✔ Some companies have rules against including a file from within an *include* file.

✔ You must take special measures to make sure that Prog4ent.h doesn't get included twice. If you do, strange and wonderful errors ensue that seem to have nothing to do with including the same file twice. ∎

Whenever you add a new *include* file to a .cpp file, you should choose Update All Dependencies from the Project menu. This choice tells Visual C++ to search the source files to determine which files include (and are therefore dependent on) which other files. If you don't, Visual C++ doesn't recompile all the source files that are necessary when the *include* file changes, and you begin to get strange link errors. ∎

The following sections discuss each of the member functions.

Adding and deleting entries

The process of adding an entry is handled by the *Add(CEntry&)* function (can't get any more logical than that). This function allocates a new *CEntry* off the heap and stores the address in a temporary *peNewEntry*. It then adds this address to the end of the *m_lEntry* list by using the *CPtrList::AddTail( )* function.

The *AddTail( )* function creates a new node, stores the given address in the node, and tacks the new node to the end of the list.

The call to *SetModifiedFlag( )* marks the document as "dirty," and the call to *UpdateAllViews( )* forces the view to redraw with the new entry added.

The *Delete( )* function reverses the steps. It first retrieves the specified entry by using *GetAt( )* and then deletes it. Deleting the object both forces the destructor for *CEntry* to be invoked and returns the *CEntry* memory to the heap. The call to *CPtrList::RemoveAt( )* removes the entry from the list and deletes it.

The *DeleteAll( )* function clears the list by repetitively deleting the first entry in the list until no entries remain.

Mapsco for entries:
GetFirst( ) / GetNext( )

The *GetFirst( )* and *GetNext( )* functions provide a way for external functions to navigate through the list of entries by means of the following pattern:

```
CEntry *pEntry;
POSITION Index;
for (pEntry = GetFirst(Index);   // Get the first entry
     pEntry;                     // Quit when entry zero
     pEntry = GetNext(Index))    // Get the next entry
{
    // ...whatever code...
}
```

If the list is empty, *GetFirst( )* returns a *NULL* pointer. If the list is not empty, *GetFirst( )* finds the position of the first element by calling *GetHeadPosition( )*. Because the argument to *GetFirst( )* is referential, *GetFirst( )* updates the *Index* passed to it to refer to this first entry. Finally, *GetFirst( )* returns the *CEntry* address stored at that position.

GetNext( ) first uses the function *CPtrList::GetNext( )* to advance the position stored in *Index* to the next entry. If the resulting *Index* is zero, you've reached the end of the list, and *GetNext( )* returns a *NULL* pointer. Otherwise, it returns the address stored at that position.

The *CProg4Doc::GetNext( )* function is subtly different from the class library *CPtrList::GetNext( )* function, but to my (feeble) mind, it's much easier to understand. *CPtrList::GetNext(Index)* returns the entry pointed at by *Index* and then updates *Index* so that it points to the next entry. Thus, *Index* and the pointer returned from *CPtrList::GetNext( )* are never in synch, which is confusing.

CProg4Doc::GetNext(Index) first increments *Index* to the next entry and then returns the entry pointed at by the new value of *Index* (or zero, if the list is exhausted). Thus, *Index* and the address that is returned remain in synch at all times. ▪

Throughput with a high-fiber serial

When the *Serialize( )* function is asked to store, it first writes the number of *CEntry* objects in the *CPtrList*. It then loops through the *CPtrList* and saves each *CEntry* by using the *CEntry::Serialize( )* function.

On the restore side, *Serialize( )* reverses the process by first reading the number of entries in the file and then reading each entry by using the *CEntry::Serialize( )* function and adding it to the document.

The call to *AfxMessageBox( )* in the event of a read error opens a simple modal dialog box with the message provided. An OK button indicating that the user has seen the message is all that's provided by default; an optional second argument enables a programmer to specify different button configurations, such as OK and Cancel or Yes, No, and Cancel.

Clearing the modified flag makes the file "clean" so that if users decide to exit from the program without making additional changes, they aren't bothered by a "Wanna save the file?" message.

Asking the *CEntry* class to serialize itself is a much better idea than saving the data members from within the document's *Serialize( )* function, for two reasons.

  ✔ The document class has no business messing with the internal details of the *CEntry* class. If the *Serialize( )* function is allowed to perform the store operation and the *CEntry* class is modified someday, the changes to *Serialize( )* are limited to the *CEntry* class and do not bleed into the document class.

  ✔ Dividing up the problem in this way simplifies both classes; the *CEntry* class can worry about entry-type things, and the *CProg4Doc* class can stay focused on document things. Their readability and maintainability are then enhanced. ▪

Creating a new entry: Just say "ID_Edit_Add"

The *OnEditAdd( )* function starts just like it did in Chapter 17, by constructing a *CProg4Dialog* object with the current time and displaying it in the Add/Modify dialog box by calling *DoModal( )*. If a user chooses OK, the dialog-box data is used to create a *CEntry* object that is then passed to the *Add( )* function to be added to the document.

Modifying an entry

Modifying a *CEntry* is only slightly more difficult than adding one. The first step is to retrieve the *CEntry* to be modified. This *CEntry* is then used to construct a new *CProg4Dialog* object. This process requires that you add the following constructor to the dialog class in both prog4dia.h and Prog4dia.cpp.

Notice how this constructor, rather than create a dialog object with the current time, builds a dialog object with the time and data specified in the provided *CEntry* object:

```
CProg4Dialog::CProg4Dialog(CEntry *pEntry)
  : CDialog(CProg4Dialog::IDD, (CWnd*)NULL)
{
    // Set the dialog from the time provided
    CTime tTime = pEntry->GetTime();

    // In dialog month it's zero-based —
    // in CTime, it's 1-based
    m_nMonth  = tTime.GetMonth() - 1;

    m_nDay     = tTime.GetDay();
    m_nYear    = tTime.GetYear();
    m_nHour    = tTime.GetHour();
    m_nMinute = tTime.GetMinute();

    m_bDisable = pEntry->GetDisabled();

    m_sText    = pEntry->GetText();
}
```

The members being initialized are contained in the *include* file prog4ent.h:

```
// Prog4dialog.h : header file
//
```

```
/////////////////////////////////////////////////////////////////
// CProg4Dia dialog

class CProg4Dialog : public CDialog
{
// Construction
public:
    CProg4Dialog(CWnd* pParent = NULL);    // standard constructor

    CProg4Dialog(CEntry *pEntry);          // optional constructor

    // Dialog Data
    //{{AFX_DATA(CProg4Dialog)
    enum { IDD = IDD_DIALOG_NSE };
    int     m_nAMPM;
    BOOL    m_bDisable;
    int     m_nMonth;
    UINT    m_nDay;
    UINT    m_nHour;
    UINT    m_nMinute;
    CString m_sText;
    UINT    m_nYear;
    //}}AFX_DATA

    // Overrides
    // ClassWizard generated virtual function overrides
    //{{AFX_VIRTUAL(CProg4Dialog)
protected:
    virtual void DoDataExchange(CDataExchange* pDX);
    //}}AFX_VIRTUAL

// Implementation
protected:

    // Generated message map functions
    //{{AFX_MSG(CProg4Dialog)
    afx_msg void OnHScroll(UINT nSBCode, UINT nPos,
                           CScrollBar* pScrollBar);
    //}}AFX_MSG
    DECLARE_MESSAGE_MAP()
};
```

The newly created dialog object is then used to pop up the Add/Modify dialog box by calling *DoModal( )*. If a user chooses OK, the old *CEntry* is deleted, and a new one is created from the information returned in the dialog box. The address of this new *CEntry* is then stored in the same node in the list that was occupied by the old entry.

Viewing That Document

The following *include* file defines the *CProg4View* class:

```
// Prog4vw.h : interface of the CProg4View class
//
/////////////////////////////////////////////////////////

class CProg4View : public CScrollView
{
    // User additions
protected:
    int      m_nCharHeight;
    int      m_nCharWidth;

    // The index of the "current" CEntry; the
    // current entry is the one that will be
    // deleted or modified if you select those
    // commands (it gets displayed in red)
    POSITION m_posCurrent;

    void Output(CDC* pDC,
             CEntry* pEntry, // entry to display
             int nOffset,   // line number
             int bCurrent); // 1->this is
                            //  the current entry

    // ...from here on, created automatically by AppWizard
    //    AppWizard and ClassWizard...
};
```

The *m_nCharHeight* and *m_nCharWidth* entries are used to save the height and average width of a character. The *m_posCurrent* entry is the index of the "currently selected" scheduler entry. The selected entry is the entry that is deleted if you choose Delete or that is modified if you choose Modify. Before making the following additions to Progvw.cpp, use the ClassWizard to add a handler for *WM_LBUTTONDOWN* to the view class:

The implementation of the view class is contained in the file Prog4vw.cpp:

```
// Prog4vw.cpp : implementation of the CProg4View class
//

#include "stdafx.h"
#include "Prog4.h"
```

```
#include "Prog4ent.h"
#include "Prog4doc.h"
#include "Prog4vw.h"

#include "Prog4dia.h"

#ifdef _DEBUG
#undef THIS_FILE
static char BASED_CODE THIS_FILE[] = __FILE__;
#endif


/////////////////////////////////////////////////////
// CProg4View

IMPLEMENT_DYNCREATE(CProg4View, CScrollView)

BEGIN_MESSAGE_MAP(CProg4View, CScrollView)
    //{{AFX_MSG_MAP(CProg4View)
    ON_COMMAND(ID_EDIT_DELETE, OnEditDelete)
    ON_COMMAND(ID_EDIT_MODIFY, OnEditModify)
    ON_UPDATE_COMMAND_UI(ID_EDIT_DELETE,
                          OnUpdateEditDelete)
    ON_UPDATE_COMMAND_UI(ID_EDIT_MODIFY,
                          OnUpdateEditModify)
    ON_WM_LBUTTONDOWN()
    //}}AFX_MSG_MAP
    // Standard printing commands
    ON_COMMAND(ID_FILE_PRINT, CScrollView::OnFilePrint)
    ON_COMMAND(ID_FILE_PRINT_PREVIEW,
               CScrollView::OnFilePrintPreview)
END_MESSAGE_MAP()

/////////////////////////////////////////////////////
// CProg4View construction/destruction

CProg4View::CProg4View()
{
    m_posCurrent = (POSITION)0;
}

CProg4View::~CProg4View()
{
}

/////////////////////////////////////////////////////
// CProg4View drawing
```

```
void CProg4View::OnDraw(CDC* pDC)
{
 CProg4Doc* pDoc = GetDocument();
    ASSERT_VALID(pDoc);

    // Get the font-size information for Output()
    // and save it in the class
    TEXTMETRIC tmDescrip;
    pDC->GetTextMetrics(&tmDescrip);
    m_nCharHeight = tmDescrip.tmHeight +
                    tmDescrip.tmExternalLeading;
    m_nCharWidth  = tmDescrip.tmAveCharWidth;

    // Loop through the scheduler entries
    CEntry* pEntry;
    POSITION Index;
    int nYOffset = 0;
    for (pEntry = pDoc->GetFirst(Index);
        pEntry;
        pEntry = pDoc->GetNext(Index))
    {
        Output(pDC, pEntry, nYOffset,
            Index == m_posCurrent);
        nYOffset++; // go to next line
    }
}

void CProg4View::OnInitialUpdate()
{
 CScrollView::OnInitialUpdate();

    // Set the scroll size to initial size of the window
    CRect rectViewSize;
    GetClientRect(&rectViewSize);

    CSize sizeTotal;
    sizeTotal.cx = rectViewSize.right;
    sizeTotal.cy = rectViewSize.bottom;
    SetScrollSizes(MM_TEXT, sizeTotal);
}

/////////////////////////////////////////////////////////
// CProg4View printing

BOOL CProg4View::OnPreparePrinting(CPrintInfo* pInfo)
{
    // default preparation
```

```
        return DoPreparePrinting(pInfo);
}

void CProg4View::OnBeginPrinting(CDC* /*pDC*/,
                                CPrintInfo* /*pInfo*/)
{
    // TODO: add extra initialization before printing
}

void CProg4View::OnEndPrinting(CDC* /*pDC*/,
                              CPrintInfo* /*pInfo*/)
{
    // TODO: add cleanup after printing
}


/////////////////////////////////////////////////////////
// CProg4View diagnostics

#ifdef _DEBUG
void CProg4View::AssertValid() const
{
    CScrollView::AssertValid();
}

void CProg4View::Dump(CDumpContext& dc) const
{
    CScrollView::Dump(dc);
}

CProg4Doc* CProg4View::GetDocument()
{
 ASSERT(m_pDocument->IsKindOf(RUNTIME_CLASS(CProg4Doc)));
    return (CProg4Doc*)m_pDocument;
}
#endif //_DEBUG


/////////////////////////////////////////////////////////
// CProg4View message handlers

void CProg4View::OnEditDelete()
{
    CProg4Doc* pDoc = GetDocument();
    ASSERT_VALID(pDoc);

    // If there is not current element...
    if (m_posCurrent == (POSITION)0)
    {
```

```
        // ...quit
        return;
    }

    // Get the next element and delete this one
    POSITION oldPosition = m_posCurrent;
    pDoc->GetNext(m_posCurrent);
    pDoc->Delete(oldPosition);
}

void CProg4View::OnEditModify()
{
    CProg4Doc* pDoc = GetDocument();
    ASSERT_VALID(pDoc);

    if (m_posCurrent == (POSITION)0)
    {
        return;
    }
    pDoc->Modify(m_posCurrent);
}

void CProg4View::OnUpdateEditDelete(CCmdUI* pCmdUI)
{
    // If the document is empty, deselect the menu item
    CProg4Doc* pDoc = GetDocument();
    ASSERT_VALID(pDoc);

    if (pDoc->GetCount())
    {
        pCmdUI->Enable(TRUE);
    }
    else
    {
        pCmdUI->Enable(FALSE);
    }
}

void CProg4View::OnUpdateEditModify(CCmdUI* pCmdUI)
{
    // Do the same thing as with the delete key
    OnUpdateEditDelete(pCmdUI);
}

void CProg4View::OnLButtonDown(UINT nFlags, CPoint point)
{
```

```
    CProg4Doc* pDoc = GetDocument();
    ASSERT_VALID(pDoc);

    // Offset the mouse position by the scroll
    // position within the logical window
    point += CSize(GetDeviceScrollPosition());

    // Convert the y offset into a line number
    int nSelectedLine = point.y / m_nCharHeight;

    // Okay, now figure out which entry is on
    // this line and make it the current entry
    CEntry *pEntry;
    int nYOffset = 0;
    m_posCurrent = (POSITION)0;
    POSITION Index;
    for (pEntry = pDoc->GetFirst(Index);
         pEntry;
         pEntry = pDoc->GetNext(Index))
    {
        if (nYOffset == nSelectedLine)
        {
            // Hey! That's us. Save off his index
            m_posCurrent = Index;
            break;
        }
        nYOffset++;
    }

    // Now force a redraw to highlight the culprit
    Invalidate(FALSE);
}

/////////////////////////////////////////////////////
//  Other functions

void CProg4View::Output(CDC*    pDC,
            CEntry *pEntry,    // CEntry to display
            int    nOffset,    // line number
            int    bSelected)  // Highlight this entry
{
    UINT nYOffset = nOffset * m_nCharHeight;

    CTime tTime = pEntry->GetTime();
    CString strTime = tTime.Format("%c");

    if (pEntry->GetDisabled())
```

```
{
    pDC->SetTextColor(RGB(0x80, 0x80, 0x80));
}
else
{
    pDC->SetTextColor(RGB(0x00, 0x00, 0x00));
}
if (bSelected)
{
    pDC->SetTextColor(RGB(0xFF, 0x00, 0x00));
}

pDC->TextOut(0, nYOffset, strTime);
CString sOut = pEntry->GetText();
pDC->TextOut(20 * m_nCharWidth, nYOffset, sOut);
}
```

In addition, you have to add the *include* file prog4ent.h from prog4.cpp and prog4dia.cpp, if you haven't already.

To display the list, the *OnDraw( )* function loops through the *CEntry* objects in the document and displays each one on its own line by using the *Output( )* function. The first three arguments to *Output( )* are the device context, the entry to display, and the line number on which to display it. The fourth argument to *Output( )* is set to *TRUE* if this is the selected entry (that is, if the current *Index* is equal to *m_posCurrent*). *Output( )* uses this flag to display the selected entry in a different color.

Skipping ahead for a moment to the *Output( )* function, the function *CTime::Format( )* is used to generate an ASCII representation of the current time. If **pEntry* is disabled, the display color is set to gray (*RGB(0x80, 0x80, 0x80)*); if **pEntry* is enabled, it's set to black. If this entry is the selected one, the color is set to red. After that's settled, the time plus a portion of the entry's text is displayed in the window.

Implementing the Modify and Delete Functions

The *OnEditModify( )* function is straightforward: If a current entry is defined, it is modified; if none is defined, the command is ignored.

The *OnEditDelete( )* is only slightly tougher. It deletes the current entry, if there is one, and makes the next *CEntry* in the list the selected entry.

Where did the selected entry come from, though? Asked another way, how do you select an entry? I implemented this in the *OnLButtonDown( )* function. As you are well aware by now, when a user clicks the left mouse button within the window, the mouse coordinates get reported in a message to this function. *OnLButtonDown( )* converts the mouse location into a line number by dividing the *y* offset by the height of a line.

Suppose that the *y* offset is reported as 35 pixels from the top of the window and that the character height stored in *m_nCharHeight* is 16 pixels. Because 35 divided by 16 is approximately 2, the mouse must be pointing at some part of the *CEntry* displayed on line 2.

The function then loops through the *CEntry* list to find the index of the *CEntry* displayed on that line, which it stores as the selected entry in *m_posCurrent*.

The *Invalidate( )* function forces a redraw of the screen to make the selected entry appear in red.

Note carefully this mouse location to document location conversion. Prog4 is a particularly simple case. In Part V, you'll see a slightly more involved case of converting a mouse location to a location within a text file. ■

The *OnUpdateEditDelete( )* and *OnUpdateEditModify( )* functions disable the Delete and Modify menu options when the document is empty and reenables them when the document is not empty.

The *OnUpdateEdit...( )* functions are called when the menu is opened, when a menu item is chosen, or whenever anything changes and the toolbar is displayed. ■

Multiple Views

Because this program is an MDI application, it is possible to open more than one view at a time. It's even possible, in fact, to open multiple views of a single document simultaneously.

Although this program doesn't provide for it, these views could be different (that is, of different classes). One view could be a list of scheduler entries, for example, and a second view might be a more detailed display of one particular entry. ■

To test this program's ability to keep its views in synch, create a few scheduler entries. Open a second view by choosing New Window from the Window menu. A new window should pop up, looking amazingly like the first one (it should be identical, in fact).

In some ways, this new view is completely independent. For example, the two views scroll independently. In addition, choosing an entry in the second view has no effect on the chosen entry in the first view. The reason is that the chosen entry is a property of the view.

When it comes to the document, however, the two views are about as independent as my wife and her sister — one never does anything without telling the other. If you delete an entry in one view, notice that the entry miraculously disappears from the other view. The same thing happens when you modify an entry. How did it know to do that?

When the view calls *CProg4Doc::Delete( )* to delete an entry, one of the last things that function does is call *UpdateAllViews( )*. This call informs the view that it's time to redraw the window because something has changed. As its name implies, however, this function is a little smarter than I've given it credit for. It doesn't just update the view that reported the change — it updates all views attached to the document. If two views are open, therefore, they both get updated, no matter which one called *Delete( )*.

By calling *UpdateAllViews( )* at the end of each document change, all views stay in synch for free. Gratis. It's not often that you get something for free.

Conclusion

This personal-scheduler program is beginning to look like a real Windows 95 application. You have a document and a view now, so you can do the following:

- ✔ Add new scheduler entries to a list maintained in the document
- ✔ Save the document to disk and restore it later
- ✔ Choose an entry to modify or delete
- ✔ Open multiple views of the same document

One feature is missing, though. Although you can view the list of entries on the screen, you can't print that list. In Chapter 19, you learn how to send output to the printer.

Chapter 19

Hot Off the Press: Printing Schedule Entries

. . . .

In This Chapter

▶ Printing scheduler entries

▶ Choosing a more appropriate font

▶ Handling multiple-page print jobs

▶ Adding page headers and footers

. . . .

*A*s much as you've worried about generating nice graphics on your screen, you have yet to address the problem of printing schedule information on your printer. It's about time for you to fix that problem. By the time the sun sets on this chapter, your personal scheduler will print with the best of them.

Printing Your List: A First Attempt

You may be surprised to realize that you've already written the code that is necessary to produce a scheduler list on your printer — sort of. Go ahead — try it. Choose either Print or Print Preview from the File menu, and let 'er rip. The output from executing Print Preview in Prog4 as it stands looks like Figure 19-1.

If you get the idea that the text looks unadorned and a little on the tiny side, you're right. The output from the printer isn't much better.

If you're disappointed, consider that you didn't have to do a single thing to get this far. You've almost finished adding print and print preview capability, and you haven't even struck a key. How did that happen?

The Printing Process

Let's look at the steps MFC goes through to print something. These steps are outlined in somewhat simplified form in Figure 19-2. Except for the step of displaying the Print dialog box, all the functions listed in the figure may be overloaded in the *CProg4View* class.

The *OnPreparePrinting( )* function is called before the Print dialog box is displayed. Its primary purpose is to communicate with MFC the data that appears in the Print dialog box, such as the number of pages in the document. (Print Preview also uses the number-of-pages information.) Whatever is done at this point, it must be reversible because the user might not complete the print process.

After a user chooses OK to begin the print process, MFC calls the *OnBegin-Printing( )* function. This function allocates any resources or performs any calculations that are necessary throughout the printing process.

After this process is complete, MFC begins invoking *OnPrepareDC( )* and *OnPrint( )* in a loop, once for each page. The *OnPrepareDC( )* function creates and sets up the device context for the print job. Any changes to the device context that are made in the *OnPrepareDC( )* function remain changed through

Multipage Output

This *OnDraw( )* function isn't adequate for printing a large number of entries. The problem is that it insists on printing all the entries in the document even if they don't fit on a single page. *OnDraw( )* doesn't recognize the little bell that rings on the typewriter when it gets to the end of the paper — it just keeps typing on the platen.

You need to add the following capabilities to *OnDraw( )*:

- To recognize the limitations of a piece of paper and stop displaying entries when it reaches the bottom of the page
- To restart on the next page where it left off at the end of the preceding page

The only changes necessary to accommodate multipage output is the addition of the page-number data member to Prog4vw.h and some code to track the number of lines per page and the current location to Prog4vw.cpp.

```
// Prog4vw.h : interface of the CProg4View class
//
/////////////////////////////////////////////////////////////

class CProg4View : public CScrollView
{
    // User-defined stuff goes first
protected:
    int     m_nCharHeight;
    int     m_nCharWidth;

    // Information used for printing
    int     m_nPageNumber; // the current page number

    // The current CEntry for Modify and Delete
    // purposes
    POSITION m_posCurrent;

protected: // create from serialization only
    CProg4View();
    DECLARE_DYNCREATE(CProg4View)
    // ...from here on, same as before...
```

You use this page number in the Prog4vw.cpp source file as follows (note that the *OnPrepareDC( )* and *OnPrint( )* functions in the following were added with the ClassWizard):

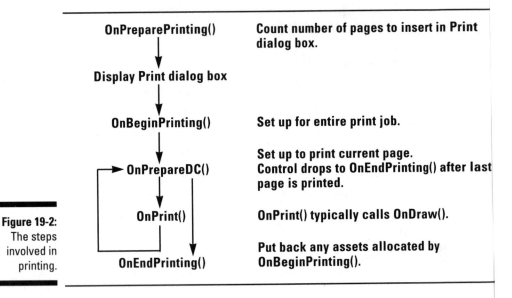

OnPreparePrinting()	Count number of pages to insert in Print dialog box.
Display Print dialog box	
OnBeginPrinting()	Set up for entire print job.
OnPrepareDC()	Set up to print current page. Control drops to OnEndPrinting() after last page is printed.
OnPrint()	OnPrint() typically calls OnDraw().
OnEndPrinting()	Put back any assets allocated by OnBeginPrinting().

Figure 19-2:
The steps involved in printing.

to the *OnPrint( )* call. In the case of the print operation, the device context tha is created refers to the printer.

Okay, this is a quiz. What does the *OnPrint( )* function do? Maybe it, I dunno, prints? It's possible to overload the *OnPrint( )* function and have it do anythin; you want; for WYSIWYG applications (which almost all Windows applications are, including yours), however, *OnPrint( )* calls *OnDraw( )* to perform the actua output.

Now you're getting to the interesting part. You may have thought that this is a somewhat roundabout way of getting to *OnDraw( )*, but the point is that, even for the print operation, you got there. When you wrote an *OnDraw( )* function to handle screen output, therefore, you were writing a function to perform printer output as well. This is the reason you can choose Print and Print Preview now and look at something other than a blank page.

This ability assumes, of course, that you enabled Print or Print Preview, as instructed, when you built the application in the AppWizard.

Also note that when you perform normal output only to the screen, only the *OnPrepareDC( )* and *OnDraw( )* functions are invoked.

The rule is easy to remember: If the name of the function has the word *Print* in it, the function is called for Print and Print-Preview output but not for nor- mal screen output. ■

```
// Prog4vw.cpp : implementation of the CProg4View class
//               This version can print a multipage doc
//

#include "stdafx.h"
#include "Prog4.h"

#include "Prog4ent.h"
#include "Prog4doc.h"
#include "Prog4vw.h"

#include "Prog4dia.h"

#ifdef _DEBUG
#undef THIS_FILE
static char BASED_CODE THIS_FILE[] = __FILE__;
#endif

// Printing constants
const UINT ENTRIES_PER_PAGE = 4;

/////////////////////////////////////////////////////
// CProg4View

    // ...this stuff stays the same

/////////////////////////////////////////////////////
// CProg4View drawing

void CProg4View::OnDraw(CDC* pDC)
{
    CProg4Doc* pDoc = GetDocument();
    ASSERT_VALID(pDoc);

    // Get the font-size information for Output()
    // and save it into the class
    TEXTMETRIC tmDescrip;
    pDC->GetTextMetrics(&tmDescrip);
    m_nCharHeight = tmDescrip.tmHeight +
                    tmDescrip.tmExternalLeading;
    m_nCharWidth  = tmDescrip.tmAveCharWidth;

    // If you aren't printing, then...
    int nSkipEntries;
    int nMaxPerPass;
    if (!pDC->IsPrinting())
    {
```

```
        // ...set the first line to display to 0...
        nSkipEntries = 0;

        // ...and set the number of lines to display
        // to be very large
        nMaxPerPass = MAXSHORT;
    }
    else
    {
        // ...otherwise, set the number per page...
        nMaxPerPass = ENTRIES_PER_PAGE;

        // ...and set the number to skip to
        // the page count times the number per page
        nSkipEntries = (m_nPageNumber - 1) * nMaxPerPass;
    }


    // Loop through the scheduler entries -- skip any entries
    // that may have already been displayed on previous pages
    CEntry* pEntry;
    POSITION Index;
    pEntry = pDoc->GetFirst(Index);
    while (nSkipEntries-- && pEntry)
    {
        pEntry = pDoc->GetNext(Index);
    }


    // Now display starting from here
    int nYOffset = 0;
    for (;
        pEntry;
        pEntry = pDoc->GetNext(Index))
    {
        Output(pDC, pEntry, nYOffset,
               Index == m_posCurrent);

        // Stop when you reach the end of the page
        nYOffset++;
        if (nYOffset >= nMaxPerPass)
        {
            break;
        }
    }
}
```

//

```
// CProg4View printing

// OnPreparePrinting -- called after the user chooses
//                        Print and before the Print dialog
//                        box appears
BOOL CProg4View::OnPreparePrinting(CPrintInfo* pInfo)
{
    CProg4Doc* pDoc = GetDocument();
    ASSERT_VALID(pDoc);

    // Set the number of pages in the Print dialog box
    int nPages =
        (pDoc->GetCount() - 1) / ENTRIES_PER_PAGE + 1;
    pInfo->SetMaxPage(nPages);

    // Now open the Page Setup window
    // (Skip Page Setup on Print Preview)
    return DoPreparePrinting(pInfo);
}

// OnBeginPrinting -- called once at the beginning of
//                        the print job after the operator
//                        enters OK in the Print dialog box
void CProg4View::OnBeginPrinting(CDC* pDC,
                                   CPrintInfo*)
{
}

// OnPrepareDC -- for drawing:
//                    called once right before OnDraw()
//                for printing:
//                    called for each page before OnPrint()
void CProg4View::OnPrepareDC(CDC* pDC,
                              CPrintInfo* pInfo)
{
    CScrollView::OnPrepareDC(pDC, pInfo);
}

// OnPrint -- is invoked right before OnDraw() once
//              for each page
void CProg4View::OnPrint(CDC* pDC,
                           CPrintInfo* pInfo)
{
    // Store the page number
    m_nPageNumber = pInfo->m_nCurPage;
```

```
        // The following calls OnDraw() to output the text
        CScrollView::OnPrint(pDC, pInfo);
}

// OnEndPrinting -- called once when printing is finished
void CProg4View::OnEndPrinting(CDC* pDC,
                                    CPrintInfo* /*pInfo*/)
{
}

/////////////////////////////////////////////////////////////
// CProg4View diagnostics

// ...from here on, the same as well...
```

The application framework that AppWizard constructs contains handlers for the functions you can't avoid overloading. I used the ClassWizard to add an *OnPrint( )* function as well. In addition, I also arranged the print functions in the order in which they're called so that, as you read beginning at *On-PreparePrint( )*, you can see the logic flow shown in Figure 19-2. See whether you can follow that flow now.

The first addition is to the *OnPreparePrinting( )* function, which is the first function called in the printing process. You calculate the number of pages it takes to print the document. I'm assuming that a fixed number of entries, *ENTRIES_PER_PAGE*, fit on a single page. The strange calculation handles the fact that the number returned from *GetCount( )* is relative to one, as is the page number. Table 19-1 shows how this calculation works, assuming that *ENTRIES_PER_PAGE* is 4.

Table 19-1 Page-Count Calculations

GetCount( ) / 4+1	GetCount( )-1	(GetCount( )-1) / 4	(GetCount( )-1)
1	0	0	1
4	3	0	1
5	4	1	2
8	7	1	2
9	8	2	3

Subtracting 1 from *GetCount( )* makes sure that, if there are exactly four entries, only a single page is produced. If there are four entries, the formula calculates one page; if there are five entries, the formula calculates two pages, and so on. (This is as close to higher math as this book gets.)

Wait a minute," you say. "I can fit more than 4 entries on a page." True, but setting the number of entries per page artificially low makes it much easier to generate multipage output. It takes a great deal of time to create 40 or 50 scheduler entries. After everything works, it's relatively easy to set this number to something more reasonable. ■

The number of pages in the document is stored in the *CPrintInfo* structure pointed at by *pInfo* by using the *SetMaxPage( )* member function. This same object is passed to all the print functions. It serves as the primary means of communication between user-written print routines and MFC. Other members include *m_nCurPage*, which is the number of the current page being printed, and *m_bPreview*, which is *TRUE* when you "print" in print-preview mode. (For a complete list, look up *CPrintInfo* in the on-line Help.)

OnPreparePrinting( ) should always invoke *DoPreparePrinting( )* and return whatever is returned by that function. It's *DoPreparePrinting( )* that displays the Print dialog box.

The next step in the process is *OnBeginPrinting( )*, which does nothing in particular in this version. *OnPrepareDC( )* invokes the *OnPrepareDC( )* function of its parent class. When you're making changes to this function, remember that it is also invoked when you're drawing to the screen.

The next function, *OnPrint( )*, is invoked once for each page. Its response is to save the current page number, which it reads from the *CPrintInfo* structure, and then proceed normally, calling the base class *OnPrint( )* function.

The *CScrollView* class inherits *OnPrint* from its parent *CView*. The *CView::OnPrint( )* function does nothing more than invoke your *OnDraw( )* function and return. Nonetheless, it's safer to call *CScrollView::OnPrint( )* than to call either *CView::OnPrint( )* or *OnDraw( )* directly. Someday the MFC designers may change things so that either *CScrollView::OnPrint( )* or *CView::OnPrint( )* does other neat things as well, and you wouldn't want to miss out. (It's not as though Microsoft never changes things.) ■

Obviously, the big changes are in the *OnDraw( )* member function.

OnDraw( ) now contains two entries, *nSkipEntries* (the number of entries to skip before beginning to display) and *nMaxPerPass* (the number of entries that fit on a "page").

If you are currently repainting the view, *nSkipEntries* is set to zero, which means that you don't skip anything, and *nMaxPerPass* is set to a ridiculously large number, which means that you display all you have. *OnDraw( )* determines whether it's printing by calling *CDC::IsPrinting( )* on the device context object that is provided.

If *OnDraw( )* is "painting" to the printer, it sets *nMaxPerPass* to *ENTRIES_PER_PAGE*, the number of entries that fit on a single page. It then sets *nSkipEntries* so that if the page number is 1, *nSkipEntries* is zero; if the page number is 2, *nSkipEntries* is *ENTRIES_PER_PAGE*; if the page number is 3, *nSkipEntries* is two times *ENTRIES_PER_PAGE*; and so on.

OnDraw( ) then loops through the first *nSkipEntries* entries in the document. After skipping those entries, *OnDraw( )* enters a second loop that displays entries as always. This time, however, it quits after displaying *nMaxPerPass* entries.

Does it work?

Create a document with four or fewer entries in it, and then choose Print Preview. Not much difference yet. The font is still too small (you can get a closer look with the magnifying glass).

Close that window and enter a few more entries so that the total number of entries exceeds four. Go back to Print Preview. Notice that you see only the first four entries in the page. Also notice that the Next Page button is enabled because Print Preview realizes that there's more than one page. Click Next Page to see the next four entries and so on until you reach the end of the document.

Exit from Print Preview and choose Print. Notice that the Print dialog box shows the number of pages to print (it also enables you to print a limited range of pages, if you prefer).

What if you don't know the number of pages?

By assuming a fixed number of entries per page, you were able to calculate in *OnPreparePrinting( )* how many pages it would take to print all the entries in the document. This assumption simplified your logic somewhat, and, thankfully, this is usually the case.

If the entries being printed are of variable length, however, you may not know in advance how many pages you need. In these types of cases, you must tell MFC when to stop printing.

Remember that *OnPrepareDC( )* is called once for each page. If this function determines that printing is not complete, it sets the flag *m_bContinuePrinting* in the *CPrintInfo* to *TRUE*. If printing seems to be finished, it sets the flag to *FALSE*.

As long as the flag remains *TRUE*, MFC invokes *OnPrint( )* to print the current page and then returns to *OnPrepareDC( )* to set up for the next page. As soon as *m_bContinuePrinting* is *FALSE*, MFC exits from the loop and calls *OnEndPrinting( )* to clean up.

Putting Up a Brave Font

Okay, so output was sent to the printer, and it was even multipage output. But I wouldn't rip the pages off the printer and go running to tell all your friends just yet.

Your friends won't be impressed. The output is horribly ugly. What can you do to make it a little more presentable?

The biggest problem with your results is that the font is too small. Although the default font is fine for displaying output on the screen, I prefer a big 18-point serif TrueType font for the printer. (Okay, italicized, underlined, Old English Gothic cursive is a little much, but I like something fancy.)

Choosing a new font is a three-step process:

1. Create a font object.
2. Find a font and attach it to the object. Remember to specify all the different options.
3. Select the font into the device context. (This step is just like selecting a pen or any other GDI object.)

In practice, it looks like the following:

```
// Create a CFont object
CFont fNewFont;

// Attach a font to it
pDC->SetMapMode(MM_TWIPS);
fNewFont.CreateFont(
        18 * 20,     // Height
        0,           // Width
        0,           // Escapement
        0,           // Orientation
        FW_NORMAL,   // Weight
        0,           // 1->italics
        0,           // Underline
        0,           // Strikeout
        ANSI_CHARSET, // Character set
```

```
                    OUT_DEFAULT_PRECIS, // Precision
                    CLIP_DEFAULT_PRECIS,// Clipping precision
                    DEFAULT_QUALITY,
                    DEFAULT_PITCH,
                    CString("MS Sans Serif"));// Font name

    // Select it into the device context
    CFont *pOldFont = pDC->SelectObject(&fNewFont);
```

The *CFont* object *fNewFont* is empty when it is created. The call to *CreateFont( )* loads into the program one of the existing fonts from the system and attaches it to the *fNewFont* object. The arguments to *CreateFont( )* specify the nature of the font you want.

Although the function offers lots of options in its arguments, the most important are the height and the name of the font you want. In this case, I've specified an 18-point version of the MS Sans Serif font (I guess that wasn't so fancy, after all).

Setting the mapping mode of the device context to *MM_TWIPS* enabled me to specify the font size in points rather than in device units of the printer. (Remember that a twip is 1/20th of a point.) The default mapping mode, *MM_TEXT*, is not convenient for supporting Print and Print Preview. All three — Print, Print Preview, and the display — have different resolutions. Switching to one of the other mapping modes, such as *MM_TWIPS*, causes sizes to be converted automatically to match the resolution of the device.

After this font object has been created, it is selected into the device context by using the *SelectObject( )* call. The return from this call is the old font object that should be restored to the device context when you're finished.

Try It!

To try out some new fonts, I made the following additions to the *CProg4View* class:

```
// Prog4vw.h : interface of the CProg4View class
//
/////////////////////////////////////////////////////////

class CProg4View : public CScrollView
{
protected:
    int     m_nCharHeight;
    int     m_nCharWidth;
```

```
        // Offset information used for printing
        int       m_nPageNumber; // the current page number

        // Use to store fonts
        CFont*    m_pTextFont;

        // Change font
        CFont* SetFont(CDC*, CFont* pNewFont = NULL);

        // The current CEntry for Modify and Delete
        // purposes
        POSITION m_posCurrent;

        void Output(CDC* pDC,
                    CEntry* pEntry,
                    int  nOffset,
                    int  bSelected); //TRUE if selected

protected: // create from serialization only
    CProg4View();
    DECLARE_DYNCREATE(CProg4View)

    // ...same from here on...
```

The member function *SetFont( )* selects the specified font into the device context and resets the *m_nCharHeight* and *m_nCharWidth* members to match the new font. It returns the old font. If no font is provided, *SetFont( )* simply calculates the character height and width based on the current font.

The following changes were necessary in the Prog4vw.cpp source file:

```
// Prog4vw.cpp : implementation of the CProg4View class
//          This version uses a better font for printing
//

#include "stdafx.h"
#include "Prog4.h"

#include "Prog4ent.h"
#include "Prog4doc.h"
#include "Prog4vw.h"

#include "Prog4dia.h"

#ifdef _DEBUG
#undef THIS_FILE
```

```
static char BASED_CODE THIS_FILE[] = _ _FILE_ _;
#endif

// Printing constants
const UINT ENTRIES_PER_PAGE = 4;
const UINT TWIPS_PER_POINT = 20;
const UINT TWIPS_PER_INCH = 72 * TWIPS_PER_POINT;

/////////////////////////////////////////////////////
// CProg4View
// ...no change until you get to the printing stuff...

/////////////////////////////////////////////////////
// CProg4View drawing

void CProg4View::OnDraw(CDC* pDC)
{
    CProg4Doc* pDoc = GetDocument();
    ASSERT_VALID(pDoc);

    // Get the font-size information for Output()
    // and save it into the class
    SetFont(pDC);

    /* Be sure and comment out or remove the following
       lines of code, because they have been replaced by
       the call to SetFont() above:
    TEXTMETRIC tmDescrip;
    pDC->GetTextMetrics(&tmDescrip);
    m_nCharHeight = tmDescrip.tmHeight +
                    tmDescrip.tmExternalLeading;
    m_nCharWidth  = tmDescrip.tmAveCharWidth;
    */

    // If you aren't printing, then...
    int nSkipEntries;
    // ...remainder of this function the same as well...

}
/////////////////////////////////////////////////////
// CProg4View printing

// OnPreparePrinting -- called after the user chooses
//                      Print and before the Print dialog
//                      box appears
BOOL CProg4View::OnPreparePrinting(CPrintInfo* pInfo)
{
```

```
        CProg4Doc* pDoc = GetDocument();
        ASSERT_VALID(pDoc);

        // Set the number of pages in the Print dialog box
        int nPages =
            (pDoc->GetCount() - 1) / ENTRIES_PER_PAGE + 1;
        pInfo->SetMaxPage(nPages);

        // Now open the Page Setup window
        // (Skip Page Setup on Print Preview)
        return DoPreparePrinting(pInfo);
}


// OnBeginPrinting -- called once at the beginning of
//                    the print job after the operator
//                    enters OK in the Print dialog box
void CProg4View::OnBeginPrinting(CDC* pDC,
                                 CPrintInfo*)
{
 pDC->SetMapMode(MM_TWIPS);
    m_pTextFont = new CFont;
    m_pTextFont->CreateFont(
                    18 * 20,    // Height
                    0,          // Width
                    0,          // Escapement
                    0,          // Orientation
                    FW_NORMAL,  // Weight
                    0,          // 1->italics
                    0,          // Underline
                    0,          // Strikeout
                    ANSI_CHARSET, // Character set
                    OUT_DEFAULT_PRECIS, // Precision
                    CLIP_DEFAULT_PRECIS,// Clipping prec.
                    DEFAULT_QUALITY,
                    DEFAULT_PITCH,
                    CString("MS Sans Serif"));
}


// OnPrepareDC -- for drawing:
//                called once right before OnDraw()
//             for printing:
//                called for each page before OnPrint()
void CProg4View::OnPrepareDC(CDC* pDC, CPrintInfo* pInfo)
{
    CScrollView::OnPrepareDC(pDC, pInfo);
}
```

```cpp
// OnPrint -- is invoked right before OnDraw() once
//            for each page
void CProg4View::OnPrint(CDC* pDC, CPrintInfo* pInfo)
{
    // Store the page number
    m_nPageNumber = pInfo->m_nCurPage;

    // Change the font for printing
    CFont *pOldFont;
    pOldFont = SetFont(pDC, m_pTextFont);

    // The following calls OnDraw() to output the text
    CScrollView::OnPrint(pDC, pInfo);

    // Restore the original font
    SetFont(pDC, pOldFont);
}


// OnEndPrinting -- called once when printing is finished
void CProg4View::OnEndPrinting(CDC* pDC,
                               CPrintInfo* /*pInfo*/)
{
delete m_pTextFont;
}


// SetFont -- change the font and get the new font-
//            size information for output purposes
CFont* CProg4View::SetFont(// Rtrns old fnt (0 if no chg)
            CDC* pDC,       // The device context
            CFont* pFont)   // The new font (0->don't
                            // change font)
{
    CFont *pOldFont = NULL;

    // Set up the Device Context
    pDC->SetMapMode(MM_TWIPS);

    // If there is a font, select it into the DC
    if (pFont)
    {
        pOldFont = pDC->SelectObject(pFont);
    }

    // Get the font-size information for Output()
    // and save it into the class.
    // (The minus sign in the calculation of m_nCharHeight
    // is to account for the fact that y increases in the
```

```
        // opposite direction in MM_TWIPS mode.)
        TEXTMETRIC tmDescrip;
        pDC->GetTextMetrics(&tmDescrip);
        m_nCharHeight = -(tmDescrip.tmHeight
                        + tmDescrip.tmExternalLeading);
        m_nCharWidth  = tmDescrip.tmAveCharWidth;

        // Return the old font (returns NULL if no
        // font change made)
        return pOldFont;
}
```

```
/////////////////////////////////////////////////////////
// CProg4View diagnostics

//   ...no changes from here down until you get to:
void CProg4View::OnLButtonDown(UINT nFlags, CPoint point)
{
        // ...one little change here...

        // Convert the y offset into a line number
        CClientDC dc(this);
        dc.SetMapMode(MM_TWIPS);
        dc.DPtoLP(&point);
        int nSelectedLine = point.y / m_nCharHeight;

        // ...the rest is the same from here on...
}
```

OnBeginPrinting( ) chooses a nice font to use for the print job. Remember that this function is called once at the beginning of the print job after you commit to printing but before you really get started. *OnBeginPrinting( )* creates the *CFont* object off the heap and stores its address in the member *m_pTextFont*.

OnPrint( ) selects the print font in the device context by calling the *SetFont( )* function before executing *OnDraw( )*. After the drawing is completed, *OnPrint( )* restores the old font.

OnDraw( ) uses *SetFont( )* to initialize the character width and height information.

After printing is completed, the *OnEndPrinting( )* returns to the heap the *CFont* object created in *OnBeginPrinting( )*.

The only other change occurs in *OnLButtonDown( )*. Because *m_nCharHeight* in now in *MM_TWIPS* units, the mouse location information, which is in device units, must be converted into logical units before a comparison can be made. (You saw this process in Chapter 4.)

Putting on a Hat and Shoes Before You Go Out

The output from this program now has a much more pleasing appearance. The appearance of the view is completely unchanged, but the print output has a font that looks attractive even on my cheap-o laser printer.

It's still not quite time to call in your friends to marvel at your lexigraphical achievement, however. Most programs display a header at the top of each page and maybe even a page number at the bottom. In addition, I'm never happy about the output jamming up against the left margin of the paper. Not to worry. A few quick adjustments should take care of these nuisances. Make the following additions:

- ✔ Add a title at the top of each page with a large, bold font.
- ✔ Add column headers with the same font as the text but underlined.
- ✔ Move the entire output over about an inch from the left margin.
- ✔ Add the page number at the bottom of the page.

To implement these enhancements, I added two more *CFont** members: one for the page header and another for the column heads as well as left and top margin offsets to the *CProg4View* class:

```
// Prog4vw.h : interface of the CProg4View class
//
/////////////////////////////////////////////////////////////

class CProg4View : public CScrollView
{
protected:
    int      m_nCharHeight;
    int      m_nCharWidth;

    // Offset information used for printing
    int      m_nLeftMargin; // left margin [twips]
    int      m_nPageOffset; // top margin [twips]
```

```
    int       m_nPageNumber; // the current page number

    // Print fonts
    CFont*    m_pHeaderFont;
    CFont*    m_pColumnHeaderFont;
    CFont*    m_pTextFont;

    // Change font
    CFont* SetFont(CDC*, CFont* pNewFont = NULL);

    // The current CEntry for Modify and Delete
    // purposes
    POSITION m_posCurrent;

    void Output(CDC* pDC,
                CEntry* pEntry,
                int  nOffset,
                int  bSelected); //TRUE if selected

protected: // create from serialization only
    CProg4View();
    DECLARE_DYNCREATE(CProg4View)

  // ...same from here on out...
```

The printing routines in Prog4vw.cpp were modified:

```
// Prog4vw.cpp : implementation of the CProg4View class
//

// ...no change here...

// Printing constants
const UINT ENTRIES_PER_PAGE = 4;
const UINT TWIPS_PER_POINT = 20;
const UINT TWIPS_PER_INCH = 72 * TWIPS_PER_POINT;

/////////////////////////////////////////////////////////////////
// CProg4View drawing

void CProg4View::OnDraw(CDC* pDC)
{
    CProg4Doc* pDoc = GetDocument();
    ASSERT_VALID(pDoc);

    // If you aren't printing, then...
    int nSkipEntries;
```

```
int nMaxPerPass;
if (!pDC->IsPrinting())
{
    // ...reset the margins...
    m_nLeftMargin = m_nPageOffset = 0;

    // ...set the first line to display to 0...
    nSkipEntries = 0;

    // ...and set the number of lines to display
    // to be very large
    nMaxPerPass = MAXSHORT;
}
else
{
    // ...otherwise, set the number per page...
    nMaxPerPass = ENTRIES_PER_PAGE;

    // ...and set the number to skip to
    // the page count times the number per page
    nSkipEntries = (m_nPageNumber - 1) * nMaxPerPass;
}

// Set the character size for the current font
SetFont(pDC);

// Loop through the scheduler entries -- skip any entries
// that may have already been displayed on previous pages
CEntry* pEntry;
POSITION Index;
pEntry = pDoc->GetFirst(Index);
while (nSkipEntries-- && pEntry)
{
    pEntry = pDoc->GetNext(Index);
}

// Now display starting from here
int nYOffset = 0;
for (;
    pEntry;
    pEntry = pDoc->GetNext(Index))
{
    Output(pDC, pEntry, nYOffset,
            Index == m_posCurrent);

    // Stop when you reach the end of the page
    nYOffset++;
```

```
        if (nYOffset >= nMaxPerPass)
        {
            break;
        }
    }
}


// ...unchanged until you get to...

/////////////////////////////////////////////////////
// CProg4View printing

// OnPreparePrinting -- called after the user selects
//                      Print and before the Print dialog
//                      box appears
BOOL CProg4View::OnPreparePrinting(CPrintInfo* pInfo)
{
    CProg4Doc* pDoc = GetDocument();
    ASSERT_VALID(pDoc);

    // Set the number of pages in the Print dialog box
    int nPages =
        (pDoc->GetCount() - 1) / ENTRIES_PER_PAGE + 1;
    pInfo->SetMaxPage(nPages);

    // Now open the Page Setup window
    // (Skip Page Setup on Print Preview)
    return DoPreparePrinting(pInfo);
}

// OnBeginPrinting -- called once at the beginning of
//                    the print job after the operator
//                    enters OK in the Print dialog box
void CProg4View::OnBeginPrinting(CDC* pDC,
                                 CPrintInfo*)

{
    // Allocate a font for the page header,
    // the column heads, and the text
    pDC->SetMapMode(MM_TWIPS);
    m_pHeaderFont = new CFont;
    m_pHeaderFont->CreateFont(
            32 * 20,   // Height
            0,         // Width
            0,         // Escapement
            0,         // Orientation
            FW_NORMAL, // Weight
            0,         // 1->italics
```

```
                0,          // Underline
                0,          // Strikeout
                ANSI_CHARSET, // Character set
                OUT_DEFAULT_PRECIS, // Precision
                CLIP_DEFAULT_PRECIS,// Clipping precision
                DEFAULT_QUALITY,
                DEFAULT_PITCH,
                CString("MS Sans Serif"));

        m_pColumnHeaderFont = new CFont;
        m_pColumnHeaderFont->CreateFont(
                18 * 20,    // Height
                0,          // Width
                0,          // Escapement
                0,          // Orientation
                FW_NORMAL,  // Weight
                0,          // 1->italics
                1,          // Underline
                0,          // Strikeout
                ANSI_CHARSET, // Character set
                OUT_DEFAULT_PRECIS, // Precision
                CLIP_DEFAULT_PRECIS,// Clipping precision
                DEFAULT_QUALITY,
                DEFAULT_PITCH,
                CString("MS Sans Serif"));

        m_pTextFont = new CFont;
        m_pTextFont->CreateFont(
                18 * 20,    // Height
                0,          // Width
                0,          // Escapement
                0,          // Orientation
                FW_NORMAL,  // Weight
                0,          // 1->italics
                0,          // Underline
                0,          // Strikeout
                ANSI_CHARSET, // Character set
                OUT_DEFAULT_PRECIS, // Precision
                CLIP_DEFAULT_PRECIS,// Clipping precision
                DEFAULT_QUALITY,
                DEFAULT_PITCH,
                CString("MS Sans Serif"));
}


// OnPrepareDC -- for drawing:
//              called once right before OnDraw()
```

```
//                for printing:
//                  called for each page right before OnPrint()
void CProg4View::OnPrepareDC(CDC* pDC, CPrintInfo* pInfo)
{
    CScrollView::OnPrepareDC(pDC, pInfo);
}

// OnPrint -- is invoked right before OnDraw() once
//            for each page
void CProg4View::OnPrint(CDC* pDC, CPrintInfo* pInfo)
{
    int nXOffset;    // Text offset from left to right

    // Set the output margins
    m_nLeftMargin =   1 * TWIPS_PER_INCH;
    m_nPageOffset =   TWIPS_PER_INCH / 2;

    // And the page number
    m_nPageNumber = pInfo->m_nCurPage;

    // Display the page header information
    CFont *pOldFont;
    pOldFont = SetFont(pDC, m_pHeaderFont);
    CString header("Personal Scheduler");
    if (m_nPageNumber > 1)
    {
        header = CString("Personal Scheduler (cont)");
    }
    nXOffset = m_nLeftMargin + 8 * m_nCharWidth;
    m_nPageOffset += m_nCharHeight; // move down a line
    pDC->TextOut(nXOffset, m_nPageOffset, header);

    m_nPageOffset += m_nCharHeight; // skip this line
    m_nPageOffset += m_nCharHeight; // add a blank line
                                    // underneath header

    // Now column headers
    SetFont(pDC, m_pColumnHeaderFont);
    CString time("Time");
    nXOffset = m_nLeftMargin;
    pDC->TextOut(nXOffset, m_nPageOffset, time);

    CString text("Text");
    nXOffset = m_nLeftMargin + 20 * m_nCharWidth;
    pDC->TextOut(nXOffset, m_nPageOffset, text);

    m_nPageOffset += m_nCharHeight; // move down a line
```

```
    // The following calls OnDraw() to output the text
    SetFont(pDC, m_pTextFont);
    CScrollView::OnPrint(pDC, pInfo);
    // And the page number at the bottom
    // Make sure that it's black
    pDC->SetTextColor(RGB(0x00, 0x00, 0x00));
    CString page;
    page.Format("Page %d of %d",
                m_nPageNumber,
                pInfo->GetMaxPage());
    nXOffset = m_nLeftMargin + 20 * m_nCharWidth;
    m_nPageOffset +=
                (ENTRIES_PER_PAGE + 2) * m_nCharHeight;
    pDC->TextOut(nXOffset, m_nPageOffset, page);

    // Put the old font back
    SetFont(pDC, pOldFont);
}

// OnEndPrinting -- called once when printing is finished
void CProg4View::OnEndPrinting(CDC* pDC,
                               CPrintInfo* /*pInfo*/)
{
    // Get rid of your fonts
    delete m_pHeaderFont;
    delete m_pColumnHeaderFont;
    delete m_pTextFont;
}

CFont* CProg4View::SetFont( // Returns old font
            CDC* pDC,       // The device context
            CFont* pFont)   // The new font (0->don't
                            // change font)
{
    CFont* pOldFont = (CFont*)NULL;

    // Set up the Device Context
    pDC->SetMapMode(MM_TWIPS);

    // If there is a font, select it into the DC
    if (pFont)
    {
        pOldFont = pDC->SelectObject(pFont);
    }

    // Get the font-size information for Output()
    // and save it into the class
```

```
        TEXTMETRIC tmDescrip;
        pDC->GetTextMetrics(&tmDescrip);
        m_nCharHeight = -(tmDescrip.tmHeight
                        + tmDescrip.tmExternalLeading);
        m_nCharWidth  = tmDescrip.tmAveCharWidth;

        // Return the previous font
        return pOldFont;
}

void CProg4View::Output(CDC*    pDC,
                CEntry *pEntry,   // CEntry to display
                int    nOffset,   // line number
                int    bSelected) // highlight this entry
{
    int nXOffset;
    int nYOffset =
                nOffset * m_nCharHeight + m_nPageOffset;

    CTime tTime = pEntry->GetTime();
    CString strTime = tTime.Format("%c");

    if (pEntry->GetDisabled())
    {
        pDC->SetTextColor(RGB(0x80, 0x80, 0x80));
    }
    else
    {
        pDC->SetTextColor(RGB(0x00, 0x00, 0x00));
    }
    if (bSelected)
    {
        pDC->SetTextColor(RGB(0xFF, 0x00, 0x00));
    }

    nXOffset = m_nLeftMargin;
    pDC->TextOut(nXOffset, nYOffset, strTime);
    nXOffset = m_nLeftMargin + 20 * m_nCharWidth;
    CString sOut = pEntry->GetText();
    pDC->TextOut(nXOffset, nYOffset, sOut);
}
```

OnBeginPrinting( ) now allocates three fonts: a large, 32-point, "daddy" font for
the page header; an 18-point, underlined, "mama" font for the column headers; and a regular, 18-point, "baby" font for the text.

The majority of the additions are in *OnPrint( )*. *OnPrint( )* begins by setting the left margin to one inch, and the top margin begins at one-half inch. (Don't like those? Change them to something else.)

OnPrint( ) then displays the string *"Personal Scheduler"* in the special header font and the strings *"Time"* and *"Text"* in their special, underlined column header font. Every time *OnPrint( )* displays another line, it first moves *m_nPage-Offset* down to skip past the line that was just printed (as a form of line-feed) and then, sometimes, to add a blank line.

Before *OnPrint( )* restores the old font, it displays the page number two paces past the last entry that was printed.

SetFont( ) remains unchanged. *Output( )* contains a few minor changes, however, to reflect the left and upper margins. *OnDraw( )* is changed to reset the *m_nLeftMargin* and *m_nPageOffset* data members in the event that output is displayed to the screen rather than to Print or Print Preview.

The zoomed Print Preview output from this program is shown in Figure 19-3.

Now you can show your friends the output.

The printed output doesn't get any better from this WinApp.

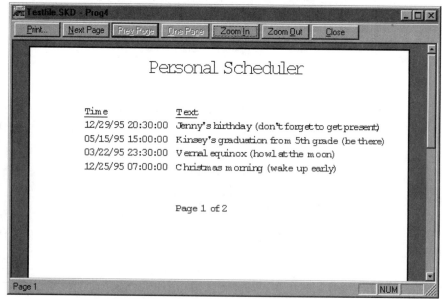

Figure 19-3:
The
(zoomed)
Print
Preview
output from
your
improved
scheduler
WinApp.

Conclusion

Your program now knows how to break up its output over several pages. It can tack margins to the sides to make the output look more centered, and it even displays attractive headers at the top and bottom of each page. What more could you ask for?

When it comes to graphical output, the improvements never stop. You could have used *CDC::GetDeviceCaps( )* to fetch the actual dimensions of the paper rather than set some fixed number of entries per page based on a standard paper size. In addition, you could have used the formatting string in the *CPrintInfo* structure to determine the format of the page number.

Your program still has a more fundamental problem, however: It doesn't do anything. No matter when you set the alarms for, they never go off because there aren't any timers. You'll add some in Chapter 20.

Chapter 20

Finishing the Personal-Scheduler Application

*T*he personal-scheduler application is great so far, except that it still doesn't do anything. Let's fix that problem so that you can declare the program done and go on to something new.

Scheduling Something

To complete this application, you have to complete these tasks:

✔ Set up a timer to prompt you periodically.

✔ Search the list for any "expired" entries.

✔ If you find one, bring your application to the top of the window heap and alert the world.

Each of these tasks is addressed in this chapter.

Using timers

A Windows timer is an input source, much like the mouse or the keyboard is. You can tell the timer to prod you every *n* milliseconds (or so) and then go away. Sure enough, every *n* milliseconds, the timer gives you a nudge, usually in the form of a *WM_TIMER* message.

There are lots of different uses for timers. For example, you can use them to implement an autosave feature in a word processor, to time out some recalcitrant device, or to alert a physically sensitive typist that it's time to change his typing position to avoid wrist strain. In this chapter, however, you use a timer to prompt the scheduler application into looking through the list of entries for one that has expired.

Setting a timer

The function *CWnd::SetTimer( )* is used to set a timer. *SetTimer( )* can be invoked in one of two different ways, as shown in the following example:

```
// prototype for callback function
void CALLBACK EXPORT Cbfn(
    HWND hWnd,       //handle of window that set timer
    UINT nMsg,       //WM_TIMER
    UINT nIDEvent,   //timer identification
    DWORD dwTime     //system time (time since bootup)
);

const UINT nID1 = 1; // Timer to use
const UINT nID2 = 2;

void fn(CWnd* pWindow, UINT nSecs)
{
    // Set a timer to send a message
    pWindow->SetTimer(nID1, nSecs * 1000, 0);

    // Set a timer to invoke a callback function
    pWindow->SetTimer(nID2, nSecs * 1000, Cbfn);
}
```

The first call to *SetTimer( )* causes Windows to send a *WM_TIMER* message every *nSecs* seconds to a window associated with the *CWnd* object pointed at by *pWindow*.

The first argument, *nID*, is simply the ID to use within the current application of the timer. The second argument is the number of milliseconds between messages. In this format, the third argument is always zero.

The number of timers under Windows 3.1 and earlier was limited systemwide to 32. The number of timers available under Windows 95 is much larger. ∎

The second call to *SetTimer( )* is similar to the first, except that it provides the address of a callback function as the third argument. In this version, the function *Cbfn( )* (in this case) is called directly to process the *WM_TIMER* message every so many milliseconds. Because this approach avoids the message-dispatch mechanism, it measures time a little more accurately.

Timer limitations

Timers have a few limitations. For one, timers are based on the programmable interval timer (PIT) chip built-in to the PC. The PIT works like a metronome, with a period of 18.2 ticks per second. That is, the PIT interrupts Windows every 55 milliseconds or so to alert it to service any waiting timers.

Even though the argument to *SetTimer( )* may specify that the application wants to be prompted every 500 milliseconds (or half a second, to mere mortals), the messages come at an interval closer to 495 milliseconds, which is the nearest multiple of 55 that is less than 500.

For most applications, a time resolution of 1/20th of a second is good enough (500 milliseconds versus 495 milliseconds isn't serious enough to warrant a court hearing for false advertising). For applications that do need the extra resolution, 18.2 ticks per second is so entrenched into the PC programming culture that it can't be changed now.

Another problem stems from the fact that the PIT is programmed when the PC is booted and is largely left alone after that. The upshot is that, when you call *SetTimer( )*, you don't know where the metronome is. It might be just about ready to click, or it may have just clicked and now requires a full swing. For long timers, the difference in one metronome swing, more or less, isn't important. For short periods, however, it can be a problem.

If you specify a 110-millisecond delay, for example, the first message may be generated anywhere from 56 to 110 milliseconds later. Subsequent messages should be generated with a period of 110 milliseconds.

A third limitation stems from the fact that the timer argument is a single unsigned *int*, which limits the duration of a timer to 65 seconds (plus change). To measure time spans longer than that, you have to implement a counter in your *WM_TIMER* message handler.

It's true that Windows 95 provides a separate timer mechanism, called a *multimedia timer*. This timer is set by using the Windows 32 API function *time-SetEvent( )*. Multimedia timers rely strictly on callback functions (described later in this section) and do not support the *WM_TIMER* message. ■

Other timely details

The *WM_TIMER* message is handled in much the same way as the *WM_PAINT* message. First, it's a low-priority message: It's processed only if no other message types are in the queue. Second, there is never more than one *WM_TIMER* message in the queue at one time. If a *WM_TIMER* message is already in the queue when the buzzer goes off, Windows just resets the buzzer without generating another message. This implies two things:

- ✔ You can't count on the *WM_TIMER* message to be timely (ironic, isn't it?). The timer message may be held up in traffic for quite some time.

- ✔ You can't even count on the *WM_TIMER* message to be there at all. If you implement a clock, for example, it's all right to use a one-second timer message to update the clock face. You cannot simply increment the seconds every time a message is received, however. If you do, your clock gets behind as *WM_TIMER* messages are swallowed up by the system during busy times. Instead, you must read the system time every time a message is received, perhaps by using the *CTime* class. (Counting messages wouldn't have worked anyway because of the 55-millisecond resolution problem mentioned earlier.)

The situation is a little better if you use the callback-function approach. Without a message queue to go through, the timer messages don't get bogged down or eaten. By avoiding the message queue, however, the callback approach seems strangely non-Windowy. ∎

A timer can be turned off by using the *CWnd::KillTimer( )* function. This function can be called from within the *OnTimer( )* timer-handler function. This capability is particularly useful for generating a one-shot: The timer is turned on somewhere in the program; after the appropriate amount of time, a *WM_TIMER* message is sent to the *OnTimer( )* function. This function kills the timer.

When the window associated with a *CWnd* object is destroyed, all alive timers associated with that window are killed automatically.

Processing a timer message

Now that you have a *WM_TIMER* message coming in to awaken you periodically, you have to use that opportunity to search the list of existing *CEntry* objects for any that may have expired.

Handle this situation by using the ClassWizard to add a message handler for the *WM_TIMER* message and then make the following additions to the *CProg4View* class in Prog4vw.cpp:

```
// Prog4vw.cpp : implementation of the CProg4View class
//

// ...initial stuff left unchanged...

// Printing constants
const UINT ENTRIES_PER_PAGE = 4;
const UINT TWIPS_PER_POINT = 20;
const UINT TWIPS_PER_INCH = 72 * TWIPS_PER_POINT;// an inch in
            TWIPs

// Timer constants
const UINT ONE_MINUTE_TIMER = 1;
const UINT SECOND = 1000;


/////////////////////////////////////////////////////////
// CProg4View

// ...nothing changed until:

void CProg4View::OnInitialUpdate()
{
    CScrollView::OnInitialUpdate();

    // Set the scroll size to initial size of the window
    CRect rectViewSize;
    GetClientRect(&rectViewSize);

    CSize sizeTotal;
    sizeTotal.cx = rectViewSize.right;
    sizeTotal.cy = rectViewSize.bottom;
    SetScrollSizes(MM_TEXT, sizeTotal);

    // Start a one-minute timer
    if (!SetTimer(ONE_MINUTE_TIMER, 1 * SECOND, NULL))
    {
        AfxMessageBox(
                "Couldn't get timer for this window",
                MB_OK | MB_ICONEXCLAMATION);
    }
}

// ...nothing else changed except for the addition
//    of the WM_TIMER message handler:

void CProg4View::OnTimer(UINT nIDEvent)
{
```

```
CProg4Doc* pDoc = GetDocument();
ASSERT_VALID(pDoc);

// Ignore any timers that go
// off while dialog box popped up
static int bIgnoreTimer = FALSE;
if (bIgnoreTimer)
{
    return;
}


// Loop through the list of entries, looking for
// one to go off
CTime tNow = CTime::GetCurrentTime();
CEntry* pEntry;
POSITION Index;
for (pEntry = pDoc->GetFirst(Index);
    pEntry;
    pEntry = pDoc->GetNext(Index))
{

    // Check the enabled entries...
    if (pEntry->GetDisabled() == FALSE)
    {

        // ...for one that's ready to go off
        if (pEntry->GetTime() < tNow)
        {

            // Found one! Sound the alarm:
            // 1) turn timers off until you're
            //     finished with this one
            bIgnoreTimer = TRUE;

            // 2) pop the window up to the front...
            //     (Get the MDI Child Frame)
            CWnd* pChildFrame = GetParentFrame();
            //     (Maximize it -- this is optional)
            pChildFrame->ShowWindow(SW_SHOWMAXIMIZED);
            //     (Now get the main frame)
            CWnd* pMainFrame =
                     pChildFrame->GetParentFrame();
            //     (Make it the foreground app)
            pMainFrame->SetForegroundWindow();
            //     (And make sure that it's visible)
            pMainFrame->ShowWindow(SW_SHOWNORMAL);

            // 3) pop up a message box...
            AfxMessageBox("Timer went off",
```

```
                                MB_OK | MB_ICONEXCLAMATION);

          // 4) disable it so that it doesn't
          //    go off again...
          pEntry->SetDisabled();
          // 5) now allow the user to see the text
          //    and potentially reset the clock
          pDoc->Modify(Index);

          // 6) turn timers back on
          bIgnoreTimer = FALSE;
       }
     }
   }
}
```

To get a feel for how the program works, compile and run it. Add an event for one minute in the future, and watch it go off. When the window is first popped up, the program sets off a timer with a frequency of one second (more or less). Again, because timers rely on windows, you cannot start a timer in the *CProg4View* constructor. The only other change to the class is the addition of the *WM_TIMER* message handler.

OnTimer( ) begins by searching through the list of *CEntry* objects and comparing the time contained in each one to the current time stored in the *CTime* object *tNow*. Disabled entries are ignored, of course.

If one of the entries contains a time earlier than the current time, the program pops itself into the foreground and opens a message box. After the message box has been acknowledged, the program disables the entry and then goes into modify mode.

Modifying the *CEntry* object does two things. First, it enables users to see the time and text with no extra work on your part (I'm all for that). Second, because this entry has expired, it's likely that a user will want to reset it, perhaps for the next day or month. If not, she can exit from modify mode by using the Cancel button and delete the entry on her own.

Notice that, during the time the *WM_TIMER* message is being processed, a flag, *bIgnoreTimer*, is set to tell the *OnTimer( )* function to ignore timer messages. This step is necessary because the dialog box that opens after the timer expires uses messages itself. A *WM_TIMER* message during this time would confuse everything. Another approach might have been to kill the timer before the dialog box was opened and then restart the timer after the box was closed.

Going to the front of the class

Making the application's window the foreground window is a multistep process that must be explained carefully. It works as shown in these steps:

1. The application first gets the view's window frame by using the *Get-ParentFrame( )* function. Because this frame is an MDI application, it is not the main frame of the entire application. It's just the child frame around this one window.

2. The application maximizes this window within the mainframe. (This step is optional.)

3. The program continues up the chain by getting the child frame's parent frame. This frame is the main frame for the entire application.

4. The program makes this window the foreground window and makes it visible, in case it has been iconified.

Making a window the foreground window does several things. First, it pops up the window to the top of the heap so that it isn't hidden. It also takes the keyboard away from whomever had it and gives it to the application. Finally, it highlights the window frame so that a user perceives that this window is the one that's "in charge."

The Idle Loop

Computers are tireless. As long as you keep the power applied, they insist on being fed a steady stream of commands. This problem is worse than you might realize. Did you know that the vast majority of your CPU's time is spent repeatedly executing the same set of "do-nothing" instructions? This set of instructions, called the *idle loop,* is executed when there's nothing else to do (probably because you're sitting there with a blank look on your face and staring at the screen, or maybe it's because you're off doing something important, such as playing with your friends).

Rather than waste this time, MFC enables you to tap in to the idle loop with the function *WinApp::OnIdle( )*. To see how *OnIdle( )* works, let's look back at the message loop buried within the MFC source code, in a function called (appropriately enough) *Run( )*.

After *Run( )* is cleaned up a little, it looks like this:

```
// main running routine until thread exits
int CWinThread::Run()
{
```

```
    ASSERT_VALID(this);

    // for tracking the idle time state
    BOOL bIdle = TRUE;

    // acquire and dispatch messages
    // until a WM_QUIT message is received.
    for (;;)
    {
        // phase1: check to see whether you can do idle work
            LONG lIdleCount = 0;
            while (bIdle &&
               !::PeekMessage(&m_msgCur, NULL, NULL,
                                        NULL, PM_NOREMOVE))
            {
                // call OnIdle while in bIdle state
                if (OnIdle(lIdleCount++) == FALSE)
                    bIdle = FALSE; // assume "no idle" state
            }

        // phase2: pump messages while available
        do
        {
            // pump message, but quit on WM_QUIT
            if (!PumpMessage())
                return ExitInstance();

            // reset "no idle" state after pumping
            // "normal" message
            if (!bIdle && IsIdleMessage(&m_msgCur))
                    bIdle = TRUE;

        } while (::PeekMessage(&m_msgCur, NULL, NULL,
                                    NULL, PM_NOREMOVE));
    }
}

// PumpMessage() -- simplified version
BOOL CWinThread::PumpMessage()
{
    // Get a message (wait if there isn't one)
    if (::GetMessage(&m_msgCur, NULL, NULL, NULL))
    {
        // It must be the the WM_QUIT message
        return FALSE;
    }
```

```
// Dispatch the message received
::TranslateMessage(&m_msgCur);
::DispatchMessage(&m_msgCur);
return TRUE;
}
```

You can see that *Run( )* implements two loops. In the first loop, *OnIdle( )* is invoked repeatedly as long as the following conditions are true:

- The input message queue is empty (that is, *PeekMessage( )* returns a *FALSE*).
- The *OnIdle( )* function continues to return a *TRUE*, indicating that it isn't finished.

As soon as either one of these conditions is no longer true, *Run( )* enters a second loop, in which it gets and dispatches messages (*PumpMessage( )*). The program stays in this loop until the message queue is emptied.

After the message queue is emptied, if the *bIdle* flag is *FALSE*, indicating that the *OnIdle( )* function does not need to be called again, the *Get Message* suspends the program, giving other applications a chance to run. If the *bIdle* flag is *TRUE*, indicating that the program doesn't want to be suspended yet, *GetMessage* isn't called unless *PeekMessage* has indicated that a message is in the queue.

Notice that if a nontrivial message is received, *bIdle* is set back to *TRUE*, enabling the program to return to the first loop. (A *nontrivial message* is any message that might have changed the state of the program. An example of a trivial message is a *WM_MOUSEMOVE* message in which the location of the mouse didn't change.)

Investing your idle time

Because the *OnIdle( )* function is virtual, it can be overloaded from the Class-Wizard for your class. So what can an *OnIdle( )* function do? Almost anything it wants, with the following caveats: It must call the *OnIdle( )* function for the base class because that is not a do-nothing function; in addition, as long as that function indicates that it still needs servicing by returning *TRUE*, your function must also return a *TRUE*.

An *OnIdle( )* function cannot do anything that will take a great deal of time or that would require message input. Remember that the program is not responsive to the outside world while it is within the *OnIdle( )* function, because that function is being called from the middle of the message-dispatch loop.

There are two ways to keep *OnIdle( )* from sucking up too much time. One is the *lCount* counter, which is incremented every time through the idle loop. *lCount* is therefore a count of the number of times *OnIdle( )* has been called since a message has been received.

You can construct your *OnIdle( )* function as follows:

```
BOOL CProg4App::OnIdle(LONG lCount)
{
    // Be sure to call the OnIdle in the base class
    // (it does other stuff)
    int bKeepItComing = CWinApp::OnIdle(lCount);

    // Every 100 loops...
    if ((++lCount % 100L) == 0)
    {
        // ...execute this one function
        bKeepItComing |= EverySoOften();
    }
    else
    {
        bKeepItComing = TRUE;
    }
    return bKeepItComing;
}
```

You can see that the program first executes *CWinApp::OnIdle( )* and retains the return value. If *lCount* is a multiple of 100, it invokes *EverySoOften( )*. If that function returns a *TRUE*, *OnIdle( )* forces *bKeepItComing* to *TRUE*, which ensures that *OnIdle( )* gets called again. As long as *OnIdle( )* is waiting for *lCount* to be a multiple of 100, it must force *bKeepItComing* to be *TRUE* — *CWinApp::OnIdle( )* may be finished, but *CProg4App::OnIdle( )* is not.

The reason *OnIdle( )* preincrements *lCount* is that it starts out with a value of zero. (Zero modulo 100 is zero.) I am assuming that you want to execute *EverySoOften( )* on the 100th call (the 99th call is close enough) and every 100th call thereafter. If you don't mind calling *EverySoOften( )* the first time *OnIdle( )* is called, the increment isn't necessary. ∎

Another way to keep your *OnIdle( )* function from using too much time is to have it simply schedule another function by posting a message to it. The work is handled by the message handler of the posted message.

Rather than set a timer, for example, you could have used the *OnIdle( )* loop to schedule your search for timed-out entries. In this case, the *OnIdle( )* function looks like the following:

```
// The following contains a pointer to the view
// that is checking for timed-out entries
CView* pTimerView;

BOOL CProg4App::OnIdle(LONG lCount)
{
    // Be sure to call the OnIdle in the base class
    // (it does other stuff)
    CWinApp::OnIdle(lCount);

    // Every 10000 loops...
    if ((++lCount % 10000L) == 0)
    {
        // ...simulate a timer message
        pTimerView->PostMessage(WM_TIMER, 0, 0);
    }

    return TRUE;   // You need to keep control coming
}
```

Every 10,000 times through the loop, this version of *OnIdle( )* posts a *WM_TIMER* message to your view, where it is processed as usual.

Comparing idle processing and timer processing

If there are two ways to get there, which way is better? The timer approach has the advantage of being more predictable. You have no guarantee that your timer function will run exactly when you requested (unless you specified a callback function). On the other hand, you do know when and how often the timer messages are generated, irrespective of how fast the processor is or what it happens to be doing.

It's difficult to determine exactly how much time transpires between messages with the *OnIdle( )* approach. If the processor is busy, no messages are generated — but that's exactly *OnIdle( )*'s advantage. *OnIdle( )* functions don't slow down the processor when it has more important things to do.

To prove this, write a small *OnIdle( )* function like the preceding one, with a count of 1000 or larger. Set a breakpoint on the *PostMessage( )* or whatever function call you happen to put within the *if* statement. Execute the program and immediately begin shaking your mouse back and forth reasonably quickly (just keep it moving — no need to shake your arm off).

As long as the mouse is moving, you won't hit your breakpoint. As long as mouse messages are arriving, the program is not idle.

Release the mouse and wait. Within a second or two after the mouse stops, the program hits your breakpoint and stops. ▪

OnIdle( ) processing is reserved for the type of task you don't mind putting off in order to get "real work" done (spell-checking a document or recalculating a spreadsheet in the background, for example).

Conclusion

That's it! Your personal scheduler is ready to use. Return to the project file, choose *Win Release* as the target by choosing Menu | Project | Targets, and rebuild the application.

The final version is then created, devoid of any excess debugging code and lacking any symbol information, which makes the executable file both smaller and faster to load and execute.

In this part, you've learned how to do many things:

✔ Open dialog boxes

✔ Manipulate menus

✔ Handle power toolbars (including balloon prompts)

✔ Maintain lists

✔ Use your mouse to choose items from a list

✔ Generate attractive output on a printer

✔ Keep time

After you've answered the questions in the following "20-Minute Workout" to see whether you really learned any of these things, continue to Part V, which mops up a few holes in your Windows background that are associated with handling text in a window.

20-Minute Workout

Questions

1 Explain the steps that occur between the time you choose the About menu item and the About dialog box appears on-screen.

2 Explain the role of the DDX_ and DDV_ functions in *DoDataExchange( )*.

3 Explain the following interesting behavior:

When you displayed a *TRACE* message from the *OnUpdateEditDelete( )* function in Chapter 17, I noted that the message appeared a number of times when the toolbar was visible. But it didn't appear forever. One additional point is that it does appear forever as long as the mouse is moving. What's going on?

4 Explain the following:

You open a window and insert a few schedule entries. You then open a new view into the same document. All the same entries appear. After you choose one of the entries, it is displayed in red in one view but not in the other. Why? Then you delete the entry. Both views are updated to show the chosen entry disappearing. Why?

5 The function *SetFont( )* sets the character height not to the sum of the height plus external leading but to the negative of that sum. Why?

6 Indicate whether each of the following tasks is best handled with a timer or with *OnIdle( )* processing:

    A. Recalculate a spreadsheet

    B. Update a clock's second hand

    C. Enable a screen saver

D. Move a sprite across the screen

E. Send low-priority data over a serial port in the background

What are the arguments for and against your decisions in question 6?

Extra-Credit Problems

Space limitations prevent me from providing solutions for the following problems; you know enough at this point, however, that you should be able to solve them:

1 Add a toolbar entry for the *modify* command.

2 Make double-clicking an entry modify that entry automatically as well.

3 Add print capability to the Etch-A-Sketch program from Part III.

Answers

1 The steps in this process were described in detail in Chapter 15, but here are the basics:

A. Choose About to cause MFC to generate a *WM_COMMAND* message with the ID set to *ID_APP_ABOUT*.

B. The following message map maps this message to the function *OnAppAbout( )*:

```
BEGIN_MESSAGE_MAP(CProg4App, CWinApp)
    //{{AFX_MSG_MAP(CProg4App)
    ON_COMMAND(ID_APP_ABOUT, OnAppAbout)
    //}}AFX_MSG_MAP
END_MESSAGE_MAP( )
```

C. *OnAppAbout( )* creates a dialog object of type *CAboutDlg* and then invokes *DoModal( )* on it to display it.

2 *DDX_* functions transfer data back and forth between a user's dialog class and the system dialog class. The system's dialog class is displayed to the user. The *DDV_* functions validate the data a user enters in the dialog box.

3 The *ON_COMMAND_UI* messages, which invoke the *OnUpdate...( )* functions, are sent from *CWnd::OnIdle( )*. This process enables the toolbar icons to be updated "as soon as the program gets around to it" without slowing down the main processing. (Nontrivial messages, such as mouse-movement messages, cause *OnIdle( )* processing to be performed again.)

4 The chosen entry is a property of the view. Choosing an entry in one view, therefore, has no effect on an entry in another view. Both views share the same document. When one view executes a *pDoc->Delete( )* function, this function calls *UpdateAllViews( )*, which forces both views to redraw (*OnDraw( )*) with the updated list.

5 In *MM_TEXT* mode, *y* starts out as 0 in the upper-left corner of the screen and increases as you move down the screen. In all other mapping modes, *y* increases as you move up the screen. To make the fewest changes possible, I set the character height to be negative to make it match the *y* direction of *MM_TWIPS*.

6
A. *OnIdle( )*

B. Timer

C. Timer

D. Timer

E. OnIdle()

7 You generally want B, C, and D to happen at some predictable rate, irrespective of how fast the processor is. For example, if you set the sprite so that it scurries across the screen by using *OnIdle( )* on a 486 computer, when the program is executed on a P6 (or whatever Intel decides to call the successor to the Pentium), the sprite is far too fast.

Part V

App3: A Text Editor

The 5th Wave   By Rich Tennant

"Careful, Sundance, this one's just started learning Windows programming and it's left him just itching for a fight."

In This Part...

*T*his application, a simple text editor, won't replace your favorite word processor. It does teach you how to read keyboard input and manipulate the text insertion marker (the caret). To decrease response time, you learn how to minimize the area of the screen that is repainted and how to read and write straight ASCII files. Finally, you learn to handle scrolling on your own.

Chapter 21

Handling the Keyboard

● ●

In This Chapter

▶ Using the *WM_KEYDOWN* and *WM_KEYUP* messages

▶ Handling the *WM_CHAR* message

▶ Receiving, storing, and displaying simple ASCII characters

● ●

E ven in this mouse-crazy world in which we live, the primary source of input for most programs is still the keyboard. Reading the keyboard is therefore an important part of any programming arsenal. This chapter begins by looking at the messages that come from the keyboard and then leads you into the next chapter, in which you write a program (called an *editor*) to store this information and manipulate it a little.

Keyboard Messages

You may not have ever thought about it, but what exactly are the steps in getting information from your fingertips to your program?

A small processor within your keyboard constantly keeps tabs on the condition of the keys. Every time the processor detects that you're leaning on one, it generates an interrupt to the main computer. This interrupt causes the processor to temporarily stop what it's doing in order to see what information the keyboard has.

The keyboard processor doesn't know anything about ASCII characters or anything like that. It couldn't care less which little symbols are painted on top of the keycaps. The information it sends to the main processor is a message that says something like, "Hey, the user just pressed the second key to the left in the third row from the top."

It doesn't really say all that, of course. Instead, each code is assigned a special code, called the *OEM scan code,* or simply the *scan code* ("OEM" is a generic term for the company that makes your computer). The keyboard processor reports the scan code to the main processor.

The main processor takes the scan-code information and puts it in a Windows message to be communicated to an application. But which one?

With the mouse-movement messages, the answer was easy — each application was associated with a window. The application that received the mouse-movement messages was the application that owned the window to which the mouse was pointing. But this solution doesn't work for keyboards because the keyboard doesn't have a pointing property.

Instead, some other rule must be used. Windows uses the following: The application that owns the active window gets the keyboard message. The active window is usually the topmost window. To make it obvious which window is active, Windows highlights its menu bar — menu bars in non-active windows are grayed-out.

The term "active" is a little clumsy, not to mention misleading (it's not active, after all — it's just sitting there). The active window is said to "have focus." It gains focus when it becomes the active window, usually because a user clicked it, and it loses focus when some other window becomes active.

Key ups and downs

The message that Windows sends to an application comes in one of four flavors:

WM_KEYDOWN (sent when a key is pressed)

WM_KEYUP (sent when a key is released)

WM_SYSKEYDOWN (sent when a "special key" is pressed)

WM_SYSKEYUP (sent when a "special key" is released)

The special keys are those keys that have special meaning to Windows. These keys are entered in combination with the Alt key, such as Alt+Tab and Alt+Esc. User applications generally ignore these messages.

If you process the system messages and don't pass them on to the default message handler, the common window-manipulation commands (such as Alt+Tab, which changes active applications) don't work when your application has focus. ■

The key-down and key-up messages usually occur in pairs. A key-down message is followed by the corresponding key-up message; if a user holds down the key long enough for the type-matic feature of the keyboard to kick in, however, you may see a series of *WM_KEYDOWN* messages before you ever see a *WM_KEYUP*.

To process the nonsystem key messages, add the functions *OnKeyDown( )* and *OnKeyUp( )* to the view with the ClassWizard (you generally need only the *OnKeyDown( )* handler because, after all, a card laid is a card played).

The first argument to the *OnKey...( )* functions is the virtual key code associated with the key that is entered. For letters of the alphabet, the virtual key code is the same as the capitalized version of the letter (irrespective of the Shift-, Ctrl-, or Alt-key state of the keyboard). The virtual key code for the letter *A,* therefore, is A. Virtual key codes for the other keys are defined in one of the Windows include files (winuser.h, to be exact). A few of the more common of these codes are shown in Table 21-1.

Table 21-1 Virtual Key Codes for Some Common Editing Keystrokes

Identifier	Keystroke
VK_CANCEL	Ctrl+Break
VK_BACK	Backspace
VK_SHIFT	Shift
VK_CONTROL	Ctrl
VK_CAPITAL	Shift Lock
VK_PRIOR	Page Up
VK_NEXT	Page Down
VK_END	End
VK_HOME	Home
VK_LEFT	Left arrow
VK_UP	Up arrow
VK_RIGHT	Right arrow
VK_DOWN	Down arrow

The second argument is the repeat count. This count is normally 1; if your program gets behind, however, and can't process keys as fast as they're sent from the keyboard, several *WM_KEYDOWN* messages may be combined (assuming that they're from the same key) and the count incremented. The repeat count for *WM_KEYUP* is always 1.

Most programs ignore the repeat count. As long as your program can keep up with the type-matic rate of the keyboard, it won't be larger than 1 anyway. If your program is slow, you may find that you still don't want to process the repeat count. For example, a user may lean on one of the arrow keys to position the cursor — not a good practice, but a common one. When the cursor gets to the spot the user wants, he releases the key. If keystrokes have backed up, the repeat count may be greater than 1. Processing these backed-up keys causes the cursor to overshoot the desired spot. ■

The third argument is a flag field whose format is shown in Table 21-2.

Table 21-2 Meaning of Flag Word to OnKey...() Functions

Bit Number	Meaning
0–7 (LSB)	OEM scan code
8	Extended key (1→Function key or numeric keypad key)
13	Context key (1→Alt key)
14	Previous key state (1→key previously down)
15	Transition state (1→key is being released)

Most programs ignore the flag field also.

DOS programs used to make heavy use of scan codes to read keys that had no ASCII equivalent; because these non-ASCII keys have been assigned virtual key codes, however, there's little reason to resort to the ostensibly machine-dependent scan code field. ■

What state are you in? (Nebraska?)

It's also possible to query the state of the keyboard via the virtual key code. When the *GetKeyState( )* function is passed a virtual key code, the function returns a nonzero if the key that corresponds to that virtual key is pressed.

A Windows application can therefore do the following:

```
// Is the Shift key currently pressed?
if (GetKeyState(VK_SHIFT))
{
    // ...yes
```

Notice that this approach is not dynamic. That is, *GetKeyState( )* represents the state as a result of messages received. You wouldn't want to sit in a tight loop waiting for a key to be pressed, as shown here:

```
// Wait for Shift key (DON'T DO THIS)
while (GetKeyState(VK_SHIFT) == 0)
{
}
```

This code is not only not Windowy in its approach, but it also represents an infinite loop. If the current shift state is 0, it will always be 0 because no message can be received to change it as long as you're stuck in this silly loop.

Another function, *GetAsyncKeyState( )*, returns the keyboard state as a result of the keyboard interrupts. You can call *GetAyncKeyState( )* in the preceding loop, but, of course, it's still not a Windows-friendly technique. ■

Notice that the *GetKeyState(VK_SHIFT)* returns a *TRUE* if either Shift key is being pressed. Special versions of these virtual key codes, *VK_LSHIFT* and *VK_RSHIFT*, can be used to query whether either the left or right Shift key is being pressed (if you care). The same is true for the *VK_CONTROL* and *VK_HOME* virtual key codes.

In addition, three special virtual key codes — *VK_LBUTTON*, *VK_RBUTTON*, and *VK_MBUTTON* — enable the program to query the state of the mouse buttons.

These three codes are useful only for querying the state of the mouse. Your *OnKey...( )* function is never called on a mouse-button transition. ■

ASCII and the WM_CHAR message

For conventional typing keys, it isn't enough simply to know their virtual key code. These keys may be capitalized, or they may even be control keys. For these keys, some translation must be performed on the *WM_KEYDOWN* message.

For some keys, such as the ones that represent the letters of the alphabet, this translation is straightforward. For example, the following translation could be used for the A key:

```
if (nVKCode == 'A')
{
    cChar = 'a';      // assume lowercase A
    if (GetKeyState(VK_SHIFT) || GetKeyState(CAPITAL))
    {
```

```
            cChar = 'A'; // Nope -- it's capitalized
    }
    if (GetKeyState(VK_CONTROL))
    {
        cChar = '\x01';  // or Ctrl+A
    }
}
```

For other keys, it isn't so easy. Keyboards from other countries map some keys differently. For example, the keystroke Shift+3 is converted to the # symbol on an American keyboard, but to £ on a British keyboard. Translating the *WM_KEYDOWN* message into its ASCII equivalent is vexing enough to make it a huge relief that you don't have to do it. Windows does it for you.

Every time a *WM_KEYDOWN* message is generated, if that key has an ASCII equivalent, Windows also generates a *WM_CHAR* message immediately following it.

The arguments to the *OnChar( )* message handler look the same as the arguments to the *OnKeyDown( )* function. The second and third arguments, the repeat count and flags, are the same, respectively. The first argument to *OnChar( )*, however, is the ASCII character that results from translating the *WM_KEYDOWN* message by using the current state of the Shift, Ctrl, and Alt keys.

In Chapter 3 (if you can remember that far back), you learned that the main message loop for all Windows programs looks something like the following (for MFC-based programs, this loop is within the *PumpMessage( )* function):

```
while (GetMessage(&msgCur, NULL, NULL, NULL))
{
    TranslateMessage(&msgCur);
    DispatchMessage(&msgCur);
}
```

You knew even then that *GetMessage( )* fetched the next message from the application's message queue and that *DispatchMessage( )* passed the message to the *WinProc* for the current application. What was never explained is the purpose of the *TranslateMessage( )* function.

At the time, something was said about going "through a translation process." Now the truth can be told. The primary purpose of *TranslateMessage( )* is to generate the proper *WM_CHAR* message as a result of *WM_KEYDOWN* messages. ∎

Most programs don't bother to handle the *WM_KEYDOWN* message for keys that also generate a *WM_CHAR* message. The *WM_CHAR* message is easier to understand and process. In practice, most programs read the *WM_KEY-DOWN* messages for the arrow keys and for the Home, End, Page Up, and Page Down keys, and they read the *WM_CHAR* messages for the other keys.

Let's See the Key Messages in Action

To get a better feel for the relationship between the different key messages, I wrote the following simple program, Prog5_1. This program handles the *WM_KEYUP*, *WM_KEYDOWN*, and *WM_CHAR* messages. For each message, the program simply displays the arguments that are received.

I built Prog5_1 in the AppWizard with all options disabled. I then added one field to the *CProg5_1View* class, which is the current output line number. Next, I used ClassWizard to add the *OnKeyDown( )*, *OnKeyUp( )*, and *OnChar( )* functions. Finally, I made the following additions:

```
// Prog5vw.h : interface of the CProg5_1View class
//
/////////////////////////////////////////////////////////

class CProg5_1View : public CView
{
protected:
    // the current outline line number
    int m_nLine;

    void OutChar(char *pMsg,
                 UINT nChar,
                 UINT nRepCnt,
                 UINT nFlags);

    // output the given string on given DC
    void Output(CString& sText, CDC *pDC);

protected: // create from serialization only
    CProg5_1View();
    DECLARE_DYNCREATE(CProg5_1View)

    // ...continues the same from here on...
```

I then made the following changes to the CProg5vw.cpp file:

```
// Prog5vw.cpp : implementation of the CProg5_1View class
//
```

```
#include "stdafx.h"
#include "Prog5_1.h"

#include "Prog5doc.h"
#include "Prog5vw.h"

#ifdef _DEBUG
#undef THIS_FILE
static char BASED_CODE THIS_FILE[] = __FILE__;
#endif

/////////////////////////////////////////////////////////
// CProg5_1View

IMPLEMENT_DYNCREATE(CProg5_1View, CView)

BEGIN_MESSAGE_MAP(CProg5_1View, CView)
    //{{AFX_MSG_MAP(CProg5_1View)
    ON_WM_KEYDOWN()
    ON_WM_KEYUP()
    ON_WM_CHAR()
    //}}AFX_MSG_MAP
END_MESSAGE_MAP()

/////////////////////////////////////////////////////////
// CProg5_1View construction/destruction

CProg5_1View::CProg5_1View()
{

}

CProg5_1View::~CProg5_1View()
{
}

/////////////////////////////////////////////////////////
// CProg5_1View drawing

CString sTitleBar("Message  Code(char) Count Flags");
void CProg5_1View::OnDraw(CDC* pDC)
{
    // On repaint, just start over
    m_nLine = 0;
    Output(sTitleBar, pDC);
}
```

```
///////////////////////////////////////////////////
// CProg5_1View diagnostics

    // ...no change here...

///////////////////////////////////////////////////
// CProg5_1View message handlers

void CProg5_1View::OnKeyDown(UINT nChar,
                            UINT nRepCnt,
                            UINT nFlags)
{
    OutChar("KeyDown", nChar, nRepCnt, nFlags);
}


void CProg5_1View::OnKeyUp(UINT nChar,
                           UINT nRepCnt,
                           UINT nFlags)
{
    OutChar("KeyUp  ", nChar, nRepCnt, nFlags);
}


void CProg5_1View::OnChar(UINT nChar,
                          UINT nRepCnt,
                          UINT nFlags)
{
    OutChar("Char   ", nChar, nRepCnt, nFlags);

}

// OutChar() -- output the keystroke along with
//              the flags passed in message
void CProg5_1View::OutChar(char *pMsg,
                           UINT nChar,
                           UINT nRepCnt,
                           UINT nFlags)
{
    CString sText;

    // If the character is printable...
    char cInterpret = ' ';
    if (isprint(nChar))
    {
        // ...then interpret it
        cInterpret = (char)nChar;
    }
```

```
    // Build a string with all data in it
    sText.Format(
            "%s    %2x    (%c)    %d    %x",
            pMsg,
            nChar, cInterpret,
            nRepCnt, nFlags);

    // Output string to view
    CClientDC cDC(this);
    Output(sText, &cDC);
}

//Output() -- output specified string
void CProg5_1View::Output(CString& sText, CDC *pDC)
{
    // Select a fixed font into the DC
    CFont fFixed;
    fFixed.CreateStockObject(ANSI_FIXED_FONT);
    CFont *pOldFont = pDC->SelectObject(&fFixed);

    // Get the font's dimensions
    TEXTMETRIC tm;
    pDC->GetTextMetrics(&tm);
    int nCharHeight = tm.tmHeight + tm.tmExternalLeading;

    // Now output the string on next line
    pDC->TextOut(0, m_nLine * nCharHeight, sText);
    m_nLine++;

    pDC->SelectObject(pOldFont);
}
```

The program's *OnDraw( )* function does nothing more than reset the line count to 0 and repaint the column headers by using the *Output( )* function.

Each of the message handlers invokes the *OutChar( )* function. *OutChar( )* prepares its arguments for printing and then uses the same *Output( )* function to display the results on the next consecutive line.

Despite what Part I said about not using spaces to align columns of characters, as you did in your DOS days, it is possible to do so if you're willing to use a fixed-point (nonproportional) font for output. Windows makes it easy, in fact, by providing a couple of fixed fonts as stock objects. I didn't bring up this subject back then because I didn't want you to stay dependent on fixed-point fonts — proportional fonts are the norm in Windows 3.1 and later. The output from this program is shown in Figure 21-1. ∎

```
Untitled - Prog5_1                          _ □ ✕
File  Edit  Help
Message    Code(char)  Count  Flags
KeyDown    41    (A)      1    1e
Char       61    (a)      1    1e
KeyUp      41    (A)      1    c01e
KeyDown    10    ( )      1    2a
KeyDown    41    (A)      1    1e
Char       41    (A)      1    1e
KeyUp      41    (A)      1    c01e
KeyUp      10    ( )      1    c02a
KeyDown    11    ( )      1    1d
KeyDown    41    (A)      1    1e
Char        1    ( )      1    1e
KeyUp      41    (A)      1    c01e
KeyUp      11    ( )      1    c01d
KeyDown    41    (A)      1    1e
Char       61    (a)      1    1e
KeyDown    41    (A)      1    401e
Char       61    (a)      1    401e
KeyDown    41    (A)      1    401e
Char       61    (a)      1    401e
```

Figure 21-1:
Some
typical
output from
Prog5_1.

Note that if you get the number of spaces wrong or if your font size is not the same, your output may not line up. Just add or remove spaces from the column headers to align the columns properly. As you can see in Figure 21-1, the first key that was pressed was the *a* key. You see the *WM_KEYDOWN* message with the virtual key code A, followed by the *WM_CHAR* message showing a letter *a*, followed finally by *WM_KEYUP* as it was released.

The next sequence shows a capital letter A. First you see the Shift key (virtual key code 10). It's followed by *WM_KEYDOWN* for the letter A, the *WM_CHAR* message, and the two *WM_KEYUP* messages.

The next sequence is Ctrl+A (the ASCII code for Ctrl+A is 0×01). Finally, I pressed and held down the *a* key, which generated multiple *WM_KEYDOWN* messages in a row without a *WM_KEYUP* message (the *WM_KEYUP* runs off the end of the window).

Conclusion

You have to be able to read the keyboard before you can generate a text editor. Now that you've surmounted that hurdle, Chapter 22 tells you how to capture some of those characters into a document.

Chapter 22

The Basic Editor

- -

In This Chapter

▶ Creating the framework

▶ Creating a document

▶ Handling tricky characters (such as Backspace and Enter)

▶ Reading and writing text files

▶ Displaying the document you've created

- -

*N*ow that you know how to read the keyboard, let's see whether you can read some of those keystrokes and do something with them. In this initial stab, you build a reasonably capable little text editor. It has no fancy features, but after you learn the basics, you can always add the fancy stuff later.

Creating the Framework

You know the drill by now. I created Prog5_2a as a normal MDI application with all the usual frills (toolbars, for example). I even registered Prog5_2a to handle .TXT files under the Advanced Options of Part 4 of AppWizard. When I finished, the new project information looked like Figure 22-1.

I then decided that, because this application was primarily textual, I would begin with the document class. Handling simple keys, such as the letters of the alphabet, is never much of a problem. The problems always occur with special keys, such as Backspace and Enter.

I could have broken up the intelligence for parsing and handling these special keys between the document and the view, but there was little reason to do that. I simply decided to make the document class the smart one this time and let the view just follow along for a change.

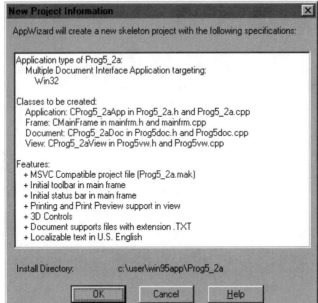

New Project Information

AppWizard will create a new skeleton project with the following specifications:

Application type of Prog5_2a:
  Multiple Document Interface Application targeting:
    Win32

Classes to be created:
  Application: CProg5_2aApp in Prog5_2a.h and Prog5_2a.cpp
  Frame: CMainFrame in mainfrm.h and mainfrm.cpp
  Document: CProg5_2aDoc in Prog5doc.h and Prog5doc.cpp
  View: CProg5_2aView in Prog5vw.h and Prog5vw.cpp

Features:
  + MSVC Compatible project file (Prog5_2a.mak)
  + Initial toolbar in main frame
  + Initial status bar in main frame
  + Printing and Print Preview support in view
  + 3D Controls
  + Document supports files with extension .TXT
  + Localizable text in U.S. English

Install Directory: c:\user\win95app\Prog5_2a

OK   Cancel   Help

Figure 22-1:
The New
Project
Information
window for
Prog5_2.

Creating the Document Class

The first thing you need in any text document class is a receptacle for the characters. You can choose from several different approaches for holding this data, but I seriously considered only two.

I first considered keeping all the characters in the document in one long string, perhaps of class *CString* or *CByteArray*. This string would have made editing relatively simple because the document class wouldn't have had to worry about line breaks caused by newlines.

The problem with this approach is that it puts an unreasonable burden on the view class. The view displays the text in lines terminated by newline characters. If the data were all strung together, the view would have to go through considerable pains to break up the data for display.

The second approach is to retain the text in an array of *CString*s, with a different *CString* for each line of text. Each line of text is terminated by a newline character. This approach makes the document class a little more difficult because it now has to process the addition and deletion of newlines; the view becomes much easier, however, because the text is already in the format that is necessary for display. To cinch the matter, the class *CStringArray* is perfect for the job.

This application is a text editor and not a word processor — no word-wrap concept exists in this Windows application. If this were a word processor, I probably would have chosen to divide the text in the document by paragraph and leave it up to the view to implement word wrapping. ∎

With this decision made, I added the member *m_saText* to the document class to hold the text:

```
// Prog5doc.h : interface of the CProg5_2aDoc class
//
/////////////////////////////////////////////////////////

class CProg5_2aDoc : public CDocument
{
// User-defined stuff
// Attributes
protected:
    // The data member to hold the text
    CStringArray m_saText;

    void AddSimpleChar(int& nLine,
                       int& nCharOff,
                       char cChar);
    void DeleteCharLeft(int& nLine, int& nCharOff);
    void AddNL(int& nLine, int& nCharOff);
    void DeleteAll();

// Operations
public:
    // The following function also interprets
    // the character that is added
    void AddChar(int& nLine, int& nCharOff, char cChar);
    CString String(int nLine);  // line number
    int  GetLength();

    // ...application-generated stuff from here on...
```

I determined that the view would need three functions from the document:

- A function with which to add a character at a given point (*AddChar( )*)
- A function to return the *CString* on a given line
- A function to return the number of lines in a document

Notice that the insertion point (*nLine* and *nCharOff*) is represented by two arguments to the *AddChar( )* function. Because *AddChar( )* updates both these parameters (that's why they are referential arguments), you might be tempted to make them members of the document. That would be incorrect, however.

Consider what would happen if you had two views open. Would you want the insertion point of one view to affect the insertion point of another view? No. The views must therefore remain as properties of the view.

The three protected member functions *DeleteCharLeft( )*, *AddNL( )*, and *Add-SimpleChar( )* are invoked depending on the type of character that is passed. In addition, *DeleteAll( )* is used to clear out the document. In the following code for the file Prog5doc.cpp, remember to use ClassWizard to add the *OnOpenDocument* and *OnSaveDocument* members before making the following additions:

```
// Prog5doc.cpp : implementation of the
//                CProg5_2aDoc class

#include "stdafx.h"
#include "Prog5_2a.h"

#include <fstream.h>

#include "Prog5doc.h"

#ifdef _DEBUG
#undef THIS_FILE
static char BASED_CODE THIS_FILE[] = __FILE__;
#endif

/////////////////////////////////////////////////////////
// CProg5_2aDoc

// ...typical stuff here...

/////////////////////////////////////////////////////////
// CProg5_2aDoc construction/destruction

CProg5_2aDoc::CProg5_2aDoc()
{
    m_saText.SetSize(0, 100);
}

CProg5_2aDoc::~CProg5_2aDoc()
{
}

/////////////////////////////////////////////////////////
```

```
// CProg5_2aDoc serialization

void CProg5_2aDoc::Serialize(CArchive& ar)
{
    // You won't be using serialization
}

// ...no changes until:
/////////////////////////////////////////////////////
// CProg5_2aDoc commands

void CProg5_2aDoc::AddChar(int& nLine,
                          int& nCharOff,
                          char cChar)
{
    // if keep is special, interpret it
    switch (cChar)
    {
      case '\n':
      case '\r':
        AddNL(nLine, nCharOff);
       break;

      case '\b':
        DeleteCharLeft(nLine, nCharOff);
        break;

      default:
        AddSimpleChar(nLine, nCharOff, cChar);
    }

    SetModifiedFlag();

    UpdateAllViews(0);
}

int CProg5_2aDoc::GetLength()
{
    return m_saText.GetSize();
}

void CProg5_2aDoc::DeleteAll()
{
    m_saText.RemoveAll();
}

void CProg5_2aDoc::AddSimpleChar(int& nLine,
```

```
                                int& nCharOff,
                                char cChar)
{
    // Is this the first character of a new line?
    if (nLine > m_saText.GetUpperBound())
    {
        // Yes -- okay, do it
        m_saText.SetAtGrow(nLine, CString(cChar));
        nCharOff = 1;
    }
    else
    {
        // No -- add to existing line; split the current
        // line at the insertion point and add your char
        CString sText = m_saText.GetAt(nLine);
        int nLength = sText.GetLength();

        CString sLeft  = sText.Left(nCharOff);
        CString sRight = sText.Right(nLength - nCharOff);
        m_saText[nLine] = sLeft
                        + CString(cChar)
                        + sRight;
        nCharOff++;
    }
    return;
}

void CProg5_2aDoc::DeleteCharLeft(int& nLine,
                                  int& nCharOff)
{
    ASSERT(nLine <= m_saText.GetUpperBound());

    // Get the current string and length
    CString& sText = m_saText[nLine];
    int nLength = sText.GetLength();

    // If this is the leftmost character...
    if (nCharOff == 0)
    {
        // ...and it's not the first line...
        if (nLine > 0)
        {
            // ...append this to the previous line
            nCharOff = m_saText[nLine - 1].GetLength();
            m_saText[nLine - 1] += sText;

            // Now move all remaining lines up
```

```
                m_saText.RemoveAt(nLine);
                nLine--;
            }
        }
    else
        {
            // Otherwise, just lose the char on the left
            CString sLeft = sText.Left(nCharOff - 1);
            CString sRight = sText.Right(nLength - nCharOff);
            m_saText[nLine] = sLeft + sRight;
            nCharOff--;
        }
}

void CProg5_2aDoc::AddNL(int& nLine, int& nCharOff)
{
    // Split the current string at the current pointer
    CString& sText = m_saText[nLine];
    int nLength = sText.GetLength();
    CString sLeft  = sText.Left(nCharOff);
    CString sRight = sText.Right(nLength - nCharOff);

    // Leave the lefthand part on this line
    m_saText.SetAt(nLine, sLeft);

    // Put the righthand part on the next line
    // (This string may be null.)
    nLine++;
    m_saText.InsertAt(nLine, sRight);

    nCharOff = 0;
}

CString CProg5_2aDoc::String(int nLine)
{
    // if this request is off the end...
    if (nLine > m_saText.GetUpperBound())
    {
        // ...return a void string
        TRACE("Request off the end of document\n");
        return CString();
    }
    return m_saText[nLine];
}

BOOL CProg5_2aDoc::OnOpenDocument(LPCTSTR lpszPathName)
{
```

```
        ifstream iFile(lpszPathName,
                    ios::in | ios::nocreate);
        if (iFile.fail())
        {
            return FALSE;
        }

        DeleteAll();

        int nLine = 0;
        char cBuffer[2048]; // just use a big buffer
        while (!iFile.eof())
        {
            iFile.getline(cBuffer, sizeof cBuffer - 1);
            m_saText.SetAtGrow(nLine++, CString(cBuffer));
        }
        return TRUE;
}
```

```
BOOL CProg5_2aDoc::OnSaveDocument(LPCTSTR lpszPathName)
{
        ofstream oFile(lpszPathName, ios::out | ios::trunc);
        if (oFile.fail())
        {
            return FALSE;
        }

        int nNoLines = m_saText.GetSize();
        int nLine;
        for (nLine = 0; nLine < nNoLines; nLine++)
        {
            oFile << String(nLine) << "\n";
        }

        // Clear the dirty flag
        SetModifiedFlag(FALSE);
        return TRUE;
}
```

(Notice that the program doesn't do anything yet — it doesn't have a view class.) Beginning with the public member function *AddChar( )*, you can see that the set of all characters is broken up into three classes:

- A newline or carriage-return character is handled by the function *AddNL( )*.
- The Backspace character is handled by the function *DeleteCharLeft( )*.
- All other characters are handled by the function *AddSimpleChar( )*.

All three functions work in somewhat the same way, so let's examine just one, *AddSimpleChar( )*, in detail. When you add the first character on the current line, *AddSimpleChar( )* must grow the *CStringArray* by one to make room for the new line.

When you add the second and subsequent character to the line, *AddSimple-Char( )* cannot just append the new character to the end of the current line, because the insertion point represented by *nCharOff* may be anywhere within the line. *AddSimpleChar( )* begins by breaking the current line in two at the insertion point and ends up with an *sLeft* lefthand string and an *sRight* right-hand string. (Either one of these strings can be zero characters long if the insertion point is at either the beginning or end of the line.) It then reassembles the two parts with the current character between them, as shown in Figure 22-2.

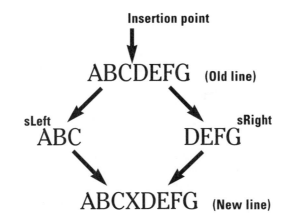

Figure 22-2:
The addition
of the
character *X*
to an
existing line.

The functions *CString::Left( )* and *CString::Right( )* operate in the same way as the Visual Basic functions *Left$* and *Right$* do. ∎

The functions *DeleteCharLeft( )* and *AddNL( )* work similarly to *AddSimpleChar( )* except that they also must deal with the possibility of existing lines being combined or split.

The functions *GetLength( )* and *DeleteAll( )* are trivial: They rely on corresponding *CStringArray( )* functions to do the work.

It isn't necessary to delete the individual *CString* objects when you delete a *CStringArray* element. Because the *CStringArray* class knows the type of object it is storing, it also knows how to dispense with them. ∎

The *String( )* function is also simple. If the specified line number is displayed off the end of the document, *String( )* returns a null *CString*. If not, it returns a copy of the requested string.

Reading and Writing Text Files

Notice that *CProg5_2aDoc* does not use the *Serialize( )* function to save or restore the document's contents. The reason is that I wanted the program to be capable of reading standard ASCII text files. *Serialize( )* is great for storing data quickly and easily. The only problem is that a programmer can't easily control the format of the resulting file. The various *Serialize( )* functions have their own idea about how they want to produce output on a disk, and there isn't much you can do to influence them.

I began by using the ClassWizard to install custom pearl-inlaid handlers for the *OpenDocument* and *SaveDocument* command messages.

The *OnOpenDocument( )* function receives the name of the file specified in the Open File dialog box. This function opens the file for input and specifies the *ios::nocreate* option because you don't want to create the file if it's not already out there. If the member function *fail( )* returns a *TRUE*, the *ifstream* object was not created properly, which almost certainly means that the open failed. In this case, *OnOpenDocument( )* fails with an ignominious error return.

If no error occurred, the function then continues to read the input file a line at a time, by using *getline( )*. Notice that *getline( )* reads until it has read the specified number of characters or encountered a newline, whichever occurs first. The size of *cBuffer* was chosen at random — it should be large enough to handle the largest anticipated single line; *getline( )* does not write past the end of the buffer, however, no matter how long the line is in the file.

After each line has been read, *OnOpenDocument( )* adds it to the document. When the end of the file has been reached, the member function *eof( )* returns a *TRUE* to tell you that it's time to stop.

The *OnSaveDocument( )* is simply the reverse process: It opens and truncates the output file and then writes each line to the file by using the *CString* inserter. (Remember that the inserter is the << operator overloaded to perform output.)

Understanding the C++ stream classes

Every time you insert an object to *cout* or extract a value from *cin*, you are using the stream classes. The classes *ifstream* and *ofstream* are related classes in the Standard C++ Library that are used for file I/O. These classes perform buffered-stream-based input and output.

Buffering means that the stream is connected to the disk file through a large RAM buffer. If the program reads a single character and the buffer is empty, C++ reads an entire block of data from the disk. Subsequent read requests are satisfied from this buffer. Only after the buffer is exhausted does *ifstream* return to read the next block from the disk. Buffering improves program performance by reducing the number of accesses to the relatively slow disk device.

The class *ifstream* provides several constructors; the most commonly used constructor is declared as follows:

```
ifstream isFile(char* pszFileName,
                int = ios::in,      // must be input
                int = filebuf::openprot);
ofstream osFile(char* pszFileName,
                int = ios::out,     // must be output
                int = filebuf::openprot);
fstream  fsFile(char* pszFileName,
                int,                // no default
                int = filebuf::openprot);

// where the second argument has the following values:
enum {
    in       = 0x01, // open for reading
    out      = 0x02, // open for output
    ate      = 0x04, // seek to eof on open
    app      = 0x08, // append
    trunc    = 0x10, // truncate
    nocreate = 0x20, // don't create if doesn't exist
    noreplace= 0x40, // don't open if file exists
    binary   = 0x80};// binary (not text) mode file
// and the third argument is always openprot
```

Because these properties are binary values, two or more properties can be combined in the second argument. For example, *ios::in | ios::nocreate* says "open the file for input, and don't create it if it doesn't exist" (in this case, the open fails).

A default constructor is also provided:

```
ifstream isFile2;
ofstream osFile2;
fstream  fsFile2;
```

An object created with the default constructor must be opened subsequently with one of the *open( )* functions. The arguments to these functions look exactly like the arguments to the first constructor shown earlier.

The destructor for these classes closes the file.

After an *fstream* object has been created, the operations in the following list (and more) are defined for it:

fail( ): Returns a nonzero if the stream has an error

operator!( ): Another name for *fail( )*

eof( ): Returns a nonzero if the stream is at end-of-file

clear( ): Clears the error flag

operator<<( ): Writes to the stream

operator>>( ): Reads from the stream

A great feature of *fstream* I/O stems from the fact that *ofstream* is a subclass of *ostream*. An *ofstream* object can therefore be passed to a function expecting to receive an *ostream* object. Specifically, an output file object may be passed to any function designed to receive *cout*, as shown in this example:

```
void OutputFn(ostream& out)
{
    out << "Some sort of output\n";
}
int main()
{
    OutputFn(cout);    // outputs to standard output

    ofstream ofFile("outfile"); // open "outfile"
    OutputFn(ofFile); // output to the file "outfile"
}                      // close the file
```

The same relationship exists between *ifstream* and *istream* and between *fstream* and *stream*.

Adding the View

With the document doing most of the work of parsing the Backspace and
Newline characters, the view class is relatively simple. The *include* file
includes members to store the font dimensions and the current insertion
point, measured in terms of line number and character offset. (Remember, as
always, to use the ClassWizard to add the *OnInitialUpdate( )* and *OnChar( )*
functions before making the following additions.)

```
// Prog5vw.h : interface of the CProg5_2aView class
//
/////////////////////////////////////////////////////////

class CProg5_2aView : public CView
{
// User-defined stuff
protected:
    // Current insert position
    int m_nLineNo;
    int m_nCharOffset;

    // Font-size information
    int m_nCharHeight;
    int m_nCharWidth;

    // Convert from/to offset measured
    // in device units to/from lines in doc
    int DPtoLine(int nDP);
    int LinetoDP(int nLine);

    // Output function
    void Output(CDC*    pDC,
                CString sText,    // text to display
                int     nOffset); // line number

// Framework-defined stuff from here on
```

The source file for *CProg5_2aView* is similarly straightforward:

```
// Prog5vw.cpp : implementation of the
//               CProg5_2aView class

#include "stdafx.h"
#include "Prog5_2a.h"

#include "Prog5doc.h"
```

```
#include "Prog5vw.h"

// ...no changes up here...

/////////////////////////////////////////////////////
// CProg5_2aView construction/destruction

CProg5_2aView::CProg5_2aView()
{
    m_nLineNo = m_nCharOffset = 0;
    m_nCharHeight = m_nCharWidth = 0;
}


CProg5_2aView::~CProg5_2aView()
{
}


/////////////////////////////////////////////////////
// CProg5_2aView drawing

void CProg5_2aView::OnDraw(CDC* pDC)
{
    CProg5_2aDoc* pDoc = GetDocument();
    ASSERT_VALID(pDoc);

    // Loop through each line, displaying them all
    int nLine;
    int nMaxLine = pDoc->GetLength();
    for (nLine = 0; nLine < nMaxLine; nLine++)
    {
        Output(pDC, pDoc->String(nLine), nLine);
    }
}


// ...no changes until:

/////////////////////////////////////////////////////
// CProg5_2aView message handlers

void CProg5_2aView::OnInitialUpdate()
{
    // Get the font-size information for Output()
    // and save it in the class
    CClientDC cDC(this);
    TEXTMETRIC tmDescrip;
    cDC.GetTextMetrics(&tmDescrip);
    m_nCharHeight = tmDescrip.tmHeight
```

```
                     + tmDescrip.tmExternalLeading;
    m_nCharWidth   = tmDescrip.tmAveCharWidth;

    CView::OnInitialUpdate();
}

// OnChar() -- process the keystroke messages
void CProg5_2aView::OnChar(UINT nChar,
                           UINT nRepCnt,
                           UINT nFlags)
{
    CProg5_2aDoc* pDoc = GetDocument();
    ASSERT_VALID(pDoc);
    pDoc->AddChar(m_nLineNo, m_nCharOffset, nChar);
}

// Output() -- output the given text at
//             the specified line number
void CProg5_2aView::Output(CDC*    pDC,
                CString sText,     // text to display
                int     nLine)     // line number
{
    int nYOffset = LinetoDP(nLine);
    pDC->SetTextColor(RGB(0x00, 0x00, 0x00));
    pDC->TextOut(0, nYOffset, sText);
}

// Convert from/to offset measured
// in device units to/from lines in doc
int CProg5_2aView::DPtoLine(int nDP)
{
    return nDP / m_nCharHeight;
}
int CProg5_2aView::LinetoDP(int nLine){
    return nLine * m_nCharHeight;
}
```

I added a handler for the *OnInitialUpdate( )* message to calculate the font-height and -width information for use by *Output( )*. The *Output( )* function is similar to the one used in the personal-scheduler application in Part IV, except that it has been considerably simplified.

The simple function *LinetoDP( )* converts the specified line number within the document into the *y* offset from the top of the window where that line should be displayed. The *DPtoLine( )* function performs the reverse operation.

It may seem silly to create a function that has only a single line of code (believe me, I've done sillier things). Nonetheless, creating a function such as *LinetoDP( )* even when it contains only a single line of code is justified whenever the function performs a single, identifiable operation. In this case, *Line-toDP( )* converts the line number to its address in the window. This process offers the following advantages:

✔ Keeping this logic separate simplifies both this function and the functions that use it.

✔ Keeping this logic in one place simplifies future changes. Suppose that future developments require a change to the way the line number is converted into the *y* offset. Without this function, this type of change may have to be made in several places throughout the program. (Remember this point — I'll return to it later.) ▪

If you're concerned about inefficiencies involved in creating a function to perform something as simple as division or multiplication, declare the function to be inline. *Inlining* a function retains the modularity advantages of a function while avoiding any overhead. ▪

Because the document does all the work of interpreting the different keys, the *OnChar( )* function I installed to handle the *WM_CHAR* message simply passes the keyboard character to the document for processing. The new character is inserted into the document at the line number and character offset specified by the view. Remember that this line and character information is updated by the document, depending on the nature of the character.

Because the document calls *UpdateAllViews( )*, each new keystroke causes the entire document to be completely redrawn. *OnDraw( )* does this by looping through each line of the document and using the *Output( )* function to display each one in the window.

Conclusion

If you compile and execute the program as it is now, you'll notice some neat features and some not-so-neat features.

First, the program enables you to enter text (that's neat). Second, you can save your files and read them back (that's pretty neat too). Because the format of the file is straight ASCII text, you can even read files created by other text editors (you can even read your own .cpp files — that's super-neat!).

Finally, you can edit your text. If you enter a newline character, your cursor moves to the next line. If you enter a backspace character, the preceding character disappears. If no more characters are on the line, entering a back-space character moves your cursor to the end of the preceding line.

You almost have to take me at my word about the editing, though, because you can't tell where you are within a document (that's not so neat). There's no cursor or anything to indicate where the next character will be inserted. In addition, there's no way to move the cursor around in the document (that's *really* not neat). You can't tell the cursor that you want to insert something at this point or that point. Nor can you scroll up or down within the document. You can make the view larger, but if you can't make the document fit entirely within the view, there's no way to get to the invisible parts.

You've come a long way, but your work in the remainder of Part V is definitely cut out for you.

Chapter 23

Improving the View

● ●

In This Chapter

▶ Adding an insertion caret

▶ Updating the caret

▶ Positioning the caret

▶ Minimizing the repaint job

● ●

*Y*our text-editor program wouldn't be too bad, if only you could tell where you are within the file. The way it is, you can't tell where the next character will be inserted until it's already there. What you need is some type of cursor.

In addition, you currently repaint the entire document even when you're adding only a single character. Even with a fast processor, this seems like extreme overkill. Isn't there a way to limit the amount you redraw?

The Caret

Windows applications use a flashing vertical bar, known as the *caret* (pronounced like the vegetable of "Bugs Bunny" fame) to indicate the position of the next character to be typed.

The caret was known historically as the *cursor;* in Windows, however, the term "cursor" is used to refer to the mouse pointer. In addition, the caret was historically a flashing underline, but this is bad for two reasons.

First, in a proportional font it's not clear how wide to make the caret. You can't be changing its width every time it changes character — that would be too much trouble.

The underline was never very good anyway because it implies that the character being underlined is about to be overwritten; yet most editors work in insert mode most of the time. The vertical caret is positioned between characters to show that the next character to be typed will squeeze in between these two brutes and force them apart.

In overwrite mode, most editors resort to a rectangular caret that flashes to cover and uncover the character to be overwritten. ■

Creating the caret is simple: The *CreateCaret( )* system call takes care of it.

But there's a problem. (Isn't there always?) Unfortunately, there's only one caret in the entire system, and all WinApps must learn to share it. This problem is primarily psychological (in the user's psyche, not in Windows'). The caret directs the user's attention to the location where the next character that is typed will be inserted. A program that doesn't have focus but that continues to flash a caret at the user is misleading. It's saying, "Hey, look over here!" when the next key will be inserted somewhere else.

Every time the program loses focus, it should destroy the caret to give the program that is gaining focus a chance to grab the caret for itself. This implies that every time the program regains focus, it must re-create and reposition the caret. To allow this to happen, Windows defines the *WM_SET-FOCUS* and *WM_KILLFOCUS* messages. The *WM_KILLFOCUS* message is sent when an application is about to lose keyboard focus. The *WM_SETFOCUS* message is sent after the application has regained focus.

If two applications use the caret, no problems occur when control switches from one to the other if both applications use the preceding messages properly. The first application gets a *WM_KILLFOCUS* message first. It responds by destroying the caret. For a short time, no caret is displayed. Only after the first application has given up focus is the second application sent the *WM_SETFOCUS* message, which causes it to re-create the caret in its own likeness. ■

Growing and eating carets

The *CreateCaret( )* API call creates the caret. When the caret is created, it is invisible. As part of the caret-creation process, it must be repositioned by using the *SetCaretPos( )* API call and then shown by using the *ShowCaret( )* Windows API call.

You can create a caret in two ways. The standard *CreateCaret( )* call accepts as its argument the address of a *CBitmap* object. To use this call, you first must create the bitmap to be used for the caret, which you can do in the App-Studio resource editor just as you would create any bitmapped icon:

```
CBitmap bmCaret;
bmCaret.LoadBitmap(IDB_BITMAP_CARET);
CreateCaret(&bmCaret);
```

After the bitmap is created, the program can load the bitmap into a bitmap object by referring to its ID (in this case, *IDB_BITMAP_CARET*) — set the bitmap ID in the properties dialog box.

A second approach is to use one of the standard carets (a simple vertical, solid bar is a popular choice for an insert caret). A special version of *Create-Caret( )* exists for this type of caret:

```
CreateSolidCaret(
          2 * GetSystemMetrics(SM_CXBORDER),
          m_nCharHeight);
```

The first argument to *CreateSolidCaret( )* is the width, and the second is the height of the caret. If you set the height to *m_nCharHeight*, the caret takes up an entire line. The width is a little different. You could simply set the width to 1 (which means one pixel). On some high-resolution displays, however, one pixel generates a razor-thin cursor. Instead, it's best to set the width to be the same as (or some multiple of) the width of the window border. You are guaranteed that Windows has calculated the window border width to be both easily visible and visually pleasing.

GetSystemMetrics( ) returns various properties about the current window. Because Windows has already gone through the work of figuring out the best width for a window border on the current display, there's no reason to repeat that work. ■

Transplanting the caret

Okay, so you know how to create a caret. How do you know where to position it? Clearly, you want to position the caret at line *m_nLineNo* and character *m_nCharOffset*. The argument to *SetCaretPos( )* is a *CPoint* containing the *x* and *y* location of the caret (in physical units). How do you convert from one to the other?

Because you can make the assumption that all lines have the same height, putting the caret on line *m_nLineNo* is easy. You just use the same calculation you use in *Output( )* to calculate the *y* offset of each line of text:

```
// Set the caret location
CPoint ptCaret;
ptCaret.y = m_nLineNo * m_nCharHeight;
```

or its logical equivalent:

```
// Set the caret location
CPoint ptCaret;
ptCaret.y = LinetoDP(m_nLineNo); // same as above
```

This calculation assumes that the display mode is *MM_TEXT*. If you're in some other mode, you also have to convert *ptCaret* from logical units to device units before using it to position the cursor. Remember that *LinetoDP( )* does nothing more at this point than multiply the line number times *m_nCharHeight*, which is the height of a line of text. ∎

Positioning the caret horizontally: The wrong way

Positioning the caret in the *x* dimension is somewhat more difficult. The simplest way to position the caret along the *x* dimension is to use the same approach used in the *y* dimension: Just multiply *m_nCharOffset* by *m_nChar-Width*:

```
// Set the cursor location -- method 1
CPoint ptCaret;
ptCaret.y = LinetoDP(m_nLineNo);
ptCaret.x = m_nCharOffset * m_nCharWidth;
SetCaretPos(ptCursor);
```

For a nonproportional font, this technique works. Even for a proportional font, it sort of works. The problem is that, although *m_nCharHeight* is the actual height of each character, *m_nCharWidth* is only the average width of all the characters in the font. Like people, characters come in different widths. Some characters, such as *W,* are much wider, and others, such as *i,* are much narrower.

With this approach, if a user types a series of *i*'s, the caret seems to race ahead of the actual typing position. If a user types all capital *W*'s, the caret lags behind the actual insert position. Even when real text is entered, the cursor often doesn't quite line up.

Positioning the caret horizontally: The right way

What you need is a way to know exactly how much room was taken up by the string of characters to the left of the caret. Fortunately, Windows provides an ideal function for this purpose: *GetTextExtent( )*. This function returns the dimensions of the provided string in the current font. You can use it to position the caret:

```
// Set the cursor location -- method 2
CPoint ptCaret;

// First the y part
ptCaret.y = LinetoDP(m_nLineNo);

// Now the x component
CClientDC cDC(this);
CSize sString = cDC.GetTextExtent(
                        pDoc->String(m_nLineNo),
                        m_nCharOffset);

ptCaret.x = sString.cx;

// Reposition caret
SetCaretPos(ptCaret);
```

The first argument to *GetTextExtent( )* is the string you're measuring (in this case, the line of text that contains the caret). The second argument is the length of the string. Because you're interested in only the width of the part of the string to the left of the caret, you pass *m_nCharOffset* as the length of the string. The function returns the size (both the height and width) of the string. You're interested only in the width contained in *cx*.

Because this technique is based on the actual width of the individual characters in the string, it can't be fooled by long sequences of *i*'s or *W*'s.

Positioning the caret with the mouse

A related problem to positioning the cursor horizontally is the problem of positioning the cursor as a result of mouse input. You want users of your text editor to be able to place the insertion caret anywhere they want within the text by simply clicking the mouse at that location.

You already know that to get the mouse location you just have to handle the *WM_LBUTTONDOWN* message. Because the mouse location is reported to *OnLButtonDown( )* as a *CPoint*, you might think that you can just store the mouse location and pass it to the caret. This method doesn't work, however, for two reasons. The obvious reason is that you still have to convert the mouse location into a line number and character offset because that's what the document understands. The second, more subtle, reason is that the mouse can move anywhere within the view window. The caret should stay aligned with the lines of text. It would be disconcerting if the caret were halfway between two lines, cutting right through a character. The user wouldn't have any idea where the next character would be inserted. (Neither would I, for that matter.)

The conversion from mouse location to caret location is therefore a two-stage process:

1. The mouse location must be converted into a line number and character offset, to give you something the document can work with.

2. The line number and character offset must then be converted back into the location of the caret, as described earlier, to ensure that the caret is displayed aligned between two text characters.

You already know how to accomplish step 2 — all you need is a function to perform step 1.

You've already seen how to convert the mouse location into a line number:

```
// point has the mouse pointer location
m_nLineNo = point.y / m_nCharHeight; // DPtoLine()
```

This code works because all lines are the same height. This calculation is contained in the function *DPtoLine( )*.

As noted, the same approach doesn't work for *m_nCharOffset* because of the variability in the character width. Again, the *GetTextExtent( )* function comes to the rescue, except that this time you have to use it in a different way:

```
// Get the line of text on this line
CProg5Doc* pDoc = GetDocument();
ASSERT_VALID(pDoc);
CString sText = pDoc->String(m_nLineNo);

// Now keep calling GetTextExtent() until you find
// the string that is just barely beyond the caret
CClientDC cDC(this);
int nCOff;
int nFudgeFactor = m_nCharWidth / 2;
int nLength = sText.GetLength();
CSize szTrial;
for (nCOff = 0; nCOff < nLength; nCOff++)
{
    szTrial = cDC.GetTextExtent(sText, nCOff);
    if (point.x <= (szTrial.cx + nFudgeFactor))
    {
        break;
    }
}

// nCOff now contains the character offset of the caret
m_nCharOffset = nCOff;
```

To see how this works, assume that the mouse cursor is pointing between the *C* and *D* in the string *ABCDEF*.

The program begins by asking whether the width of the string *A* is greater than the mouse cursor's *x* offset. It isn't, of course, so the program then compares the width of the string *AB* to the mouse's *x* offset. Still no dice. *ABC*? Close, but not yet. Finally, the program finds that the string *ABCD* extends beyond the mouse cursor's *x* location. The mouse cursor must therefore be between the *C* and the *D*.

The small fudge factor is there only to force the caret evenly to one side or the other when the cursor is pointing somewhere in the middle of a character. Without this factor, the caret always falls to the right of the character that is being pointed at.

Minimizing the Repaint

Another problem with this initial foray into text editing was that it repainted the entire document after every keystroke. This section explains why.

After *AddChar( )* has added a character to the current line, it invokes *UpdateAllViews(0)* — the zero indicates that *UpdateAllViews( )* should not exclude any views from the update. This function calls the *Update( )* function for each view. The default *CView::Update( )* function invalidates the entire window, which forces a complete repaint.

Notice, however, that the documentation for *UpdateAllViews( )* lists its arguments:

```
void UpdateAllViews(CView* pSender,   // view to skip
            LPARAM lHint = 0L,    // optional hints
            CObject* pHint = NULL );
```

The second and third arguments are optional hints that the document function can provide to alert the view to what has changed. These hints are passed on to *Update( )*:

```
virtual void OnUpdate(CView* pSender, // same as...
            LPARAM lHint,       // ...passed to...
            CObject* pHint );   // ...UpdateAllViews
```

What kind of hints might the document pass *OnUpdate( )*? You might pass along some indication of what changed in the document so that the view doesn't have to repaint the entire window.

In this case, typing a simple character updates only a single line. Repainting the entire window just because a single character has been added seems like a terrible waste. Passing the line number in *lHint* would allow *Update( )* to repaint just the single line rather than the entire window.

You could get fancy and pass the location of just the single character that has changed. Many programs do exactly that. For simple characters, it wouldn't be a bad idea, but for more complex characters, such as newline and delete, it can lead to a great deal of fancy logic for not much gain. If you limit the repaint to the line containing the character, it handles even complex cases with little extra logic and is plenty fast enough. ■

You implement minimal update in the next version of your text editor.

Text Editor: The Sequel

This second version of the text editor requires no change to the document *include* file and only a minor change to the document source file. That change is in the *AddChar( )* function to implement update hinting:

```
void CProg5_2bDoc::AddChar(int& nLine,
                           int& nCharOff,
                           char cChar)
{
    // Keep track of where you started
    int nLineHint = nLine;

    // If keep is special, interpret it
    switch (cChar)
    {
      case '\n':
      case '\r':
        AddNL(nLine, nCharOff);
       break;

      case '\b':
        DeleteCharLeft(nLine, nCharOff);
        break;

      default:
        AddSimpleChar(nLine, nCharOff, cChar);
    }

    SetModifiedFlag();
```

```
// Use the hint to indicate which line changed
// If more than one line affected...
if (nLineHint != nLine)
{
    // ...update from here down
    nLineHint = min(nLineHint, nLine);
    nLineHint = ~nLineHint;
}
UpdateAllViews(0, nLineHint);
}
```

Remember that I'm using version letters to differentiate the numerous versions of the text editor. You will want to edit the existing Prog5_2 program without the version letter (or just stick with Prog5_2a). ■

The function begins by memorizing the current line number. It then goes through the process of processing the new character. If the line number didn't change, *AddChar( )* assumes that only the current line number could have been affected by the new character. Therefore, it passes just the one line number to *UpdateAllViews( )* for repainting.

If the line number is different, one of two things has happened: The user has either backspaced over a newline so that the current line is being concatenated with its predecessor or the user has entered a new line, which splits the preceding line in two. In either case, the current line (or, sometimes, the line before the current line) and all subsequent lines have to be repainted.

The lines after the current line must be repainted because inserting or removing a line causes the rest of the lines to scroll either up or down.

Because the line number cannot be negative, let's use negative values of *nLineHint* to indicate "from here down."

Notice that I used the complement operator (~) rather than the negative operator (−) to generate the negative. The reason is that −0 is indistinguishable from 0; however, ~0 is different from 0. Therefore, 0 means "repaint line 0," whereas ~0 (or 0xFFFFFFFF) means "repaint from line 0 down" (repaint the entire document). ■

The only change to the view *include* file is the addition of the prototype for the *UpdateCaret( )* function, which repositions the caret according to the value of *m_nLine* and *m_nCharOffset*.

```
// Prog5vw.h : interface of the CProg5_2bView class
//
////////////////////////////////////////////////////////////////
```

```
class CProg5_2bView : public CView
{
// User-defined stuff
protected:
    // Current insert position
    int m_nLineNo;
    int m_nCharOffset;

    // Font-size information
    int m_nCharHeight;
    int m_nCharWidth;

    // Position the caret between characters properly
    void UpdateCaret();

    // Convert from/to offset measured
    // in device units to/from lines in doc
    int DPtoLine(int nDP);
    int LinetoDP(int nLine);

    // Output function
    void Output(CDC*    pDC,
                CString sText,     // text to display
                int     nOffset);  // line number
    // Framework-defined stuff
```

The source code for the view shows more substantial changes in places, however (remember to use *ClassWizard* to add *OnUpdate*, *OnLButtonDown*, *OnSet-Focus*, and *OnKillFocus* before making the following additions):

```
// Prog5vw.cpp : implementation of the
//               CProg5_2bView class
//

// ...no change until you get to drawing routine...

/////////////////////////////////////////////////////////
// CProg5_2bView drawing

void CProg5_2bView::OnDraw(CDC* pDC)
{
    CProg5_2bDoc* pDoc = GetDocument();
    ASSERT_VALID(pDoc);

    // First get the clipping region
    CRect rectInvalid;
```

```
    pDC->GetClipBox(&rectInvalid);

    // Now convert the display region into line
    // numbers within the document (include any partial
    // lines)
    int nMinLine = DPtoLine(rectInvalid.top);
    int nMaxLine =
        DPtoLine(rectInvalid.bottom + m_nCharHeight - 1);

    // Make sure that nMax doesn't exceed the number of
    // lines in the document
    nMaxLine = min(nMaxLine, pDoc->GetLength());

    int nLine;
    // Note: remove declaration of nMaxLine from here;
    // (it's declared earlier)
    for (nLine = nMinLine; nLine < nMaxLine; nLine++)
    {
        TRACE("Updating line %d\n", nLine);
        Output(pDC, pDoc->String(nLine), nLine);
    }
    TRACE("Finished OnDraw()\n");
}

// ...no more changes until the message handlers...
/////////////////////////////////////////////////////////
// CProg5_2bView message handlers
void CProg5_2bView::OnInitialUpdate()
{
    // Get the font-size information for Output()
    // and save it into the class
    CClientDC cDC(this);
    TEXTMETRIC tmDescrip;
    cDC.GetTextMetrics(&tmDescrip);
    m_nCharHeight = tmDescrip.tmHeight
                  + tmDescrip.tmExternalLeading;
    m_nCharWidth  = tmDescrip.tmAveCharWidth;

    CView::OnInitialUpdate();
}

// OnUpdate -- repaint just the parts of the window that
//             need to be repainted. The LPARAM
//             hint is the line number that needs to be
//             repainted; if negative, then repaint from
//             here down
```

```
void CProg5_2bView::OnUpdate(CView* pSender,
                             LPARAM lHint,
                             CObject* pHint)
{
    // Figure out how much to repaint
    // Construct the invalid rectangle starting with
    // the entire client window
    CRect rectInvalid;
    GetClientRect(&rectInvalid);

    // Now recalculate the top and bottom based
    // on line number in the hint. If the line number is
    // negative...
    int nLine = (int)lHint;
    if (nLine < 0)
    {
        // ...then start at the specified line and
        // go all the way to the bottom
        nLine = ~nLine;
        rectInvalid.top = LinetoDP(nLine);
    }
    else
    {
        // If positive, just this line
        rectInvalid.top = LinetoDP(nLine);
        rectInvalid.bottom =
                            rectInvalid.top + m_nCharHeight;
    }

    InvalidateRect(rectInvalid);
}

void CProg5_2bView::OnChar(UINT nChar,
                           UINT nRepCnt,
                           UINT nFlags)
{
    CProg5_2bDoc* pDoc = GetDocument();
    ASSERT_VALID(pDoc);
    pDoc->AddChar(m_nLineNo, m_nCharOffset, nChar);
    UpdateCaret();
}

void CProg5_2bView::OnSetFocus(CWnd* pOldWnd)
{
    CView::OnSetFocus(pOldWnd);

    CreateSolidCaret(
```

```
        2 * GetSystemMetrics(SM_CXBORDER),
        m_nCharHeight);
    UpdateCaret();
    ShowCaret();
}


void CProg5_2bView::OnKillFocus(CWnd* pNewWnd)
{
    CView::OnKillFocus(pNewWnd);
    HideCaret();
    DestroyCaret();
}


void CProg5_2bView::OnLButtonDown(UINT nFlags,
                                  CPoint point)
{
    // Find where this is:
    // Line number is easy
    m_nLineNo = DPtoLine(point.y);

    // Char is interesting -- first get the string
    CProg5_2bDoc* pDoc = GetDocument();
    ASSERT_VALID(pDoc);
    CString sText = pDoc->String(m_nLineNo);

    // Use the string to recursively zero in on
    // the caret position
    CClientDC cDC(this);
    int nCOff;
    int nFudgeFactor = m_nCharWidth / 2;
    int nLength = sText.GetLength();
    CSize szTrial;
    for (nCOff = 0; nCOff < nLength; nCOff++)
    {
        szTrial = cDC.GetTextExtent(sText, nCOff);
        if (point.x <= (szTrial.cx + nFudgeFactor))
        {
            break;
        }
    }
    m_nCharOffset = nCOff;

    // Now update caret with new location
    UpdateCaret();
}


//UpdateCaret() -- update the caret location based on
```

```
//                    the line number and char offset.
//                    Make sure that the caret is
//                    between characters.
void CProg5_2bView::UpdateCaret()
{
    CProg5_2bDoc* pDoc = GetDocument();
    ASSERT_VALID(pDoc);

    // Keep character offset within range of a line
    CString sOutString = pDoc->String(m_nLineNo);
    m_nCharOffset = min(m_nCharOffset,
                        sOutString.GetLength());
    m_nCharOffset = max(m_nCharOffset, 0);

    CPoint ptCaret;
    CClientDC cDC(this);
    CSize sString = cDC.GetTextExtent(
                        sOutString,
                        m_nCharOffset);

    ptCaret.x = sString.cx;
    ptCaret.y = LinetoDP(m_nLineNo);

    // Reposition caret
    SetCaretPos(ptCaret);
}
```

```
// Output -- display the given text at the specified line number
void CProg5_2bView::Output(CDC*   pDC,
                        CString sText, // text to display
                        int     nLine) // line number
{
    int nYOffset = LinetoDP(nLine);

    pDC->SetTextColor(RGB(0x00, 0x00, 0x00));
    pDC->TextOut(0, nYOffset, sText);
}

// Convert from/to offset measured
// in device units to/from lines in doc
int CProg5_2bView::DPtoLine(int nDP)
{
    return nDP / m_nCharHeight;
}
int CProg5_2bView::LinetoDP(int nLine){
    return nLine * m_nCharHeight;
}
```

Minimal update

Of course, the built-in *CView::OnUpdate( )* knows nothing about any hint you might be passing through *UpdateAllViews( )*. The default version just invalidates the entire window.

To make use of the hint information, I added a new *OnUpdate( )* function with the ClassWizard. This version begins by finding the size of the client area of the view window. This size represents the maximum size of the area that needs to be repainted.

OnUpdate( ) then moves the top of the repaint area down to the line indicated in *lHint*. If *lHint* is nonnegative, it also sets the bottom of the repaint area to be the top of the next line. The repaint area then includes just the strip that contains the current line.

If the hint is negative, *OnUpdate( )* leaves the bottom of the repaint area as the bottom of the client window, which forces the program to repaint from line *lHint* to the bottom of the window.

After the calculation is complete, *OnUpdate( )* invalidates the calculated rectangle. Both these conditions are shown in Figure 23-1.

If you invalidate only the necessary portions of the output view, you speed up redrawing without any changes to *OnDraw( )*. (Remember that Windows pays about as much attention to attempts to display to areas of the window not within an invalid region as my son does to requests to feed our dogs.)

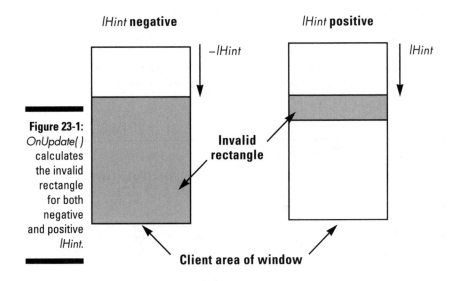

Figure 23-1:
OnUpdate( )
calculates
the invalid
rectangle
for both
negative
and positive
lHint.

Nevertheless, *OnDraw( )* shouldn't even generate requests to display lines that are completely outside the invalid rectangle: It's a waste of perfectly good CPU cycles.

To avoid drawing lines that are not within an invalid region, *OnDraw( )* first queries the device context for the invalid rectangle by using the *GetClipBox( )* function. *GetClipBox( )* returns the smallest rectangle that completely encompasses all clipping regions.

MFC has functions to read the invalid rectangle from the current window rather than from the device context; it's too late, however, to use any of these functions. The *BeginPaint( )* operation that is invoked before calling *OnDraw( )* combines any invalid window rectangles into the clipping region of the device context and then zeroes them out. If you ask the window for its invalid rectangle from within *OnDraw( )*, the answer always comes back *NULL*, meaning that the window is completely valid. ■

OnDraw( ) then converts the top of the clipping rectangle into the corresponding document line number by using the *DPtoLine( )* function. It does the same for the bottom, being careful to include any partially visible lines (by adding *m_nCharHeight-1* to the bottom of the rectangle). Finally, the program loops from the top line to the bottom line of the invalid rectangle.

The calls to *TRACE( )* are there only to prove to you that the minimum redraw algorithm really works. After you're convinced, you should remove these calls.

Remember that calls to *OnDraw( )* don't originate only with changes to the document. *WM_PAINT* messages that end up in *OnDraw( )* requests may be generated by Windows as a result of a window's being resized, reshown, or unobscured by a superior window, for example. You should prove to yourself that the minimal repaint algorithm works reasonably well for all redraws.

If the client area is partially obscured and then brought to the front, for example, *OnDraw( )* repaints only the lines that are necessary to refresh the window. ■

Caret capabilities

The updated text editor also includes the caret capabilities discussed earlier in this chapter. The *OnChar( )* function updates the caret location after each character by calling *UpdateCaret( )*.

The *OnSetFocus( )* function, which is called when the window gains focus, creates a solid vertical caret, positions it by using the *UpdateCaret( )* function, and then makes it visible by calling *ShowCaret( )*. The *OnKillFocus( )* function merely hides and destroys the caret.

The *OnLButtonDown( )* function converts the mouse location into a line number and character offset by using the algorithm discussed earlier in this chapter. The *UpdateCaret( )* function also was discussed earlier in this chapter. The check to keep the caret within the confines of the line keeps the caret from extending to the right of the line into unoccupied space.

Conclusion

The addition of the caret enables a user to see where the next character will be inserted. Grabbing the *WM_LBUTTONDOWN* message from the mouse enables the program to position the caret wherever the user wants.

You can reduce drastically the amount of repainting that is done within *OnDraw( )* by providing a hint to the *UpdateAllViews( )* function to indicate the line number or line numbers that need to be repainted. This is particularly important for the text editor because the window must be repainted after every character is typed.

Note again that you could have tried to limit the area that was redrawn to just the tiny rectangle that includes only the single character that was typed. This can lead to some rather tortured logic when you are forced to handle special characters, such as delete and newline. Limiting the repaint to just the line that contains the new character greatly simplifies the logic and is almost as efficient.

Only one feature remains to be added to the text editor: scrolling. Chapter 24 explains how to do it.

Chapter 24

Scrolling Your Own

●●

In This Chapter

▶ Implementing your own scrolling capability

▶ Handling scroll bars and arrow keys

●●

*S*o far, your editor is limited to displaying whatever fits in a single window. To view files larger than the available window space, you must implement some sort of scrolling capability.

In Part III, you added scrolling capability to the Etch-A-Sketch program by basing the application's view class on *CScrollView* rather than on the normal *CView*. *CScrollView* handled all the dirty work for you. This method is fine for applications with small documents, but for applications with potentially large documents, it's not satisfactory.

The problem is that the Etch-A-Sketch program repainted the entire drawing on a virtual window and let *CScrollView* map the visible portion on the physical window. But what if that virtual window consists of a document with thousands of lines of text? Repainting the entire document, even for something as trivial as an extra keystroke, makes Johnny a very slow application.

Adding Scrolling Capability

Your program shares the burden of implementing scrolling with Windows. Any window created with the *WS_VSCROLL* window style, which includes the view windows created by MFC, can have a vertical scroll bar (*WS_HSCROLL* for horizontal scroll bars). It just has to be turned on to become visible.

Each scroll bar has two properties:

✔ A range
✔ A position

The position of the scroll bar is a value that corresponds to the position of the scroll thumb along the track. The range of the scroll bar represents the legal limits of the position. If the range of the scroll bar is 0 through 100, for example, the position of the thumb can be anywhere between 0 and 100. Position 0 corresponds to the thumb all the way at the top of the range; position 100, all the way to the bottom; and position 50, exactly in the middle.

Windows is responsible for the following tasks:

- Handling the interaction of the mouse with the scroll bar
- Handling changes in the appearance of the scroll bar because of clicking the buttons
- Moving the thumb
- Sending scroll messages to the application and informing it of any changes

Your application is responsible for these tasks:

- Setting the scroll range
- Updating the scroll position
- Scrolling the text within the view window as a result of the scroll messages
- Implementing scrolling from the keyboard (optional)

MFC creates windows with the range set to (0, 0), which has the effect of hiding the scroll bar. Your application must set the scroll range as soon as it determines that the text no longer fits within the window. Doing so unhides the scroll bar. You can set the scroll bar range back to (0, 0) and therefore rehide the scroll bar if either the window expands or the document shrinks so that the document does fit within the window.

When a user clicks one of the scroll bar *gadgets* (a generic term for the buttons and troughs that make up a scroll bar), the program receives two WM_VSCROLL messages: one when the gadget is pressed and one when it's released. (The scroll messages are described in Chapter 16, in the discussion of the horizontal scroll bars associated with the time fields in the dialog box.)

To implement scrolling, you should view the document as existing in some potentially extremely long logical window that is large enough to hold the entire document. Some portion of this logical window is mapped to the physical window, which is the part you see. The program maintains the offset of the physical window within the logical window. Scrolling consists of moving the physical window around within the logical window by increasing or decreasing the offset.

Cruising the Scroll Bars

Let's see what scrolling looks like in practice. The scroll offset, *m_nViewOffset*, is added to the view class to hold the offset of the physical view within the document:

```
// Prog5vw.h : interface of the CProg5_2cView class
//
/////////////////////////////////////////////////////////////

class CProg5_2cView : public CView
{
// User-defined stuff
protected:
    // Current insert position
    int m_nLineNo;
    int m_nCharOffset;

    // Font-size information
    int m_nCharHeight;
    int m_nCharWidth;

    // Offset of view within the document
    int m_nViewOffset;

    // Return the line number of the bottom of the
    // window
    int GetWindowHeight();
    int GetDocHeight();

    // Convert from/to offset measured
    // in device units to/from lines in doc
    int DPtoLine(int nDP);
    int LinetoDP(int nLine);

    // Update scroll bars
    void UpdateScrollBar();

    // Position the caret between characters properly
    void UpdateCaret();

    // Output function
    void Output(CDC*    pDC,
                CString sText,    // text to display
                int     nOffset); // line number
// Framework-defined stuff from here on...
```

The additional function *GetWindowHeight( )* calculates the height of the view (the physical window) in device units. The function *GetDocHeight( )* calculates the "height" of the document (the logical window), also in device units.

Stated another way, *GetDocHeight( )* calculates the height of the smallest window that would completely contain the document.

The *UpdateScrollBar( )* function updates the range of the scroll bar and the position of the scroll thumb, as you'll see later in this chapter.

The source file, Prog5vw.cpp, implements the scroll bar additions (use Class-Wizard to add the *OnVScroll( )* and *OnSize( )* message-handler functions):

```cpp
// Prog5vw.cpp : implementation of the
//               CProg5_2cView class
//

// ...no changes to this initial stuff...

/////////////////////////////////////////////////////////
// CProg5_2cView construction/destruction

CProg5_2cView::CProg5_2cView()
{
    m_nLineNo = m_nCharOffset = 0;
    m_nCharHeight = m_nCharWidth = 0;
    m_nViewOffset = 0;
}

CProg5_2cView::~CProg5_2cView()
{
}


/////////////////////////////////////////////////////////
// CProg5_2cView drawing

void CProg5_2cView::OnDraw(CDC* pDC)
{
    CProg5_2cDoc* pDoc = GetDocument();
    ASSERT_VALID(pDoc);

    // First get the clipping region
    CRect rectInvalid;
    pDC->GetClipBox(&rectInvalid);

    // Convert the display region into line numbers
    // within the document (include any partial
```

```
        // lines)
        int nMinLine = DPtoLine(rectInvalid.top);
        int nMaxLine =
            DPtoLine(rectInvalid.bottom + m_nCharHeight - 1);

        // Make sure that nMaxLine doesn't exceed the number of
        // lines in the document
        nMaxLine = min(nMaxLine, pDoc->GetLength());

        int nLine;
        for (nLine = nMinLine; nLine < nMaxLine; nLine++)
        {
            Output(pDC, pDoc->String(nLine), nLine);
        }
}

// ...no changes until message handlers...

/////////////////////////////////////////////////////////
// CProg5_2cView message handlers

void CProg5_2cView::OnInitialUpdate()
{
    // Get the font-size information for Output()
    // and save it into the class
    CClientDC cDC(this);
    TEXTMETRIC tmDescrip;
    cDC.GetTextMetrics(&tmDescrip);
    m_nCharHeight = tmDescrip.tmHeight
                    + tmDescrip.tmExternalLeading;
    m_nCharWidth  = tmDescrip.tmAveCharWidth;

    CView::OnInitialUpdate();
}

// OnUpdate -- repaint just the parts of the window that
//             need to be repainted. The LPARAM
//             hint is the line number that needs to be
//             repainted; if negative, then repaint from
//             here down
void CProg5_2cView::OnUpdate(CView* pSender,
                             LPARAM lHint,
                             CObject* pHint)
{
    // First update the scroll bars based on the number
    // of lines in the document
    UpdateScrollBar();
```

```
        // Second, figure out how much to repaint
        // Construct the invalid rectangle starting with
        // the entire client window
        CRect rectInvalid;
        GetClientRect(&rectInvalid);

        // Now recalculate the top and bottom based
        // on line number in the hint. If the line number is
        // negative...
        int nLine = (int)lHint;
        if (nLine < 0)
        {
            // ...then start at the specified line and
            // go all the way to the bottom
            nLine = ~nLine;
            rectInvalid.top = LinetoDP(nLine);
        }
        else
        {
            // If positive, just this line
            rectInvalid.top = LinetoDP(nLine);
            rectInvalid.bottom =
                            rectInvalid.top + m_nCharHeight;
        }

        InvalidateRect(rectInvalid);
}

void CProg5_2cView::OnChar(UINT nChar,
                           UINT nRepCnt,
                           UINT nFlags)
{
    CProg5_2cDoc* pDoc = GetDocument();
    ASSERT_VALID(pDoc);
    pDoc->AddChar(m_nLineNo, m_nCharOffset, nChar);
    UpdateCaret();
}

void CProg5_2cView::OnSetFocus(CWnd* pOldWnd)
{
    CView::OnSetFocus(pOldWnd);

    CreateSolidCaret(
        2 * GetSystemMetrics(SM_CXBORDER),
        m_nCharHeight);
    UpdateCaret();
    ShowCaret();
```

```
    }

void CProg5_2cView::OnKillFocus(CWnd* pNewWnd)
{
    CView::OnKillFocus(pNewWnd);
    HideCaret();
    DestroyCaret();
}

void CProg5_2cView::OnLButtonDown(UINT nFlags, CPoint point)
{
    // Find where this is:
    // Line number is easy
    m_nLineNo = DPtoLine(point.y);

    // Char is interesting -- first get the string
    CProg5_2cDoc* pDoc = GetDocument();
    ASSERT_VALID(pDoc);
    CString sText = pDoc->String(m_nLineNo);

    // Use the string to zero in on it
    CClientDC cDC(this);
    int nCOff;
    int nFudgeFactor = m_nCharWidth / 2;
    int nLength = sText.GetLength();
    CSize szTrial;
    for (nCOff = 0; nCOff < nLength; nCOff++)
    {
        szTrial = cDC.GetTextExtent(sText, nCOff);
        if (point.x <= (szTrial.cx + nFudgeFactor))
        {
            break;
        }
    }
    m_nCharOffset = nCOff;

    // Now update caret with new location
    UpdateCaret();
}

void CProg5_2cView::OnVScroll(UINT nSBCode,
                              UINT nPos,
                              CScrollBar* pScrollBar)
{
    // Set new offset
    switch(nSBCode)
    {
```

```
      case SB_LINEDOWN:
        m_nViewOffset += 1;
        break;

      case SB_LINEUP:
        m_nViewOffset -= 1;
        break;

      case SB_THUMBTRACK:
        m_nViewOffset = nPos;
        break;

    default:
        return;
    }

    // Make sure that this isn't out of range
    int nMin;
    int nMax;
    GetScrollRange(SB_VERT, &nMin, &nMax);
    m_nViewOffset = max(m_nViewOffset, nMin);
    m_nViewOffset = min(m_nViewOffset, nMax);

    // Now update the scroll bar position
    SetScrollPos(SB_VERT, m_nViewOffset);

    // Keep caret in same place in document
    UpdateCaret();

    // And repaint with the scrolled value
    Invalidate();
}

void CProg5_2cView::OnSize(UINT nType, int cx, int cy)
{
    if (m_nCharHeight)
    {
        UpdateScrollBar();
    }
}

//UpdateCaret() -- update the caret location based on
//                 the line number and char offset.
//                 Make sure that the caret is
//                 between characters.
void CProg5_2cView::UpdateCaret()
{
```

```
        CProg5_2cDoc* pDoc = GetDocument();
        ASSERT_VALID(pDoc);

        // Keep character offset within range of a line
        CString sOutString = pDoc->String(m_nLineNo);
        m_nCharOffset = min(m_nCharOffset,
                            sOutString.GetLength());
        m_nCharOffset = max(m_nCharOffset, 0);

        CPoint ptCaret;
        CClientDC cDC(this);
        CSize sString = cDC.GetTextExtent(
                            sOutString,
                            m_nCharOffset);

        ptCaret.x = sString.cx;
        ptCaret.y = LinetoDP(m_nLineNo);

        // Reposition caret
        SetCaretPos(ptCaret);
    }


// Output() -- output the text at the specified line number
void CProg5_2cView::Output(CDC*   pDC,
                        CString sText, // text to display
                        int     nLine) // line number
{
    int nYOffset = LinetoDP(nLine);
    pDC->SetTextColor(RGB(0x00, 0x00, 0x00));
    pDC->TextOut(0, nYOffset, sText);
}


//GetWindowHeight() -- return height of window
//                     in device units
int CProg5_2cView::GetWindowHeight()
{
    // Divide the height of the window by
    // the height of a character
    CRect rectView;
    GetClientRect(&rectView);

    // Note that rectView.top is always 0.
    return rectView.bottom;
}


//GetDocHeight() -- Return the length of the
//                  document in device units
```

```cpp
int CProg5_2cView::GetDocHeight()
{
    CProg5_2cDoc* pDoc = GetDocument();
    ASSERT_VALID(pDoc);

    return pDoc->GetLength() * m_nCharHeight;
}


//UpdateScrollBar() -- update the scroll bars
//              based on a change in either
//              the size of the window or the
//              number of lines in document
void CProg5_2cView::UpdateScrollBar()
{
    // If all the lines are visible...
    int nVisible = GetWindowHeight();
    int nMax = GetDocHeight();
    if (nVisible >= nMax)
    {
        // ...hide the scroll bar
        SetScrollRange(SB_VERT, 0, 0);

        // if you're going to hide the scroll bar,
        // you have to make sure that everything's
        // visible
        m_nViewOffset = 0;
        UpdateCaret();
    }
    else
    {
        // Not all lines visible -- set scroll range
        SetScrollRange(SB_VERT, 0,
                    nMax - nVisible, FALSE);
        if (m_nViewOffset > (nMax - nVisible))
        {
            m_nViewOffset = nMax - nVisible;
            UpdateCaret();
        }
        SetScrollPos(SB_VERT, m_nViewOffset);
    }
}

// DPtoLine() -- convert the offset from the top
//               of the window into line number offset
//               from beginning of document
int CProg5_2cView::DPtoLine(int nDP)
{
```

```
    // Add in the scrolling bias to account for
    // the fact that the top of the window may
    // be offset into the document
    nDP += m_nViewOffset;

    // Now convert the device units into line number
    return nDP / m_nCharHeight;
}


//LinetoDP() -- convert the line number in document
//              into an offset from the top of the
//              window
int CProg5_2cView::LinetoDP(int nLine)
{
    // Convert from line number to device units
    int nDP = nLine * m_nCharHeight;
    // Now bias this by the offset of the top
    // of the window
    return nDP - m_nViewOffset;
}
```

To follow the scroll bar story, let's begin with *UpdateScrollBar( )*. This function first finds the height of the view by using the *GetWindowHeight( )* function and the height of the document by using the *GetDocHeight( )* function. If the entire document can be displayed within the view, the function hides the vertical scroll bar by setting its range to (0, 0). The call to *UpdateCaret( )* makes sure that the caret stays in the same place relative to the document in case the *m_nViewOffset* changes.

If the entire document cannot be displayed, the function sets the range to be from 0 to *GetDocHeight( ) - GetWindowHeight( )*.

I could have set the range as follows:

```
SetScrollRange(SB_VERT, 0, GetDocHeight(), FALSE).
```

This line enables the offset, *m_nViewOffset*, to attain any value between 0 and the length of the document. It also enables a user to scroll the view to the point that the document completely (even if just barely) scrolls off the top of the view (shown as case 1 in Figure 24-1).

That method doesn't seem very useful to me. I like to limit the range of *m_nViewOffset* so that the most a user can scroll the view is to the point that the last line of the document becomes the last line in the view. For this reason, I limit *m_nViewOffset* to *GetDocHeight( ) - GetWindowHeight( )* (shown as case 2 in Figure 24-1). ∎

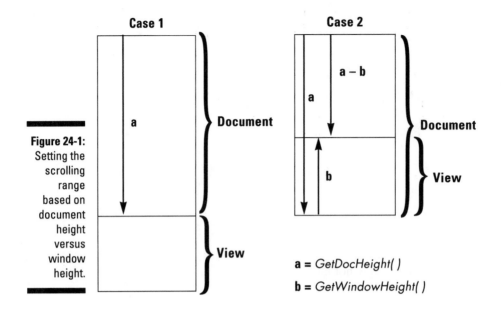

Figure 24-1:
Setting the
scrolling
range
based on
document
height
versus
window
height.

$a = GetDocHeight( )$

$b = GetWindowHeight( )$

After the range has been set, the current offset contained in *m_nViewOffset* is
forced within this range. Whenever *m_nViewOffset* is changed, *UpdateCaret( )* is
called to keep the caret tracking with the document.

The scroll bar range should be updated under either of these two conditions:

  ✔ *If the document height changes:* This condition may be the result of either
  adding lines because of a new line or removing lines by using a backspace. This condition is handled by adding a call to *UpdateScrollBar( )* to
  the beginning of *OnUpdate( )*, because *OnUpdate( )* is called whenever the
  document changes.

  ✔ *If the size of the window changes:* This condition is handled by adding
  the *OnSize( )* function to handle the *WM_SIZE* message that would
  accompany a resizing of the window.

The scroll messages are handled by *OnVScroll( )*. The *nSBCode* argument to
OnVScroll( ) indicates what the user did to the scroll bar. The various codes
and their meanings are shown in Table 24-1 (this information for the horizontal scroll bar is shown in Chapter 16).

The program responds to the line-up and line-down actions by decrementing
and incrementing *m_nViewOffset*, respectively. The program responds to the
thumb track code by taking the scroll position directly from *nPos*.

Table 24-1 Legal SB Codes in WM_VSCROLL Message

SB Code	User Action
SB_LINEDOWN	Clicks down arrow
SB_LINEUP	Clicks up arrow
SB_PAGEDOWN	Clicks trough below scroll thumb
SB_PAGEUP	Clicks trough above scroll thumb
SB_THUMBTRACK	Grabs scroll thumb and moves it
SB_THUMBPOSITION	Releases scroll thumb
SB_ENDSCROLL	Releases mouse button; is then sent on any of the up or down messages

I have intentionally not handled the *SB_PAGEUP* and *SB_PAGEDOWN* codes here; they are included as one of the questions in the "20-Minute Workout" at the end of this part of the book. ∎

The resulting value of *m_nViewOffset* is first bounded to make sure that it does not exceed the range of the scroll bar and then is used to reposition the scroll thumb.

Invalidating the window causes the window to be redrawn with the new value of *m_nViewOffset*, which implements the text scroll.

Vindicating little functions

A couple of design points are worthy of note (actually, I just can't resist bragging).

Although the addition of scrolling capability adds a few functions to your editor, it changes the existing code very little. This is desirable because it's generally considered easier to add new code to an existing program than it is to change what's already there.

Changes to the existing code are minimal because of the (clever) decision to create the *DPtoLine( )* and *LinetoDP( )* functions to convert the view offset to document line number and back. These functions isolated the logical-window- (document) to-physical-window (view) mapping into one set of functions that enabled the scrolling to be implemented in one place.

Actually, I'm not quite that clairvoyant. The first version of this set of text editor programs did not have separate *DPtoLine( )* and *LinetoDP( )* functions. To implement scrolling in this version of *Prog5_2c*, *m_nViewOffset* appeared in seven or eight places throughout the program, not including *OnVScroll( )* and *UpdateScrollBar( )*. (It took the better part of a night to find all the proper places and decide when to add *m_nViewOffset* and when to subtract it.)

With the addition of *DPtoLine( )* and *LinetoDP( )*, *m_nViewOffset* appears in just the two places, other than *OnVScroll( )* and *UpdateScrollBar( )*. (Making these additions took the better part of five minutes.) ■

Multiple views

Because this text editor supports multiple views, this is another good opportunity to examine the effect of opening multiple views into the same document. Let's try opening two views into an empty document.

Notice that typing in one view causes the additional text to appear in both views. The reason is that *UpdateAllViews( )* invokes the *OnUpdate( )* function for each view object separately.

If you reinsert the *TRACE( )* calls to the *OnDraw( )* function, you notice that the repaints of both windows are minimal (only the necessary lines of each window are redrawn). The reason is that the *OnUpdate( )* function calls receive the same hint. Each view decides on its own how to interpret it.

Place one of the view windows so that it partially eclipses the other. Then move the window up or down slightly so that only one line in the background window is affected. Again, you should notice that only the single line is redrawn, because your new *OnDraw( )* function is smart enough to interpret the invalid rectangle information that Windows provides.

Scrolling one view has no effect on the other view because *m_nViewOffset* is a property of the view object.

Handling Arrow Keys

Although Windows is perfectly willing to handle interactions with the scroll bar, it's about as responsive to the keyboard arrow keys as my weight is to my attempts to diet.

The arrow keys normally don't implement scrolling directly. Instead, they are used to update the caret. After the caret has reached the edge of the view, the application scrolls the view in order to keep the caret visible.

The following *WM_KEYDOWN* message-handler function, *OnKeyDown( )* (which is added with ClassWizard), processes the common arrow keys:

```
void CProg5_2dView::OnKeyDown(UINT nChar,
                              UINT nRepCnt,
                              UINT nFlags)
{
    CProg5_2dDoc* pDoc = GetDocument();
    ASSERT_VALID(pDoc);

    // Get the height of the window in both
    // device units and lines
    int nWindowHeight = GetWindowHeight();
    int nWindowLH = nWindowHeight / m_nCharHeight;

    // Handle the arrow keys -- everything else
    // just pass through
    switch(nChar)
    {
      case VK_RIGHT:
        m_nCharOffset++;
        break;

      case VK_LEFT:
        m_nCharOffset--;
        break;

      case VK_UP:
        m_nLineNo--;
        break;

      case VK_DOWN:
        m_nLineNo++;
        break;

      case VK_PRIOR:
        m_nLineNo -= (nWindowLH / 2);
        break;

      case VK_NEXT:
        m_nLineNo += (nWindowLH / 2);
        break;

      default:
        // Use default processing if it's not one of
        // the keys above
        CView::OnKeyDown(nChar, nRepCnt, nFlags);
```

```
        return;
    }

    // Make sure that the line number is still reasonable
    if (m_nLineNo < 0)
    {
        m_nLineNo = 0;
    }
    int nBottomLimit = pDoc->GetLength();
    if (m_nLineNo > nBottomLimit)
    {
        m_nLineNo = nBottomLimit;
    }


    // Now make sure that the caret stays visible
    // Is it off the top of the window?
    int nCaretOffset = LinetoDP(m_nLineNo);
    if (nCaretOffset < 0)
    {
        // Yes -- move the window up
        m_nViewOffset += nCaretOffset;
        UpdateScrollBar();
        Invalidate();
    }

    // How about off the bottom?
    int nWindowBottom = nWindowHeight - m_nCharHeight;
    if (nCaretOffset > nWindowBottom)
    {
        // Yes -- move the window down
        m_nViewOffset += (nCaretOffset - nWindowBottom);
        UpdateScrollBar();
        Invalidate();
    }

    // Now update the caret with the new line number
    // and character offset
    UpdateCaret();
}
```

The function begins by requesting the height of the window, in both device units and lines of text. It then looks at the virtual key code passed to the function in the argument *nChar*. The codes for left, right, up, and down are handled by incrementing or decrementing the proper offset. The *VK_PRIOR* and *VK_NEXT* cases implement page-up and page-down capability, respectively. In this case, the function increments the pointer by half the height of the window. A fixed jump size could have been used instead.

Any keys other than those mentioned here are processed in the normal manner, by being passed to *CView::OnKeyDown( )*.

The next section of the function checks to make sure that the offsets don't move out of range. You don't have to worry about *m_nCharOffset* because *UpdateCaret( )* keeps it in check. You do have to make sure, however, that the line offset does not go off the top (*m_nLineNo < 0*) or bottom (*m_nLineNo > nBottomLimit*) of the document.

The final checks make sure that the caret remains visible. The first test, for example, converts *m_nLineNo* into the *y* offset from the top of the view window. If this offset is negative, the current line number is above the top of the window, so the function scrolls the view down enough that *m_nLineNo* is the topmost visible line in the window.

Window scrolling is performed in this case by updating the *m_nViewOffset* and then invalidating the window. Calling *UpdateScrollBar( )* keeps the scroll bar in synch with the value of *m_nViewOffset*.

Conclusion

This is about as far as I want to take this little text editor program. Obviously, many features can be added, some of which you add as part of the following "20-Minute Workout." Text editors are an example of one of those programs that never stops growing.

The point of this program (and this book) has been to give you a firm foundation in Windows programming — one that you can use as a basis for your continuing mastery of Windows 95 and beyond.

You've learned how to accomplish these tasks:

- ✔ Handle live and dangerous keyboard input
- ✔ Process ASCII text within a document
- ✔ Update multiple views
- ✔ Minimize the amount of the view being repainted to speed the refresh rate of the resulting application
- ✔ Scroll text within a small window as a result of both mouse input and keyboard input

Perhaps you never thought that you would make it this far, but here you are, a Windows 95 programmer.

20-Minute Workout

Questions

1 The DPtoL*ine( )* and *LinetoDP( )* functions in this part make the assumption that all lines are the same height. What if this weren't true? What would be the implication?

2 What if the text editor couldn't keep up with the cursor thumb as it rocketed up and down the scroll bar? Is there something you could do to make your application more acceptable to the user (other than drop the price)?

3 The constructor for the *Prog5_2Doc* class includes the following line:

```
m_saText.SetSize(0, 100);
```

What purpose does this call serve? (Notice that the program works even without this call.)

4 Explain the following code, taken from the *OnOpenFile( )* function:

```
ifstream iFile(lpszPathName,
               ios::in | ios::nocreate);
if (iFile.fail())
{
    return FALSE;
}
```

5 Prog5_2 does not handle page-up and page-down tasks as part of its scroll capability. Add this capability to *OnVScroll( )*. (This problem is a relatively simple one.)

6 Prog5_2 does not implement the Delete Right keystroke. Implement this feature as well. ***Hint:*** You normally would use the Del key to implement Delete Right; this key does not generate a *WM_CHAR* message, however, because it has no ASCII equivalent, making it necessary to handle Del on the *WM_KEY-DOWN* message. Instead, follow the lead of some now-ancient word processors and use Ctrl-G (ASCII '\x7') to implement Delete Right. This problem is somewhat more challenging, but you should attempt it — it's definitely educational.

Answers

1

If different lines were of different heights, *LinetoDP( )* would have to loop through each line, measuring its height and adding it to a total. *GetTextExtent( )* works this way when it loops through each character in the string, adding the character's width to some total.

By the same token, *DPtoLine(x)* would have to use the same approach as *OnLButton( )*: It would have to start at line zero and convert each line to its offset in device units until it had "bracketed" *x*.

2

Whenever your program cannot keep up with the onslaught of *SB_THUMB-TRACK* messages, it can always process the single *SB_THUMBPOSITION* message, which does not occur until the user releases the cursor thumb.

3

The call to *SetSize(0, 100)* sets the current size to 0, which it already is. More important, however, it sets the growth to 100. Every time the *CStringArray* needs to grow, it grows by 100 positions. This reduces by a factor of 100 the number of times the *CStringArray* must undergo the relatively painful skin-shedding operation of growing.

4

This code creates an input stream object with the name *iFile*, opening the file whose name is pointed at by the ASCIIZ character string *lpszPathName*. The file is opened for input but is not created if it does not already exist. If the open fails, probably because the file doesn't exist, the function returns a *FALSE*.

5

The following modifications to *OnVScroll( )* implement page-up and page-down scrolling by clicking in the scroll trough:

```
void CProg5_2dView::OnVScroll(UINT nSBCode, UINT nPos, CScrollBar*
        pScrollBar)
{
    // Set new offset
    switch(nSBCode)
    {
      case SB_LINEDOWN:
```

```
              m_nViewOffset += 1;
              break;

          case SB_LINEUP:
              m_nViewOffset -= 1;
              break;

          case SB_THUMBTRACK:
              m_nViewOffset = nPos;
              break;

          case SB_PAGEDOWN:
              m_nViewOffset += GetWindowHeight() / 2;
              break;

          case SB_PAGEUP:
              m_nViewOffset -= GetWindowHeight() / 2;
              break;

          default:
              return;
      }

      // Make sure that this isn't out of range
      int nMin;
      int nMax;
      GetScrollRange(SB_VERT, &nMin, &nMax);
      m_nViewOffset = max(m_nViewOffset, nMin);
      m_nViewOffset = min(m_nViewOffset, nMax);

      // Now update the scroll bar position
      SetScrollPos(SB_VERT, m_nViewOffset);

      // Keep caret in same place in document
      UpdateCaret();

      // And repaint with the scrolled value
      Invalidate();
  }
```

 The following change to *AddChar( )* plus the additional function *DeleteChar-Right( )* implement the Delete Right function.

```
void CProg5_2dDoc::AddChar(int& nLine,
                           int& nCharOff,
                           char cChar)
```

```
{
    // Keep line of where you started
    int nLineHint = nLine;

    // If keep is special, interpret it
    switch (cChar)
    {
      case '\n':
      case '\r':
        AddNL(nLine, nCharOff);
       break;

      case '\b':
        DeleteCharLeft(nLine, nCharOff);
        break;

      case '\x7':
        DeleteCharRight(nLine, nCharOff, nLineHint);
        break;

      default:
        AddSimpleChar(nLine, nCharOff, cChar);
    }

    SetModifiedFlag();

    // Use the hint to indicate which line changed
    // If more than one line affected...
    if (nLineHint != nLine)
    {
        // ...update from here down
        nLineHint = min(nLineHint, nLine);
        nLineHint = ~nLineHint;
    }
    UpdateAllViews(0, nLineHint);
}

void CProg5_2dDoc::DeleteCharRight(int& nLine,
                                   int& nCharOff,
                                   int& nLineHint)
{
    ASSERT(nLine <= m_saText.GetUpperBound());

    // Get the current string and length
    CString& sText = m_saText[nLine];
    int nLength = sText.GetLength();
```

```
    // If this is the rightmost character...
    if (nCharOff == nLength)
    {
        // ...and it's not the last line...
        if (nLine < m_saText.GetUpperBound())
        {
            // ...append this to the next line
            m_saText[nLine] += m_saText[nLine + 1];

            // Now move all lines after the next one up
            m_saText.RemoveAt(nLine + 1);
            nLineHint++;
        }
    }
    else
    {
        // Otherwise, just lose the char on the right
        CString sLeft = sText.Left(nCharOff);
        CString sRight =
                    sText.Right(nLength - nCharOff - 1);
        m_saText[nLine] = sLeft + sRight;
    }
}
```

The *DeleteCharRight( )* function is modeled directly after the *DeleteCharLeft( )* function, except that it's simpler. The only additional difficulty stems from the fact that neither *nLine* nor *nCharOff* changes when characters to the right are deleted. This confuses the *AddChar( )* function into not repainting the entire view even when it needs to be repainted.

To avoid this problem, I resorted to the slight kludge of passing the *nLineHint* to *DeleteCharRight( )*. When the entire view needs repainting, *DeleteCharRight( )* changes *nLineHint* so that it is no longer equal to *nLine*.

Part VI
The Part of Tens

The 5th Wave

Buddy Diskk COMPUTER COMEDIAN

"SO I ASK THIS 'HIGH-TECH FORTUNE TELLER' HOW SHE'S ABLE TO PREDICT THE PAST, PRESENT, AND FUTURE AT THE SAME TIME? AND SHE SAYS SHE USES MULTITASKING TEA LEAVES IN ALL OF HER CERAMICWARE. SERIOUSLY! SERIOUSLY!"

In This Part...

What ...*For Dummies* book would be complete without a Part of Tens?

This part starts out by examining the C++ errors that are so troublesome you can find them plastered to the post-office wall, right next to the mugs of the FBI's most-wanted criminals. These errors are so common and so difficult to find that all C++ programmers have to be aware of them.

The chapters in this part look at some of the compiler switches with which you can change the way the Visual C++ compiler operates and outlines some of the places you can look when you run up against a programming nut that just refuses to give.

Chapter 25

Top Ten C++ Programming Errors

In This Chapter

▶ Common pointer errors

▶ Errors stemming from operator confusion

▶ Errors related to 0

▶ Declaration-related problems

*T*he syntax of C++ is a funny thing. To beginning C++ programmers, it seems obscure. The functional programming features left over from C tend to confuse purely object-oriented programmers. At the same time, the new object-oriented features confuse functional programmers. After a few months of using C++, however, the semantics seem to fall into place. Nonetheless, plenty of snares in the forest can trap an unsuspecting C++ novice. Familiarity with some of these traps might help you avoid falling into them so easily.

Forgetting to Initialize a Pointer

This error is just a special version of the generic "forgetting to initialize a variable" error; what makes this one worse is that the consequences are often much worse:

```
void SomeFunction()
{
    int *pnVar;
    int nVal;
    nVal = *pnVar;   // bad enough
    *pnVar = nVal;   // much worse
}
```

The pointer variable *pnVar* in this example is never assigned a value. You must assume, therefore, that it contains garbage. Reading from a garbage pointer is bad enough because the results are certain to be garbage. Writing to a garbage pointer is much worse, however, because it results in data being overwritten at some unknown location.

If the area that is overwritten is unused, no harm is done. If the area is in use, however, the data is lost. What makes finding this type of error so difficult is that the problem doesn't become apparent until the program tries to make use of the data that is now lost. This problem may occur many minutes after the data is lost.

Because this problem is difficult to diagnose manually, the Visual C++ compiler goes through some pains to avoid it. For example, a warning would be generated when you compile the preceding function. In this case, the compiler can tell that the variable has not been assigned a value before being used. In many cases, it is not possible to tell.

The Windows 95 operating system tries to help out by protecting memory to a certain extent: If an application attempts to read or write from memory that doesn't belong to it, Windows can often trap the request and terminate the program immediately. Unfortunately, Windows 95 cannot trap an invalid access to memory that the application owns. Nor can it trap all illegal accesses, because certain holes had to be left open in the name of compatibility with Windows 3.1.

Forgetting to Return Heap Memory

I've already mentioned this problem in Chapter 14; it's such a serious and common problem, however, that this warning bears repeating. In addition to those everyday laws we all have to live with, such as the one that says "What goes up must come down," is the law that says "Any memory that gets allocated from the heap must be returned to the heap."

If you fail to return heap memory after you're finished with it, the system becomes more and more starved for memory until, finally, your program can go no farther and drops dead. Like a man in the desert dying of thirst, this type of program can progress slowly, swerving unsteadily in fits and stops until it finally takes its last breath.

This problem occurs in situations such as the following:

```
Car* GetANewCar(int nOccupants)
{
    Car* pCar;
    if (nOccupants < 4)
    {
```

```
            pCar = new Car(2);    // get a two-door
        }
        else
        {
            pCar = new Car(4);   // otherwise, a four-door
        }
        return pCar;
    }

    void GoToTheStore(int nOccupants)
    {
        // get a car
        Car* pCar = GetANewCar(nOccupants);

        // now drive to the store
        if (pCar)
        {
            pCar->Drive(Store);
        }
    }
```

In this example, the function *GoToTheStore( )* begins by allocating a new car to make the drive — which is somewhat wasteful, but you would certainly agree that the algorithm should work. If a new car *is* allocated, it is used to drive to the store, indicated by the call *pCar->Drive(Store)*.

The problem is that the function doesn't destroy the *Car* object after it has arrived safely at its destination. Instead, the function simply exits, leaving the memory lost.

It's obvious that the programmer is counting on the destructor *~Car* to return the memory when the object *pCar* goes out of scope at the end of the program. It doesn't happen, however, because the type of *pCar* is not *Car* — it's *Car**. No destructor is invoked when *pCar* goes out of scope.

The corrected function appears as follows:

```
    void GoToTheStore(int nOccupants)
    {
        // get a car
        Car* pCar = GetANewCar(nOccupants);

        // now drive to the store
        if (pCar)
        {
            pCar->Drive(Store);
        }
```

```
// now delete the object, returning the memory
delete pCar;
}
```

There are a million stories in the big city. This has been just one of them. Similarly, there are a million different ways to lose heap memory. You must be on guard against all of them.

Returning a Reference to Local Memory

Another common memory problem is returning from a function the address of a local memory object. When the function returns, the object is no longer valid. The next time a function is called, this memory location is likely to be given to this new function for its use. Continuing to use this memory pointer writes into the local memory of the new function.

This common problem occurs in this way:

```
Car* GetANewCar(int nOccupants)
{
    Car* pCar;
    if (nOccupants < 4)
    {
        pCar = &Car(2);    // get a two-door
    }
    else
    {
        pCar = &Car(4);    // otherwise, a four-door
    }
    return pCar;
}
```

Notice how the pointer *pCar* is assigned the address of a local, unnamed object created by the constructor *Car( )*. In principle, there's no problem. There is a problem, however, with returning this address from the function, because the temporary object is destructed at the closed brace.

Confusing Operators

C++ inherits a rather cryptic set of operators from its progenitor, C. This, combined with the flexibility of the syntax rules, makes it easy for a programmer to get confused and use the wrong operator.

The most famous example of this situation is exemplified by the following:

```
if (nVal = 0)
{
    // do something if nVal is nonzero
}
```

The programmer obviously intended to write *if (nVal == 0)*. Unfortunately, the preceding statement is a perfectly legal, if nonsensical, C++ statement that assigns 0 to *nVal* and then tests to see whether the result is nonzero (which is impossible). The result is that the code within the braces is never executed.

Other pairs of easily confused operators are *&* and *&&* and *|* and *||*.

The Four Faces of 0

The constant 0 has four possible meanings, depending on how it is used:

- ✔ The integer zero
- ✔ The address that cannot be the address of an object
- ✔ Logical *FALSE*
- ✔ The terminator of a string

I can prove to you that these differences in meaning are actually observed. For example, the following assignment is legal:

```
int *pInt;
pInt = 0;  // this is legal
```

And the following is not:

```
int *pInt;
pInt = 1;  // this is not
```

The first assignment is legal because of the second definition in the list: The constant 0 can be an address. The constant 1 cannot, however.

This multiplicity of meaning can lead to some errors that are difficult to find:

```
// copy a string from pSource to pTarget -- incorrect version
while (pSource)
{
    *pTarget++ = *pSource++;
}
```

The *while* loop in this example attempts to copy the source string pointed at by *pSource* to the block of memory pointed at by *pTarget*. Unfortunately, the conditional has been written incorrectly. It should have been written this way:

```
// copy a string from pSource to pTarget
while (*pSource)
{
    *pTarget++ = *pSource++;
}
```

You can see that the terminating condition occurs when the character pointed at by *pSource* is a *NULL*. This is the fourth definition of 0. The code as written, however, checks to see whether the address *pSource* is 0, which is definition number 2.

The net result is that the *while( )* loop continues writing over memory until the program crashes.

Confusion between the other definitions of 0 is also possible. The only defense is simply to be careful when you use the constant 0.

Declaration Confusions

Compound declarations are confusing enough, but C++ — in its zeal to maintain backward compatibility with C — creates several declaration inconsistencies you must avoid:

```
class MyClass
{
public:
    MyClass(int nArg1 = 0, int nArg2 = 0);
};
MyClass mcA(1, 2);
MyClass mcB(1);
MyClass mcC();
```

mcA is an object constructed with the arguments *1* and *2*, and *mcB* is an object constructed with the arguments *1* and *0*. You might assume, therefore, that *mcC* is an object constructed with the arguments *0* and *0*; this is not the case, however. Instead, *mcC( )* is a function that takes no arguments and that returns an object of class *MyClass* by value.

Other confusion stems from the use of the initialization operator =:

```
MyClass mcB = nA;   // same as MyClass mcB(nA);
```

This use of = is allowed in order to enhance compatibility with C; you should avoid this construct, however, because it's not applied consistently. For example, the following does not have the intended effect:

```
MyClass mcA = nA, nB;
```

Rather than declare an object *mcA(nA, nB)*, this declares an object *mcA(nA)* followed by a separate object *nB*, using the default constructor.

Stick with the C++ format — it's much safer.

Order of Evaluation Confusion

The precedence of the C and C++ operators (discussed in Appendix A) enables you to know how to evaluate expressions such as the following:

```
a = b * c + d;
```

That is, is *d* added to the product of *b* and *c*, or is *b* multiplied by the sum of *c* and *d*? (The answer is the former, of course.)

Precedence does not affect the order of evaluation of the subexpressions, however. Let's change the sample expression in a seemingly trivial way:

```
a = b() * c() + d();
```

Now the question is, in which order are the functions *b( )*, *c( )*, and *d( )* called? The answer is that the order is completely indeterminate. Worse, the order cannot be made determinate by the use of parentheses. The following expression, therefore, has no effect:

```
a = (b() * c()) + d();
```

The order of evaluation of the functions normally isn't of any interest. If these functions have side effects that affect each other in some way (called *mutual side effects*), however, the order *is* important. If these functions change the same global variable, for example, the results are different depending on the order in which the functions are called.

Mutual side effects can raise their ugly head even when function calls are not involved:

```
int nI = 0;
cout << "nA [0]=" << nA[nI++] << "nA[1]=" << nA[nI++] << "\n";
```

In this expression, the problem is that the single expression contains two subexpressions that have a mutual side effect — the variable *nI* is incremented. Which *nA[nI++]* is executed first: the left one or the right one? It's impossible to say. The preceding code may or may not work as expected.

Declaring Virtual Member Functions

To overload a virtual member function in a subclass, both the arguments to the function in the subclass and the returned type must be declared identically to the function in the base class. This is not always obvious. For example, the following code seems to make sense:

```
class Base
{
public:
    virtual void AFunc(Base *pB);
};

class Subclass : public Base
{
public:
    virtual void AFunc(Subclass *pS);
};
```

This code does compile, but there is no late binding. The argument to the function *Base::AFunc( )* is of type *Base**, whereas the argument to the function *Subclass::AFunc( )* is *Subclass**, which is different.

The only exception to this rule is the following, which is allowed under the ANSI C++ standard:

```
class Base
{
public:
    virtual Base* AFunc();
};

class Subclass : public Base
{
public:
    virtual SubClass* AFunc();
};
```

In this example, each function returns the address of an object of its own type. This technique is so common that the standards committee decided to allow it.

Calls to Virtual Member Functions from Within the Constructor

Calls to virtual member functions made from within a constructor are bound early, which short-circuits what would otherwise be a neat capability:

```
class Base
{
public:
    Base();
    virtual void BuildSection();
};
class Subclass : public Base
{
public:
    Subclass();
    virtual void BuildSection();
};
Base::Base()
{
    BuildSection();
}
```

In this example, the programmer wants the constructor to invoke *BuildSection( )* polymorphically, calling *Base::BuildSection( )* when the object being constructed is a *Base* object and calling *Subclass::BuildSection( )* when the object is of class *Subclass*.

This example doesn't work, however, for the following simple reason: At the time the call to *BuildSection( )* is made, the object being constructed is only a *Base* object. Even if the object eventually will be a *Subclass* object, the constructor for *Subclass* has yet to have a go at it. Calling *Subclass::BuildSection( )* might be fatal under these circumstances. Even if the object will eventually be a *Subclass*, at the point of the call to *BuildSection( )*, the object is only a *Base*, and the call must be bound early to the function *Base::BuildSection( )*.

Pointer Alignment

This problem isn't fatal when you execute your program on 80×86 processors (such as the chip that drives your PC). It is fatal, however, on most other processors and may get in the way of your ability to port your application to some other environment. In addition, this problem can lead to substandard performance, even on an Intel processor.

When you cast a pointer from one type to another, it's possible to end up with what's called a *misaligned pointer.* A processor generally wants to address blocks of memory which are aligned on a boundary that matches the size of the block being accessed. For example, words can be accessed only on word boundaries (addresses that are multiples of two), double words on double word boundaries (addresses that are multiples of four), and so on.

The compiler normally ensures that this rule is observed. When you cast from one pointer type to a larger pointer type, however, you can easily violate this rule:

```
char  cA;
char* pC = &cA;

int*  pI;
pI = (int*)pC;
*pI = 0;          // this may be fatal
```

Because a char is only one byte long, the address *&cA* may have any value, including an odd value. In contrast, *pI* should contain only addresses that are multiples of four. The assignment of *pC* to *pI* is allowed because of the cast. If the address is not a multiple of four, however, the subsequent assignment may cause the program to crash.

On an Intel processor, the assignment is not fatal even if the value of *pC* is odd; the assignment takes more than twice as long, however, as it would if the assignment were properly aligned. Be on your guard against misaligned pointers.

This situation can occur only when you're casting from a pointer to one type to a pointer to a larger type. ■

Chapter 26

Top Ten Compiler Settings

In This Chapter

▶ Using switches to reduce compilation time

▶ Using switches to reduce the size of the executable file

▶ Customizing the compiler toolbar

*V*isual C++ defines a plethora of different options. Although some of these compiler settings have little or no effect, others are critically important to the proper functioning of your program. This chapter lists the ten (or so) most important compiler settings.

Each of these options is listed by the menu sequence used to arrive at that option. Most of them are properties of the individual project, which means that different projects may have different options set.

Project Settings | Microsoft Foundation Classes

This setting determines whether the library that contains the MFC code is linked to become a part of your program at link-time or left as a Dynamic Link Library (DLL) to be loaded when the program is executed.

A *DLL* is a library that stays in the Windows directory to be loaded only when the program needs it. DLLs have the additional advantage that multiple programs can share the same DLL in memory. ■

Linking the MFC library with your application statically makes your .EXE executable file larger, but it makes it independent of any other files.

Choosing the other option of Dynamic Linking makes the .EXE file considerably smaller because it doesn't have to include the MFC library code. It makes the program somewhat slower to load, however, because the DLL must be loaded and linked at execution time. It also makes the program dependent on the existence of the MFC DLL in the Windows system directory.

Project Settings | C/C++ | Code Generation | Processor

Choosing this option determines which type of processor instructions you want to set. Choosing 486 or Pentium enables the Visual C++ compiler to use instructions that may not be in the 386 repertoire. Although this setting may enhance performance, it limits the number of different types of PCs on which the program can run. Choose 386 for the greatest applicability (but at the cost of performance).

Project Settings | C/C++ | Precompiled Header | Use .PCH

Choosing this option enables the compiler to save the results of compiling the common .h files in a file normally called stdafx.pch. When you compile subsequent files, the compiler skips the step of compiling these initial .h files and simply loads the .pch file, thereby picking up where it left off. Because these initial .h files (which include windows.h) are lengthy, this option can save considerable compilation time. This option should be enabled.

Project Settings | C/C++ | Code Generation | Calling Convention

This option determines the calling convention for functions that are not otherwise declared *cdecl*, *pascal*, or *winapi*. Because the MFC and Standard C libraries assume *cdecl*, this option should always be set to *cdecl* unless you will link your code with a Pascal or Fortran program (which is highly unlikely).

Project Settings | C/C++ | C++ Language | Enable Exception Handling

The exception-handling capability enables a function to declare an error condition that is then fielded at some higher level. A discussion of this capability is beyond the scope of this book; MFC uses it extensively, however, so you should leave this option enabled.

Project Settings | Link | Customize | Link Incrementally

During the process of recompiling and relinking, Visual C++ attempts to replace only those .OBJ files that have changed without rebuilding the entire .EXE file. This process is called an *incremental link,* as opposed to a *full link.*

Incremental links are faster than full links. Enabling the incremental link feature can therefore save time when you make minor changes.

It's usually not possible to perform an incremental link when you're making substantial changes. In this case, the Visual C++ compiler starts out by attempting an incremental link, only to be forced to give up and start over with a full link because of the large number of changes. The net result is increased link-time when compared to not attempting an increment link.

You should enable incremental linking when you're making small changes but disable this feature when you're making wholesale changes.

Project Settings | Browse | Generate Browse Info File Only on Demand

The final step in the build process is normally the building of the browse information file. It takes almost as long to generate this file as it does to create the .EXE executable. Generating this file is usually a waste of time because you don't often use the browse feature. Setting the option to Generate Browse Info File Only on Demand reduces build-time by not building the browse file automatically; it means that you must manually update the browse file, however, when you want to use the browse feature.

Tools | Customize | Toolbars

Visual C++ enables you to customize the toolbar by choosing toolbar icons from the other toolbars and adding them to your own. Customizing the toolbar by adding the functions you use the most can be a great labor-saving device. For example, I combine the main Debugger commands and the Class-Wizard icon with the main File and Search icons in my toolbar, to give me most of the features I need.

Chapter 27

Top Ten Places to Get Help

In This Chapter

▶ On-line sources of help

▶ Printed sources

▶ Human aids

▶ Divine sources of Windows assistance

C++, Visual C++, MFC, and Windows all have learning curves that must be conquered. The combination can be bewildering enough to make you wonder why you ever considered programming in the first place. Knowing where to go to get help can reduce both your frustration and your blood pressure.

On-Line Help

The first place to look for help with any problem is in the On-Line Help. With the massive amounts of storage available on CD-ROM, Microsoft has managed to amass an impressive amount of information there, most of it organized reasonably well.

If you can afford the hefty price tag, the Microsoft Developer's CD is another great source of information.

Books

Another place you can look for help is in books. You should always keep a few good language reference books handy. The best ones are from IDG books, of course. For help with C++, check out *C++ For Dummies, Borland C++ For Dummies,* and *Visual C++ For Dummies.*

Although it's difficult to read, the definitive reference for C++ is still *The Annotated C++ Reference Manual,* from Ellis and Stroustrup. No similar definitive work for Windows exists.

Magazines

Subscribe to a good Windows programming magazine. At first these magazines are difficult to read, and you may not get much from them, but persevere. As you learn the lingo and figure out the concepts, you'll get more and more from the articles.

Depending on your level of expertise, you might prefer certain magazines over others. *Microsoft Systems Journal* is the standard for heavy-metal programmers, and I recommend *Windows Tech Journal* as the best all-around publication. Aimed at somewhat less intense Windows programmers, it's still full of good information.

Magazines such as *Dr. Dobbs Journal* and *PC Tech Journal* are also full of Windows programming articles, although they aren't devoted strictly to Windows. This lack of focus may be an advantage because it gives readers a broader background.

Users' magazines are also a useful source of information. These magazines are meant more for sophisticated computer users than for programmers. Now that I've thrown in the word *sophisticated,* however, I should mention that they like to include programming articles as well, including such topics as upcoming Windows standards. *PC Magazine* and *Byte* are the flagships in this fleet.

My personal preference is to subscribe to one or two Windows-specific magazines supplemented by one generic programming magazine and one users' magazine.

On-line Forums

On-line computer services are another good source of help for the confused and wayward. Forums devoted to such topics as Windows programming, Win32 programming, Windows NT, C++, and more are available on BIX, CompuServe, America Online (AOL), and other on-line services. To enhance your education, be sure to read regularly the messages posted here.

Forums are interactive: You can post your message today and log on tomorrow to find an answer (hopefully). In addition, the other people who read the forums tend to be relatively nice, so you generally can get a helpful answer of some kind.

To access these on-line services, you need a modem and an account, of course. Don't be afraid of these services — they are now easy to use. The first time I tried CompuServe, many years ago, I found it hopelessly arcane and difficult to navigate. Somehow the designers of that service and I just didn't think alike. After a few months, I gave up and canceled my subscription.

I recently returned to CompuServe to try again. Fortunately, one of the first things I did was to get WinCIM, one of the CompuServe navigators (DOSCIM and MacCIM are also available). I was amazed at the difference. Accessing CompuServe from the WinCIM interface makes it extremely user-friendly and easy to use. Although I don't frequent the other services, I am told that the same is also true of them.

USENET Groups on the Internet

The Internet has a message facility known as the USENET, which is divided into areas of special interest to which you can subscribe. Subscribing enables you to participate in sometimes lively discussions about topics of interest. The USENET is another area in which you can post a question and receive an answer within a few days.

Dozens of different USENET groups contain more messages than you would really want to read in a sitting. I subscribe to the following groups:

comp.lang.c++ (generic C++ information)

comp.os.ms-windows.announce (general information)

*comp.os.ms-windows.programmer.** (a series of groups devoted to different aspects of Windows programming, including Win32)

comp.std.c++ (an exchange devoted to work being done on the ANSI C++ standard)

To access the USENET, all you need is some form of Internet access. All university students have access to the Internet. In addition, the Internet is accessible from most commercial on-line services such as CompuServe, Delphi, and America Online. The rules for getting on the Internet are different, depending on the service. After you get there, however, you first must subscribe to the USENET groups in which you're interested. After you've subscribed, messages should begin rolling in.

The primary rule for "surfing" the Internet is simple: Look before you leap. The Internet has been around a long time; programmers who have "grown up with it" know all its ins and outs, but they're not sure how they feel about the recent influx of newcomers. If you're one of those newcomers, look and listen for a few days — if not a week or two — before you venture into posting your own messages.

Also ask about FAQs (Frequently Asked Questions). The groups maintain these files of commonly asked questions to avoid having to answer the same question repeatedly. Unless your question is particularly difficult, it may well be in one of the FAQs.

Microsoft's On-line Service

Microsoft has opened its own on-line service with the introduction of Windows 95. Win95 includes a communications package, called Microsoft Exchange, that allows connections to this network. The service was still brand-new when this book was being written, so I don't know much about its usefulness or cost. In addition, there is some question about whether Microsoft will be allowed to offer this type of service, because it may compete unfairly with other on-line service providers. If it still exists when you read this book, it does seem worth a try.

The Nearest Computer Nerd

Don't overlook your friends. My friends call me regularly, asking for advice and help with their programs. Most computer nerds don't mind these types of requests, as long as you've made a reasonable attempt to find the answer yourself and you haven't abused the privilege.

A few gifts wouldn't hurt, of course. You might try bringing a Jolt cola and a Twinkie with you when you ask for assistance. And don't forget to add those people to your Christmas-card list — an extra pocket protector can always be put to good use.

Computer Clubs

Computer clubs are just a collection of nearby computer nerds. These clubs serve different functions; one of the most important is to disseminate knowledge about new products, which may or may not interest you.

Another function of these computer clubs is to provide a meeting place for programmers to get together and have classes (for large clubs, such as those associated with cities) or swap war stories (such as recent mouse-finger strains). Get to know these people — they are a storehouse of Windows and C++ knowledge.

Telephone Help

Telephone help is your absolute last alternative. I've included this section only to warn you that it really is no alternative at all. On-line telephone support from companies such as Microsoft is notoriously expensive and slow, and you spend hours waiting in a telephone queue and listening to elevator music. Look for computer geek instead. Try bribing him this time — an entire pizza is still cheaper than a telephone bill for on-line support.

Divine Intervention

Or you can always hope for divine intervention — it's sure to work better than telephone support does. I call this the "sleep on it" approach. When I have a problem I just can't work out after a few hours of pounding on it, I generally just get up and leave it alone. Then I sleep on it a day or so and return to it. I don't know whether it's divine intervention or my subconscious at work, but often the solution comes to me within minutes.

Appendix

Visually Basic C

● ●

*I*f you're a Visual Basic programmer, this appendix should teach you
enough C to enable you to work through the example programs in this
book. By working through them and referring back to this appendix as necessary, you should end up as a reasonably accomplished C programmer.

When I say "C," I'm referring to Standard C as defined by the American
National Standards Institute (otherwise known as ANSI C). Visual C++ is completely compliant with this standard. ▨

Because you already have experience in Visual Basic, I use that experience in
teaching you C. I compare and contrast the two languages to reduce the
learning curve you must climb.

C++, the basis of Microsoft Foundation Classes, is discussed in Chapter 6.
To avoid overwhelming you, this discussion is limited to C; whenever some
small feature differs between C and C++, however, I'll try to remember to
point it out here.

Some BASIC History

BASIC was conceived as a small, simple language that Dartmouth College
could use to teach programming to its students in the early 1960s. Because
BASIC is a small language, it didn't take much of a computer to run it. That
was fortunate because even mainframes of the day weren't much in the way
of computers. As mainframe computers became more powerful, BASIC began
to slip into obscurity.

The invention of the microprocessor in the '70s brought the price of computers down to where the average hacker could afford to buy one (as long as he
was willing to get a second mortgage on his house and forgo eating for a few
months, which he was). Unfortunately, these computers were not very powerful — just like the original mainframes. This coincidence did not slip the
notice of a certain Bill Gates and Paul Allen, who wrote a version of BASIC

that could run on one of these microprocessors in a scant 4K of RAM and without a disk. They founded a company to sell that BASIC and called it Microsoft — maybe you've heard of it.

BASIC was never embraced by hackers. As personal computers became more powerful, the hacker community moved on to other languages. Perhaps out of loyalty, however, Microsoft never let BASIC die.

For the PC, there was first GW-BASIC (also known as BASICA) and then Quick-Basic. As Windows began to catch on, Microsoft wanted a vehicle to bring Windows programming to the masses. What better medium than BASIC, now renamed Visual Basic?

Some BASIC Comparisons

Visual Basic is not your grandmother's BASIC anymore. Over the years, Microsoft's vision of BASIC has fallen more in line with that of other computer languages.

With Visual Basic, the genre took a "Mother, may I?" jump in the direction of C. I personally suspect that Visual Basic was written by a bunch of C programmers. As you'll see as you learn C, Visual Basic shows considerable similarities to its linguistic cousin. Although moving from Visual Basic to C involves a learning curve, it's not as steep as you might think.

The ways in which Visual Basic and C differ are discussed in the following sections.

Compiled versus interpreted languages

Before a computer can execute your program, it must convert the Visual Basic or C statements into the only language it understands: machine language. It goes about this task in one of two ways:

- ✔ *The compiler approach:* Converts the entire program into machine language and saves the results in an executable file. A programmer or user then can execute the file as often as she wants. (In Windows, the executable file carries the extension .EXE.)

- ✔ *The interpreter approach:* Converts each source line into machine instructions as the program comes to it and then executes the instructions immediately.

The two processes are analogous to the two ways I might approach an encyclopedia written in a foreign language I don't understand. One approach is to hire someone to translate the entire encyclopedia for me and, after the translation is complete, read the translation at my convenience without having to refer to the original. This resembles the compiler approach.

A disadvantage of this approach is that the entire encyclopedia must be translated, even though I may be interested in only a few articles. On the other hand, after the encyclopedia has been translated, I don't have to keep dragging the translator around with me every time I want to use the encyclopedia (that's good, because he's a real bore). In addition, ever since I took that Evelyn Wood class, I can read much faster than the translator can translate, so this approach is more economical if I intend to use the encyclopedia frequently.

In the second approach, to avoid translating the entire encyclopedia, I can hire the translator to translate for me out loud. I can then direct the translator to read whatever I want to hear. This approach avoids having to translate the entire encyclopedia and is similar to the interpreter approach.

The advantage of this approach is that I can begin to work immediately. I don't have to wait for the translator to translate the entire encyclopedia. On the other hand, the translator translates much slower than I can read, and the encyclopedia is useless to me without the translator.

Visual Basic supports both compiler and interpreter modes. While you are writing and debugging your program, Visual Basic runs in interpretive mode. This mode is ideal because you're interested more in getting your program running than in how fast it might be. In addition, any problems you find can be fixed "on the spot" — the change takes effect immediately.

Not until you ask Visual Basic to generate a stand-alone .EXE file does it act like a compiler, by converting the entire program into an executable file.

By comparison, C is strictly a compiled language. Before you can execute your program in Visual C++, you must compile all the source files into an executable file. If you make any change in a module, no matter how slight, you must recompile the entire module before you can test your change.

Minimal versus do-it-all languages

Some languages are "do it all" languages. To make things as easy as possible for programmers, they pack a great deal of punch into each expression. Other languages take the minimalist approach: Give programmers all the power they need to get the job done, but if it takes one expression or two, who cares?

Visual Basic takes the benign approach, doing as much as it can for programmers. C takes the minimalist approach as much as possible. C has no *String* type, for example, instead forcing programmers into manipulating arrays of characters manually.

Given a choice between an easy-to-use language and a "down and dirty" minimalist language, why would anyone choose the latter? Power. Higher-level languages force you to do things in a certain way — the way foreseen by the language. Low-level languages give you the basic tools and let you have at it — do whatever it takes to get the effect you want. Minimalist languages such as C can augment their capabilities by using extensive libraries of functions that perform most of the operations commonly required during a typical programming day.

Terse versus blabby languages

Visual Basic uses more English words in its instruction set: C uses cryptic symbols to do the same thing. Compare the following *If* statement in Visual Basic:

```
If Value < 0 Then
    Value = -Value
EndIf
```

to the same *if* statement in C:

```
if (Value < 0)
{
    Value = -Value;
}
```

C's terseness often turns off beginning programmers. After all, how can you possibly be expected to understand such cryptic gibberish? After you know what each of the symbols means, however, C is just as easy to read as any other language (trust me on this one).

One extra confusion factor is that C is case sensitive: *if* is not the same as *IF*, which is not the same as *If*. This is contrary to the way people think. People change the capitalization of words all the time without affecting their meaning (consider the word *people* in this sentence and in its predecessor). Fortunately, C is consistent — all C keywords are in lowercase.

Going to C

There's an old German saying, "The first step is always the hardest step." (I hear old Germans saying it all the time.) So let's get the difficult step over with.

Fundamentally, a C program consists of a series of statements. A statement is either a comment, a declaration, or an expression. Expressions consist of combinations of objects and operators.

The following sections look more closely at each of these terms.

Comments

The simplest statement is a comment. A *comment* in C is any string of text (including newlines) that begins with /* and ends with */. Compare the following:

```
/* This is a C comment */
```

with its Visual Basic equivalent:

```
' This is a Visual Basic comment
```

A comment is the only statement in C that does not end with a semicolon.

Although C++ accepts the C comment style, it introduces a second comment that's more similar to Visual Basic's. The C++ comment, which appears in the following example, also stops at the end of the line (it's the only statement in C or C++ that does so):

```
// This is a C++ comment
```

Also note that, with the exception of the // comment, C and C++ throw newlines in with tabs and spaces and calls them all *whitespace*. All forms of whitespace are interchangeable. Anywhere you see a space, you can put a newline or a tab and vice versa. The program then has complete freedom in formatting the C source statements. ■

Objects

Both C and Visual Basic have two kinds of objects: *constants* and *variables*. Constants in C look like their Visual Basic equivalents except for the octal and hexadecimal versions:

```
10   /* the constant 10; type is VB Integer */
10.0 /* a floating point 10; type is VB Double */
010  /* an octal 10, 8 decimal; same as VB &O10 */
0x10 /* a hexadecimal 10, 16 decimal; same as VB &H10 */
```

In addition, C provides for the definition of single-character constants using single quotes or arrays of characters using double quotes. Nonprinting characters are defined by including a backslash followed by either a special symbol or the numeric value of the character:

```
'A'    /* the character A */
'\t'   /* the character Tab */
'\x41' /* the character whose value is hex 41 --
          this is the same as 'A' */
'\\'   /* the special character \ */
"Array of characters" /* Looks the same as in Visual Basic */
```

The array of characters in C looks and acts much like the Visual Basic *String*, but it's not identical, as you'll see later in this appendix.

Have you any objects to declare?

C variables use the same basic naming rules as their Visual Basic equivalents do, except that C variable names are case sensitive. As with Visual Basic, a C variable may not carry the same name as a *reserved word,* which is a word that already has a meaning in the language, such as *for* or *if*.

C has no provision for using a reserved word as a variable name and then enclosing it in brackets, as Visual Basic does (that's a stupid idea anyway). ▪

All C variables must be declared — C does not share Visual Basic's default declarations based on the last letter of the variable name or based on some *Def*-type statement.

A C declaration consists of a variable type followed by one or more variable names separated by commas. Table A-1 lists the C types and their Visual Basic equivalents.

The actual sizes of the different types are not specified in the C standard; the sizes shown in Table A-1 are for Win32 Visual C++ 2.0 on the PC. ▪

Table A-1: Visual C++ and Corresponding Visual Basic Variable Types

C Type	Visual Basic Equivalent	Size [bytes]
char	Byte	1 byte
int	Integer	4 bytes*
short (int)	Integer	2 bytes
long (int)	Long	4 bytes
float	Single	4 bytes
double	Double	8 bytes
No equivalent	Currency	—
No equivalent	String	—
No equivalent	Variant	—

* 2 bytes in Visual Basic and Win16 versions of Visual C++.

All the following declarations are typical:

```
char cACharacter;
int nAnInteger;
int nInteger1, nInteger2; /* line 3 -- bad practice */

float fASinglePrecision;
double dADoublePrecision;
```

It's possible to declare more than one variable of the same type in a single statement, as shown in line 3 of this example; because this is considered bad programming practice, however, you should avoid it.

The types *short* and *long* are considered special types of integers rather than separate types themselves. Thus, the following declarations are equivalent:

```
long int lV1;
long lV2;
```

In addition, the *int* and *char* types may be flagged as either *signed* or *unsigned*. An unsigned variable has twice the range, but may not be negative. In practice, you seldom if ever see *signed*, because it's the default.

It's possible to initialize a variable when it is created:

```
int nSomeVar = 10;  /* starts life with the value 10 */
```

In the absence of this kind of initialization, global and static variables are initialized to 0, whereas local variables contain some unspecified value — the technical C term is "garbage."

C does not share Visual Basic's concept of *Empty* and *Null*. Just as everybody's gotta be somewhere, all C variables have some value. In addition, when C programmers say "NULL," they mean literally 0 and not "no value." ▪

It's also possible to rename existing types by using the reserved word *typedef*. Consider the following definition:

```
typedef unsigned int UINT;
UINT uNumber;  /* equivalent to unsigned int uNumber */
```

The *typedef* has declared *UINT* to be another name for *unsigned int*. Notice that this is not a new type — it's just a new name for an existing type. ▪

Scope rules

In addition to type, variables have a property called *scope* (sometimes called *storage class*). There are two different types of variable scope:

- ✔ *Global variables:* Defined outside any function. In C, these variables may be defined anywhere within any module. Global variables are created when the program starts executing and are not destroyed until the program terminates. Global variables are accessible to functions in any module in the program.

- ✔ *Local variables:* Defined at the beginning of a C function. Local variables are created when the function is called and are destroyed when the function exits. They are accessible only within that function.

In C, a variable is automatically global if it is declared outside a function. There is no *Global* reserved word. Also, a global variable can be defined within any module.

The reserved word *static* can be applied to either global or local variables; it has a completely different meaning, however, in the two cases. A global variable is normally accessible to any function within the program. Declaring a global variable static limits its scope to just those functions defined within the same module as the static global declaration.

A static local variable is created the first time that the function containing the variable is called, but it is not destroyed until the program terminates. Static local variables retain their value when the function exits.

Arrays of hope in a C of objects

Arrays of objects are declared in C by using brackets:

```
int nArray[10];  /* elements numbered from 0 to 9 */
nArray[0] = 0;   /* zero first element */
nArray[1] = 0;   /* zero second element */
```

The array *nArray* in this example has 10 members, numbered 0 through 9. (In Visual Basic, an array declared *nArray(10)* has 11 members, numbered 0 through 10.)

nArray[10] is not a valid member of the array int *nArray[10]* in C (even though it is valid in Visual Basic). ▪

Individual members of a C array are accessed in the same way as in Visual Basic.

User-defined types

C enables programmers to define their own data types in addition to the intrinsic types listed earlier, by using the C *struct*. The C *struct* bears a considerable similarity to the Visual Basic *Type*. For example, the following Visual Basic *Type* declaration:

```
Type Element
    nAtomicNumber As Integer
    fAtomicWeight As Single
    dHalfLife As Double
    nElectronsPerOrbital(6) As Integer
End Type

Sub SomeSub()
    Dim Chlorine As Element
    ReDim Elements(1 to 103) As Element

    Chlorine.nAtomicNumber = 17
    Chlorine.fAtomicWeight = 35.453
    Chlorine.nElectronsPerOrbital(0) = 2
    Chlorine.nElectronsPerOrbital(1) = 7

    Elements(1).nAtomicNumber = 1     ' Hydrogen
    Elements(1).fAtomicWeight = 1.00797
    Elements(1).nElectronsPerOrbital(0) = 1
    ' and so on
End Sub
```

looks similar in C:

```c
struct Element              /* the name of the new type */
{
    int nAtomicNumber;      /* the members */
    float fAtomicWeight;
    int nElectronsPerOrbital[10];
};
void fn()
{
    struct Element chlorine;/* declare Element object */
    Element elements[103];  /* struct optional in C++ */

    chlorine.nAtomicNumber = 17;
    chlorine.fAtomicWeight = 35.453;
    chlorine.nElectronsPerOrbital[0] = 2;
    chlorine.nElectronsPerOrbital[1] = 7;

    elements[0].nAtomicNumber = 1;     /* Hydrogen */
    elements[0].fAtomicWeight = 1.00797;
    elements[0].nElectronsPerOrbital[0] = 1;
    /* and so on */
}
```

You can see from this example that members of C structures are accessed almost identically to members of Visual Basic types.

Because Visual Basic allows programmers to start arrays with 1, you can assign *Hydrogen* to *Elements(1)*. Because C has no such option, however, you are forced to assign *Hydrogen* to *Elements[0]*.

Of course, you can just allocate an extra element in your array and ignore element 0. If you want to declare an array to describe the first 103 elements, for example, you can declare the array as follows:

```c
int nElement[104];
```

and then access *nElement[1]* through *nElement[103]*. Of course, you waste *nElement[0]*, but what's a single integer compared to enhanced readability? ∎

All arrays in C are declared the same, whether they're global or local. ∎

The *typedef* reserved word is often used in connection with structures:

```
typedef struct
{
    /* ...whatever members... */
} MyDef;
MyDef mydefObject; /* 'struct' not necessary even in C */
```

Typedef structures do not require the *struct* reserved word, even in C. ■

String 'em up

Notice that C has no *String* type. In place of the *String*, C uses an array of characters with a *NULL* character as a terminator. C defines a constant character string as follows:

```
char cArrayOfChars[11] = "0123456789";
```

This line defines the array *cArrayOfChars* beginning with *cArrayOfChars[0]* with a value of '*0*' extending through *cArrayOfChars[9]* with a value of '*9*'; the last character in the string is *cArrayOfChars[10]*, which contains the terminating null character, normally written '\x0'. You'll return to this point later in this appendix, in the section "A few C pointers."

Missing types

Neither Visual Basic nor C defines a Boolean type — both use integers instead.

Visual Basic 4.0 defines a Boolean type, but that version had not been shipped at the time this book was written. ■

In C, 0 is considered *False*, and nonzero is considered *True*. The comparison operators generate either a 0 or a 1 (Visual Basic comparisons generate either 0 or –1), as shown in this example:

```
int a, b, c;
a = 0;
b = 2;
if (a < b)          /* comparison generates a 1 */
{
    /* This is executed.*/
}
if (a)              /* 0 is considered False */
{
    /* This code is never executed. */
```

```
}
if (b)              /* Nonzero is True */
{
    /* This code is never executed. */
}
a = a < b;         /* 'a' now has the value 1 */
a = (a < b) * 5;   /* 'a' now has the value 5 */
```

C has nothing similar to the *Variant* data type. C insists on knowing exactly which type of object it's dealing with.

Finally, C has no *Currency* type, and, because time is money, it has no *Time* type either.

Smooth operators

The C operators are shown in Table A-2. If Visual Basic has an equivalent (or near equivalent) operator, it is listed also.

Table A-2 is sorted in order of precedence, with operators near the top of the list having higher precedence than those farther down. In the expression *2 + 3 * 4*, multiplication is performed first because * has higher precedence than does +, so the resulting value is 14. Enclosing a subexpression in parentheses forces that subexpression to be evaluated first. Thus, *(2 + 3) * 4* forces the addition to be performed before the multiplication, which results in a value of 20.

The precedence rules for C are, on the whole, the same as the precedence rules for Visual Basic. ∎

Table A-2 C Operators and Their Visual Basic Equivalents

Precedence	Symbol	Type of Operation	Visual Basic Equivalent
1 (Highest)	[ ]	Index array	( )
	( )	Invoke function	( )
	.	Get data member	.
	–>	Get data member from ptr	.
	postfix ++	Post-increment	I = I + 1
	postfix – –	Post-decrement	I = I – 1
2	prefix ++	Pre-increment	I = I + 1
	prefix – –	Pre-decrement	I = I – 1
	sizeof	Declare size of object	Len( )

Table A-2 *Continued*

Precedence	Symbol	Type of Operation	Visual Basic Equivalent
	&	Return address of	None
	*	Dereference pointer	None
	+	Plus	None
	–	Minus	–
	~	Bitwise NOT	Not
	!	Logical NOT	Not
3	(type)	Type cast	CInt, CLng, CSng, and so on
4	*	Multiply	*
	/	Divide	\ or /
	%	Modulo	Mod
5	+	Add	+
	–	Subtract	–
6	<<	Left shift	None
	>>	Right shift	None
7	< > <= >=	Relational operators	< > <= >=
8	==	Equality	=
	!=	Inequality	< >
9	&	Bitwise AND	And
10	^	Bitwise XOR	Xor
11	|	Bitwise OR	Or
12	&&	Logical AND	None
13	||	Logical OR	None
14	? :	Ternary	None
15	=	Assignment	=
	*= /= %= += –= <<= >>= &= ^= |=	Compound assignment	None
16 (Lowest)	,	Sequence operator	None

The following section discusses the different operators in more detail.

Assignment operators

C uses a simple but powerful approach to evaluating expressions: Every expression has both a value and a type. This approach is best seen in the assignment operators. First, C is probably unique among languages in even considering assignment to be an operator. The simple equal-sign assignment operator (=) says, "Take the value on the right and store it in the object on the left; return the resulting value and type." The following expression, therefore, has the effect you expect:

```
int n;
n = 10;  /* what is the value of this expression? */
```

What you may not expect is that the value of this expression is 10 and its type is *int*.

Defining assignment to be an operator allows for constructs such as the following:

```
if (n = fn())   /* call fn() and save results in n... */
{               /* ...if result is nonzero then...   */
                /* ...do whatever. */

}
```

This statement does the following: "Call the function *fn( )*, and store the result in the variable *n*. If the resulting value of *n* is *True* (nonzero), execute the code within the block."

Note that it does *not* compare *n* with the value returned from *fn( )*, which would be written as follows:

```
if (n == fn())  /* if n is equal to fn()... */
{
```

This mistake is a common one, especially among Visual Basic programmers. ■

The various compound assignment operators are merely shorthand for the binary operators, as shown in this example:

```
a += b;   // is equivalent to:
a = a + b;
```

Casting light on the cast operator

C is a strongly typed language, which means that each object has not only a value but also a type, such as *int* or *float*. Mixed mode operations, as exemplified by the following code segment, are allowed:

```
int n;
float f1, f2;
f1 = n + f2;
```

In this case, *n* is automatically converted into a *float* before the addition is performed. (C programmers say that *n* was *promoted*.)

You can make this conversion explicit by enclosing the new type within parentheses in front of the object. It's considered better style to write the preceding code segment this way:

```
int n;
float f1, f2;
f1 = (float)n + f2;
```

Adding up the arithmetic operators

The simple arithmetic operators, such as +, –, *, and /, are similar to their Visual Basic equivalents. One minor difference is that in C *int* / *int* produces an *int*. To create a floating-point result, one or the other of the arguments must be promoted to a *float* or *double*:

```
int n1;
int n2 = 3;
int n3 = 2;
float f;
n1 = n2 / n3;        /* equals 1, as you would expect */
f = n2 / n3;         /* f is now 1.0 */
f = (float)n2 / n3;  /* f now equals 1.5 */
```

A few of the arithmetic operators are unique to C. The following three expressions, for example, are identical:

```
n = n + 1;
n += 1;
n++;
```

You might ask why anyone would have three statements that do the same thing (go ahead, ask away). In the days when compilers were stupid and programmers were supposed to be smart, it was possible for *n++* to generate fewer machine instructions and, therefore, to execute faster than *n = n + 1*.

Even stranger, there are two ++ operators: One is called pre-increment; the other, post-increment. Although both increment their argument, the difference lies in the value of the expression, which works as follows:

```
int n1 = 3;
int n2 = 3;
int nValue;

nValue = ++n1;   /* nValue is now equal to 4 */
nValue = n2++;   /* nValue is now equal to 3 */
/* both n1 and n2 are now 4 */
```

Both *n1* and *n2* end up with the value 4; the value of the expression *++n1*, however, is 4 (the value of *n1* after being incremented), whereas the value of the expression *n2++* is 3 (the value of *n2* before being incremented).

The same holds true for the pre-decrement and post-decrement operators, *--n* and *n--*.

Comparing comparison operators

The comparison operators <, <=, >, and >= have the same look and feel in Visual Basic as they do in C. In both languages, the operators compare two numerical values and return either a *True* or a *False*.

The comparison for equality in C is the == operator. The single = version is called the assignment operator, as mentioned. The inequality operator is *!=*.

Is there any logic to logical operators?

The logical operators *!*, *&&*, and *||* treat their arguments as logical values (*True* and *False*). They always generate either a 0 or a 1. Consider the following cases using the *!* (pronounced "bang") operator:

```
int n1 = 0;
int n2 = 5;
int n;
n = !n1;    /* n is now 1 */
n = !n2;    /* n is now 0 */
n1 = !!n1;  /* n1 is now 0 */
n2 = !!n2;  /* n2 is now 1 */
```

The logical *AND* and logical *OR* operators are also interesting in that they perform *short-circuit evaluation.* That is, C doesn't evaluate the second argument if that argument wouldn't affect the outcome of the overall expression, as shown in this example:

```
if (e1 && e2)
{
    /* ...whatever... */
}
```

Expression *e2* isn't evaluated if expression *e1* is *False* because the value of *e2* could not possibly affect the value of the overall expression. This can be useful:

```
if ((d != 0) && (n / d < limit))
{
    /* ...whatever... */
}
```

If *d* is equal to zero, the result of the first comparison is *False*. If the lefthand argument to *&&* is *False*, there's no need to evaluate the righthand argument — *False AND Anything* is *False*. Thus, the division on the right side is not performed, which is good because the denominator is 0. The preceding example is a common case in which the programmer relies on short-circuit evaluation to avoid a divide overflow.

Short-circuit evaluation can cause problems, however, as shown in this example:

```
if (g() && h())
{
/* ...whatever... */
}
```

If function *g( )* returns a 0, function *h( )* is not called, no matter what wonderful things function *h( )* might have done.

Short-circuit evaluation for the logical *OR* works in exactly the opposite way, as you would expect:

```
if (e1 || e2)
{
    /* ...whatever... */
}
```

Expression *e2* is not evaluated if expression *e1* is *True* because the value of *e2* could not possibly affect the value of the overall expression.

Picking bitwise operators to bits

The bitwise operators ~, &, |, and ^ work exactly the same as their respective Visual Basic analogs, *Not*, *And*, *Or*, and *Xor*. Each works on a bit-by-bit basis, and none performs short-circuit evaluation, like their logical counterparts do.

Using the bitwise operators as logical comparators can generate unexpected results:

```
int n1 = 0x55;     /* following bit pattern: 0101 0101 */
int n2 = 0x22;     /*                        0010 0010 */

int n = n1 &  n2;  /* result is False =   0000 0000 */
n = n1 && n2;      /* result is True */
```

Notice that the result of *n1 && n2* is 1, *True*, because both *n1* and *n2* are *True*, nonzero; the result of *n1 & n2* is 0, and therefore *False*, because *n1* and *n2* have no bits set in common.

Understanding those shifty shift operators

The shift operators, << and >>, enable you to shift the lefthand argument by the number of bits specified by the righthand argument. Both arguments must be integers.

Shifting an integer left has the effect of multiplying the number by the corresponding power of 2. Shift left 1, therefore, multiplies the number by 2, shifting by 2 multiplies it by 4, and so on, except that the shift operation is much quicker. Shifting a nonnegative integer right divides by the corresponding power of 2.

If the resulting number is too large to be contained within the variable, the most significant bits are lost.

Taming the twisted ternary

The *ternary* is a real oddball: It's the only operator that has three arguments. It works as follows:

```
e1 ? e2 : e3
```

First, *e1* is evaluated. If it is *True*, *e2* is evaluated and used as the value of the expression; otherwise, *e3* is evaluated and used as the value of the expression. The type of the result is a type that is compatible with both *e2* and *e3*. In this example,

```
int n;
int a, b;
float f;
(a > b) ? n : f;
```

if *a* is greater than *b*, the value of the expression is the value contained in *n*; otherwise, it's the value contained in *f*. Either way, the type of the expression is *float*.

Controlling program flow

C defines a set of flow-control statements similar to those offered in Visual Basic. The statements are summarized in Table A-3.

Table A-3: Flow-Control Statements and Their Visual Basic Equivalents

C	Visual Basic
if()	If...Then...Else
while()	Do While...Loop
do...while()	Do...Loop While
for()	For...Next
switch()	Select Case
break	Exit Do, Exit For
continue	(None)
goto	GoTo

The first three control structures in this table work much like their Visual Basic counterparts do. In its simplest form, the *if* statement appears as follows:

```
if (e1)
{
    s1;
    s2;
    /* ...takes a licking and keeps on ticking... */
}
else          /* from here down is optional */
{
```

```
    s3;
    s4;
    /* ...and so it goes... */
}
```

Expression *e1* is evaluated. If it is *True* (nonzero), then the block of statements containing *s1* and *s2* is executed. If the condition is *False*, the block
containing *s3* and *s4* is executed. The *else* clause is optional.

If only a single statement appears within the braces, the braces are optional.
Because it's considered good programming practice, however, to include the
braces, I always show them, regardless of whether they're required. ∎

The *while* and *do...while* statements appear as follows:

```
/* check the condition first */
while(e1)
{
    s1;
    s2;
    /* ...they lived happily ever after... */
}

/* check the condition at the end of the loop */
do
{
    s1;
    s2;
    /* ...goooood, day!... */
} while (e1);
```

Both the *while* and *do...while* statements continue to execute the set of
instructions in a loop as long as *e1* evaluates to *True*. The only difference is
that the *while* evaluates *e1* before starting through the loop, whereas
do...while waits until the end of the loop to test *e1*.

The *break* statement is similar to the *Exit* statement in that it passes control
to the next statement outside the control structure that contains it. The
break is always associated with an *if* statement of some type:

```
while(e1)
{
    s1;
    if (e2)          /* if e2 is true... */
    {
        break;       /* ...then exit the loop */
```

```
        }
    s2;
}
```

Here *e1* is evaluated; if it is *True*, *s1* is executed. *e2* is then evaluated; if it is *True*, control passes to the *break*, which passes control outside the loop. If not, execution continues with *s2* and back up to *e1* to repeat the cycle.

There is only one type of *break*, irrespective of the type of loop being exited. ■

The *continue* statement is similar to the *break* except that, rather than pass control outside the loop, *continue* passes control to the conditional. That is, the *continue* statement causes the program to immediately begin another pass through the loop.

For the love of Pete!

The *for* statement is a strange beast, but it approaches most things in the same way as C does. In its most general form, it looks like this:

```
for (e1; e2; e3)
{
    s1;
    /* ...and that's the way it was... */
}
```

This *for* loop is equivalent to the following *while* loop:

```
e1;
while(e2)
{
    s1;
    /* ...and that's the way it was... */
    e3;
}
```

That is, first *e1* is evaluated. *e2* is then evaluated, and, if it is *True*, control passes to the statements within the loop. Finally, before control passes back to *e2*, *e3* is evaluated.

This looks strange indeed, until you see what a typical *for* loop looks like:

```
for (n = 0; n < 10; n++)
{
```

```
        nArray[n] = 0; /* zero out the elements of array */
    }
```

You can see that *e1* is used to initialize *n* to zero, *e2* is used to terminate the *for* loop, and *e3* is used to increment *n* each pass through the loop. The equivalent Visual Basic *For...Next* loop appears as follows:

```
For n = 0 To 9
    nArray(n) = 0
Next n
```

The Visual Basic *For...Next* loop seems easier to read, but the C *for* loop is much more powerful. Consider that the following C *for* loop has no Visual Basic equivalent:

```
/* read from 'filename' until End-Of-File */
for (hF = open(filename); !eof(hF); read(hF, block))
{
    /* ...We stay in touch, so you stay in touch... */
}
```

Some folks (myself included) would consider this to be abuse of a *for* loop, punishable by one "all-nighter" spent trying to find some obscure bug these types of statements invariably cause, but be aware that you do see it. ∎

Switch me back to sanity

The *switch* construct is reasonably straightforward:

```
switch(e1)
{
  case c1:
        s1;
        /* ...and so on... */
        break;  /* exit switch (this is optional) */

  case c2:        /* repeat this as often as you like */
        s2;
        /* ...while(nE1Cares) { continue; } */
        break;

  default:
        s3;
        /* ...more of the same... */
}
```

Each *case* statement is followed by a constant. When control passes to the *switch* statement, *e1* is evaluated and the result compared to each case. If it is equal to one of the constants, control passes to the statement following that case. If *e1* is not equal to any of the constants, control passes to the statement following the *default*.

The strange thing about the C *switch* statement is that control doesn't automatically exit the *switch* statement when control reaches the end of a case. Instead, control just continues down through the next cases. To force control to exit the *switch*, the last statement in each *case* statement should be a *break*.

Functions

C functions and Visual Basic functions differ in some important ways, both in the way they're declared and the way they're used.

Consider the following simple example Visual Basic function:

```
Function Min(n1 As Integer, n2 As Integer) As Integer
    If n1 < n2 Then
        Min = n1
    Else
        Min = n2
    End If
End Function
```

The same C function looks like this:

```
/* Min -- returns the smaller of two arguments */
int Min(int n1, int n2)
{
    int nMinValue;
    if (n1 < n2)
    {
        nMinValue = n1;
    }
    else
    {
        nMinValue = n2;
    }
    return nMinValue;
}
```

Notice the following differences:

✔ The return type of the C function precedes the function name.

✔ There is no special reserved word *Function.*

✔ The body of the C function is contained within braces.

✔ The return value of a C function is specified by the *return* statement.

In particular, notice that *return* is normally followed by an expression of some sort. A *return* can appear anywhere within the function, and a function can have more than one *return* statement (just as Visual Basic functions can have multiple *Exit Function* statements). The *Min( )* function in the preceding example could have been written as follows:

```
/* Min -- returns the smaller of two arguments */
int Min(int n1, int n2)
{
    if (n1 < n2)
    {
        return n1;
    }
    else
    {
        return n2;
    }
}
```

Interestingly, C has nothing that corresponds to a Visual Basic subroutine. Instead, C simply uses a function that returns nothing. (If you think about it, what's the difference between a subroutine and a function that doesn't return anything?) The C reserved word for "nothing" is *void.* The following function is really C's version of a subroutine:

```
void CheckForNegValue(int nValue)
{
    if (nValue < 0)  /* if argument is negative... */
    {
        exit(-1);    /* ...terminate program */
    }
    return;          /* the 'return' here is optional */
}
```

Notice that the *return* in this example is not followed by an expression because the function doesn't return anything. The return isn't even necessary. When control passes to the closed brace, the function returns anyway.

C weenies don't say "the function returns nothing"; instead, they say "the function returns *void*." (This sounds a little like the little boy who claims that he didn't clobber his sister.) ◾

Using C functions

C functions are invoked in the same way as Visual Basic functions, as shown in the following code segment:

```
int a, b, c;
a = Min(b, c);
```

Because it's possible to ignore the value returned from a C function, the C compiler accepts the following gibberish:

```
Min(b, c);
```

Even though this particular statement is nonsense, returned error codes are often ignored (whether they should be is a different story).

C always passes arguments to functions by value. Visual Basic passes by value only when the argument is declared *ByVal*; otherwise, Visual Basic passes by reference. Because C++ can pass arguments either by value or by reference, this particular aspect of function behavior is discussed in Chapter 6. ◾

Typical prototype type declarations

A function is considered to have a type in C, just as variables and constants have a type. The type of the *Min( )* function defined earlier, for example, is *int Min(int, int)*. You read this as "a function *Min* that takes an *int* and an *int* and returns an *int*."

A function should be declared before it is used. This process is normally handled by the *prototype declaration,* which appears as a function with no body.

Suppose that you have purchased a library of math routines, one of which was a natural log function, *Ln( )*. The following code segment uses this function to create a base 10 log function, *Log( )*:

```
/* Ln -- returns the natural log */
double Ln(double x);  /* the prototype declaration */

/* Log -- returns the base 10 log */
double Log(double x)
{
```

```
/* divide the natural log of x by the natural
   log of 10 to get the base 10 log of x */
return Ln(x) / Ln(10);
}
```

The *Log( )* function first takes the natural log of *x*. It then divides that number by the natural log of *10*. Notice, however, that *10* is an *int* and that the function *Ln( )* expects a *double* as its argument. No problem — C promotes the integer 10 into a double 10 before making the call. But how did it know that *Ln( )* expects a *double* argument? The same way that you did — the prototype declaration said so.

Defining prototype declarations at the beginning of the module avoids argument type mismatches that are tedious to debug.

A few C pointers

Variables are much like post boxes at the post office. Each one is a little receptacle capable of holding a single value. Both variables and post boxes have addresses — in the case of small-town post boxes, they're painted right on the front.

Visual Basic enables you to access the address of a variable implicitly. For example, when you pass a variable to a function in Visual Basic, you are passing the address off the front of its post box. That function can change the value of the variable by storing back into the address provided, as shown in Figure A-1.

C, however, enables you to access the address of a variable explicitly by using the *&* operator. This operator returns the address of its argument. The inverse operation is performed by the *** that finds the value contained in the address provided.

In C, an address is usually called a *pointer.* Fetching the value pointed at by a pointer is called *dereferencing the pointer.* ▪

In the following example:

```
char c;
char *pC;  /* declare a pointer variable */
pC = &c;   /* set the value of pC to the address of c */
*pC = 'A'; /* store an A at the char pointed at by pC */
```

pC is declared to be a pointer to a *char*. The first assignment stores the address of *c* in the pointer *pC*. The next assignment stores the value *'A'* in the *char* pointed at by *pC*, which just happens to be the same as *c* (see Figure A-2).

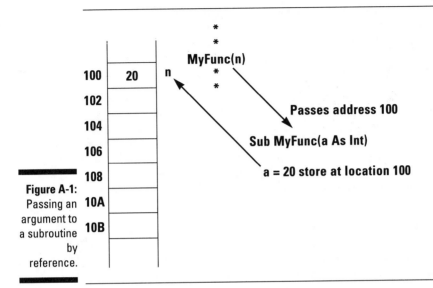

Figure A-1:
Passing an argument to a subroutine by reference.

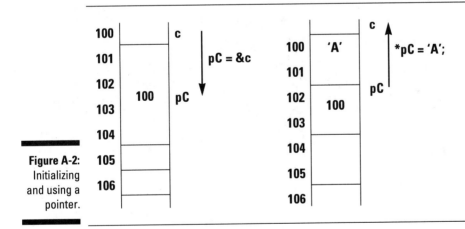

Figure A-2:
Initializing and using a pointer.

It's possible to define pointers to composite types, as shown in this example:

```
struct MyStruct
{
    int n;
    double d;
};
void fn()
{
```

```
        MyStruct ms;    /* remember that 'struct' is optional
                           in Visual C++ even in C mode */
        MyStruct *pMS;  /* define pointer to a MyStruct */

        ms.n = 0;       /* access member with an object */

        pMS = &m;
        pMS->n = 1;     /* access member with a pointer */
        pMS->d = 10.0;
    }
```

The only feature that's different from what you might have expected is the new operator ->, which is used to access a structure member from a pointer.

Pointer arithmetic

Consider again the pointer *pC*, which is defined in Figure A-2. Look at what would happen if you did something crazy:

```
    char cArray[13] = "Dummies rule";
    pC = &cArray[0];    /* pC points to the 'D' */
    *pC = 'T';          /* replace 'D' with 'T' */
    pC = pC + 1;        /* pC now points at 'u' */
```

The assignment *pC = &array[0]* causes *pC* to point to the beginning of the array. (The assignment **pC = 'T'* changes the phrase into one that's more applicable to my house.) Adding a 1 to *pC* causes it to "move over" to the next character in the array so that it points to the *'u'*.

This is somewhat remarkable the first time you see it. C programmers love to write loops like the following:

```
    /* convert the cArray string to all uppercase */
    for (pC = &cArray[0]; *pC; pC++)
    {
        *pC = toupper(*pC); /* convert single char to uc */
    }
```

This *for* loop works by setting the pointer at the beginning of the loop (*pc = &cArray[0]*). It then checks to see whether the character pointed at by *pC* is a 0. Remember that C strings automatically are terminated by a *NULL* character (which has the value 0). The loop then converts the current character (the character **pC*) to uppercase before moving the pointer *pC* over to the next character by incrementing it.

"So," you ask, "what's wrong with the following?"

```
for (n = 0; cArray[n]; n++)
{
    cArray[n] = toupper(cArray[n]);
}
```

Not a thing, except that the pointer version executes just a skosh faster and that C programmers are keen to get every last bit of performance from their programs.

Speaking of arrays, what really is the difference between the following two assignments?

```
char cArray[13] = "Dummies rule";
pC = &cArray[0];    /* pC points to the 'D' */

cArray[9] = 'o';    /* replace 'u' with 'o' */
*(pC + 9) = 'o';    /* does the same */
```

If *pC* points to *cArray[0]*, then *pC + 9* points to *cArray[9]*. The value of the expression **(pc + 9)* is simply the character pointed at by *pC + 9*. The answer is "none," which leads to the following rule:

An array name without any index is taken to be the address of the first element of the array. ■

Okay, this is nice for pointers to *chars*, but it works only because a *char* takes only one byte. What about other types of objects that take more than a single byte? The designers of C thought that pointer addition was such a neat capability that they decided to retain it for all object types; therefore, the second rule:

Addition to a pointer is always defined in terms of the size of the thing that's pointed at. ■

This rule works just like street addresses: Incrementing the street address moves you down to the next house, no matter how big the house may be.

In defense of pointers

Other than shaving a few milliseconds off the response time of your Windows program, what good are pointers? First, sometimes those milliseconds are in critical places, such as graphics routines. The ability to shave those milliseconds can save you from resorting to assembly language or something else that's really awful.

Other conditions occur that are difficult to handle in most languages but that are handled simply and elegantly with pointer variables — dynamic memory allocation, for example.

Windows provides a library function called *GlobalAlloc( )* that can allocate large blocks of memory. Associating these memory blocks with objects in the program is impossible in languages such as Visual Basic. In C, however, the following is just what the doctor ordered:

```
void fn()
{
    int *pnBlock;
    pnBlock = GlobalAlloc(GMEM_FIXED, SIZE_TO_ALLOC);
    /* now pnBlock points to large block of memory */
}
```

As you work through the example Windows programs in this book, you see countless ways in which pointer variables come to the rescue.

Programming tips

I've used a few special techniques in the Windows programs in this book. You should follow these techniques in writing your own programs.

Prototyping

Use prototypes early and often. Why wait to find a silly error by hand that the compiler could have found for you automatically with a prototype?

Package programming

The best programmers collect their functions in packages. These packages usually provide some set of related capabilities, such as a memory manager package or a communications package.

The prototypes for the public functions that make up this package are normally collected in an *include* file. Anyone who wants to use the package uses the *#include* directive to include the prototypes in his own code.

The *#include* directive inserts the contents of the specified file at the point of the *#include* as though they had been typed there. By convention, *include* files end with a .h extension. ■

For example, the standard Visual C++ *include* file for Windows is called windows.h. This file contains prototypes for all the standard Windows API functions.

Adopt a standard style

Because C ignores newlines, it doesn't really care how the source statements are formatted. Over the years, programmers have gravitated to a common convention for what C source code should look like. In this book, I've attempted to follow that standard as much as possible. You should too.

Even if you don't follow the standard standard, you should at least make up a clear, straightforward standard of your own and follow it. It makes finding errors much easier for both you and the people who have to come along behind you and read what you've written.

KISS (Keep it simple, stupid)

In the early days of C programming, compilers were stupid. They tended to convert each instruction into machine code without any meaningful attempt at optimization. It was often necessary for programmers to take extreme measures to generate the fastest code possible. Nowadays, however, compilers are much better at optimizing the machine code they produce. In addition, processors are so much faster these days that it usually doesn't make any difference.

When you do come across so-called clever code, it's educational to try to understand it. Don't copy it, though — it just encourages them.

Conclusion

It's difficult to cover in one appendix what most authors take an entire book to describe. I've tried to hit the high points and arm you with enough knowledge to take on the Windows programs in the remainder of this book.

Sally forth into Part I — be brave of heart. Although your course may seem difficult at times and full of peril, your persistence will be rewarded.

Index

Type & Learn Windows Programming USING WinScope™
by Tom Swan

ISBN: 1-56884-071-3
$34.95 USA/$44.95 Canada

Software included.

Type & Learn C™
by Tom Swan

ISBN: 1-56884-073-X
$34.95 USA/$44.95 Canada

Software included.

Heavy Metal™ Visual C++ Programming
by Steve Holzner

ISBN: 1-56884-196-5
$39.95 USA/$54.95 Canada

Software included.

Heavy Metal™ OLE 2.0 Programming
by Steve Holzner

ISBN: 1-56884-301-1
$39.95 USA/$54.95 Canada

Software included.

The Type & Learn Programming Series is the complete starter kit for first-time programmers.

The Type & Learn Programming Series features books bundled with bestselling special edition products from leading companies like Borland International and The Periscope Company. New programmers get a cutting edge book, a proven, effective teaching method, *and* the critical software needed in order to start programming right away.

Bend the rules to your advantage with the Heavy Metal Series and take your programs from professional to legendary!

The Heavy Metal Series is the programmer's vehicle to learning precision programming techniques. These books, geared especially for the intermediate to advanced programmer, teach how to delve deep into programs to reclaim the power lost when they stick to conventional programming techniques.

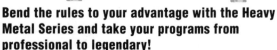

Detour: The Truth About the Information Superhighway
by Michael Sullivan-Trainor

ISBN: 1-56884-307-0
$22.99 USA/$32.99 Canada

Lotus Notes Application Development Handbook
by Erica Kerwien

ISBN: 1-56884-308-9
$39.99 USA/$54.99 Canada

Covers versions 3.01 and 3.1.
Software included.

The UNIX-Haters Handbook
by Simson Garfinkel, Daniel Weise & Steven Strassmann

ISBN: 1-56884-203-1
$16.95 USA/$22.95 Canada

Macworld Ultimate Mac Programming: How to Write High-Performance Code
by Dave Mark

ISBN: 1-56884-195-7
$39.95 USA/$54.95 Canada

Software included.

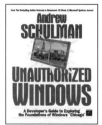

Unauthorized Windows 95: A Developer's Guide to Exploring the Foundations of Windows 95
by Andrew Schulman

ISBN: 1-56884-169-8
$29.99 USA/$39.99 Canada

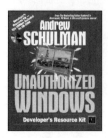

Unauthorized Windows 95: Developer's Resource Kit
by Andrew Schulman

ISBN: 1-56884-305-4
$39.99 USA/$54.99 Canada

Includes Software.

FOR MORE INFORMATION OR TO ORDER, PLEASE CALL ▶ 800. 762. 2974

For volume discounts & special orders please call
Tony Real, Special Sales, at 415. 655. 3048

Order Center: **(800) 762-2974** *(8 a.m.–6 p.m., EST, weekdays)*

5/8/95

Quantity	ISBN	Title	Price	Total

Shipping & Handling Charges

	Description	First book	Each additional book	Total
Domestic	Normal	$4.50	$1.50	$
	Two Day Air	$8.50	$2.50	$
	Overnight	$18.00	$3.00	$
International	Surface	$8.00	$8.00	$
	Airmail	$16.00	$16.00	$
	DHL Air	$17.00	$17.00	$

*For large quantities call for shipping & handling charges.
**Prices are subject to change without notice.

Ship to:

Name _____

Company _____

Address _____

City/State/Zip _____

Daytime Phone _____

Payment: □ Check to IDG Books (US Funds Only)

       □ VISA   □ MasterCard   □ American Express

Card # _____ Expires _____

Signature _____

Subtotal _____

CA residents add
applicable sales tax _____

IN, MA, and MD
residents add
5% sales tax _____

IL residents add
6.25% sales tax _____

RI residents add
7% sales tax _____

TX residents add
8.25% sales tax _____

Shipping _____

Total _____

Please send this order form to:

IDG Books Worldwide
7260 Shadeland Station, Suite 100
Indianapolis, IN 46256

Allow up to 3 weeks for delivery.
Thank you!

IDG BOOKS WORLDWIDE REGISTRATION CARD

RETURN THIS REGISTRATION CARD FOR FREE CATALOG

Title of this book: Windows 95 Programming For Dummies

My overall rating of this book: ❑ Very good [1] ❑ Good [2] ❑ Satisfactory [3] ❑ Fair [4] ❑ Poor [5]

How I first heard about this book:

❑ Found in bookstore; name: [6]

❑ Advertisement: [8]

❑ Word of mouth; heard about book from friend, co-worker, etc.: [10]

❑ Book review: [7]

❑ Catalog: [9]

❑ Other: [11]

What I liked most about this book:

What I would change, add, delete, etc., in future editions of this book:

Other comments:

Number of computer books I purchase in a year: ❑ 1 [12] ❑ 2-5 [13] ❑ 6-10 [14] ❑ More than 10 [15]

I would characterize my computer skills as: ❑ Beginner [16] ❑ Intermediate [17] ❑ Advanced [18] ❑ Professional [19]

I use ❑ DOS [20] ❑ Windows [21] ❑ OS/2 [22] ❑ Unix [23] ❑ Macintosh [24] ❑ Other: [25]_____

(please specify)

I would be interested in new books on the following subjects:

(please check all that apply, and use the spaces provided to identify specific software)

❑ Word processing: [26]

❑ Data bases: [28]

❑ File Utilities: [30]

❑ Networking: [32]

❑ Other: [34]

❑ Spreadsheets: [27]

❑ Desktop publishing: [29]

❑ Money management: [31]

❑ Programming languages: [33]

I use a PC at (please check all that apply): ❑ home [35] ❑ work [36] ❑ school [37] ❑ other: [38] _____

The disks I prefer to use are ❑ 5.25 [39] ❑ 3.5 [40] ❑ other: [41]_____

I have a CD ROM: ❑ yes [42] ❑ no [43]

I plan to buy or upgrade computer hardware this year: ❑ yes [44] ❑ no [45]

I plan to buy or upgrade computer software this year: ❑ yes [46] ❑ no [47]

Name: _____ Business title: [48] _____ Type of Business: [49]

Address (❑ home [50] ❑ work [51]/Company name: _____)

Street/Suite#

City [52]/State [53]/Zipcode [54]: _____ Country [55]

❑ **I liked this book!** You may quote me by name in future IDG Books Worldwide promotional materials.

My daytime phone number is _____

IDG BOOKS

THE WORLD OF COMPUTER KNOWLEDGE

❏ YES!

Please keep me informed about IDG's World of Computer Knowledge.
Send me the latest IDG Books catalog.